Big Data Beyond the Hype

About the Authors

Paul Zikopoulos is the Vice President of Technical Professionals for IBM's Information Management division and leads its World-Wide Competitive Database and Big Data teams. Paul is an award-winning writer and speaker with more than 20 years of experience in information management and is seen as a global expert in Big Data and Analytic technologies. Independent groups often recognize Paul as a thought leader with nominations to SAP's "Top 50 Big Data Twitter Influencers," Big Data Republic's "Most Influential," Onalytica's "Top 100," and Analytics Week's "Thought Leader in Big Data and Analytics" lists. Technopedia listed him a "Big Data Expert to Follow," and he was consulted on the topic by the popular TV show *60 Minutes*. Paul has written more than 350 magazine articles and 18 books, some of which include *Hadoop for Dummies, Harness the Power of Big Data, Understanding Big Data, DB2 for Dummies,* and more. Paul has earned an undergraduate degree in Economics and an MBA. In his spare time, he enjoys all sorts of sporting activities, including, apparently, hot yoga. Ultimately, Paul is trying to figure out the world according to Chloë—his daughter. Follow him on Twitter @BigData_paulz.

Dirk deRoos is IBM's World-Wide Technical Sales Leader for IBM's Big Data technologies. Dirk has spent the past four years helping customers build Big Data solutions featuring InfoSphere BigInsights for Hadoop and Apache Hadoop, along with other components in IBM's Big Data and Analytics platform. Dirk has co-authored three books on this subject area: *Hadoop for Dummies, Harness the Power of Big Data,* and *Understanding Big Data.* Dirk earned two degrees from the University of New Brunswick in Canada: a bachelor of computer science and a bachelor of arts (honors English). You can reach him on Twitter @Dirk_deRoos.

Christopher Bienko covers the Information Management Cloud Solutions portfolio for IBM's World-Wide Technical Sales organization. Over the better part of two years, Christopher has navigated the cloud computing domain, enabling IBM customers and sellers to stay abreast of these rapidly evolving technologies. Prior to this, Christopher was polishing off his freshly minted bachelor of computer science degree from Dalhousie University. Christopher also holds a bachelor of science degree from Dalhousie University, with a double major in biology and English. You can follow his musings on Twitter @ChrisBienko and see the world through his lens at http://flickr.com/photos/chrisbienko/.

Rick Buglio has been at IBM for more than eight years and is currently a product manager responsible for managing IBM's InfoSphere Optim solutions, which are an integral part of IBM's InfoSphere lifecycle management portfolio. He specializes in Optim's Data Privacy and Test Data Management services, which are used extensively to build right-sized, privatized, and trusted nonproduction environments. Prior to joining the Optim team at IBM, he was a product manager for IBM's Data Studio solution and was instrumental in bringing the product to market. Rick has more than 35 years of experience in the information technology and commercial software industry across a vast number of roles as an application programmer, business analyst, database administrator, and consultant, and has spent the last 18 years as a product manager specializing in the design, management, and delivery of successful and effective database management solutions for numerous industry-leading database management software companies.

Marc Andrews is an IBM Vice President who leads a worldwide team of industry consultants and solution architects who are helping organizations use increasing amounts of information and advanced analytics to develop industry-specific Big Data and Analytics solutions. Marc meets with business and technology leaders from multiple industries across the globe to share best practices and identify how they can take advantage of emerging Big Data and Analytics capabilities to drive new business value. Marc is a member of the IBM Industry Academy and has been involved in several multibillion-dollar acquisitions in the information management and analytics space. He has a bachelor of economics degree from the Wharton Business School at the University of Pennsylvania and holds three patents related to information integration. You can reach him at marc.andrews@us.ibm.com.

About the Technical Editor

Roman B. Melnyk is a senior member of the DB2 Information Development team. Roman edited *DB2 10.5 with BLU Acceleration: New Dynamic In-Memory Analytics for the Era of Big Data; Harness the Power of Big Data: The IBM Big Data*

Platform; Warp Speed, Time Travel, Big Data, and More: DB2 10 for Linux, UNIX, and Windows New Features; and *Apache Derby: Off to the Races.* Roman co-authored *Hadoop for Dummies, DB2 Version 8: The Official Guide, DB2: The Complete Reference, DB2 Fundamentals Certification for Dummies,* and *DB2 for Dummies.*

Big Data Beyond the Hype

A Guide to Conversations
for Today's Data Center

Paul Zikopoulos
Dirk deRoos
Christopher Bienko
Rick Buglio
Marc Andrews

New York   Chicago   San Francisco
Athens   London   Madrid   Mexico City
Milan   New Delhi   Singapore   Sydney   Toronto

Book number 19: One day I'll come to my senses. The time and energy needed to write a book in your "spare time" are daunting, but if the end result is the telling of a great story (in this case, the topic of Big Data in general and the IBM Big Data and Analytics platform), I feel that it is well worth the sacrifice.

Speaking of sacrifice, it's not just the authors who pay a price to tell a story; it's also their loved ones, and I am lucky to have plenty of those people. My wife is unwavering in her support for my career and takes a backseat more often than not—she's the "behind-the-scenes" person who makes it all work: Thank you. And my sparkling daughter, Chloë, sheer inspiration behind a simple smile, who so empowers me with endless energy and excitement each and every day. Over the course of the summer, we started to talk about Hadoop. She hears so much about it and wanted to know what it is. We discussed massively parallel processing (MPP), and I gave her a challenge: Create for me an idea how MPP could help in a kid's world. After some thought, she brought a grass rake with marshmallows on each tine, put it on the BBQ, and asked "Is this MPP, BigDaDa?" in her witty voice. That's an example of the sparkling energy I'm talking about. I love you for this, Chloë—and for so much more.

I want to thank all the IBMers who I interact with daily in my quest for knowledge. I'm not born with it, I learn it—and from some of the most talented people in the world…IBMers.

Finally, to Debbie Smith, Kelly McCoy, Brad Strickert, Brant Hurren, Lindsay Hogg, Brittany Fletcher, and the rest of the Canada Power Yoga crew in Oshawa: In the half-year leading up to this book, I badly injured my back…twice. I don't have the words to describe the frustration and despair and how my life had taken a wrong turn. After meeting Debbie and her crew, I found that, indeed, my life had taken a turn…but in the opposite direction from what I had originally thought. Thanks to this studio for teaching me a new practice, for your caring and your acceptance, and for restoring me to a place of well-being (at least until Chloë is a teenager). Namaste.

—Paul Zikopoulos

To Sandra, Erik, and Anna: Yet again, I've taken on a book project, and yet again, you've given me the support that I've needed.

—Dirk deRoos

To my family and friends who patiently put up with the late nights, short weekends, and the long hours it takes to be a part of this incredible team: Thank you. I would also like to thank those who first domesticated Coffee arabica for making the aforementioned possible.

—Christopher Bienko

I would like to thank my immediate family for supporting my contribution to this book by putting up with my early and late hours and, at times, my stressed-out attitude. I especially want to thank my wife, Lyndy, my in-house English major, who helped edit and proofread my first draft and this dedication. I would also like to thank Paul Zikopoulos for providing me with the opportunity to be part of this book, even though there were times when I thought I was crazy for volunteering. Finally, I would like to thank my entire Optim extended family for "having my back" at work and for allowing me to "go stealth" as needed so that I could focus on making this project a reality.

—Rick Buglio

I would like to thank all of our clients for taking the time to tell us about their challenges and giving us the opportunity to demonstrate how we can help them. I would also like to thank the entire IBM Big Data Industry Team for their continued motivation and passion working with our clients to understand their business needs and helping them to find ways of delivering new value through information and analytics. By listening to our clients and sharing their experiences, we are able to continuously learn new ways to help transform industries and businesses with data. And thank you to my family, Amy, Ayla, and Ethan, for their patience and support even when I am constantly away from home to spend time with companies across the world in my personal pursuit to make an impact.

—Marc Andrews

CONTENTS AT A GLANCE

PART III
Calming the Waters: Big Data Governance

CONTENTS

PART II

Watson Foundations

PART III
Calming the Waters: Big Data Governance

FOREWORD

Through thousands of client engagements, we've learned organizations that outperform are using data for competitive advantage. What sets these leaders apart? It's their ability to get three things right. First, they drive business outcomes by applying more sophisticated analytics across more disparate data sources in more parts of their organization—they infuse analytics everywhere. Second, they capture the time value of data by developing "speed of insight" and "speed of action" as core differentiators—they don't wait. Third, they look to change the game in their industry or profession—they shift the status quo. These game changers could be in how they apply Big Data and Analytics to attract, grow, and retain customers; manage risk or transform financial processes; optimize operations; or indeed create new business models. At their very core, they directly or indirectly seek to capitalize on the value of information.

If you selected this book, you likely play a key role in the transformation of your organization through Big Data and Analytics. You are tired of the hype and are ready to have a conversation about seizing the value of data. This book provides a practical introduction to the next generation of data architectures; introduces the role of the cloud and NoSQL technologies; and discusses the practicalities of security, privacy, and governance. Whether you are new to this topic or an expert looking for the latest information, this book provides a solid foundation on which to grow.

Our writers are accomplished scientists, developers, architects, and mathematicians. They are passionate about helping our clients turn hype into reality. They understand the complexities of rapidly shifting technology and the practicalities of evolving and expanding a data architecture already in place. They have worked side-by-side with clients to help them transform their organization while keeping them on a winning path.

I'd like to acknowledge Paul, Dirk, Chris, Rick, and Marc for sharing their deep knowledge of this complex topic in a style that makes it accessible to all of us ready to seize our moment on this Big Data journey.

Beth

Beth Smith
General Manager, IBM Information Management

ACKNOWLEDGMENTS

Collectively, we want to thank the following people, without whom this book would not have been possible: Anjul Bhambhri, Rob Thomas, Roger Rea, Steven Sit, Rob Utzschneider, Joe DiPietro, Nagui Halim, Shivakumar Vaithyanathan, Shankar Venkataraman, Dwaine Snow, Andrew Buckler, Glen Sheffield, Klaus Roder, Ritika Gunnar, Tim Vincent, Jennifer McGinn, Anand Ranganathan, Jennifer Chen, and Robert Uleman. Thanks also to all the other people in our business who make personal sacrifices day in and day out to bring you the IBM Big Data and Analytics platform. IBM is an amazing place to work and is unparalleled when you get to work beside this kind of brain power every day.

Roman Melnyk, our technical editor, has been working with us for a long time—sometimes as a coauthor, sometimes as an editor, but always as an integral part of the project. We also want to thank Xiamei (May) Li who bailed us out on Chapter 14 and brought some common sense to our Big Match chapter. Bob Harbus helped us a lot with Chapter 8—the shadow tables technology—and we wanted to thank him here too.

We want to thank (although at times we cursed) Susan Visser, Frances Wells, Melissa Reilly, and Linda Currie for getting the book in place; an idea is an idea, but it takes people like this to help get that idea up and running. Our editing team—Janet Walden, Kim Wimpsett, and Lisa McCoy—all played a key role behind the scenes, and we want to extend our thanks for that. It's also hard not to give a special sentence of thanks to Hardik Popli at Cenveo Publisher Services—the guy's personal effort to perfection is beyond apparent. Finally, to our McGraw-Hill guru, Paul Carlstroem—there is a reason why we specifically want to work with you—you did more magic for this book than any other before it…thank you.

INTRODUCTION

The poet A.R. Ammons once wrote, "A word too much repeated falls out of being." Well, kudos to the term *Big Data*, because it's hanging in there, and it's hard to imagine a term with more hype than *Big Data*. Indeed, perhaps it is repeated too much. *Big Data Beyond the Hype: A Guide to Conversations for Today's Data Center* is a collection of discussions that take an overused term and break it down into a confluence of technologies, some that have been around for a while, some that are relatively new, and others that are just coming down the pipe or are not even a market reality yet. The book is organized into three parts.

Part I, "Opening Conversations About Big Data," gives you a framework so that you can engage in Big Data conversations in social forums, at keynotes, in architectural reviews, during marketing mix planning, at the office watercooler, or even with your spouse (nothing like a Big Data discussion to inject romance into an evening). Although we talk a bit about what IBM does in this space, the aim of this part is to give you a grounding in cloud service delivery models, NoSQL, Big Data, cognitive computing, what a modern data information architecture looks like, and more. This chapter is going to give you the constructs and foundations that you will need to engage conversation that indeed can hype Big Data, but allow you to extend those conversations beyond.

In **Chapter 1**, we briefly tackle, define, and illustrate the term *Big Data*. Although its use is ubiquitous, we think that many people have used it irresponsibly. For example, some people think Big Data just means Hadoop—and although Hadoop is indeed a critical repository and execution engine in the Big Data world, Hadoop is not solely Big Data. In fact, without analytics, Big Data is, well, just a bunch of data. Others think Big Data just means more data, and although that *could be* a characteristic, you certainly can engage in Big Data without lots of data. Big Data certainly doesn't replace the RDBMS either, and admittedly we do find it ironic that the biggest trend in the NoSQL world is SQL.

We also included in this chapter a discussion of *cognitive computing*—the next epoch of data analytics. *IBM Watson* represents a whole new class of industry-specific solutions called Cognitive Systems. It builds upon—but is not meant to replace—the current paradigm of programmatic systems, which will be with us for the foreseeable future. It is often the case that keeping pace with the demands of an increasingly complex business environment requires a paradigm shift in what we should expect from IT. The world needs an approach that recognizes today's realities as opportunities rather than challenges, and it needs computers that help with probabilistic outcomes. Traditional IT relies on search to find the location of a key phrase. Emerging IT gathers information and combines it for true discovery. Traditional IT can handle only small sets of focused data, whereas today's IT must live with Big Data. And traditional IT is really just starting to ubiquitously work with machine language, whereas what we as users really need is to be able to interact with machines the way we communicate—by using natural language. All of these considerations, plus the cancer fighting, *Jeopardy!* winning, wealth managing, and retail-assisting gourmet chef known as IBM Watson itself, are discussed in this chapter.

After providing a solid foundation for how to define and understand Big Data, along with an introduction to cognitive computing, we finish this chapter by presenting to you our Big Data and Analytics platform manifesto. This vendor-neutral discussion lays out the architectural foundation for an information management platform that delivers dividends today and into the future. IBM has built such a platform, and we cover that in Part II of this book. If you're taking a journey of discovery into Big Data, no matter what vendor (or vendors) you ultimately partner with, you will need what we outline in this part of Chapter 1.

Chapter 2 introduces you to something we call *polyglot persistence*. It's an introduction to the NoSQL world and how that world is meant to complement the relational world. It's about having access to a vast array of capabilities that are "right-fit, right-purpose" for you to deliver the kinds of solutions you need. There are well over 150 NoSQL databases, so we break them down into types and discuss the "styles" of NoSQL databases. We also discuss things like CAP and ACID, which should give you a general understanding of what differentiates the NoSQL and SQL worlds. We assume you have a pretty good knowledge of the relational world, so we won't be focusing on relational databases here (although it's definitely part of a polyglot architecture). Entire books have been written about NoSQL, so consider this chapter a primer; that said, if you thought NoSQL was something you put on your resume if you don't know SQL, then reading this chapter will give you a solid foundation for understanding some of the most powerful forces in today's IT landscape.

In the cloud, you don't build applications; you *compose* them. "Composing Cloud Applications: Why We Love the Bluemix and the IBM Cloud" is the title for our dive into the innovative cloud computing marketplace of *composable services* (**Chapter 3**). Three key phrases are introduced here: *as a service, as a service*, and *as a service* (that's not a typo, our editors are too good to have missed that one). In this chapter, we introduce you to different cloud "as a service" models, which you can define by business value or use case; as your understanding of these new service models deepens, you will find that this distinction appears less rigid than you might first expect. During this journey, we examine IBM SoftLayer's flexible, bare-metal infrastructure as a service (IaaS), IBM Bluemix's developer-friendly and enterprise-ready platform as a service (PaaS), and software as a service (SaaS). In our SaaS discussion, we talk about the IBM Cloud marketplace, where you can get started in a freemium way with loads of IBM and partner services to drive your business. We will also talk about some of the subcategories in the SaaS model, such as data warehouse as a service (DWaaS) and database as a service (DBaaS). The IBM dashDB fully managed analytics service is an example of DWaaS. By this point in the book, we would have briefly discussed the IBM NoSQL Cloudant database—an example of DBaaS. Finally, we will tie together how services can be procured in a PaaS or SaaS environment—depending on what you are trying to get done. For example, IBM provides a set of services to help build trust into data; they are critical to building a data refinery. The collection of these services is referred to as IBM DataWorks and can be used in production or to build applications (just like the dashDB service, among others). Finally, we talk about the IBM Cloud and how IBM, non IBM, and open source services are hosted to suit whatever needs may arise. After finishing this chapter, you will be seeing "as a service" everywhere you look.

Part I ends with a discussion about where any organization that is serious about its analytics is heading: toward a data zones model (**Chapter 4**). New technologies introduced by the open source community and enhancements developed by various technology vendors are driving a dramatic shift in how organizations manage their information and generate insights. Organizations have been working hard to establish a single, trusted view of information across the enterprise but are realizing that traditional approaches lead to significant challenges related to agility, cost, and even the depth of insights that are provided. A next generation of architectures is emerging, one that is enabling organizations to make information available much faster; reduce their overall costs for managing data, fail fast, and archive on day zero; and drive a whole new level of value from their information.

A modern architecture isn't about the death of the enterprise data warehouse (EDW); it's about a polyglot environment that delivers tangible economies of scale alongside powerful capabilities as a whole. This confluence results in deeper insights, and these insights are materialized more quickly. So, is the EDW dead? Not even close. However, there is a move away from the traditional idea of EDWs as the "center of the universe" to the concept of an environment in which data is put into different "zones" and more fit-for-purpose services are leveraged on the basis of specific data and analytic requirements.

Chapter 4 talks about the challenges most companies are trying to overcome and the new approaches that are rapidly evolving. Read about sandboxes, landing zones, data lakes (but beware of the data swamp), fail-fast methodologies, day zero archives, data refineries, and more. We also discuss the elephant in the room: Hadoop.

What is a data refinery? It's a facility for transforming raw data into relevant and actionable information. Data refinement services take the uncertainty out of the data foundation for analysis and operations. Refined data is timely, clean, and well understood. A data refinery is needed to address a critical problem facing today's journey-bound Big Data organizations: Data seems to be everywhere *except* where we need it, *when* we need it, and in the *reliable* form that we need. That refinery also has to be available as a set of services such that the information flows can be composed in the cloud with discrete pieces of refinery logic—and traditionally available on premise too. The data holds great potential, but it's not going to deliver on this potential unless it is made available quickly, easily, and cleanly to both people and systems. A data refinery and the zone architecture we cover in this chapter go hand in hand when it comes to a next-generation information management architecture.

Part II, "IBM Watson Foundations," covers the IBM Big Data and Analytics platform that taps into all relevant data, regardless of source or type, to provide fresh insights in real time and the confidence to act on them. IBM Watson Foundations, as its name implies, is the place where data is prepared for the journey to cognitive computing, in other words, IBM Watson. Clients often ask us how to get started with an IBM Watson project. We tell them to start with the "ground truth"—your predetermined view of good, rational, and trusted insights—because to get to the start line, you need a solid foundation. IBM Watson Foundations enables you to infuse analytics into every decision, every business process, and every system of engagement; indeed, this part of the book gives you details on how IBM can help you get Big Data beyond the hype.

As part of the IBM Big Data and Analytics portfolio, Watson Foundations supports all types of analytics (including discovery, reporting, and analysis) and predictive and cognitive capabilities, and that's what we cover in **Chapter 5**. For example, Watson Foundations offers an enterprise-class, nonforked Apache Hadoop distribution that's optionally "Blue suited" for even more value; there's also a rich portfolio of workload-optimized systems, analytics on streaming data, text and content analytics, and more. With governance, privacy, and security services, the platform is open, modular, trusted, and integrated so that you can start small and scale at your own pace. The following illustration shows an overview map of the IBM Watson Foundations capabilities and some of the things we cover in this part of the book.

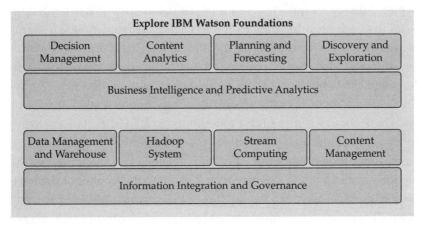

Chapter 6 describes Hadoop and its related ecosystem of tools. Hadoop is quickly becoming an established component in today's data centers and is causing significant disruption (in a good way) to traditional thinking about data processing and storage. In this chapter, you'll see what the buzz is all about as we delve into Hadoop and some big changes to its underlying architecture. In addition to its capabilities, Hadoop is remarkable because it's a great example of the power of community-driven open source development. IBM is deeply committed to open source Hadoop and is actively involved in the community. You'll also learn about IBM's Hadoop distribution, called *IBM InfoSphere BigInsights for Hadoop* (BigInsights), which has two main focus areas: enabling analysts to use their existing skills in Hadoop (such as SQL, statistics, and text analytics, for example) and making Hadoop able to support multitenant environments (by providing rich resource and workload management tools and an optional file system designed for scalability, multitenancy, and flexibility). If you are looking for 100 percent pure open source Hadoop, BigInsights has it (we call it "naked Hadoop"). Like other vendors (such as Cloudera), IBM offers optional proprietary Hadoop extensions that we think deliver greater value, such as visualization, security, SQL programmability, and more. We like to refer to this as "Blue Suit Hadoop." So if you want to leverage open source Apache Hadoop without any fancy add-ons but with full support that includes all the back testing and installation complexities handled for you, BigInsights does that—and it also lets you dress it up with enterprise-hardening capabilities.

Chapter 7 describes how you can analyze data before it has landed on disk—it's the "analytics for data in motion" chapter (sometimes, it seems that analytics for data at rest gets all the attention). This is an area in which IBM has differentiated itself from any other vendor in the marketplace. In fact, few Big Data vendors even talk about data in motion. IBM is well traveled in this area, with a high-velocity Big Data engine called *InfoSphere Streams*. Think about it: From EDWs to RDBMSs to HDFS, the talk is always centered on harvesting analytics "at rest." Conversations about Big Data typically end here, forgetting about how organizations can really benefit by moving their at-rest analytics (where they *forecast*) to the frontier of the business (where they can *nowcast*). We call this *in-the-moment analytics*. The irony is that we all operate "in the moment" every time we write an email, yet we don't demand it of our analytics systems. For example, when you misspell a word, does it get flagged with a disapprovingly red squiggly underline as you type? That's in the moment. How many of us configure our spelling analytics engine to engage only after the entire email has been written? Not many. In fact, it's more likely the case that you have autocorrect turned on, and if a spelling error is discovered as you type, it's automatically corrected. What's more, as you spot words the analytics dictionary doesn't recognize, you can opt to "learn" them (harvesting them at rest), and subsequent occurrences of the same misspelled words are corrected or highlighted (in motion).

Did you know that it takes between 300 and 400 milliseconds to blink the human eye? When you hear that analytics is occurring "in the blink of an eye," it certainly sounds fast, doesn't it? What you might not know is that BLU Acceleration analytics, in its sweet spot, is about *700 million times faster* than the blink of an eye (yes, you read that right), and this is the focus of **Chapter 8**. You also might not know that BLU Acceleration is a technology and not a product—so you are going to find it in various on-premise products and off-premise services (we talk about that in this chapter too). BLU Acceleration is a confluence of various big ideas (some new and some that have been around for a while) that together represent what we believe to be the most powerful in-memory analytics system in today's competitive marketplace. In this chapter, we introduce you to those ideas. BLU Acceleration technology first debuted in an on-premise fashion in the DB2 10.5 release. What we find even more exciting is its availability in both PaaS and SaaS provisioning models as a newly hosted or managed (depending if you leverage the service from the IBM Cloud Marketplace or Bluemix) analytics service called dashDB!

One of the things that makes BLU Acceleration so special is that it is optimized to work *where the data resides,* be it on a traditional spinning disk, a solid-state disk (SSD), in system memory (RAM), or even in the CPU cache (L1, L2, and so on). Let's face it, in a Big Data world, not all of the data is going to fit into memory. Although some nameplate vendors have solutions that require this, the BLU Acceleration technology does not. In fact, BLU Acceleration treats system memory as the "new disk." It really doesn't want to use that area to persist data unless it needs to because RAM is too darn slow! (Now consider those vendors who talk about their "great" in-memory system RAM databases.) This is yet another differentiator for the BLU Acceleration technology: It's built from the ground up to leverage 700 million times faster storage mechanisms than the blink of an eye.

If you are using the BLU Acceleration technology on premise through DB2, you simply must take notice of the fact that it has also been extended to bring reporting directly on top of OLTP systems with *shadow table* support in the DB2 Cancun release (10.5.0.4). Clients testing this new capability have seen incredible performance improvements in their latency-driven extract, transform, and load (ETL) protocols, not to mention a jaw-dropping performance boost to their reports and analytics, without sacrificing the performance of their OLTP systems.

The IBM PureData System for Analytics (PDA), powered by Netezza technology, is a simple data appliance for serious analytics. It simplifies and optimizes the performance of data services for analytic applications, enabling complex algorithms to run in minutes, not hours. We don't mind saying that the Netezza technology that powers this system pretty much started the appliance evolution that every major database vendor now embraces. And although there is a lot of imitation out there, we don't believe that other offerings are in the PDA class when it comes to speed, simplicity, and ease of operation in a single form factor; deeply integrated analytics; and the flattening of the time-to-value curve. **Chapter 9** describes the *IBM PureData System for Analytics.*

In this chapter, you learn about patented data filtering by *field programmable gate arrays* (FPGAs). You will also learn about PDA's rich built-in analytical infrastructure and extensive library of statistical and mathematical functions—this capability is referred to as IBM Netezza Analytics (INZA). INZA is an embedded, purpose-built, advanced analytics platform—delivered *free* with every system. It includes more than 200 scalable in-database analytic functions that execute analytics in parallel while removing the complexity of parallel programming from developers, users, and DBAs. In short, it lets you predict with more accuracy, deliver predictions faster, and respond rapidly to changes. In fact, we don't know of any competing vendor who offers this type of technology in their warehousing appliances. The second best part (it is hard to beat free) is that some of these functions are part of dashDB, and more and more of them will make their way over to this managed analytics service. In fact, so will the Netezza SQL dialect, making dashDB the analytics service to burst Netezza workloads into the cloud.

Chapter 10 is the "build more, grow more, sleep more" chapter that covers *IBM Cloudant.* This chapter continues the exploration of JSON and NoSQL databases (covered in Chapter 2) with additional detail and a touch of technical depth about the IBM Cloudant DBaaS solution—another kind of SaaS offering. Cloudant's earliest incarnation was as a data management layer for one of the largest data-generating projects on Earth: the Large Hadron Collider (LHC), operated by the European Organization for Nuclear Research (CERN). Among the many subject areas that particle physicists investigate with the LHC are the origin of the universe and how to replicate the conditions around the Big Bang, to name but a few. This data store technology matured into Cloudant, a fully managed NoSQL data-layer solution that eliminates complexity and risk for developers of fast-growing web and mobile applications. We examine how the flexibility of a JSON document data model ensures that you can perform powerful indexing and query work (including built-in Apache Lucene and geospatial searches) against nearly any type of structured or unstructured data, on an architecture that is a managed and scaled database as a service for off-premise, on-premise, and occasionally connected mobile environments.

Part III, "Calming the Waters: Big Data Governance," covers one of the most overlooked parts of any Big Data initiative. In fact, if you're moving on a Big Data project and you aren't well versed with what we talk about in this part of the book, you're going to get beyond the hype alright, but where you end up isn't going to be what you had in mind when you started. Trust us. In fact, it's so overlooked that although it's part of Watson Foundations from a product perspective, we decided to give this topic its own part. We did this out of a concern for what we are seeing in the marketplace as companies run to the pot of gold that supposedly lies at the end of the Big Data rainbow. Although, indeed, there is the potential for gold to be found (assuming you infuse your Big Data with analytics), when you run for the gold with a pair of scissors in your hand, it can end up being painful and with potentially devastating consequences. In this part, we cover the principles of information governance, why security must *not* be an afterthought, how to manage the Big Data lifecycle, and more.

Chapter 11 describes what really sets IBM apart in the Big Data marketplace: a deep focus on data governance. There is universal recognition in the relational database space that the principles of data governance (such as data quality, access control, lifecycle management, and data lineage) are critical success factors. IBM has made significant investments to ensure that the key principles of data governance can be applied to Big Data technologies. This is not the chapter to miss—we can't think of a more important chapter to read before beginning any Big Data conversation. Think of it this way: If you were to plan a trip somewhere, would you get there faster, safer, and more efficiently by using a GPS device or intuition? Governance is about using a GPS device for turn-by-turn directions to effective analytics.

Chapter 12 is the "security is *not* an afterthought" chapter in which we discuss the importance of security in a Hadoop environment and the ever-changing world of Big Data. We share some of our personal field experiences on this topic, and we review the core security requirements for your Hadoop environment. If data is sensitive and needs to be protected in an RDBMS, why do some folks think it doesn't have to be protected in HDFS (Hadoop's file system)? As more and more organizations adopt Hadoop as a viable plat-form to augment their current data housing methods, they need to become more knowledgeable about the different data security and protection meth-ods that are available, weighing the pros and cons of each.

We finish this chapter with a somewhat detailed introduction to the IBM services that are available for this domain, including their abilities to govern, protect, and secure data in Hadoop environments as it moves through the data lifecycle—on or off premise. We cover the *InfoSphere Guardium* and *Info-Sphere Optim* family of data lifecycle management services. There is so much talk about "data lakes" these days, but without an understanding of the material that we cover in this chapter, it's more likely to be a data swamp!

Chapter 13 extends the conversation from the safeguarding of information to making the data trusted—and there's a big difference. As lines of business, data scientists, and others get access to more and more data, it's essential that this data be surfaced to them as artifacts for interrogation, not by its location in the polyglot environment (for example, sentiment data in Hadoop and mobile interaction data in Cloudant). This enables you to see a manifest of data artifacts being surfaced through a Big Data catalog and to access that data through your chosen interface (Excel spreadsheet, R, SQL, and so on). To trust the data, you need to understand its provenance and lineage, and that has everything to do with the metadata. Let's face it, metadata isn't sexy, but it's vitally important. Metadata is the "secret sauce" behind a successful Big Data project because it can answer questions like "Where did this data come from?" and "Who owns this metric?" and "What did you do to present these aggregated measures?"

A business glossary that can be used across the polyglot environment is imperative. This information can be surfaced no matter the user or the tool. Conversations about the glossarization, documentation, and location of data make the data more trusted, and this allows you to broadcast new data assets across the enterprise. Trusting data isn't solely an on-premise phenomenon; in our social-mobile-cloud world, it's critical that these capabilities are provided as services, thereby creating a data refinery for trusted data. The set of products within the *InfoSphere Information Server* family, which is discussed in this chapter, includes the services that make up the IBM data refinery and they can be used traditionally through on-premise product installation or as individually composable discrete services via the IBM DataWorks catalog.

Master data management (matching data from different repositories) is the focus of **Chapter 14.** Matching is a critical tool for Big Data environments that facilitate regular reporting and analytics, exploration, and discovery. Most organizations have many databases, document stores, and log data repositories, not to mention access to data from external sources. Successful organizations in the Big Data era of analytics will effectively match the data between these data sets and build context around them at scale and this is where IBM's Big Match technology comes to play. In a Big Data world, traditional matching engines that solely rely on relational technology aren't going to cut it. IBM's Big Match, as far as we know, is the only enterprise-capable matching engine that's built on Hadoop, and this is the focus of the aptly named "Matching at Scale: Big Match" Chapter 14.

Ready...Set...Go!

We understand that when all is said and done, you will spend the better part of a couple of days of your precious time reading this book. But we're confident that by the time you are finished, you'll have a better understanding of requirements for the right Big Data and Analytics platform and a strong foundational knowledge of available IBM technologies to help you tackle the most promising Big Data opportunities. You will be able to get beyond the hype.

Our authoring team has more than 100 years of collective experience, including many thousands of consulting hours and customer interactions. We have experience in research, patents, sales, architecture, development, competitive analysis, management, and various industry verticals. We hope that we have been able to effectively share some of that experience with you to help you on your Big Data journey beyond the hype.

P.S. It's a never-ending one!

Part I

Opening Conversations About Big Data

1

Getting Hype out of the Way: Big Data and Beyond

The term *Big Data* is a bit of a misnomer. Truth be told, we're not even big fans of the term—despite that it is so prominently displayed on the cover of this book—because it implies that other data is somehow small (it might be) or that this particular type of data is large in size (it can be, but doesn't have to be). For this reason, we thought we'd use this chapter to explain exactly what Big Data is, to explore the future of Big Data (cognitive computing), and to offer a manifesto of what constitutes a Big Data and Analytics platform.

There's Gold in "Them There" Hills!

We like to use a gold mining analogy to articulate the opportunity of Big Data. In the "olden days," miners could easily spot nuggets or veins of gold because they were highly visible to the naked eye. Let's consider that gold to be "high value-per-byte data." You can see its value, and therefore you invest resources to extract it. But there is more gold out there, perhaps in the hills nearby or miles away; it just isn't visible to the naked eye, and trying to find this hidden gold becomes too much of a gambling game. Sure, history has its gold rush fever stories, but nobody ever mobilized millions of people to dig everywhere and anywhere; that would be too expensive. The same is true for the data that resides in your enterprise data warehouse today. That data has been invested in and is trusted. Its value is obvious, so your business invested

3

in cleansing it, transforming it, tracking it, cataloging it, glossarizing it, and so on. It was harvested…with care.

Today's miners work differently. Gold mining leverages new age capital equipment that can process millions of tons of dirt (low value-per-byte data) to find nearly invisible strands of gold. Ore grades of 30 parts per million are usually needed before gold is visible to the naked eye. In other words, there's a great deal of gold (high value-per-byte data) in all of this dirt (low value-per-byte data), and with the right equipment, you can economically process lots of dirt and keep the flakes of gold that you find. The flakes of gold are processed and combined to make gold bars, which are stored and logged in a safe place, governed, valued, and trusted. If this were data, we would call it *harvested* because it has been processed, is trusted, and is of known quality.

The gold industry is working on chemical washes whose purpose is to reveal even finer gold deposits in previously extracted dirt. The gold analogy for Big Data holds for this innovation as well. New analytic approaches in the future will enable you to extract more insight out of your forever archived data than you can with today's technology (we come back to this when we discuss cognitive computing later in this chapter).

This is Big Data in a nutshell: It is the ability to retain, process, and understand data like never before. It can mean more data than what you are using today, but it can also mean different kinds of data—a venture into the unstructured world where most of today's data resides.

If you've ever been to Singapore, you're surely aware of the kind of downpours that happen in that part of the world; what's more, you know that it is next to impossible to get a taxi during such a downpour. The reason seems obvious—they are all busy. But when you take the "visible gold" and mix it with the "nearly invisible gold," you get a completely different story. When Big Data tells the story about why you can't get a cab in Singapore when it is pouring rain, you find out that it is *not* because they are all busy. In fact, it is the opposite! Cab drivers pull over and stop driving. Why? Because the deductible on their insurance is prohibitive and not worth the risk of an accident (at fault or not). It was Big Data that found this correlation. By rigging Singapore cabs with GPS systems to do spatial and temporal analysis of their movements and combining that with freely available national weather service data, it was found that taxi movements mostly stopped in torrential downpours.

Why Is Big Data Important?

A number of years ago, IBM introduced its Smarter Planet campaign ("Instrumented, Interconnected, and Intelligent," for those of you who didn't get the T-shirt). This campaign anticipated the Big Data craze that hit the IT landscape just a few short years later.

From an instrumentation perspective, what *doesn't* have some amount of coding in it today? In a Big Data world, we can pretty much measure anything we want. Just look at your car; you can't diagnose a problem these days without hooking it to a computer. The wearables market is set to explode too; even fashion house Ralph Lauren developed a shirt for the U.S. Open tennis championship that measures its wearer's physiological markers such as heart rate, breathing, stress levels, and more. You can imagine how wearables can completely change the way society treats cardiac patients, post-traumatic stress disorders, train engineers, security forces, and more. As you can imagine, instrumentation has the ability to generate a heck of a lot of data. For example, one electric car on the market today generates 25GB of data during just one hour of charging.

One important Big Data capability is capturing data that is getting "dropped to the floor." This type of data can yield incredible insights and results because it enriches the analytics initiatives that are going on in your organization today. *Data exhaust* is the term we like to use for this kind of data, which is generated in huge amounts (often terabytes per day) but typically isn't tapped for business insight. Online storefronts fail to capture terabytes of generated clickstreams that can be used to perform web sessionization, optimize the "last mile" shopping experience, understand why online shopping baskets are getting abandoned, or simply understand the navigational experience. For example, the popular Zynga game FarmVille collects approximately 25TB of log data per day, and the company designs iterations of the game based on these interactions. We like to think of this data as digital body language because it shows you the path that a client took to reach a destination—be that the purchasing of a pair of socks or the selling of cheese in an online game. Stored log files are a corpus of data describing the operational state (and outages for that matter) of your most important networks—you could analyze this data for trends when nothing obvious has gone wrong to find the "needle in the stack of needles" that reveals potential downstream problems. There's an "if" here that tightly correlates with the promise of Big Data: "*If* you could collect and analyze all the data...." We like to refer to the capability of analyzing all of the data as *whole-population analytics*. It's one of the value propositions of Big Data; imagine the kind of predictions and insights your analytic programs could make if they weren't restricted to samples and subsets of the data.

In the last couple of years, the data that is available in a Big Data world has increased even more, and we refer to this phenomenon as the *Internet of Things (IoT)*. The IoT represents an evolution in which objects are capable of interacting with other objects. For example, hospitals can monitor and regulate pacemakers from afar, factories can automatically address production-line issues, and hotels can adjust temperature and lighting according to their guests' preferences. This development's prediction by IBM's Smarter Planet agenda was encapsulated by the term *interconnected*.

This plethora of data sources and data types opens up new opportunities. For example, energy companies can do things that they could not do before. Data gathered from smart meters can provide a better understanding of customer segmentation and behavior and of how pricing influences usage—but only *if* companies have the ability to use such data. Time-of-use pricing encourages cost-savvy energy consumers to run their laundry facilities, air conditioners, and dishwashers at off-peak times. But the opportunities don't end there. With the additional information that's available from smart meters and smart grids, it's possible to transform and dramatically improve the efficiency of electricity generation and scheduling. It's also possible to determine which appliances are drawing too much electricity and to use that information to propose rebate-eligible, cost-effective, energy-efficient upgrades wrapped in a compelling business case to improve the conversion yield on an associated campaign.

Now consider the additional impact of social media. A social layer on top of an instrumented and interconnected world generates a massive amount of data too. This data is more complex because most of it is unstructured (images, Twitter feeds, Facebook posts, micro-blog commentaries, and so on). If you eat Frito-Lay SunChips, you might remember its move to the world's first biodegradable, environmentally friendly chip bag; you might also remember how loud the packaging was. Customers created thousands of YouTube videos showing how noisy the environmentally friendly bag was. A "Sorry, but I can't hear you over this SunChips bag" Facebook page had hundreds of thousands of Likes, and bloggers let their feelings be known. In the end, Frito-Lay introduced a new, quieter SunChips bag, demonstrating the power and importance of social media. It isn't hard to miss the careers lost and made from a tweet or video that went viral.

For a number of years, Facebook was adding a new user every three seconds; today these users collectively generate double-digit terabytes of data every day. In fact, in a typical day, Facebook experiences more than 3.5 billion posts and about 155 million "Likes." The format of a Facebook post is indeed structured data. It's encoded in the JavaScript Object Notation (JSON) format—which we talk about in Chapter 2. However, it's the *unstructured* part that has the "golden nugget" of potential value; it holds monetizable intent, reputational decrees, and more. Although the structured data is easy to store and analyze, it is the unstructured components for intent, sentiment, and so on that are hard to analyze. They've got the potential to be very rewarding, *if*....

Twitter is another phenomenon. The world has taken to generating over 400 million daily expressions of short 140 character or less opinions (amounting to double-digit terabytes) and commentary (often unfiltered) about sporting events, sales, images, politics, and more. Twitter also provides enormous amounts of data that's structured in format, but it's the unstructured part within the structure that holds most of the untapped value. Perhaps more accurate, it's the combination of the structured (timestamp, location) and unstructured (the message) data where the ultimate value lies.

The social world is at an inflection point. It is moving from a text-centric mode of communication to a visually centric one. In fact, the fastest growing social sites (such as Vine, Snapchat, Pinterest, and Instagram, among others) are based on video or image communications. For example, one fashion house uses Pinterest to build preference profiles for women (Pinterest's membership is approximately 95 percent female). It does this by sending collages of outfits to clients and then extracting from the likes and dislikes preferences for color, cut, fabric, and so on; the company is essentially learning through error (it's a methodology we refer to as *fail fast* and we talk about it later in this book). Compare this to the traditional method whereby you might fill in a questionnaire about your favorite colors, cuts, and styles. Whenever you complete a survey, you are guarded and think about your responses. The approach that this fashion house is using represents unfiltered observation of raw human behavior—instant decisions in the form of "likes" and "dislikes."

Most of today's collected data is also temporally and spatially enriched. For example, we know where one of the stars of the television show *Myth Busters* lives, not because he told us, but because he tweeted a picture of his car with location-based services (LBS) enabled on his smart device and ended up sharing his home's geographic location with more than a million of his closest friends! Most people don't know what LBS is, but they have it turned on because they're using some mobile mapping application. These days, folks let you know when they have checked in at the gym or what restaurant they are in through their social apps.

Such data, with its built-in location awareness, represents another tremendous opportunity for finer granularities of personalization or profiled risk assessment, *if*…. Today, a number of major credit card companies have programs that are based on this approach. For example, if you purchase a coffee using your credit card, the company will profile your location (through LBS) and your purchase history and then communicate an offer from a retailer near your current location that is tailored to you or vice versa.

Brought to You by the Letter *V*: How We Define Big Data

Somehow Big Data got tagged with the stem letter *V* to describe its attributes. We've seen some definitions use so many *V*s that we are tempted to add "V for Vendetta" to rise up against this trend and revolt. With that said, we're not going to invent a new nomenclature to describe Big Data, but we will limit ourselves to just four *V*s: *volume, variety, velocity,* and *veracity*.

No Question About It: Data Volumes Are on the Rise

Volume is the obvious Big Data attribute. At the start of this chapter, we gave you all kinds of statistics that were out of date the moment we sent the manuscript to the printers! We've already mentioned some of the causes for data explosion, which we categorize as *social-mobile-cloud* and the *Internet of Things*. So, we'll just leave you with one more statistic that will be out of date by the time you get this book: 5PB of data is generated *every day* from mobile devices alone. That's about 10,000 Blu-ray Discs. Don't forget—volume is relative. So if your analytical models are measured in gigabytes, then terabytes represent Big Data in your world from a volume perspective. Don't fall in the "I have more data than you have" trap. It's not always about how much data you have; it's what you do with it that counts. Like we always say, Big Data without analytics is…well…just a bunch of data.

Variety Is the Spice of Life

The *variety* characteristic of Big Data is really about trying to capture all of the data that pertains to our decision-making process. Making sense out of unstructured data, such as opinion and intent musings on Facebook or analyzing images, isn't something that comes naturally for computers. However, this kind of data complements the data we use to drive decisions today. Most of the data out there is semistructured or unstructured. (To clarify, all data has some structure; when we refer to *unstructured data*, we are referring to the subcomponents that don't have structure, such as the free-form text in a comments field or the image in an autodated and geocoded picture.)

Consider a customer call center. Imagine being able to detect the change in tone of a frustrated client who raises his voice to say, "This is the third outage I've had in one week!" A Big Data solution would identify not only the terms *third* and *outage* as negative events trending to a consumer churn event, but also the tonal change as another indicator that a customer churn incident is about to happen. A Big Data solution could do more than just deescalate such a scenario—it could prevent it.

All of this insight can be gleaned from unstructured data. Now combine this unstructured data with the customer's system of record data such as transaction history (the structured data with which we're familiar), and you've got a personalized model of this consumer: his value, how "brittle" he is becoming as your customer, and much more. (You could start this analysis by attempting to analyze recorded calls, not in real time, and evolve the solution to one that analyzes the spoken word in real time.)

Adelos has developed one of the most sophisticated sound classification systems in the world. This system is used for real-time perimeter security control; a thousand sensors are buried underground to collect and classify detected sounds so that appropriate action can be taken (dispatch personnel, dispatch aerial surveillance, and so on) depending on the classification. Consider the problem of securing the perimeter of a nuclear reactor that's surrounded by parkland. The Adelos system could almost instantaneously differentiate the whisper of the wind from a human voice or the sound of a human footstep from the sound of running wildlife. In fact, if a tree were to fall in one of its protected forests, Adelos can affirm that it makes a sound and classify what the sound was (in this case a falling tree), even if no one is around to hear it. Image and sound classification is a great example of the variety characteristic of Big Data.

How Fast Can You Analyze? The Velocity of Your Data

One of our favorite but least understood characteristics of Big Data is *velocity*. We define velocity as the rate at which data arrives at the enterprise and the time that it takes the enterprise to process and understand that data. We often ask our clients, "After data arrives at your enterprise's doorstep, how long does it take you to do something about it or to even know that it has arrived?" (We don't like most of the answers we get to this question.)

Think about it for a moment. The opportunity-cost clock on your data starts ticking the moment the data hits the wire. As organizations, we're taking far too long to spot trends or to pick up valuable insights. It doesn't matter what industry you are in; being able to more swiftly understand and to respond to data signals puts you in a position of power. Whether you are trying to understand the health of a traffic system, a patient, or apply a stress test to a position in a booked loan portfolio, reacting faster gives you an advantage. Velocity is one of the most overlooked areas in the Big Data craze, and it's an area in which we believe IBM is unequalled in the capabilities and sophistication that it provides.

You might be thinking that velocity can be handled by Complex Event Processing (CEP) systems, and although they might seem applicable on the surface, in the Big Data world, they fall short. Stream processing enables advanced analysis across diverse data types (not just relational data) with high messaging data rates and low latency. For example, one financial services sector (FSS) client analyzes and correlates more than 5 million market messages per second to execute algorithmic option trades with an average latency of 30 microseconds. Another client analyzes more than 500,000 Internet Protocol detail records (IPDRs) per second, which equals more than 6 billion IPDRs per day, on more than 4PB of data per year to understand trending and the current health of its networks. Consider an enterprise network security problem. In this domain, threats come in microseconds, so you need technology that can respond and keep pace. However, you also need something that can capture lots of data quickly and analyze it to identify emerging signatures and patterns on the network packets as they flow across the network infrastructure.

Finally, from a governance perspective, consider the added benefit of a Big Data analytics velocity engine. If you have a powerful analytics engine that can apply complex analytics to data as it flows across the wire and you can glean insight from that data without having to land it, you might not have to subject this data to retention policies, which can result in huge savings for your IT department.

Today's CEP solutions are targeted to approximately tens of thousands of messages per second at best, with seconds-to-minutes latency. Moreover, the analytics are mostly rules based and applicable only to traditional data types (in contrast to the Adelos example earlier). Don't get us wrong; CEP has its place (which is why IBM Streams ships with a CEP toolkit), but it has fundamentally different design points. CEP is a nonprogrammer-oriented solution for applying simple rules to discrete and "complex" events.

Not a lot of people are talking about Big Data velocity because there aren't a lot of vendors that can deal with it, let alone integrate at-rest technologies with velocity to deliver economies of scale for an enterprise's current investment. The ability to have seamless analytics for both at-rest and in-motion data moves you from the *forecast* model that's so tightly aligned with traditional warehousing and energizes the business with a *nowcast* model. The whole point is getting the insight that you learn at rest to the frontier of the business so that it can be analyzed and understood as it happens.

Data Here, Data There, Data, Data Everywhere: The Veracity of Data

Veracity is a term that's being used more and more to describe Big Data; it refers to the quality or trustworthiness of the data. Tools that help handle Big Data's veracity discard "noise" and transform the data into trustworthy insights.

A Big Data platform gives businesses the opportunity to analyze all of their data (whole population analytics) and to gain a better understanding of their business, their customers, the marketplace, and so on. This opportunity leads to the Big Data conundrum: Although the economics of deletion have caused a massive spike in the data that's available to an organization, the percentage of the data that an enterprise can understand is on the decline. A further complication is that the data that the enterprise is trying to understand is saturated with both useful signals and lots of noise (data that can't be trusted or that isn't useful to the business problem at hand).

Embedded within all of this noise are potential useful signals: The person who professes a profound disdain for her current smart phone manufacturer and starts a soliloquy about the need for a new one is expressing monetizable intent. Big Data is so vast that quality issues are a reality, and *veracity* is what we generally use to refer to this problem domain; no one believes everything they read on the Internet, do they? The fact that one in three business leaders don't trust the information that they use to make decisions is a strong indicator that veracity needs to be a recognized Big Data attribute.

Cognitive Computing

Technology has helped us go faster and go further—it has literally taken us to the moon. Technology has helped us to solve problems previous generations couldn't imagine, let alone dream about. But one question that we often ask our audiences is "Can technology think?" Cognitive systems is a category of technologies that uses natural language processing and machine learning (we talk about these disciplines in Chapter 6) to enable people and machines to interact more naturally and to extend and magnify human expertise and cognition. These systems will eventually learn, think, and interact with users to provide expert assistance to scientists, engineers, lawyers, and other professionals in a fraction of the time it now takes.

When we are asked the "Can technology think?" question, our answer is "Watson can!" Watson is the IBM name for its cognitive computing family that delivers a set of technologies unlike any that has come before it. Rather than forcing its users to think like a computer, Watson interacts with humans…on human terms. Watson can read and understand natural language, such as the tweets, texts, studies, and reports that make up the majority of the world's data—a simple Internet search can't do that. You likely got your first exposure to cognitive computing when IBM Watson defeated Brad Rutter and Ken Jennings in the *Jeopardy!* challenge. This quiz show, known for its complex, tricky questions and smart champions, was a perfect venue for the world to get a first look at the potential for cognitive computing.

To play, let alone win, the *Jeopardy!* challenge, Watson had to answer questions posed in every nuance of natural language, including puns, synonyms and homonyms, slang, and jargon. One thing you might not know is that during the match, Watson was not connected to the Internet. It knew only what it had amassed through years of interaction and learning from a large set of unstructured data. Using machine learning, statistical analysis, and natural language processing to find and understand the clues in the questions, Watson compared possible answers by ranking its confidence in their accuracy. What's more, without machine learning to build confidence in its answers, Watson wasn't going to beat any *Jeopardy!* challenge winner.

Back when Watson was a trivia guru, it could sort through the equivalent of 200 million pages of data to uncover an answer in three seconds. Today, the Watson technology is available on the cloud as a service, 24 times faster, and has gone from the size of a master bedroom to three stacked pizza boxes! Read that sentence again, and now imagine what your Big Data world is going to look like in a couple of years. This exponential increase in capacity has changed what Watson can do today, the things that IBM has planned on the horizon for tomorrow, and the things that Watson will do in the far future that we don't even know about yet.

Watson represents a first step into cognitive systems, a new era of computing. While it makes use of programmatic computing (more on that in a bit), it adds three additional capabilities that make Watson truly unique: natural language processing, hypothesis generation and evaluation, and dynamic learning. Although none of these capabilities by itself is unique to Watson, the combination delivers the power to move beyond programmatic computing and to unlock the world of global unstructured data. Watson technology empowers you to move from a keyword-based search that provides a list of locations to an intuitive, conversational means of discovering a set of confidence-ranked responses.

When asked a question, Watson generates an hypothesis and comes up with both a response and a level of confidence. Watson, however, also shows you the steps that it took to get to that response, which is a form of reasoning. You don't program Watson; you work with it. Through these interactions, it learns much like humans do. Every experience makes it smarter and faster.

Watson can also teach. For example, new generations of doctors are helping Watson learn the language of medicine. In turn, Watson is helping to teach doctors by providing possible treatment options. Watson (and Watson-like technologies) are now assisting doctors at Memorial Sloan Kettering with diagnostics by providing a variety of possible causes for a set of symptoms. Watson can help doctors narrow down the options and pick the best treatments for their patients. The doctor still does most of the thinking; cognitive computing doesn't replace human intelligence—it augments it. Watson is there to make sense of the data and to help to make the process faster and more accurate.

Watson is also learning the language of finance to help wealth management advisors plan for their clients' retirement. For example, the IBM Watson Engagement Advisor can react to a caller's questions and help front-line service personnel find the right answers faster. The IBM Watson Discovery Advisor helps researchers uncover patterns that are hiding in mountains of data and then helps them share these new insights with colleagues. With Watson Analytics, you can ask Watson a question, and Watson then shows you what the data means in a way that is easy for anyone to understand and share—no techie required. Watson Data Explorer helps you to search, interrogate, and find the data wherever it might be—and this capability is a pillar to any Big Data and Analytics platform (we talk about this in the "A Big Data and Analytics Platform Manifesto" section in this chapter). Finally, there is also IBM Watson Developer's Cloud that offers the software, technology, and tools that developers need to take advantage of Watson's cognitive power over the cloud anytime.

For city leaders, such new systems can help them to prepare for major storms by predicting electrical outages. They can also help them to plan evacuations and prepare emergency management equipment and personnel to respond in the areas that will need help the most. These are just a few examples that show how Watson and cognitive computing are game changers. Personalization applications that help you to shop for clothes, pick a bottle of wine, and even invent a recipe (check out Chef Watson: www.bonappetit .com/tag/chef-watson) are another area in which IBM cognitive computing capabilities are redefining what Big Data solutions *can* do and what they *should* do.

The one thing to remember about Watson long after you've read this book is that *Watson provides answers to your questions.* Watson understands the nuances of human language and returns relevant answers in appropriate context. It keeps getting smarter, learning from each interaction with users and each piece of data it ingests. In other words, you don't really program Watson; you learn with it.

You might be familiar with Apple's Siri technology. People often ask us, "What's the difference?" Siri is preprogrammed, and all possible questions and her answers must be written into the application using structured data. Siri does not learn from her interactions either. Watson, on the other hand, reads through all kinds of data (structured, semistructured, and unstructured) to provide answers to questions in natural language. Watson learns from each interaction and gets smarter with time through its machine learning capabilities. We were pretty excited when IBM and Apple recently announced their partnership because we believe that Siri and Watson are going to go on a date and fireworks are going to happen! We also see the potential for IBM technologies such as the NoSQL Cloudant document store to get deeply embedded into iOS devices, thereby changing the game of this technology for millions of users.

Why Does the Big Data World Need Cognitive Computing?

You can more or less categorize the last century and a bit of computing into three eras.

- **The Tabulating System Era**   Circa 1900 onward. Think tabulation machines and calculators.

- **The Programmable System Era**   Circa 1950 onward. Programmable computers to run analyses in a deterministic manner.

- **Today's Cognitive Systems Era**   Circa 2011 onward. Systems that learn and interact with users through natural language, as well as some other technologies under the IBM Watson brand.

The systems of yesterday and today delivered tremendous business value and societal benefits by automating tabulation and harnessing computational power to boost both enterprise and personal productivity. Cognitive systems will forever change the way people interact with computing systems. People will extend their expertise across any domain of knowledge and make complex decisions involving the extraordinary volumes and types of data that can be found on the domain in the fast-moving world of Big Data.

The need for cognitive computing comes from the Big Data world in which we live. Figure 1-1 shows why cognitive computing is *the* requirement for the next generation of understanding, insight, and productivity.

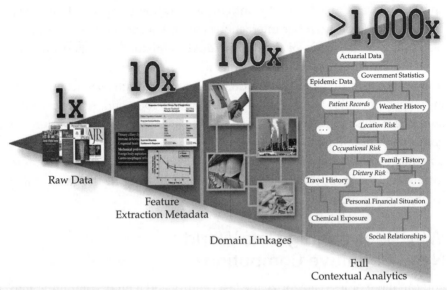

Figure 1-1 *Big Data analytics and the context multiplier effect*

Let's assume you use a wearable device that tracks your steps during the day and sleep patterns at night. In this case, the raw data is the number of steps and hours of sleep. From this raw data, the device can calculate the number of calories burned in a day; this is an example of *feature extraction*. You can also use this device's software to see at what points in the day you are active; for example, you were highly active in the latter part of the day and sedentary in the morning. During your sleeping hours, the device is able to leverage the metadata to map your sleeping habits. This device's accompanying application also enables you to log what you eat in a day and how much you weigh; this is a great example of *domain linkages*. You are mixing information about diet with physical markers that describe your overall sleep and activity levels. There might also be a social ecosystem where others share information such as occupation, location, some family medical history (such as "My dad died of a heart attack"), travel information, hobbies, and so on. Such a community can share information and encourage friendly competition to promote health. Such an infrastructure can represent a corpus for full contextual analytics. It can factor in other variables, such as the weather, and uncover trends, such as low activity, and alert you to them. This is a simple example, the point is that as interest in such a problem domain grows, so too does the data. Now think about the field of cancer research. Consider how many publications in this area are generated every day with all the clinical trials and the documentation behind both successes *and* failures. Think about all the relevant factors, such as a patient's family history, diet, lifestyle, job, and more. You can see that when you want to connect the dots—including dots that you can't even see at first—the data is going to get unmanageable and cognitive help is needed.

That help can come in the form of the new class of industry-specific solutions called cognitive systems, of which IBM Watson is a good example. The next generation of problem solvers is going to learn much faster than we ever did with cognitive computing technologies like Watson, and, in turn, Watson will learn much faster with our help. Cognitive computing will enable developers to solve new problems and business leaders to ask bigger questions. Together, people and technology will do things that generations before could not have imagined.

A Big Data and Analytics Platform Manifesto

To help an analytics-focused enterprise reach its potential, it is important to start with a checklist of "imperatives" for a Big Data and Analytics platform. We know that the trusted platforms of yesterday and, in some cases, today have limitations. We see these limitations daily as companies strive to transform themselves into data-driven, decision-making organizations. The limitations of traditional approaches have resulted in failed projects, expensive environments, nonscalable deployments, and system slowdowns.

You can't have a Big Data platform without relational database management systems (RDBMSs) or Hadoop. You need a framework to process and understand natural language. The data in your platform has to be governed and integrated; some data must have a sense of veracity to it, while others you cannot necessarily trust in the name of discovery. Moreover, there is no point in hosting a lot of data if you can't find it. In a Big Data world, it's no longer a "find the needle in a haystack" challenge; it's a "find the needle in a stack of needles" challenge.

The Big Data and Analytics platform that you build has to tackle *from the beginning* one of the biggest challenges that we have seen yet: how to realize

24/7 *decisioning* (rather than just 24/7 data collection). A big part of that capability, and surely the focus of the next inflection point, is cognitive computing.

When putting together the building blocks of a Big Data and Analytics platform, it is imperative that you start with the requirement that the platform *must* support all of your data. It must also be able to run all of the computations that are needed to drive your analytics, taking into consideration the expected service level agreements (SLAs) that will come with multitiered data. Figure 1-2 shows a vendor-neutral set of building blocks that we feel are "must have" parts of a true Big Data platform—it's our Big Data and Analytics Manifesto.

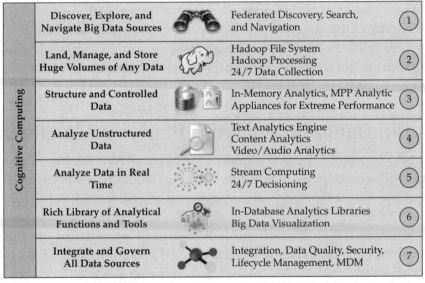

Figure 1-2   *A Big Data and Analytics platform manifesto: imperatives and underlying technologies*

1. Discover, Explore, and Navigate Big Data Sources

We believe that when it comes to boosting your analytics IQ, we are all guilty of the same thing: not knowing the things that we could already know. Considering the amount of data that is continually pouring into organizations, data collection is not the issue. Tools such as Google Desktop or Apple Spotlight are designed to find "stuff" on your laptop that you don't know or forgot you have. It's the same in the analytics world. With all the hype about Big Data, it's easy to see why companies can't wait to analyze new data types and make available new volumes of data with dreams of epiphanies that are just "around the corner." But any Big Data project should start with the "what you could already know" part. From personalized marketing to finance to public safety, your Big Data project should start with what you have. In other words, know what you have before you make big plans to go out and get more. Provision search, navigation, and discovery services over a broad range of data sources and applications, both inside and outside of your enterprise, to help your business uncover the most relevant information and insights. A plan to get more mileage out of the *data that you already have* before starting other data gathering projects will make understanding the new data that much easier.

The process of data analysis begins with understanding data sources, figuring out what data is available within a particular source, and getting a sense of its quality and its relationship to other data elements. This process, known as *data discovery,* enables data scientists to create the right analytic models and computational strategies. Traditional approaches required data to be physically moved to a central location before it could be discovered. With Big Data, this approach is too expensive and impractical.

To facilitate data discovery and unlock resident value within Big Data, the platform must be able to discover data that is *in place*. It has to be able to support the indexing, searching, and navigation of different sources of Big Data. Quite simply, it has to be able to facilitate discovery in a diverse set of data sources, such as databases, flat files, or content management systems—pretty much any persistent data store (including Hadoop) that contains structured, semistructured, or unstructured data.

And don't forget, these cross-enterprise search, discovery, and navigation services must strictly adhere to and preserve the inherent security profiles of the underlying data systems. For example, suppose that a financial document is redacted for certain users. When an authorized user searches for granular details in this document, the user will see all the details. But if someone else with a coarser level of authorization can see only the summary when directly accessing the data through its natural interfaces, that's all that will be surfaced by the discovery service; it could even be the case that the search doesn't turn up any data at all!

In a Big Data world, it's not just about being able to search your data repositories (we cover these repositories in Chapter 4); it's also about creating a platform that promotes the rapid development and deployment of search-based applications that leverage the Big Data architecture that you've put in place—and that's the point, right? You aren't investing in Big Data because you don't want people to use the data. These aren't data science projects; they are strategic business imperatives.

When you invest in the discovery of data that you already have, your business benefits immensely. Benefits include enhanced productivity with greater access to needed information and improved collaboration and decision making through better information sharing.

It's simple. In the same manner that humans forget stuff they used to know as they get older, organizations forget things too. We call it organizational amnesia and it's way more of an epidemic than you think. Keeping in mind that innovation is facilitated by making information available to empowered employees, when you start having conversations about getting beyond the Big Data hype, don't forget to include the information you already have—the information that you may have just forgotten about.

2. Land, Manage, and Store Huge Volumes of Any Data

Few technologies have gotten more buzz over the past few years than Hadoop (the subject of Chapter 6). When coupled with Big Data, you have enough hype to write a whole library of trendy technical books. There's a reason for all the excitement around these technologies. Traditional data storage and analytics tools have not been cutting it when dealing with Big Data. From a *volume* perspective, many tools start to become impractical when thresholds in the dozens of terabytes are exceeded. Sometimes, "impractical" means that the technology simply won't scale any further or that a tipping point is reached in terms of how much time it takes to work with data sets. And sometimes, "impractical" means that although the technology can scale, the licensing, administrative, and hardware costs to deal with increased data volumes become unpalatable. From a *variety* perspective, traditional analytic tools work well with only structured data, which represents, at most, 20 percent of the data in the world today.

Considering the pressing need for technologies that can overcome the volume and variety challenges for data at rest, it's no wonder that business magazines and online tech forums alike are buzzing about Hadoop. And it's not all talk either. The IT departments in most Fortune 500 companies have done more than a little experimentation with Hadoop. The problem is that many of these initiatives have stagnated in the "science project" phase. The challenges are common: It is easy and exciting to start dumping data into these repositories; the hard part comes with what to do next. The meaningful analysis of data that is stored in Hadoop requires highly specialized programming skills, and for many algorithms, it can be challenging to put them into a parallelizable form so that they can run in Hadoop. And what about information governance concerns, such as security and data lifecycle management, where new technologies like Hadoop don't have a complete story?

Some traditional database vendors consider Hadoop to be no more than a data preparation opportunity for their data warehousing projects. We disagree with that view and discuss how we see Hadoop at play for analytics, data integration, operation excellence, discovery and more in Chapter 6.

It is not just Hadoop that's at play here. The JSON specification is ubiquitous for how mobile information is encoded today. Understanding relationships between entities (people, things, places, and so on) is something that requires the use of graphs. Some data needs to "bit bucket" to just store any data and retrieve it via a simple key. All of these fall under the NoSQL database genre, and we cover that in Chapter 2.

3. Structured and Controlled Data

Despite what some might want you to believe, we are not seeing the end of the RDBMS era. In fact, it is quite the opposite. A Big Data and Analytics platform needs to be *polyglot* (see Chapter 2), and that means you are going to end up using NoSQL, Hadoop, *and* RDBMS technologies. These technologies support various information management *zones*, which we introduce you to in Chapter 4. One of the zones requires that data be highly structured, controlled, and harvested.

If we had to pick an area that comes close to being as hot as Hadoop or Big Data, it would be *in-memory columnar databases*. In-memory computing offers the advantage of speed in data-intensive processing for analytics and reporting. As the cost of computer memory drops, in-memory processing "obliterates the wait" for business answers, and RDBMS technologies are behind this success. What's more, as the memory in CPU caches continues to expand, there is even more opportunity to get data into the CPU cache, which is inordinately faster than system RAM. These technologies are appealing because they typically require much less DBA involvement compared to traditional solutions. For example, performance-tuning objects such as indexes are not needed or created, which allows data scientists and line-of-business (LOB) owners to self-serve their analytics. Just load the data and go! Indeed, the future buyer of IT is the LOB, and collectively, they are driving the demand for software as a service (SaaS) analytics; IBM dashDB and Amazon Redshift are perfect examples of cloud-driven SaaS analytics services (we talk about this in Chapter 3).

Some of your data might be populated from the Hadoop repository, as discussed in the previous section, but some of it might come from another source that is trending in the structured and controlled data world: the analytical appliance (Chapter 9). Traditional architectures decoupled analytical environments from data environments. Analytical software would run on its own infrastructure and retrieve data from back-end data warehouses or other systems to perform complex analytics. The rationale was that data environments were optimized for faster data access but not necessarily for advanced mathematical computations. Hence, analytics were treated as a distinct workload that had to be managed in a separate infrastructure. This architecture was expensive to manage and operate, created data redundancy, and performed poorly with increasing data volumes. The analytic architecture prescribed in this manifesto is one that can run both data processing and complex analytics on the same platform. It needs to deliver petabyte-scale throughput by seamlessly executing analytic models inside the platform, against the entire data set, without replicating or sampling data. It must also enable data scientists to iterate through different models more quickly to facilitate discovery and experimentation with a "best fit" yield.

4. Manage and Analyze Unstructured Data

For a long time, data has been classified on the basis of its type—structured, semistructured, or unstructured. Existing infrastructures typically have barriers that prevent the seamless correlation and holistic analysis of these data classifications, and independent systems have been used to store and manage these different data types. We've also seen the emergence of hybrid systems that can be disappointing because they don't natively manage all data types. For the most part—there are some exceptions—we find the "trying to fit a circle shape through a square hole" approach comes with a lot of compromise.

Of course, organizational processes don't distinguish among data types. When you want to analyze customer support effectiveness, structured information about a customer service representative's conversation (such as call duration, call outcome, customer satisfaction survey responses, and so on) is as important as unstructured information gleaned from that conversation (such as sentiment, customer feedback, and verbally expressed concerns). Effective analysis needs to factor in *all* components of an interaction and to analyze them within the same context, *regardless* of whether the underlying data is structured or not. A Big Data and Analytics platform must be able to manage, store, and retrieve both unstructured and structured data, but it must also provide tools for unstructured data exploration and analysis. (We touch on this in Chapter 6, where we cover Hadoop.)

This is a key point that we do not want you to miss because it is often overlooked. You likely do not have the appetite or the budget to hire hundreds of expensive Java developers to build extractors. Nor are you likely a LinkedIn- or Facebook-like company; you have a different core competency—your business. To process and analyze the unstructured data that is found in call logs, sentiment expressions, contracts, and so on, you need a rich ecosystem in which you can develop those extractors. That ecosystem must start with a tool set: visually rich tooling that enables you to compose and work with the extractions. You will want to compose textual understanding algorithms through a declarative language; in other words, you should not have to rely on bits and bytes Java programming, but rather on an app-based composition framework that is more consumable throughout the enterprise. If you want to query Hadoop data at rest, you are likely looking for an SQL-like interface to query unstructured data. This way, you can leverage the extensive skills in which you have invested. Finally, the ecosystem should have the ability to compile the higher-level declarations (the queries that you write) into code that can be executed in an efficient and well-performing manner, just like the SQL that is optimized under the covers by every RDBMS vendor.

Of course, you can apply the same requirements to video and audio, among other data types. For example, IBM hosts what we believe to be the world's largest image classification library. Pictures are retrieved on the basis of attributes that are "learned" through training sets. Imagine combing through thousands of photos looking for winter sports without having to tag them as winter sports. You can try it for yourself at http://mp7.watson.ibm.com/imars/.

5. Analyze Data in Real Time

Performing analytics on activity as it unfolds presents a huge untapped opportunity for the enterprise. For the most part, we still see analytic models and computations running on at-rest data that's stored in repositories (traditional databases, Hadoop, and so on). Although this works well for transpired events that occurred a few minutes, hours, or even days before, these repositories generally rely on disk drives to store and retrieve data. Even the best-performing disk drives and memory-optimized databases have unacceptable latencies when reacting to certain events in real time.

Enterprises that want to boost their analytics IQ need the ability to analyze data *as it is being generated* and then take appropriate action. The idea is to derive insight *before* the data is stored. We refer to this type of data as *streaming data* and the analysis of it as the *analytics of data in motion*. Depending on the time of day or other contexts, the volume of the data stream can vary dramatically. For example, consider a stream of data that is carrying stock trades in an exchange. Depending on trading events, that stream can quickly swell from 10 to 100 times its normal volume. This implies that a Big Data platform not only has to support analytics on data at rest, but also has to effectively manage increasing volumes of data streams and support analytics on data in motion. To get beyond the Big Data hype, you have to ensure you are not just having conversations about analytics on data at rest You have to converse about how insights gleaned through analytics on at-rest data get applied to data in motion. We cover this topic in Chapter 7.

6. A Rich Library of Analytical Functions and Tools

One of the key goals of a Big Data and Analytics platform should be to reduce the *analytic cycle time*, the amount of time that it takes to discover and transform data, develop and score models, and analyze and publish results. When your platform empowers you to run extremely fast analytics, you have the foundation on which to support multiple analytic iterations and speed up model development. Although this is the goal, there needs to be a focus on improving developer productivity. By making it easy to discover data, develop and deploy models, visualize results, and integrate with front-end applications, your organization can enable practitioners, such as analysts and data scientists, to be more effective. We refer to this concept as the *art of consumability*. Consumability is key to democratizing Big Data across the enterprise. You shouldn't just *want*; you should *always demand* that your Big Data and Analytics platform flatten the time-to-analysis curve with a rich set of accelerators, libraries of analytic functions, and a tool set that brings agility to the development and visualization process. Throughout this book, we illustrate how this part of the manifesto is rooted across the IBM Big Data and Analytics platform.

A new take on an old saying is appropriate here: *"A picture is worth a thousand terabytes."* Because analytics is an emerging discipline, it is not uncommon to find data scientists who have their own preferred approach to creating and visualizing models. It's important that you spend time focusing on the visualization of your data because that will be a key consumability attribute and communication vehicle for your platform. It is *not the case* that the fancier the visualization, the better—so we are not asking you to use your Office Excel 3D mapping rotations here. That said, Big Data does offer some new kinds of visualizations that you will want to get acquainted with, such as Streamgraphs, Treemaps, Gantt charts, and more. But rest assured, your eyes will still be looking over the traditional bar charts and scatter plots too.

Data scientists often build their models by using packaged applications, emerging open source libraries, or "roll your own" approaches to build models with procedural languages. Creating a restrictive development environment curtails their productivity. A Big Data and Analytics platform needs to support interaction with the most commonly available analytic packages. There should also be deep integration that facilitates the pushing of computationally intensive activities, such as model scoring, from those packages into the platform on premise or in the cloud. At a minimum, your data-at-rest and data-in-motion environments should support SAS, SPSS, and R. The platform also needs to support a rich set of "parallelizable" algorithms (think: machine learning) that has been developed and tested to run on Big Data (we cover all of this in Chapter 6), with specific capabilities for unstructured data analytics (such as text analytic routines) and a framework for developing additional algorithms. Your platform should provide the ability to visualize and publish results in an intuitive and easy-to-use manner.

7. Integrate and Govern All Data Sources

Over the last few years, the information management community has made enormous progress in developing sound data management principles. These include policies, tools, and technologies for data quality, security, governance, master data management, data integration, and information lifecycle management. These principles establish veracity (trust) in the data and are extremely critical to the success of any analytics program. For example, if a certain masking policy is used for credit card data in the RDBMS, why isn't the same policy used to mask the data when it resides in Hadoop's HDFS file system? If you want to know where a certain set of data comes from and what was done to it before you draw inferences from it, does it matter where the data resides? No! Unfortunately, from what we can tell, although many agree with our mindset here, many don't practice it.

We struggled when it came to the location of this part of the manifesto in Figure 1-2. Its current location suggests that the entire Big Data and Analytics platform should sit on the ability to integrate and govern all data sources— which is our intent. On the other hand, we see too many people treat this topic as an afterthought—and that leads to security exposure, wasted resources, untrusted data, and more. We actually think that you should scope your Big Data architecture with integration and governance in mind from the very start. In fact, you should probably do this for all the data assets in your organization. Think about it this way: Deciding *not* to govern some "toss-away" data is actually a governance decision. By handling all data that you are keeping for analytics as though it will be governed, you are on the right path to a modern information management architecture.

We get it. Governance can be akin to when your mother asked you to clean up your room; you didn't like it, but at the same time, you now know how good it was for you. We will tell you this: Organizations that do more than take a minimal effort to comply with an approach to governance end up creating regulatory dividends by repurposing the same data for other uses. A Big Data and Analytics platform should embrace these principles and treat them as foundational and intrinsic to the platform itself, which is a guideline that represents the main theme of Part III.

Cognitive Computing Systems

As we discussed earlier in this chapter, cognitive computing systems learn from and interact naturally with people to extend what either humans or machines could do on their own. They help human experts to make better decisions by penetrating the complexity of Big Data. When you look at the capabilities that are outlined in our Big Data and Analytics platform manifesto, it becomes obvious how these capabilities can feed cognitive systems so that artificial intelligence meets business intelligence. That is where the next frontier of discovery is to be found, be it a cure for cancer or concierge shopping services. For IBM, the place where data is prepared for cognitive systems is Watson Foundations, the focus of Part II.

Of Cloud and Manifestos...

We didn't explicitly come out and say it (yet), but the cloud is going to play a big part of your Big Data and Analytics platform. Whether you are using it for bursty workloads that need the scalability relief that this deployment model can offer or for turnkey discovery, you should ensure that the capabilities that are described in this manifesto are available as composable services in the cloud if it makes sense to do so.

When you assemble your Big Data and Analytics platform, ensure that the vendors with which you partner showcase their ability to deliver the services that are outlined in this manifesto, in multiple modalities, to suit your business needs.

Cloud-based delivery models for IT infrastructure, frictionless development, and service-provisioned capabilities are so critical to a Big Data strategy that we dedicated an entire chapter to it in this book! For the most part, the IBM Information Management capabilities cloud service offerings (such as IBM DataWorks and dashDB) will drive the innovations that you will see in its on-premise appliance and software solution offerings (such as the BLU Acceleration technology in DB2). This is all part of a *cloud-first* strategy that is born "agile" and drives IBM's ability to more quickly deliver Big Data analytic capability to the marketplace in the manner in which it will be consumed.

Now reflect on some of the required Big Data and Analytics platform capabilities we outlined in our manifesto. It means you may want to leverage a cloud service to perform one of the many data refinery activities available in the IBM Cloud. The catalog of these services is collectively known as IBM DataWorks. IBM BLU Acceleration technology is available as a turkey analytics powerhouse service called dashDB. (dashDB also includes other services, some of which are found in the IBM DataWorks catalog, along with Netezza capabilities and more.)

The cloud-first strategy isn't just for IBM's Information Management brand either. Watson Analytics is a set of services that provide a cloud-based predictive and cognitive analytics discovery platform that's purposely designed for the business user (remember the new buyer of IT we talked about earlier in this chapter).

Need a JSON document store to support a fast-paced and agile app dev environment? It's available in the IBM cloud as well; Hadoop cluster, yup; SQL data store, yup—you get the point. From standing up computing resources (infrastructure as service), to composing applications (platform as a service—think IBM Bluemix), to running them (the IBM Cloud marketplace SaaS environment), the richest capability of service we know of is available from IBM. These services are mostly available in a freemium model to get going with options for enterprise-scale use and sophistication. Finally, the IBM Cloud services catalog doesn't just contain IBM capabilities, it includes services delivered through a rich partner ecosystem and open source technologies too.

Wrapping It Up

In this chapter, we introduced you to the concept of Big Data. We also highlighted the future of analytics: cognitive computing. Finally, we shared with you our Big Data and Analytics platform manifesto.

We kept most of this chapter vendor agnostic. We wanted to give you a solid background against which you can evaluate the vendors that you choose to help you build your own Big Data and Analytics platform and to describe the things to look for when you design the architecture. In short, this chapter gave you the key points to guide you in any Big Data conversation. The remaining chapters in this part of the book cover NoSQL and the cloud.

By the time you finish this part, you will have a solid understanding of the main topics of discussion in today's data-intensive analytics landscape.

Of course, it goes without saying that we hope you will agree that IBM is a Big Data and Analytics partner that has journeyed further with respect to strategic vision and capabilities than any other vendor in today's marketplace. And although we would love you to implement every IBM solution that maps to this manifesto, remember that the entire portfolio is modular in design. You can take the governance pieces for database activity monitor and use those on MongoDB or another vendor's distribution of Hadoop. Whatever vendor, or vendors, you choose to partner with on your Big Data journey, be sure to follow this Big Data and Analytics manifesto.

2

To SQL or Not to SQL: That's Not the Question, It's the Era of Polyglot Persistence

The word *polyglot* is used to refer to an individual who knows multiple languages. What does this have to do with information technology? Well, this is the term that's been adopted to describe what IBM calls a *Next Generation Data Platform Architecture*, one that combines the use of multiple persistence (storage) techniques to build, store, and manage data applications (apps) in the most efficient way possible. We believe that apps will become polyglot in the sense that end users interact with a single interface, while the back-end app is a combination of persistence technologies and APIs working in harmony "under the covers." If you look at the IBM Bluemix platform as a service (PaaS) model, which we talk about in the next chapter, it becomes apparent how next-generation apps will be composed of a set of polyglot services. What's more, consuming functionality through the use of an API service is the future of app development—the API economy we call it. So beyond just data, the apps of the future (and many of today) are polyglot.

Polyglot persistence is a handyman's toolbox approach to solving complex data-layer problems. The data platform (toolbox) of tomorrow—which was really needed yesterday—has to bring various technologies (tools) to support a polyglot environment. This enables organizations to break down complicated data-layer problems into segments and to select the best technology for each problem segment. No technology completely replaces another; there are existing investments in database infrastructure, skills honed over decades, and existing best practices that cannot (and should not) be thrown away. Innovation around polyglot solutions and NoSQL technologies will be *complementary* to existing SQL systems. The question is and always has been "What is available to help the business, and what is the problem that we are trying to solve?" If you're having a Big Data conversation that's intended to get beyond the hype, you need to verse yourself with polyglot concepts—the point of this chapter.

The easiest way to look at polyglot persistence is first to understand the emergence of the two most ubiquitous data persistence architectures in use today: SQL and NoSQL. (We are setting aside for the moment another, more recent approach, which is aptly named NewSQL.) NoSQL is not just a single technology, a fact that makes any conversations on this topic a bit more complicated than most. There are many kinds of NoSQL technologies. Even the NoSQL classification system is full of complexity (for example, the data model for some columnar family stores is a key/value format, but there are key/value databases too). In fact, the last time we looked, there were more than 125 open source NoSQL database offerings! (For a summary of the current landscape, see 451 Group's Matt Aslett's data platforms landscape map at http://tinyurl.com/pakbgbd.)

The global NoSQL market has been forecasted to be $3.4 billion by 2020, experiencing 21 percent compounded annual growth rates (CAGRs) between 2015 and 2020, according to the value-added reseller firm Solid IT. The bottom line is that NoSQL technologies continue to gain traction (some much more than others); but the majority have ended up as spins-offs or off-shoots or have just faded away. In this chapter we are going to talk about the styles of NoSQL databases and refer to some of the ones that have made their mark and didn't fade away.

You likely interact with NoSQL databases (directly or indirectly) on a daily basis. Do you belong to any social sites? Are you an online gamer? Do you buy things online? Have you experienced a personalized ad on your mobile device or web browser? If you answered "yes" to any of these questions, you've been touched by NoSQL technology. In fact, if you're a Microsoft Xbox One gamer, have leveraged the Rosetta Stone learning platform to make yourself a polyglot, bought concert tickets through Ticketmaster, or put a document in Dropbox, you're actually interacting with one of IBM's NoSQL offerings, Cloudant, which handles more than 10 billion transactions per day and supports millions of databases (see Chapter 10). NoSQL comes from an evolution in the IT landscape that is characterized by massive amounts of data around *interactions*—not just transactions. This is the rapid-fire "fuzzy" data that powers today's *systems of engagement* (more about these systems later), smart devices, and web apps. To address this shift, new models of app development, data storage, and data access are needed. In fact, you will find that NoSQL has an even larger role to play as we move from people-driven systems of engagement to the engagement of "things"—the Internet of Things.

In this chapter, we introduce you to the world of polyglot persistence and why it's critical for enterprises to adopt this methodology. We dispel some doomsday myths and articulate how the IBM Big Data and Analytics platform's DNA has been engineered for this specific methodology. We focus on NoSQL in this chapter because that area is likely newer for most readers. We assume that relational database management systems (RDBMSs) are well understood in the organization where you build, test, and deploy apps, so won't talk about them here unless it helps the NoSQL discussion.

By the time you finish reading this chapter, you will have a firm understanding of what NoSQL is all about, including its applicability in a Big Data world (hint: it's not what you put on your résumé if you don't have any SQL skills). You'll also appreciate how a polyglot environment can deliver enormous benefits and economies of scale to your business and that single technology approaches are not always up to the task for the requirements at hand; indeed, the "one ring to rule them all" approach is best left to Tolkien books.

Core Value Systems: What Makes a NoSQL Practitioner Tick

One of the key reasons behind the emergence of NoSQL is its practitioners. Consider database administrators (DBAs), developers, and the term *performance*. Performance to a DBA typically means in relation to a service level agreement (SLA): "Is it running as fast as I promised that it would run?" To developers performance means: "How fast can I build my app?"

Think about it—today's social-mobile-cloud apps evolve so rapidly, and the barrier to entry for new apps is so flat, thanks to the cloud, that developers need two things: an endless supply of super-caffeinated beverages and an app lifecycle that supports a near-continuous innovation and integration of code changes.

Developers deserve and expect better than "good enough" technologies, and their tools and infrastructure must continually improve. At first, this doesn't sound like great news for folks on the operations side of the house. Developers have become so influential in our social-mobile-cloud world that the emergence of as-a-service cloud models and the marriage between developers and operations personnel (DevOps) directly reflect the need for businesses to be agile if they want to be innovative. The IBM Bluemix platform as a service (PaaS) development ecosystem is all about agility—it provides developers with hundreds of IBM, non-IBM, and open source services to compose apps in a hosted environment powered by Softlayer—and that includes a number of NoSQL services. (We talk about Bluemix and the cloud in Chapter 3.)

Developers are the most visible force driving NoSQL technologies because line-of-business (LOB) owners are asking for quick delivery, and developers are the ones building the apps. There's an undeniable confluence between the changing nature of the data in a Big Data world and emerging technologies that seek to quench the thirst by developers for better ways to not only persist that data, but work with it in an agile manner too. Make no mistake about it: NoSQL is here to stay.

To better appreciate a developer's demand for agility, let's assume you're a developer who is enhancing a mobile shopping cart app for your company. You've been tasked with personalizing this app by an executive team that believes this enhancement will help drive users to make more "no-thought, on-the-spot" purchases. You've been on this project for two months, coming off the heels of an earlier project that took three months to complete. Your life is characterized by these types of project-to-project assignments. As you design the personalization aspects of your app, you decide that it's a great idea to add a Facebook ID field so that tailored offers can be shared within the user's network.

Traditionally, if the data is stored in an RDBMS, the developer has to go to the DBA and request a database schema change. The DBA schedules the work required to fulfill the request. Perhaps the developer will see something in the test system within a day or two ("We'll let you know when it's done" is the stuff that makes developers cringe). Now, think about this app in production...your change request to surface the new Facebook scoring module falls into the realm of DBA "limbo." Ask colleagues who have been in similar situations how long this might take and the answer might shock you. In some companies, it's months! (Additional data modeling could create even further delays.)

Developers want to be able to add, modify, or remove data attributes at will, without having to deal with middlemen or "pending approval" obstacles. They want to experiment, learn from failure, and be agile. If they are to fail, they want to fail fast (we talk about this methodology in Chapter 4). Agility is prized because mobile app users expect continuous functional enhancements, but the friction of traditional development approaches typically doesn't allow for that. In most environments, developers have to keep "in sync" with DBA change cycles.

NoSQL databases appeal to these developers because they can evolve apps rapidly without DBA or data modeler intervention. There are other scenarios as well. Speed of transaction matters in a social-mobile-cloud world; depending on the app, many developers are willing to serve up "stale" results (by using data that might be slightly out of date and will in all likelihood eventually be right, it's just not right now) in exchange for more responsive and faster apps—in some cases they are okay if the data is lost—we discuss these trade-offs later in this chapter. We think Big Data conversations that include polyglot open the door to a more satisfactory trade-off between consistency and availability.

This agility scenario sums up what we believe are the fundamental differences between the SQL and NoSQL worlds. There are others. For example, in the SQL world, a lot of the work to store data has to be done up front (this is often referred to as *schema-first* or *schema-on-write*), but getting data out is pretty simple (for example, Excel easily generates SQL queries). In the NoSQL world, however, it's really easy to store data (just dump it in), and much of the work goes into programming ways to get the data out (*schema-later* or *schema-on-read*).

As previously mentioned, NoSQL was born out of a need for scalability. Most (not all) NoSQL technologies run on elastic scale-out clusters, but most RDBMSs are hard-pressed to scale horizontally for transactions. Microsoft SQL Server doesn't have anything here that isn't some kind of workaround; at the time of writing, SAP HANA doesn't support scale-out for OLTP, and those with experience trying to get Oracle RAC to scale know the effort that is involved. From a transactional perspective, it's fair to give IBM's DB2 for System z and DB2 pureScale offerings due credit here. Their well-proven transactional scale-out and performance-optimizing services are made possible by IBM's Coupling Facility technology for bringing in and removing resources without having to alter your apps to achieve the near-linear performance gains that you would expect when scaling a cluster. It's also fair to note that almost every RDBMS vendor has at least a semi-proven solution for scaling out business intelligence (BI) apps—but these are very focused on structured data.

Table 2-1 lists a number of other differences between the NoSQL and SQL worlds. We aren't going to get into the details for each of them (or this would be solely a NoSQL book), but we touch on some throughout the remainder of this chapter. Take note that what we're listing in this table are general tendencies—there are exceptions.

The NoSQL World (Schema Later)	The SQL World (Schema First)
New questions? No schema change	New questions? Schema change
Schema change in minutes, if not seconds	Schema: permission process (we're not talking minutes here)
Tolerate chaos for new insights and agility (the cost of "getting it wrong" is low)	Control freaks (in many cases for good reasons)
Agility in the name of discovery (easy to change)	Single version of the truth
Developers code integrity (yikes!)	Database manages integrity (consistency from any app that access the database)
Eventual consistency (the data that you read might not be current)	Consistency (can guarantee that the data you are reading is 100 percent current)
All kinds of data	Mostly structured data
Consistency, availability, and partition tolerance (CAP)	Atomicity, consistency, isolated, durable (ACID)

Table 2-1 *Characteristics of the NoSQL and SQL Worlds*

What Is NoSQL?

In our collective century-plus experience with IT, we honestly can't recall a more confrontational classification for a set of technologies than NoSQL. More ironic is the popular trend of adopting SQL practices and terminology in NoSQL solutions. We're sure that there are practitioners who feel that the name is apt because, as they see it, a war is coming—a sort of *Game of Thrones* ("The Database") where the Wildings of the North (the NoSQL "barbarians") are set to take over the regulated (and boring) world of RDBMSs. Although this sounds pretty exciting, it's simply not going to happen. The term *NoSQL* was the happy (some would say not happy) result of a developer meet-up that was pressed to come up with a name for SQL-alternative technologies.

Popular NoSQL products—which we classify later in this chapter— include Cloudant, MongoDB, Redis, Riak, Couchbase, HBase, and Cassandra, among others. These products almost exclusively run on Linux, leverage locally attached storage (though sometimes network-attached storage), and scale out on commodity hardware.

SQL, which has been around for 40 years, is the biggest craze in the NoSQL Hadoop ecosystem space. SQL is so hot because it's incredibly well suited to querying data structures and because it is a declarative language, which is so important because it enables you to get an answer without having to program *how* to get it.

This matters. It matters when it comes to broadening insights about your organization. A terrific example of this involves the IBM SQL on Hadoop engine (called Big SQL) available in InfoSphere BigInsights for Hadoop—a "just the query engine" stand-alone MPP Hadoop SQL processing engine that quite simply is the best in its class. The IBM approach is different than other vendors such as Oracle, Teradata, Pivotal, and Microsoft; they focus on a "use the RDBMS to either submit a remote query or run the entire query with the involvement of a database" approach. A true Hadoop query engine runs the MPP SQL query engine on Hadoop, uses Hive metadata, and operates on data stored in Hadoop's file system using common Hadoop data types. (For details on SQL on Hadoop and Big SQL see Chapter 6).

We believe that Big SQL can deliver incredible performance benefits and is more suitable over anything we've seen in the marketplace, including Cloudera Impala. Why? First, IBM has been in the MPP SQL parallelization game for more than four decades; as you can imagine, there's decades of experience in the Big SQL optimizer. Second, IBM's Big SQL offers the richest SQL support that we know of today in this space—it supports the SQL used in today's enterprises. That's very different from supporting the SQL that's easiest to implement, which is the tactic of many other vendors, like those that support query-only engines. If Hadoop SQL compatibility were a golf game, we'd say that the IBM Big SQL offering is in the cup or a tap-in birdie, whereas others are in the current position of trying to chip on to save a bogey.

Don't lose sight of the motivation behind polyglot persistence: attaching the right approach and technology for the business problem at hand. Conversations around SQL and NoSQL should focus more on how the two technologies complement one another. In the same way that a person living in Canada is better served by speaking English *and* French, a data architecture that can easily combine NoSQL and SQL techniques offers greater value than the two solutions working orthogonally. In our opinion—and there are those who will debate this—the rise of NoSQL has really been driven by developers and the requirements we outlined earlier in this chapter. New types of apps (online gaming, ad serving, and so on), the social-mobile-cloud phenomenon, and the acceptance of something we call *eventual consistency* (where data might not necessarily be the most current—no problem if you are counting "Likes" on Facebook but a big deal if you're looking at your account balance) are all significant factors.

Is Hadoop a NoSQL Database?

Having referenced Hadoop in this chapter already, it is worth taking a moment to tackle a question that we get quite often: "Is Hadoop a NoSQL store?" This question can confuse a lot of people. We already touched on how Hadoop and IBM's Big SQL technologies are a great example of the ubiquitous demand for SQL support across almost all emerging data-related technologies, so it's a natural question to ask.

We classify Hadoop as an ecosystem of software packages that provides a computing framework. These include MapReduce, which leverages a K/V (key/value) processing framework (don't confuse that with a K/V database); a file system (HDFS); and many other software packages that support everything from importing and exporting data (Sqoop) to storing transactional data (HBase), orchestration (Avro and ZooKeeper), and more. When you hear that someone is running a Hadoop cluster, it's likely to mean MapReduce (or some other framework like Spark) running on HDFS, but others will be using HBase (which also runs on HDFS). Vendors in this space include IBM (with BigInsights for Hadoop), Cloudera, Hortonworks, MapR, and Pivotal. On the other hand, NoSQL refers to non-RDBMS SQL database solutions such as HBase, Cassandra, MongoDB, Riak, and CouchDB, among others.

At least for now, Hadoop is mostly used for analytic workloads. Over time, we expect that to change; indeed, parts of its ecosystem, such as HBase, are being used for transactional work and have emerging database properties for transactional control. Like NoSQL databases, Hadoop is implemented on commodity clusters that scale out and run on Linux (although Hortonworks did port its Hortonworks Data Platform (HDP) to Windows in partnership with Microsoft). The disk architecture behind this ecosystem is almost always locally attached disks.

Different Strokes for Different Folks: The NoSQL Classification System

As it turns out, NoSQL is a broad topic. To make it easier to talk about NoSQL, we will introduce you to the four "flavors" that the marketplace has settled on when it comes to classifying NoSQL databases. That being said, keep in mind that some of the classification lines are blurred because some flavors are being mixed for interoperation. For example, the NoSQL HBase database (shipped as part of the IBM InfoSphere BigInsights for Hadoop offering) has both key/value and columnar influences within its capabilities.

Give Me a Key, I'll Give You a Value: The Key/Value Store

A *key/value* (K/V) database provides access to a value primarily through a key. As a simple analogy, think of the way you interact with files on your laptop as a key/value store (it isn't...but as an analogy it works). Let's assume you want to open a picture called `AnnaErikChloePicnic.jpg` located in the `c:\temp` directory. To work with this file, you would use the `c:\temp` key to locate it and then pull *all of the file* into your app for viewing. In a nutshell, that's a K/V store. Values in a K/V store are generally said to be *opaque binary objects* because you can't really see into them unless you pull all the values out, but you can pretty much store anything you want in them (we say "generally" because some K/V stores offer the ability to support partial key retrieval through manually defined metadata). Keeping in mind our analogy, for the most part, you can drop anything you want into a file system directory (text files, graphic files, audio) and locate the information by using the key, which in this analogy's case is the directory pathname. In the same way you don't load half a photo, in a true K/V store, you don't fetch a portion of the values. (If you want to do that, you should likely be using a NoSQL document database, which we cover in the next section.) K/V stores are less suited for complex data structures as well; they typically can't be used as a substitute for JSON-encoded NoSQL document database stores, such as IBM Cloudant, which is more suited for persisting complex data structures.

K/V stores are popular for user sessions and shopping cart sessions because they can provide rapid scaling for simple data collections. For example, you might use a K/V store to create a front end for a retail web site's product catalog (this is information that doesn't change very often); if inconsistent changes do occur, they're not going to create major problems that grind service to a halt. NoSQL's eventually consistent data model applies conflict resolution strategies under the covers while the distributed database "agrees" (eventually) to a consistent view of your data. Data that is typically found in K/V stores isn't highly related, so practitioners rely on basic programmatic CRUD (create, read, update, delete) interfaces to work with them.

We estimate that K/V stores represent about 24 percent of the NoSQL market. Examples of K/V databases include MemcacheDB, Redis, Riak, Amazon DynamoDB, and the one we aren't supposed to say out loud (Voldemort), among others. IBM provides HBase (packaged with the InfoSphere BigInsights for Hadoop offering, available on premise and off premise through the IBM Cloud), which includes a number of enterprise-hardening and accessibility features such as SQL and high-availability services. (HBase has columnar characteristics as well, so we return to that product in our discussion about columnar stores.) Finally, it's fair to note that IBM's Cloudant document store has been used with great success for many of the use cases mentioned earlier.

The Grand-Daddy of Them All: The Document Store

The *document store* is basically a K/V store, but instead of the value being a smattering of numbers, web session token IDs, or a string, it's a document, such as a customer record or even a book. It has structure that you can see and work with, and it is the most intuitive way for persisting objects that we can see and think about in the real world. Document stores are by far the most popular

NoSQL technology deployed today. Our research suggests that document stores represent more than 63 percent of today's NoSQL revenue landscape.

What you store in a NoSQL document database can be any kind of data at all, so you'll sometimes see this genre competing with the K/V store that we talked about in the previous section. In fact, we've seen ever-increasing adoption of document stores over K/V stores for apps that require a NoSQL data layer solution. For example, Cloudant (a JSON document data store) has rich-text searching facilities, geospatial capabilities, geoload balancing, and a *masterless* (not master-slave) architecture that is ideally suited for the data layer tasks that can hamper a K/V store. We've seen a number of clients implement Cloudant instead of Amazon Dynamo DB because of the markedly better performance and flexibility of Cloudant's data layer (flip to Chapter 10 for a detailed look at Cloudant). Other examples of document databases include Couchbase, MarkLogic, and MongoDB. As well, there are RDBMS solutions such as DB2 and Informix, which have introduced JSON services within their relational engines.

The key thing to remember about a document store is that it's a way to store and retrieve documents by way of a primary key, which serves as the document ID. The corresponding value is the document itself. Technologies in this space typically enable you to index the documents, and those documents can be nested (think of a family tree as an example). And as long as the incoming data meets some loose definition of a document, you are able to store that data in a document database. You can see some overlap with the pure K/V use cases right away; this type of NoSQL database is great for a product catalog, especially a frequently changing one! NoSQL document data stores are characteristically flexible: They are ideal for persisting objects where the schema is not well defined or is likely to change in the future; now reflect back on the kinds of apps we noted are being built for the social-mobile-cloud Big Data world. And moreover, you don't need a DBA to jump in and go through the mundane work of redefining a database schema—the schema for each document is self-describing, so that one document's schema can be altered without having to lock down the entire database to make the change. These are some of the reasons why the document store is the kingpin of the NoSQL world at this time. What kind of document gets stored in a document store? The document store genre of the NoSQL world is dominated by one word: *JSON*.

What Is JSON, and Why Is It the "New Cool"?

If you know what JSON is, you can skip this section. If you think that JSON is the name of the person in the corner office, please read on. We're not going to cover all the details of JSON in this section, so if you want to learn more about it than what we cover here, check out www.JSON.org.

JSON stands for JavaScript Object Notation. It has become the de facto lightweight data interchange format and is predominantly used to exchange data between programs that were written in virtually any modern programming language. JSON has trumped XML as the industry's darling markup language because of JSON's readability (for both humans and machines), a self-describing schema, hierarchical data structures (you can have values nested within complex objects, such as having separate mobile and office phone numbers in a phoneNumber object), it's less verbose, and more. JSON's syntax will be familiar to anyone who has worked with a modern programming language, and it is designed to be minimalist (it's shorter and more compact, which is great when you are sending data everywhere in a mobile world). For example, the XML representation of <name>John</name> can alternatively be expressed in JSON as "name" : "John"; you can appreciate how JSON not only presents data in a more readable format, but also significantly reduces the footprint of your documents.

We have mentioned that NoSQL databases typically have no predefined and rigid schemas for storing data; this leads to another benefit: modeling. It seems to us that using a single JSON document to define a product catalog is a lot easier than shredding and joining a number of tables in a third normal form (3NF) database schema. Because there is no predefined schema with JSON, it can represent an endless number of data structures. If a developer is able to persist multiple classes of data structures within the same database, then the process of designing a database to fit a client's business model is simplified. For example, imagine a commercial retail store that wants to model its inventory; the fields and descriptors needed for products in the home cleaning supplies section will require very different data representations than a widescreen television from the electronics department. Using JSON, these two different product taxonomies can be stored side by side, thanks to the flexibility of JSON's document-specific schema.

JSON is well suited to the NoSQL world because that world is not cluttered by the overuse of NULL values that you typically find in relational database tables that store sparse data sets. (In a social-mobile-cloud world, there are hundreds or thousands of stored attributes, and not all of them have data values. Think of a detailed social profile that is barely filled out—this is an example of a sparse data set.)

The multitude of data types that you can represent with JSON are intuitive and comprehensive: strings, numbers, Booleans, nulls, arrays, and objects (nested combinations of these data types). JSON is composed with curly brackets ({ }) and can contain arrays (unlike XML), which are denoted with square brackets ([ ]). You use double quotation marks (" ") to denote a string. For example, 35 is a number on which you can perform arithmetic operations, whereas "35" is a string—both could be used for age, but the data type that you choose has implications for what you can do with the data.

In almost every use case that we've seen, JSON processing is much faster than XML processing; it's much easier to read and write too. As its name implies, it's closely related to the ubiquitous JavaScript programming language—ubiquitous in the mobile apps space. XML, on the other hand, is fairly difficult for JavaScript to parse; its processing involves a lot of infrastructure overhead.

Today we are in a world that IBM calls the "API economy," which serves as the backbone to the as-a-service model that dominates today's cloud (we talk about this in Chapter 3). JSON is a natural fit for these services—in fact, if you programmatically interact with Facebook, Flickr, or Twitter services, then you're familiar with how these vendors leverage JSON-based APIs for sending data to and receiving data from end users. By the time the RDBMS world got sophisticated with XML, developers had moved to JSON because it is so naturally integrated with almost any programming language used today (not just JavaScript). JSON has a much simpler markup and appearance than XML, but it is by no means less sophisticated in terms of functionality. This app shift has led developers to request that their data be stored in JSON document store NoSQL databases.

Most new development tools support JSON but not XML. In fact, between 2009 and 2011, one in every five APIs said "good-bye" to XML, and 20 percent of all new APIs supported *only* JSON (based on the 3,200 web APIs that were listed at Programmable Web in May 2011).

"Less is better: The less we need to agree upon for interoperation, the more easily we interoperate," said Tim O'Reilly (the personality behind those tech books with animal covers). The logical representation, readability, and flexibility of JSON are compelling reasons why JSON is the de facto data interchange format for the social-mobile-cloud world. These are the drivers behind JSON's success—they directly map to the developer's value system we commented on earlier—and are precisely the reason why NoSQL document stores such as IBM Cloudant are dominating the NoSQL marketplace today.

Enough Already: What Does a JSON Document Actually Look Like?

The following is an abbreviated example of a JSON document. It shows the profile of a business that is returned from a spatially aware Google-based API search for highly rated health and wellness vendors. This search has also pulled in reviews for the business from popular social sites such as Yelp and Facebook—all stitched together through the API economy.

```
{
"ownerName"                    : "Debbie",
      "ownerlastName"          : "Smith",
      "age"                    : 35,
      "businessProfile"        : "Hot Yoga",
      "businessName"           : "Power Yoga Canada",
      "address"                :
      {
      "streetAddress"          : "22 Stevenson Road South",
      "city"                   : "Oshawa",
      "province"               : "ONT",
      "postalCode"             : "L1J5L9"
      },
      "socialScores"           :
         [

      {"yelpScore"             : "*****"},
      {"facebookReview"  : "5/5"}
         ]
  }
```

As you can see, a JSON document is pretty simple. And if you want to add another set of attributes to this generated document, you can do so in seconds. For example, you might want to add an Instructors array with corresponding bios and certification information. A developer could do this with a few simple keystrokes, thereby avoiding the begging and bribing rituals around DBA-curated schema change requests of the past.

But I Still Use XML!

We didn't say that XML was dead; it has just assumed a different place in IT architectures. Standard data interchanges for finance and healthcare (among others) are still heavily vested in XML. You will find XML being used for many different things—from documentation to database manipulation and more. We are not dismissive of XML's value in these use cases, but rather we are suggesting why JSON has risen to the top of the food chain. It is simple: JSON is dead easy for programmers to work with. JSON's integration into modern-day programming languages means that you don't, for example, have to concern yourself with document object model (DOM) or simple API for XML (SAX) parsers.

XML deserves a document store too! IBM first debuted a document database almost a decade ago in the DB2 9 release with its pureXML technology. Unlike most RDBMS vendors that have the facilities to store XML documents, the "pure" part of the pureXML name was purposeful. It is a true XML document store with its own engine and processing framework for working with XML documents. This engine can stand alone as an XML database or seamlessly interoperate with DB2's relational side. pureXML is widely used today, supports XQuery and schema validations, and is freely available in all editions of DB2. You can also, of course, store XML in Hadoop or NoSQL databases.

As we said, you don't hear as much about XML these days, but it's still widely used. If Jonathan Goldsmith (the Dos Equis beer spokesperson, otherwise known as the "World's Most Interesting Man") were to comment here, he'd say, "I don't always use XML, but when I do, I use DB2 pureXML. Keep interchanging data, my friends."

IBM has a number of solutions in the JSON persistence area (some of which are part of the traditional RDBMS landscape technology, such as Informix and DB2). However, the most proven, scalable, and turnkey NoSQL document store that IBM provides is a fully managed service called Cloudant (see Chapter 10). You can leverage Cloudant services off premise through a hosted and fully managed database as a service model (DBaaS)—a deriviate of software as a service (we cover details about as-a-service models and the cloud in Chapter 3). In addition, IBM recently announced a new on-premise Cloudant offering too!

Column Family, Columnar Store, or BigTable Derivatives: What Do We Call You?

Another type of NoSQL database genre is referred to as *columnar*. Although the storage mechanics indeed include column orientation, the term *columnar*, as used elsewhere, means quite a bit more. With that said, the market has labeled this NoSQL genre as *columnar*, so we'll stick with that.

Columnar databases can be found in both RDBMS and NoSQL worlds (for example, we talk about the dashDB analytics service—which is a columnar database—throughout this book). In the NoSQL world, this database genre accounts for about 10 percent of the revenue share of the NoSQL database landscape.

You'll find that columnar NoSQL databases are quite popular for apps that require high-volume, low-latency writes; indeed, there are petabyte-scale use cases associated with these databases. They are specifically designed to store millions of columns with billions of rows. In fact, HBase documentation recommends RDBMS technology unless you are into the hundreds of millions of rows and up territory. Various use cases around the Internet of Things (IoT)—sensor data, user activity logs, and typical telecommunications call detail record (CDR) apps—come to mind as usage domains for this type of technology.

Columnar databases are noted for their *column families*. As the name suggests, columns belong to a column family. Similar to a K/V store, data is retrieved though a key, which in this case is a column lookup; furthermore, columns that are frequently accessed together are likely to belong to the same column family. For example, if you want a client's first name, you would get that by accessing the FirstName column. However, it's reasonable to assume that you might also want to access that person's last name and billing address as a way of describing the client—these fields would therefore likely belong to the same column family.

If you went looking for the birthplace of the NoSQL columnar movement, you'd find yourself knocking at Google's doorstep, reading their research publication entitled *BigTable: A Distributed Storage System for Structured Data* (2006). Curiously enough, Google didn't call BigTable a database in this paper; it called it "a distributed storage system for managing structured data that is designed to scale to a very large size: petabytes of data across thousands of commodity servers." Like other NoSQL technologies, BigTable is schema-less—you can define columns within rows and on the fly. Perhaps puzzling to RDBMS practitioners is the fact that one row can have a different number of columns than another row that belongs to the same database.

HBase and Cassandra are probably the most popular names in the NoSQL columnar space—both descend from BigTable. There is a lot of fierce competition between them in the marketplace, with zealots on each side claiming victory. Both technologies have a lot in common. They both log but don't support "real" transactions (more about this topic later), they both have high availability and disaster recovery services that are implemented through replication, both are Apache open source projects, and more. We examined the strengths and weaknesses of both technologies, but we tend to favor HBase (and not just because IBM ships it as part of BigInsights for Hadoop). HBase is a more general-purpose tool, and it's also an established part of the Hadoop ecosystem. For example, when you install HBase through BigInsights for Hadoop, you don't need to iteratively download, install, configure, and test other open source components. Instead, simply launch the installer, and it performs the necessary work on single-node and cluster environments. After installation, the tool automatically performs a "health check" to validate the installation and report on the results. Monitoring of your environment is centralized and ongoing administration is simplified because it's integrated into the Hadoop management tooling that is provided by IBM. Ultimately, HBase just feels like a much richer and more integrated experience, especially for users of Hadoop. Cassandra can also run on Hadoop, but we are told it runs best in standalone mode, where it's really good at high-velocity write operations.

Don't Underestimate the Underdog: The Graph Store

Graph stores have been different from the start. For example, although most NoSQL solutions are all about scaling out, graph databases are all about interactions and relationships: who knows who, what is related to what, and so on. The key point is that in a graph database, the relationships among data points are mirrored in the modeling and structure of that data within the database itself. In essence, you can trace the relationships between data based on how it is persisted. Typically, graph stores are found servicing apps whose data is highly interconnected and in situations where tracing data point relationships is key, such as a web site recommendation engine for purchasing that is based on social circles and influencers. Graph store databases are like those tiny fish in a big aquarium that look really cool—they aren't plentiful, but we are going to keep a watchful eye because we expect great things from them.

As you can imagine, in the IoT world where we live, graph database technologies are poised to become a big deal. We think that Social Network Analysis (SNA) is a front-runner for graph database apps—it maps and measures relationship flows between entities that belong to groups, networks, operational maps, and so on. If you're an online dater, there's no question that you've been "touched" by a graph database. The social phenomenon Snap AYI (Are You Interested) has socially graphed hundreds of millions of profiles for its matchmaking recommendations engine to statistically match people that are more likely to be compatible. (Imagine what Yenta could have done with this technology—think *Fiddler on the Roof*...wait for it...got it? Good. If not, Google it.)

Although online dating might not be your cup of tea, we are almost sure that our readers participate in professional social forums such as LinkedIn or Glassdoor; both use graph store technologies. Glassdoor's social graph has nearly a billion connections, and it openly talks about the accuracy of its recommendations engine (which is powered by graph database technology). Twitter? It released its own graph store, FlockDB, to the open source community.

Imagine the usefulness of graph databases for solving traffic gridlock problems by using location data from smart phones to orchestrate the speeds and paths that drivers should take to reach their destinations; as creepy as that sounds, it's still a graph database use case. The classic traveling salesperson problem, network optimization, and so on—these kinds of problems are aptly suited for graph databases. For a great example of how this type of analysis can have a true impact on a business, consider a company like UPS—the "What can brown do for you?" delivery folks. If every UPS driver drove one extra mile a day, it would mean an average of 30,000 extra miles for UPS—at a cost of $10,000,000 per year! Graph database technology could identify the relationships among drivers, fuel, and costs sooner. Ten million dollars in annual savings is certainly a strong incentive for companies that are on the fence about what NoSQL technology can do for their business.

Finally, IBM Watson (briefly discussed in Chapter 1) uses graph stores to draw conclusions from the corpus of data that it uses to identify probable answers with confidence. There is a lot of math going on behind the scenes in a graph database, but hey, that's what computers are for.

Graph processing is heating up and is the fastest-growing database in the NoSQL space. Some RDBMS vendors are incorporating graph technology as part of their database solution. For example, both IBM DB2 and Teradata have at one time or another announced such capabilities to the marketplace. That said, we believe graph store technologies belong squarely in the NoSQL realm and out of the RDBMS world, for reasons that are beyond the scope of this book.

There are a number of graph databases available to the NoSQL market today. For example, Apache Giraph is an iterative graph processing system that is built for high scalability and that runs on Hadoop. Other examples include Titan and Neo4J. IBM is working closely with graph stores in Watson, as mentioned previously, and in social apps that are deployed across the company. We wanted to formally state IBM's direction in the graph store space, but as it stands today our lawyers see fit to give us that loving mother stare of "We know better" on this topic (at least we thought it was loving), so we'll leave it at this: Expect potentially big "titan-sized" things around the time that this book is in your hands (or sometime thereafter).

How Graph Databases Work

Unlike other databases, which store data in columns, rows, or key/value pairs, graph stores identify data through nodes and edges, each of which has its own defining properties.

It's really easy to evolve a "schema" with these databases; just add a new edge or node (that's the agility part of NoSQL). The performance benefit of graph databases stems from the fact that other databases have to perform numerous joins to bring together the data connection (a hint at why we think graph capability doesn't belong in the RDBMS world), whereas a graph database traverses from object to object. Remember, graph stores don't just store data; they store the relationships between things of interest, be it people, products, destinations, and so on.

There are frameworks around which graph database metadata and languages are programmed; Resource Description Framework (RDF) is one of them. Another one is called the Web Ontology Language (OWL—a curious acronym considering the name); *ontology* is a fancy word for describing conversations that precisely describe things and their relationships. OWL is actually built on top of RDF and was designed to process information on the web. Its inspiration was the W3C work on the semantic web. (The inclusion of semantic data in web pages so that they could become a "web" of data, be linked together, and thus be searchable by those paths was the graph database "aha!" moment.) The ability of computers to use such metadata to understand information about web resources is the idea behind the semantic web, and RDF emerged as a W3C standard for describing web resources.

Graph databases describe an entity (called a *node* in the graph world) with properties, along with that entity's connections (referred to as *edges*), through an ontology of linked fields. These types of data entities, expressed in the form of subject-predicate-object, are called *triples,* and they are stored in specialized triple-store databases: graph stores.

Consider the relationship statement "IBM is a company." In a triple, "IBM" is the subject, "is a" represents the predicate, and "company" represents the object. When you combine this triple with other triples that deal with the same subject, you have a graph in which the edges define the relationships among the items that you are describing.

Within IBM, graph databases are used to better connect groups. Consider the classic organization chart; you've seen them a hundred times. If you've ever heard the phrase "Love (or something like that) flows down from the top," this is where it comes from. Ironically, this is *not* how organizations tend to operate in interconnected environments. They don't take direction according to a rigid structure; this is often referred to as *matrix management*. For example, in many countries, company employees must report to someone in their local country, and as a result, you'll often find a reporting structure in which an employee reports to an executive, even if they don't work for that executive or in the executive's organization. In reality, people are linked to many other persons in multiple ways. Matrix management makes things more interconnected and more complex. For this reason, we decided to use it as our sample problem domain for illustrating how graph databases work.

IBM is a company of more than 400,000 people, and as you can imagine, when it comes to enablement activities across the enterprise, getting the Information Management brand's story to the rest of the company involves social complexities. A graph database can be exceptionally helpful in this area. SmallBlue is an internal IBM app that enables you to find colleagues—both from your existing network of contacts and also from the wider organization—who are likely to be knowledgeable in subject areas that interest you. This app can suggest professional network paths to help you reach out to colleagues more accurately (from an interest perspective) and more quickly. Figure 2-1 uses our group's real app to show you how a graph store works.

A graph always has an ordered pair (just like the K/V stores we talked about earlier): a vertex (node) and edge. A graph is defined by its vertices and edges. Nodes can be about anything that interests you, and that's why we often refer to them as *entities*. As you can see in Figure 2-1, a graph can have many nodes and edges that are connected in multiple ways. This figure shows a general graph from which you can learn a lot of things. For example, who might be the best gatekeeper for a certain class of information in the network? In other words, who is the key group connector? That individual should be the one with the shortest path to the highest *degree* (number of linkages) to other persons.

Figure 2-1 *Using a graph database to discover and understand relationships in a large organization*

A basic graph has details about every node and vertex (vertices are bidirectional). For example, the fact that Dirk knows Paul doesn't necessarily mean that Paul knows Dirk until a vertex showing that Paul knows Dirk is added. In a graph store, it's important to understand that these connections are weighted; not all connections are equal. Weightings can help you to understand the relationships and how they affect a network. Weightings can also use color or line thickness to articulate attributes. For example, in Figure 2-1, Dirk has a larger circle connecting him to Paul than Chris does. Although they both work for Paul, Dirk and Paul have worked together for many years, published books together, and previously worked side-by-side in development—all this strengthens their relationship. Marc Andrews is a vice president in a different segment and therefore has a different relationship with Paul; although that relationship doesn't have similar attributes to what Dirk and Paul have, Marc and Paul work closely together and have equal hierarchal standing at IBM. Rick Buglio is in a different relationship altogether; he doesn't report to Paul, neither is he part of the department, but something connects them (for example, this book), and so on.

We created this visualization by searching our graph store for Big Data attributes; we were specifically looking for the strongest spoke of the book's authors into a new group, or an individual with the greatest number of spokes, into Big Data domains that we aren't already a part of—all in an effort to spread our gospel of Big Data. Any time you try to figure out multiple entry points into a community—be it for internal enablement, charity fundraising, or to get a date from a pool of people—it's a graph problem. This domain of analysis involves concepts such as closeness centrality, "betweeness" centrality, and degree centrality. As it turns out, Lori Zavattoni works in IBM's Watson division; we identified her by using a social graph within IBM to find an enablement leader who seems to be a major influencer and shares spokes with other groups. We kept this graph simple, so keep in mind that a "true" graph can contain thousands (and more likely millions) of connections. We also left the connection graph at a coarse degree of separation (2, as shown on the right side of this figure); you can throttle this (and other) attributes up or down. We reached out to Lori to see what we can do around Big Data and Watson and the result was a section on the topic in Chapter 1.

There are graph subtypes such as a *tree* and a *linked list*. A tree graph enables any node to talk to any other node, but it cannot loop back (cycle) to the starting node except by retracing its exact steps through the path it took to get there (this kind of breadcrumb trail is popular for web page navigation analysis). If a connection were made between Paul and Lori, the only way to Lori's connections is through Paul; therefore, Dirk must go through Paul to get to Lori. Of course, Dirk could just send Lori a quick email—but if this were a voter identification list, a political party would use Paul to get to Lori and gain access to her connections only through that first link with Paul. In fact, this *exact* technique was used by the reelection team for Barack Obama's second presidential campaign.

The best way to describe a linked list (which is more restrictive than a tree graph) is to think of a graph that resembles a connect-the-dots picture. Each node sequentially connects to another node, though in this case you might not end up with a pretty picture. Examining a company's supply chain or procurement channel might produce a linked list graph. For example, the only way to get a doctor's appointment with a specialist in Canada is to get a referral by your general practitioner; so if you've got a skin issue, your family doctor is part of the linked list to the dermatologist—there is only one kind of graph in a linked list.

As you've seen, graph databases are great for highly connected data because they are powerful, come with a flexible data model, and provide a mechanism to query connected data in a highly performing manner. They are, however, not perfect. Aside from the fact that they are still maturing, the schema that is produced by a graph database can get complex in a hurry, and transactions aren't always ACID-compliant (more on this in a bit). What's more, because they can grow rapidly, one of the traditional challenges with graphs has been (and still is) the processing time that is required to work through all of the data permutations that even relatively small graphs can produce (we think that this is a short-term challenge). That said, we feel that the greatest short-term weakness of graph databases is that they require a new way of thinking—a paradigm where everything that you look at is a graph. The open source movement is taking the lead and you can see quarterly gains in graph database adoption as a reflection of those efforts. We think that this is a great example of why polyglot persistence is key to your strategy—an architecture that leverages multiple capabilities (in a variety of different forms) can provide the most value as businesses make the jump to NoSQL.

From ACID to CAP

To better understand some of the characteristics of NoSQL databases, it's best to start with traditional RDBMS technology. *Atomicity, consistency, isolation*, and *durability* (commonly referred to as the ACID properties of a relational database) are cornerstones of the traditional SQL world. These properties help to guarantee that database transactions are processed reliably. There are entire books with chapters dedicated to each ACID property, but we limit this discussion to those details that help to clarify NoSQL characteristics. It's important to understand trade-offs between how relational databases work and how NoSQL databases work; these aren't "one is better than the other" kinds of discussions—it's more like a "one is better suited to solving a particular problem" discussion.

Atomicity means that a transaction should be committed or undone as a whole. In the event of a failure, all operations that were "in flight" should be undone, and any changes should be rolled back to the previous state. Have you ever wanted to buy something online and clicked Buy, only to find your Internet connection dropped and the purchase didn't go through? Atomicity means that this transaction never happened and that your credit card won't be charged for a purchase that didn't happen because the transaction could not be completed successfully without interruption.

Consistency means that a transaction that is applied to a system in a consistent state should leave the system in a consistent state, and data that is modified by the transaction should be validated according to any business rules that are defined in the database (we alluded to this in Table 2-1). Imagine that two business partners, Adam and Bob, share the same checking account. Consistency means that at any time and from any location or device that is connected to the bank's network, Adam and Bob should be able to see how much money is in their account, and both should see the same balance in that account. Triggers offer another example of consistency. Suppose that a defined database trigger fires whenever a client delete operation occurs. For this transaction to complete successfully, the client record must be inserted into a callback table. The delete isn't considered successful if the trigger didn't fire.

Isolation means that when concurrent transactions run on a database, they operate independently of one another and can't interfere with each other. If both transactions want to access the same data value, what happens next depends on the concurrency model that is in effect; one transaction waits until the other one completes, or it simply reads an older copy of the data, among other options (each option has potential consequences, such as a phantom read or nonrepeatable read, among others). Isolation is used to deliver performance and consistency in an RDBMS system.

The fourth ACID property of a relational database is *durability*, which means that completed transactions should remain permanent and be protected from system failures. All major RDBMS vendors offer some sort of mechanism that logs transactions on disk (ironically, all vendors in this space pretty much follow the IBM-invented ARIES logging protocol). For example, if you receive verification that you have successfully paid a bill, that bill is paid, and if the database has to re-create the transaction after a failure, it has all the information on disk to successfully replay the transaction.

In summary, ACID databases mostly prize consistency of the data over the availability of the data. (There are some exceptions that require more explanation. For example, both Oracle and DB2 support a "readers don't block writers and writers don't block readers" operational model. But this is outside the scope of this book.)

CAP Theorem and a Meatloaf Song: "Two Out of Three Ain't Bad"

The acronym CAP stands for *consistency, availability,* and *partition tolerance. Consistency* here is similar to the ACID property. Some might think of it as single-copy consistency because they define it at the single partition level in a database cluster. We believe it to mean that all nodes in the same system see the same data at the same time. Think back to Adam and Bill having the same view of their checking account.

Availability is a guarantee that every request to the database receives a response, either success or failure. That's a very different view of availability than what many think of in the RDBMS world. For example, if you can ping your RDBMS server, does that mean it's available? Ping always returns a response—the packet was either successfully delivered or not. For others, availability means that a transaction can be processed.

Partition tolerance means that a clustered system continues to operate even in the presence of lost messages or failures that occur in parts of the system; in other words, node failures shouldn't cause the whole database to collapse.

Being partition tolerant also means being able to scale into distributed systems; you can see how RDBMSs traditionally place less emphasis on partition tolerance, given how difficult many of these systems are to scale horizontally. Partition tolerance helps with the elastic scalability of NoSQL databases (those that scale out). Although the SQL world is weaker in the partition tolerance transactional area (with the exception of DB2 pureScale and DB2 for System z technologies that are based on IBM's Coupling Facility, which was designed for this purpose), the NoSQL world prioritizes partition tolerance.

The CAP theorem (first proposed by Eric Brewer in his "Principles of Distributed Computing" keynote address and later refined by many) states that you can guarantee only two out of the three CAP properties simultaneously—and that's not bad according to the hit song writer, Meatloaf. In other words, if your database has partitions (particularly if it's distributed), do you prioritize consistency or the availability of your data? (We should note that trade-offs between consistency and availability exist on a continuum and are not an "all-or-nothing" proposition.)

Clearly, reduced consistency and weakened transactional "ACIDity" don't sound like a good idea for some banking use cases that we can think of—and yet there are many apps where high availability trumps consistency if your goal is to be more scalable and robust. As you might expect, in a social-mobile-cloud world, systems of engagement and systems of people apps could very well make this kind of trade-off. For example, if you're checking how many Repins you have on Pinterest, does it matter if that number is accurate at a specific point in time? Or can you settle for being eventually consistent, if it means that your users get values (whether or not they are the most up to date) on demand?

NoSQL practitioners are, more often than not, willing to trade consistency for availability on a tunable spectrum. In fact, one NoSQL database with a "mongo" footprint is well known for data writes that can just disappear into thin air. Ultimately, the NoSQL solution that you select should be based on business requirements and the type of apps that you're going to support.

There is a subset of the CAP theorem that refers to a persistence layer being basic availability, soft state, and eventual consistency—BASE. We're not going to get into these finer-level details in this chapter because our goal was to give you a basic overview, which we feel we've done.

Let Me Get This Straight: There Is SQL, NoSQL, and Now NewSQL?

So far, we've mainly discussed NoSQL databases—the focus of this chapter. But NewSQL is certainly an emerging topic—the next hot topic if you will. Because we only wanted to focus on NoSQL in this chapter, we include only a short primer on NewSQL technology, but keep your eyes on this space. NewSQL is the NoSQL of the SQL age (insert cheeky emoticon here).

We know where the name NewSQL comes from: a research paper penned by 451 Group's Matt Aslett. He refers to a new class of operational databases that can't use NoSQL solutions because the apps that they support have stringent transactional and consistency requirements. Indeed, the flexibility and scalability of NoSQL databases comes with a trade-off between consistency and availability. In some spaces, this just isn't acceptable. In his paper, Matt Aslett states that NewSQL databases differ greatly with respect to their internals (architecture, implementation), but they share two distinguishing features: They all support the relational data model and use SQL as their primary interface.

NewSQL's intent is to deliver on all three aspects of the CAP theorem; as you can imagine, because there are a number of people who think a database can deliver only one or two—but not all three—of the CAP theorem properties, this area is the subject of hot debate. Some NewSQL databases use HDFS as the underlying file system, others support a proprietary file system, and others let you choose. Much like NoSQL servers, you're likely to find NewSQL implemented on Linux in a scale-out cluster with locally attached disks; you will also find network-attached storage. Off-premise cloud deployment is common for this technology because the design favors high-speed interconnections within and between clusters. The calling card of NewSQL is the marriage between agility and scalability while still emphasizing the importance of ACID-compliant transactions.

Although the name implies that these databases use a new kind of SQL, NewSQL databases use the SQL that we have known and loved for half a century. The focus for this class of database system is the automatic resharding and balancing of data across geographically dispersed machines. You can see the allure of NewSQL. One of the drivers for NoSQL databases is seamless scalability, which can be hampered in the SQL world by the inherent write latency that is a side effect of high-consistency data requirements.

Wrapping It Up

In this chapter, we covered SQL, NoSQL, and even touched on NewSQL database technologies as options for today's data centers. We also discussed the concept of polyglot persistence. Supporting a polyglot Big Data and Analytics platform means selecting a variety of data-layer technologies that address the widest array of use cases that your apps might encounter. We also talked about how in the API economy, these layers will be fully abstracted—we talk more about this in the next chapter. Elsewhere in this book, you'll read about NoSQL technologies such as the Cloudant document store, HBase, the Hadoop ecosystem, in-memory columnar database technology, and traditional RDBMS technologies across all form factors: from off-premise hosted or fully managed services, to "roll-your-own" on-premise solutions, and appliances. Together, these polyglot tools represent the next generation of data-layer architectures and solutions for tomorrow's Big Data and Analytics challenges.

3

Composing Cloud Applications: Why We Love the Bluemix and the IBM Cloud

A journey toward the adoption of the "cloud" to meet business targets is in many ways a transition from traditional systems of record to systems of engagement and systems of people. Consider the emergence of social media—it's hard to pinpoint exactly when *selfies* and *tweets* became part of our vocabulary. Just like the Web evolved from being a rigid set of pages to a space that's much more organic, interactive, and integrated, we are bearing witness to a transformation in computing from hardened silos to flexible "as a service" models. Why? Three words: social-mobile-cloud.

Social-mobile-cloud has dramatically accelerated social change in totally unanticipated ways; in fact, it has completely changed and altered the flow of information on the entire planet. Information used to flow from a few centralized sources out to the masses. Major media outlets like The BBC, CNN, NY Times, and Der Spiegel were dominant voices in society, and were able to control conversations about current events. Social-mobile-cloud has obliterated the dominance of mass media voices and changed the flow of information to a many-to-many model. In short, the spread of mobile technology and social networks, as well as unprecedented access to data is changing how individuals, groups, and organizations engage. We call this mode of engagement *The Why*.

Of course, all this new data has become the new basis for competitive advantage. We call this data *The What*. All that's left is *The How*. And this is where the cloud comes in. This is where you deploy infrastructure, software, and even services that deliver analytics and insights in an agile way. In fact, if you're a startup today, would you go to a venture investment firm with a business plan that includes the purchase of a bunch of hardware and an army of DBAs to get started? Who really does that anymore? You'd get shown the door, if you even make it that far. Instead, what you do is go to a cloud company like SoftLayer (the IBM Cloud), swipe your credit card to get the capacity or services, and get to work. It allows you to get started fast and cheap (as far as your credit card is concerned). You don't spend time budgeting, forecasting, planning, or going through approval processes: You focus on your business.

The transformational effects of The How (cloud), The Why (engagement), and The What (data) can be seen across all business verticals and their associated IT landscapes. Consider your run-of-the-mill application (app) developer and what life was like before the cloud era and "as a service" models became a reality. Developers spent as much time navigating roadblocks as they did writing code. The list of IT barriers was endless: contending with delays for weeks or months caused by ever-changing back-end persistence (database) requirements, siloed processes, proprietary platform architectures, resource requisitions, database schema change synchronization cycles, cost models that were heavily influenced by the number of staff that had to be kept in-house to manage the solution, processes longer than this sentence, and more. Looking back, it is a wonder that any code got written at all!

Development is a great example. Today we see a shift toward agile processes. We call this *continual engineering*. In this development operations (DevOps) model, development cycles get measured in days; environment stand up times are on the order of minutes (at most hours); the data persistence layer is likely to be a hosted (at least partially) and even a fully managed service; the platform architecture is loosely coupled and based on an API economy and open standards; and the cost model is variable and expensed, as opposed to fixed and capital cost depreciated over time.

As is true with so many aspects of IT and the world of Big Data, we anticipate this wave of change has yet to reach its apex. Indeed, there was too much hype around cloud technologies, and practitioners had to get beyond that just like Big Data practitioners are now facing the hype barrier. But today there is no question about it, the cloud is delivering real value and agility. It has incredible momentum, it is here to stay, and the conversation is now well beyond the hype. The cloud was once used for one-off projects or test workloads, but now it's a development hub, a place for transactions and analytics, a services procurement platform where things get done. In fact, it's whatever you decide to make it. That's the beauty of the cloud: All you need is an idea.

At Your Service: Explaining Cloud Provisioning Models

We broadly categorize the cloud's provisioning models and concepts into the three domains that are shown in Figure 3-1, which serve as the focus for much of this chapter: infrastructure as a service (IaaS), platform as a service (PaaS), and software as a service (SaaS).

The provisioning models in this figure all stand in contrast to traditional IT, where you'd have to manage the entire technology stack. We call the traditional approach an *on-premise* solution (in your place of work), while the "as a service" models are *off-premise* solutions (they reside "in the cloud").

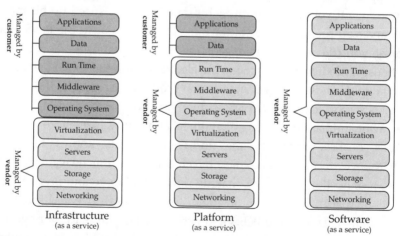

Figure 3-1 *A high-level comparison of vendor and customer responsibilities at each as-a-service level*

To help you better understand the practical differences between an on-premise solution and the "as a service" models listed in Figure 3-1, we've come up with the following analogy (we'd like to thank IBMer Albert Barron for this story's inspiration).

Imagine you have a son who's just started his sophomore year at university, and is living in your home. He just mentioned how he found a tequila lime chicken recipe he got from the Chef Watson's bon appetit site (http://bonappetit.com/tag/chef-watson) and wants to use it to impress a date. You laugh and remind him that you taught him how to boil an egg over the summer. After some thought, your son concludes that making a gourmet dish is too much work (cooking, cleaning, preparation, and so on) and his core competencies are nowhere to be found in the kitchen; therefore, he decides to instead take his date to a restaurant. This is similar to the SaaS model, because the restaurant manages everything to do with the meal: the building and kitchen appliances, the electricity, the cooking skills, and the food itself. Your son only had to make sure he cleaned himself up.

A year passes and your son is now in his junior year, but is still living in your home (we can hear the painful groan of some of our readers who know this situation too well). He's got another date and wants to arrange for a more intimate setting: your house. He buys all the ingredients and digs out the recipe, but pleads for help with making the meal. Being a loving parent, you also want your son to impress his date (this may speed up his moving out), and you prepare the meal for him. This is similar to the PaaS model, because you (the vendor) managed the cooking "platform": You provided the house and kitchen appliances, the electricity, and the cooking skills. You even bought candles! However, your son brought the food and the recipe.

In his senior year, you're pleased that your son has moved into his own apartment and has been taking on more responsibility. Just before he moved, he tells you he's found "the one" and wants to really impress this person with his favorite tequila lime chicken recipe. But this time he wants to class it up, so he's hosting it and he's making it. He's had to go and find a place to live (floor space), and his rent includes appliances (a stove and fridge) and utilities. He takes a trip to IKEA and gets some tasteful place settings and a kitchen table and chairs (your 20-year-old couch wouldn't be suitable for such an important guest to sit and eat). Once he's settled into his apartment, he goes to the grocery store to get the ingredients, and then comes home and cooks the meal—he essentially owns the process from start to finish. Your son owns everything in the food preparation process except for the core infrastructure, which he's renting: This is IaaS. As an aside, since he has sole access to all of the resources in his apartment, this IaaS model would be called *bare-metal* infrastructure in cloud-speak.

In this IaaS scenario, imagine if your son shared an apartment with roommates. Everything from the contents in the fridge, to the stove, to place settings, to the tables and chairs are potentially shared; we call this a *multitenant* infrastructure in cloud-speak. Those roommates? They can literally be what we call "noisy neighbors" in the cloud space. In so many ways, they can get in the way of an expected planned experience. For example, perhaps they are cooking their own food when he needs access to the stove, they planned their own important date on the very same evening, they might have used the dishes and left them dirty in the sink, or worse yet…drank all the tequila! In a multitenanted cloud environment, you share resources; what's different in our analogy is the fact that you don't know who you're sharing the resources with. But the key concept here is that when you share resources, things may not operate in a manner in which you expected or planned.

A few years later, your son has a stable job (finally!) and has just bought his own house. He's newly married, and for old-time's sake, wants to make his spouse the tequila lime chicken recipe that started their romance. This time, he truly owns the entire process. He owns the infrastructure, he's cooking the meal, and he bought the ingredients. In every sense, this is similar to an on-premise deployment.

Notice what's common: In every one of these scenarios, at the end of the evening, your son eats tequila lime chicken. In the on-premise variation of the story, he does all of the work—in some scenarios he has to share the resource and in others he doesn't. There are scenarios in which he has other people take varying amounts of responsibility for the meal. Today, even though your son is now independent and has the luxury of his own infrastructure, he still enjoys occasionally eating at restaurants; it's definitely easier for him to go out for something like sushi or perhaps he is just too tired to cook after a long week. This is the beauty of the "as a service" models—you can consume services whenever the need arises to offload the management of infrastructure, the platform, or the software itself; in cloud-speak you'll hear this referred to as *bursting*.

As your understanding of these service models deepens, you will come to realize that the distinctions among them can begin to blur. Ad hoc development strategies of the past have given way to predefined development "stacks," and going forward, we will see these stacks refined into development "patterns" that are available as a service. Today, the expert integrated IBM PureSystems family (PureFlex, PureApplication, and PureData systems) combines the flexibility of a general-purpose system, the elasticity of an on-premise cloud, and the simplicity of an appliance. These systems are integrated by design and are finely tuned by decades of experience to deliver a simplified IT experience. You can think of these as foolproof recipes. For example, a data warehouse with a BLU Acceleration pattern (we talk about this technology in Chapter 8) is available for a PureFlex system, which equates to tracing paper for a beautiful picture (in this case, a high-performance turn-key analytics service). Patterned solutions are not exclusive to on premise: Pattern design thinking is driving service provisioning for cloud-based environments. For example, IBM makes the BLU Acceleration technology available in PaaS and SaaS environments through a hosted or managed analytics warehousing service called dashDB.

From small businesses to enterprises, organizations that want to lead their segments will quickly need to embrace the transition from low-agility software development strategies to integrated, end-to-end DevOps. The shift toward cloud models ushers in a new paradigm of "consumable IT"; the question is, what is your organization going to do? Are you going to have a conversation about how to take part in this revolutionary reinvention of IT? Or will you risk the chance that competitors taking the leap first will find greater market share as they embrace the cloud?

Setting a Foundation for the Cloud: Infrastructure as a Service

The key business initiative driving IaaS adoption is the need to flatten IT expenditures by leveraging cloud-based data centers in place or in support of on-premise IT investments. Those who relish the terminology of finance might express this strategy as a transfer of capital expenditure (CAPEX) to operational expenditure (OPEX). From an accounting perspective, CAPEX cannot be fully written off in the period during which the expense was incurred. It has to be amortized. OPEX costs, on the other hand, are deductible in the accounting period during which they were incurred. This is an attractive proposition, and there is certainly a financial edge to be gained by moving to the cloud. But this isn't the true reason for the cloud's momentum. Moving to the cloud gives you increased agility and the opportunity for capacity planning that's similar to the concept of using electricity: It's "metered" usage that you pay for as you use it. In other words, IaaS enables you to consider compute resources as if they are a utility like electricity. Similar to utilities, it's likely the case that your cloud service has tiered pricing. For example, is the provisioned compute capacity multi-tenant or bare metal? Are you paying for fast CPUs or extra memory? Never lose sight of what we think is the number-one reason for the cloud and IaaS: it's all about *how fast can you provision the computing capacity.*

When organizations can quickly provision an infrastructure layer (for example, the server component for IaaS shown in Figure 3-1), the required time to market is dramatically reduced. Think of it this way: If you could snap your fingers and have immediate access to a four-core, 32GB server that you could use for five hours, at less than the price of a combo meal at your favorite fast-food restaurant, how cool would that be? Even cooler, imagine you could then snap your fingers and have the server costs go away—like eating the combo meal and not having to deal with the indigestion or calories after you savor the flavor. Think about how agile and productive you would be. (We do want to note that if you are running a cloud service 24x7, 365 days a year, it may not yield the cost savings you think; but agility will always reign supreme compared to an on-premise solution.)

A more efficient development and delivery cycle leads to less friction and lowers the bar for entry when it comes to innovation and insights: Imagine the opportunities and innovations that your organization can realize when the traditional pain points and risk associated with costly on-premise IT infrastructures are reduced by a cloud-based, scalable, "as a service" solution.

We often talk about three significant use-case patterns emerging for adopters of IaaS data layers, and we think they should be part of your Big Data conversations too. The first involves a discussion on ways for organizations to reduce their large and ongoing IT expenses through the optimization of their existing data centers. When such companies move their infrastructure to a managed cloud, they begin to enjoy consolidation of services, virtualized deployments that are tailored to their storage and networking requirements, and automatic monitoring and migration.

The second pattern involves the ability to accelerate the time to market for new applications and services. Clients can leverage new environments and topologies that are provisioned on the cloud with ease, often by simply select-ing the sizing that is appropriate for their workloads and clicking "Go" to kick off the compute resource spin-up process. It might not be real magic, but a couple of swipes and gestures can be just as impressive.

The third pattern involves an environment that is running a client's apps and services on top of an IaaS layer. These clients can gain immediate access to higher-level enterprise-grade services, including software for *composing* (developing) apps in the cloud or *consuming* cloud apps such as IBM's dashDB analytics warehouse or IBM's DataWorks refinery services, and so on. These are the PaaS and SaaS flavors of the cloud. Each service builds on the other and delivers more value in the stack. It's kind of like a set of Rus-sian dolls—each level of beauty gets transferred to the next and the attention to detail (the capabilities and services provided from a cloud perspective) increases. In other words, the value of IaaS gives way to even more value, flexibility, and automation in PaaS, which gives way to even more of these attributes in SaaS (depending on what it is you are trying to do).

What are some of the available services for organizations that leverage an IaaS methodology? Figure 3-2 shows IaaS at its most fundamental level. A vendor delivers complete management of the hardware resources that you request for provisioning over the cloud: virtual machine (VM) provisioning, construction and management of VM images, usage metering, management of multitenant user authentication and roles, deployment of patterned solu-tions, and management of cloud resources.

Earlier in this chapter we referred to cloud services as hosted or managed. With *managed* IaaS providers, you gain access to additional resources such as patching and maintenance, planning for capacity and load, managed responses to data-layer events (including bursts in activity, backup, and disaster recovery), and endpoint compliance assurances for security—all of which are handled for you! In a *hosted* environment, these responsibilities fall on you. It's the difference between sleeping over at mom's house (where you

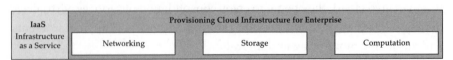

Figure 3-2   *Infrastructure as a service (IaaS) provides the foundational level for any service or application that you want to deploy on the cloud.*

are expected to still do a lot of work—you are hosted) or sleeping at a resort (managed—it's all done for you in a luxurious manner).

Finally, IaaS providers like IBM are increasingly supplying integration support with on-premise infrastructure to offer hybrid cloud deployments, advanced security (threat and vulnerability assessments), tailored provisioning (for storage and networking requirements), and full orchestration to ensure that services on the cloud work in concert.

IaaS for Tomorrow...Available Today: IBM SoftLayer Powers the IBM Cloud

Regardless of what analysts say, the cloud is not a commodity. And no matter what provisioning model you use, the physical hardware—along with hundreds of miles of networking cable, among other things—lives in some brick-and-mortar facility. One thing we want you to know when it comes to cloud discussions is that no two clouds are built the same way. We believe the IBM Cloud (powered by SoftLayer) offers its clientele the highest-performing cloud infrastructure available. It's a cloud platform that started as a cloud platform and was built from the ground up to be a managed cloud service. Because it's a managed service, you have the assurance that IBM SoftLayer manages and maintains this infrastructure layer for you.

As we mentioned earlier, the IBM Cloud (across the spectrum of IaaS, PaaS, and SaaS provisioning options) is powered by SoftLayer. It can provision private, public, or hybrid cloud services. To date, IBM has invested more than $1 billion (US) to extend SoftLayer's data centers across the globe. By the time this book goes to print, there will be about 40 geographically dispersed server farms worldwide. Each data center is built, outfitted, and operated with the same consistent level of service, giving you consistent capabilities and availability anywhere in SoftLayer's footprint. From what we can tell, it has more global data centers than any other vendor in its peer group; in fact, in many parts of the world, where regulations for some entities mandate that data stay within its country of origin, SoftLayer is the *only* "big name" choice.

One of the things that sets SoftLayer's data centers apart is the consistently high performance clients experience when provisioning services at any of its locations worldwide. SoftLayer's data centers operate with first-class computing, storage, and networking gear. All of these pieces come together to enable the industry's most advanced "network within a network." SoftLayer's fast, resilient private network backbone forms the core of its triple-network architecture. Specifically, its data centers are connected by three distinct (yet deeply integrated) public, private, and internal management networks to deliver lower total networking costs, better access, and higher data transfer rates. In our experience, we've seen the IBM Cloud push 2TB of data per second between locations around the world (they weren't close to each other) into a private network with less than 40ms of latency. Unlike other competitors who made their name selling books online, SoftLayer won't lock you into one vendor's technology. For example, the other cloud vendor we just hinted at mandates that the data has to be loaded from their provisioned storage in order to get it into their analytic service. Perhaps you want to load it directly from your own on-premise data repository. Why should you be forced to stage your data on a cloud storage tier (for a fee, of course), only to move it again?

SoftLayer is an all-in-one, automated platform—all the services that you require are delivered within a single management system that's entirely consumable through web services. All the SoftLayer data centers and networks share a single management touch point; one tool ties it all together and gives you control over everything—each bare-metal server, virtual server, storage device, you name it—from a single pane of glass.

Disaster and *downtime* are words that no one wants to hear in any IT setting. Indeed, talk of availability and disaster recovery can stir up feelings of anxiety for companies that are not prepared for the volatile web. SoftLayer's strategy for building a global infrastructure footprint that's managed as a service doesn't just prepare for outages and disasters to happen—it expects them! As a SoftLayer customer, your data and infrastructure are more robust because of this posture.

SoftLayer can provision services in a dedicated or shared multitenant environment (more on that in a bit). We think that SoftLayer's provisioning versatility is unique in the industry when you consider that analyst firm Gartner commented that "by 2017… half of all large enterprises would have a hybrid cloud deployment." Think about it. Long before IBM bought SoftLayer as the backbone for its cloud service, it had decades of experience in on-premise deployments. Next, IBM deployed a number of expert-designed systems that provide on-premise clouds. Today, IBM is leading the industry when it comes to off-premise deployments on SoftLayer technology. What's more, IBM has embraced the hybrid cloud; for example, you can seamlessly burst work into the IBM Cloud and back to the ground again if required. The tally of vendors who can do this as seamlessly and efficiently as IBM is small, and we think this places IBM at the top of the short list for hybrid cloud architectures. It's important that the conversations you have about Big Data not be limited to the cloud, but rather include a discussion of a *hybrid* ecosystem. (In case it's a point of confusion, a hybrid cloud means a mixture of off-premise and on-premise investments, as we refer in our examples. A hybrid cloud's definition also includes a mix of clouds; for example, private and public. If a private cloud is set up for your company by your company, then we classify it as on premise, because the servers are owned by your company and reside on company property. Their capacity is provisioned across the company as a cloud model, and thus it's a private cloud, but it is still an on-premise investment.)

We see a lot of marketing around hybrid cloud from various vendors, but more often than not, the words ring hollow. These vendors require customers to completely change the way their apps work and need to be deployed in order to "fit" into their cloud model. *True* hybrid architectures, such as what the IBM SoftLayer infrastructure provides, are able to adapt and integrate with the existing on-premise infrastructure. If your IaaS solution requires that you change your apps to fit rigidly constrained models, or force fits you into a cost-metered staging area, we suggest reassessing the merits of that provider. Having a flexible cloud infrastructure that adapts to your business requirements (and not the other way around) is going to matter as you grow your Big Data platform.

Noisy Neighbors Can Be Bad Neighbors: The Multitenant Cloud

Before we cover the other "as a service" models, it's worth taking a moment to examine a fundamental aspect of SoftLayer's deployment options: bare-metal infrastructure for private single-tenant cloud environments.

Bare metal is not an '80s big hair–band satellite radio channel, but a term that describes completely dedicated infrastructure on the cloud. Many of the largest vendors that offer cloud services today do it solely over a shared, public, multitenant, and often virtualized environment. One obvious concern in this environment is privacy—forced multitenancy (sharing cloud infrastructure) is a major pain point for companies that want to host sensitive data on the cloud.

But there are more issues at stake. Performance on a bare-metal server will always outperform the same provisioned infrastructure if it's virtualized—there is always some performance loss in a virtualized environment. For situations where fastest performance is a must, you will want a bare-metal server, and that's not an option with every cloud provider. Provisioning multitenant resources also means having to contend with the reality of shared resources; performance is never consistent and might not necessarily live up to the full potential that was promised on paper. We attribute this unpredictability to the "noisy neighbors" effect. In a shared cloud service, the noisy neighbor is exactly what you might imagine: Other users and applications sharing the same provisioned infrastructure on a multitenant environment can bog down performance and potentially ruin the experience for everyone else (think back to our example of a young man hosting a date at a shared residence). Perhaps those neighbors are generating a disproportionate amount of network traffic or are heavily taxing the infrastructure to run their apps. The end result of this effect is that all other users of the shared environment suffer degraded performance. In this kind of setting, you can't be assured of consistent performance, which means you can't pass the assurance of predictable behavior down to your customers. In the same manner that inconsistent query response times foreshadow the death of a warehouse, the same applies for services in the cloud.

In a provisioned multitenant cloud environment, you don't know who your neighbors are. Imagine for a moment that you are unknowingly sharing your cloud with some slick new gaming company that happened to hit the jackpot: Their app has "gone viral." Who knew that an app for uploading pictures of your boss to use in a friendly game of "whack-a-mole" would catch on? Within days, millions join this virtual spin on a carnival classic. All this traffic creates a network-choking phenomenon. Why do you care? If this gaming studio and its customers happen to be sharing the same multitenant environment as you are, then the neighborhood just got a lot noisier, and your inventory control system is going to run a lot like the aforementioned game—up and down.

The IBM Cloud gives clients the option to provision a true bare-metal, dedicated IaaS that removes "noisy neighbors" and privacy concerns from the equation altogether. It can provision and manage an infrastructure layer that is exclusively dedicated to your company's cloud services or hosted apps. Your services benefit from the guaranteed performance and privacy that come from a bare-metal deployment. IBM is uniquely positioned to seamlessly integrate bare-metal and virtual servers, all on demand, as part of a unified platform. SoftLayer also provides autoscaling, load balancing, different security models (for open and commercial technologies), and a variety of server provisioning options (dedicated and multitenant). Every client has a preference; some might have a business need that fits a hybrid model of multitenancy and dedicated bare metal working side by side; others might be fine with virtualization for all their servers. SoftLayer offers the IaaS flexibility to meet and exceed the requirements of any client—including those who don't want to live beside noisy neighbors.

Building the Developer's Sandbox with Platform as a Service

We get a little more technical in this section, so let's ease into the discussion with a look at what defines platform as a service (PaaS) and how IBM's Bluemix fits into that framework. Grab your shovel—it's time to hit the PaaS sandbox.

Bluemix is IBM's PaaS for composing, managing, and running applications that work in many settings—from web, mobile, Big Data, smart devices, Internet of Things, and more—all supported by an open standards environment based on Cloud Foundry. Bluemix enables you to provision complete development environments faster than it takes for you to reboot your laptop after a blue screen. Choose a language run time, or bring your own, and run with it! The catalog of IBM, third-party, and open source API-fronted services enables you to work without ever needing to step outside of the Bluemix environment. Enterprises and businesses today also want to integrate with their on-premise infrastructure; Bluemix can make that happen with support for environments. Do you want to connect to existing on-premise assets; link those to public and private clouds; and do so with a fully supported development, deployment, monitoring, and logging toolkit (DevOps)? Bluemix can do that too! What's more, IBM hardens your entire solution with enterprise-grade security, so there is no need to fret about the volatile world of the cloud. Lastly, the way you pay for using Bluemix is much like how you're billed for electricity—you pay for what you use. And if you are using one of the many freemium services that are available on Bluemix, unlike your electricity, you don't pay anything at all!

If You Have Only a Couple of Minutes: PaaS and IBM Bluemix in a Nutshell

When you go to any cloud provider (for example, IBM SoftLayer, Amazon, or Microsoft Azure), you can provision a hardware layer with a couple of mouse gestures, grab a coffee, and voilà: a server! What IaaS gives you is the shell: the infrastructure layer that supports the software or services you build and run. Storage, firewalls, load balancers, CPU, memory—all of these components are provisioned in IaaS and are at your disposal. But consider for a moment what's missing from this picture. If you recall from Figure 3-1, not even the operating system (OS) shows up until the PaaS pillar. So, when we say that IaaS gives you *all* the parts that you need to start installing software, we are talking about the absolute *minimum*—it's like buying a laptop with no OS.

Quite simply, IBM Bluemix enables clients to rapidly compose, deploy, and manage cloud applications. We like to tell clients that Bluemix allows you to go live in seconds because a developer can choose any language or run time, or even bring their own. In fact, you can use Bluemix to build, manage, and run all manner of apps for web, mobile, and Big Data solutions. It ties together development backbones such as node.js, Java, mobile back-end services, application monitoring, analytics service, database services, and more. Bluemix takes the work out of standing up a dev environment, or forcing developers to deal with virtual machine images or hardware to get stuff done (you don't have to prepare the tequila lime chicken, thinking back to our university student analogy). With a few swipes or keystrokes, you can provision instances of your applications with the necessary development services to support them. This streamlining translates into countless hours saved when compared to traditional app dev preparation such as installation, configuration, troubleshooting, and the seemingly endless amounts of time spent reacting to never-ending changes in requirements; instead, Bluemix lets you relentlessly innovate. Indeed, Bluemix lets developers go from zero to production in one command!

IBM envisions Bluemix as a ecosystem that answers the needs and challenges facing developers, while at the same time empowering and enabling businesses to leverage their resources in the most efficient way possible. This means Bluemix provides organizations with a cloud platform that requires very little in-house technical know-how, as well as cost savings. At the same time, Bluemix lets organizations dynamically react to users' demands for new features. The Bluemix platform and the cloud provide the elasticity of compute capacity that organizations require when their apps explode in popularity.

As a reflection of IBM's commitment to open standards, there are ongoing efforts to ensure Bluemix is a leader when it comes to the open standards that surround the cloud. As such, Bluemix is an implementation of IBM's Open Cloud Architecture, leveraging Cloud Foundry to enable developers to rapidly build, deploy, and manage their cloud applications, while tapping a growing ecosystem of available services and run-time frameworks.

The API economy is at the core of Bluemix. It includes a catalog of IBM, third-party, and open source services and libraries that allows developers to compose apps in minutes. Quite simply, Bluemix offers the instant services, run times, and managed infrastructure that you need to experiment, innovate, and build cloud-first apps. Bluemix exposes a rich library of IBM proprietary technologies. For example, the BLU Acceleration technology behind the dashDB analytics service, the Cloudant NoSQL document store, IBM DataWorks refinery services, and more. IBM partner-built technologies (like Pitney Bowes location services) as well as open source services (like MongoDB and MySQL, among others) are also part of its catalog. The Bluemix catalog is by no means static—Bluemix continues to add services and shape the platform to best serve its community of developers.

In practical terms, this means that cloud apps built on Bluemix will reduce the time needed for application and infrastructure provisioning, allow for flexible capacity, help to address any lack of internal tech resources, reduce TCO, and accelerate the exploration of new workloads: social, mobile, and Big Data.

Bluemix is deployed through a fully managed IBM Cloud infrastructure layer. Beyond integration in the IBM Cloud, Bluemix has integration hooks for on-premise resources as well. Flexibility is the design point of Bluemix and it lets you seamlessly pull in resources from public and private clouds or other on-premise resources.

Layered security is at the heart of Bluemix. IBM secures the platform and infrastructure and provides you with the tools you need to secure the apps that you compose. IBM's pedigree in this area matters, and this is baked into the apps you compose on this platform.

Bluemix has a dynamic pricing scheme that includes a freemium model! It has pay-as-you go and subscription models that offer wide choice and flexibility when it comes to the way you want to provision Bluemix services. What's more, and perhaps unlike past IBM experiences, you can sign up and start composing apps with Bluemix in minutes!

Digging Deeper into PaaS

What are the key business drivers behind the market demand for PaaS? Consider an application developer named Jane. PaaS provides and tailors the environment that Jane needs to compose and run her apps, thanks to the libraries and middleware services that are put in her development arsenal. Jane and other end users don't need to concern themselves with how those services are managed or organized "under the covers." That complexity is the responsibility of the PaaS vendor (IBM) to manage and coordinate. More than anything, this new development paradigm decreases the time to market by accelerating productivity and easing deployment of new apps over the cloud. Are you a mobile game developer? If so, you can provision a robust and rich back-end JSON data store for your app in seconds, attach to it a visualization engine, and perform some analytics. It's like baking a cake—simply grab the premeasured and taste-tested ingredients, and bake away!

The Bluemix PaaS model platform enables new business services to be built and delivered without significant operational and capital expenditures, thanks to a platform that runs on top of a managed SoftLayer infrastructure and integrates cleanly between services. The traditional components of a development stack—the operating system, the integrated development environment (IDE), the change management catalog, the bookkeeping and tooling that every developer needs—can be provisioned with ease by using the PaaS architecture of Bluemix. If you are a developer of apps that are born and launched over the cloud, PaaS is your playground. Continuous delivery and code iteration become a reality when your apps and services can be implemented on a platform that supports the full DevOps process from beginning to end.

PaaS offers such tremendous potential and value to users like Jane because there are more efficiencies to be gained than just provisioning some hardware. Take a moment to consider Figure 3-3. Having access to subsystems and linkages to databases, messaging, workflow, connectivity, web portals, and so on—this is the depth of customization that developers crave from their environment. It is also the kind of tailored experience that's missing from IaaS-only vendors. The layered approach shown in Figure 3-3 demonstrates how PaaS is, in many respects, a radical departure from the way in which enterprises and businesses traditionally provision and link services over distributed systems. Traditionally, classes of subsystems would be deployed independently of the app that they are supporting. Similarly, their lifecycles would be managed independently of the primary app as well. If Jane's app is developed out of step with her supporting network of services, she will need to spend time (time that would be better spent building innovative new features for her app) ensuring that each of these subsystems has the correct versioning, functionality mapping for dependencies, and so on. All of this translates into greater risk, steeper costs, higher complexity, and a longer development cycle for Jane.

With a PaaS delivery model like Bluemix, these obstacles are removed: App developers and users don't need to manage installation, licensing, maintenance, or availability of underlying support services. The platform assumes responsibility for managing subservices (and their lifecycles) for you. When the *minutiae* of micromanaging subservices are no longer part of the equation, the potential for unobstructed, end-to-end DevOps becomes possible. With a complete DevOps framework, a developer can move from concept to full production in a matter of minutes. Jane can be more agile in her development, which leads to faster code iteration and a more polished product or service for her customers. We would describe this as the PaaS approach to *process-oriented design and development.*

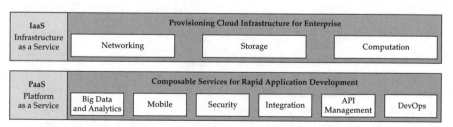

Figure 3-3 *Platform as a service (PaaS) provides an integrated development environment for building applications that are powered by managed services.*

Being Social on the Cloud: How Bluemix Integrates Platforms and Architectures

The cloud is a vast space, and the apps that you develop for it could very well need to reach out and "mingle" with other apps. Bluemix comes fully equipped with a catalog of integration and coordination services for external applications and other public clouds so that your apps can stay social. Later in this chapter, we discuss deployable PaaS and design patterns that make it easy to expose catalogs of apps and services. This style of automated deployment is ideally suited for PaaS and is paving the way for the *composable business*.

There are three potential PaaS configurations that you can run purely on the cloud. These three models have had the most success and widespread adoption among PaaS developers. A key differentiator for the IBM Cloud is that it can support all three of them (which is not the case with most other vendors).

In Figure 3-4 you can see the three main types of PaaS configurations. Common to all three of these PaaS configurations is that our developer Jane is at the top of the stack. Jane needs to compose new cloud applications with as little friction as possible, and so with each configuration (Types I–III), we have two clouds—Cloud A and Cloud B—running on top of an IaaS layer. Cloud A is running completely different services (mobile back-end libraries, Internet of Things device connectivity services) than Cloud B (database back ends, NoSQL document data stores). However, to power Jane's app, she

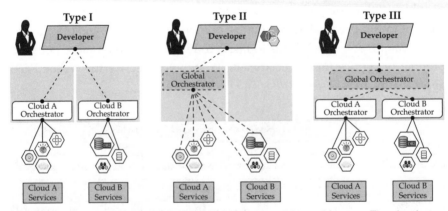

Figure 3-4 *Three configurations of a platform as a service architecture. The cloud services can be governed by cloud-specific (Type I), global (Type II), or a hybrid of orchestrators (Type III).*

needs to tap into both Cloud A and B. How she does that integration and how these required services are coordinated between those clouds (something we refer to as *orchestration*) is where we start to differentiate between the PaaS approaches. Whether Jane provisions services through a "single pane of glass" (a global orchestrator that has a predefined assortment of services to choose from) or defines linkages with these cloud services directly (even if they live on clouds that are separate from her PaaS environment) determines the type of PaaS architecture her solution requires.

Need a breather? Remember that this layer of complexity—how the pieces of PaaS and its services fit together—are not the concern of the developer. This is what's great about PaaS after all! IBM handles the integration of services behind the scenes and determines how those services come together. In other words, the PaaS infrastructure in Bluemix determines how Jane's instructions to a "single pane of glass" are translated across multiple cloud environments (internal or even external public clouds) to deliver the functionality that her apps need. We just added this tech section here in case you want a taste of the details that are going on behind the scenes, but never lose sight that with Bluemix, you don't have to care about such details.

Understanding the Hybrid Cloud: Playing Frankenstein Without the Horror

What exactly do we mean by *hybrid cloud deployments*? It's a term that is commonly heard in conversations about bridging on-premise and off-premise deployments. There is a huge elephant in the room any time we talk about moving services to the cloud, and that elephant is named "current investments." Companies with an invested on-premise infrastructure are understandably reluctant to rip out those systems and migrate completely to the cloud, unless there is a sound business plan that surrounds the suggestion. We don't think companies should rip and replace stuff. They need to come up with a strategic plan and, where it makes sense, leverage the cloud, and where it doesn't, leverage what they have. Anyone who decrees "rip and replace everything" is pulling back into the cloud's hype phase. Quite simply, as should be the case with any initiative, ensure that there is a sound business plan that surrounds the strategy.

A hybrid cloud environment that's stitched together cross-premise can be either marvelous or monstrous. The key to leadership and innovation around infrastructure hybridization is to start thinking in terms of "composite templates." When workload requirements are well defined, you can leverage services in a way that plays to their strengths. For example, perhaps an off-premise cloud infrastructure would be well suited for experimental batch operations and an on-premise infrastructure would be well suited for performance-critical tasks. At the same time, perhaps governance regulations dictate a completely different premise location criterion. Also, never forget that without a network connection, the hybrid cloud model falls apart. A robust network is a must.

The key is to design hybrid access to services across infrastructures (on the cloud and on the ground). Composite templates are akin to the IBM PureSystems deployable patterns that we mentioned earlier. When hybrid services and access patterns are well defined and understood, companies such as IBM can wrap provisioning and architecture expertise into repeatable, deployable patterns.

The picture that we are painting is less the image of Frankenstein's creature and much more a carefully crafted model made out of Lego bricks. Consider Figure 3-5: The concept of composable services is central to Bluemix

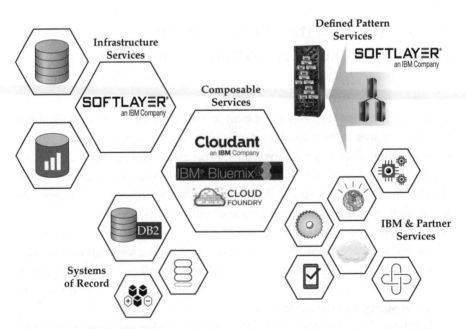

Figure 3-5   *IBM Bluemix's catalog of composable services is central to the integration of on-premise and off-premise infrastructure services.*

and the IBM Cloud as a whole. What differentiates IBM's platform from competitors is the continuum of services that can be accessed across both on-premise *and* off-premise resources. Cloud-ready solutions such as SoftLayer make this possible, bursting data on demand to the cloud, as needed.

Tried and Tested: How Deployable Patterns Simplify PaaS

At its core, PaaS gives you control over the provisioning and automation of a mind-boggling number of patterned middleware services (development environments, run times, packaged services, business patterns, and so on) and the metering of application usage. For managed PaaS solutions, you can perform monitoring on a per-app basis (with respect to usage and performance), manage app and service licenses, conduct identity and security management, and manage push/pull access from mobile devices.

Truly advanced PaaS solutions such as IBM Bluemix provide data caching services, autoscaling in response to increasing (or decreasing) demand for services that are running on top of the platform, workload automation, and cloud bursting (for example, to a dedicated IaaS bare-metal environment like IBM SoftLayer) as needed. Bluemix's selection of reusable design patterns and automated service composition adds value, whereas its open ecosystem of services (including non-IBM proprietary and open source services) and integration patterns with traditional repositories add capability. A PaaS such as Bluemix enables organizations to offer their development teams a full-featured, end-to-end, continuous delivery environment where services can be provisioned and are composable on the cloud.

One question that you might be asking is "What is the relationship between PaaS and patterns?" Patterns enable you to encode business and development best practices into a deliverable that you can manage and deploy in a repeatable way. They are typically applied to existing problems that have been part of a marketplace or environment for a period of time. Only after a business's pain points have been thoroughly studied and understood can you have hardened best practices and access patterns to overcome those challenges—these are the "standard operating procedures" that are well suited for translation into deployable patterns. An apt analogy is vaccination against disease: There might be an experimental vaccine for a new disease that seems to improve a patient's health, but it is not until the efficacy

and safety of the treatment are well understood that the vaccine is mass produced for the general population.

To apply this analogy to business patterns, let's consider Figure 3-6.
Although there might exist several ad hoc one-off strategies for solving a
particular business use case, it isn't until the strategy demonstrates successful results over a period of time that IBM will consider it to be an expert
deployable "patterned" solution for clients. IBM's entire PureSystems family
is built around this concept of standardization and proven patterns to address
business challenges of innovation, speed, and time to market. What's more,
all of the expertise and effort that went into developing these on-premise patterned expert-baked solutions are now being leveraged for the Bluemix PaaS
environment.

The challenge with deploying patterns to a cloud environment is that,
from a design perspective, patterns are geared more toward existing technologies and are not necessarily optimized for iterative deployment of ever-
evolving applications and architectures. For example, what is the pattern for
taking a cookie-cutter implementation and days later stitching in a new service that just changed the scope of what your app is all about? We are getting
at the fact that the cloud is a highly dynamic environment. The idea of establishing a hardened pattern around an environment where new code is
deployed on the first day, a new database is added on the second day, a queuing system and then a monitoring system are tacked on after that, and who
knows what else, becomes seemingly impossible.

So if apps that are born and developed on the cloud are built iteratively and
gradually, how can design patterns ever get traction in such an environment?
The answer is PaaS, because PaaS can be broken down and modeled in much
the same way as *subpatterns*. There is a surprising amount of synergy between
design patterns and the way that practitioners provision environments and
services over the cloud. With this in mind, let's explore a layered approach to
application development in the cloud.

At the top of Figure 3-6, developer Jane is actively making use of the Bluemix core services to compose and run cloud-native apps; this is what we refer
to as the *Bluemix Fabric*. Meanwhile, Jane is taking advantage of a large catalog
of external services (available through the API economy; more on this topic in
a bit) such as database back ends, queuing services, and so on. The key idea
here is that these back-end external services *can be provisioned using patterns*.

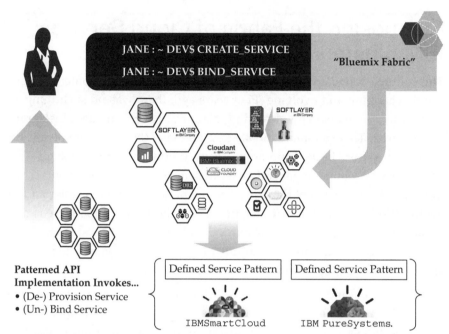

Figure 3-6 *The PaaS "Bluemix Fabric" leverages design patterns to create a frictionless and productive environment for developers through services that are provisioned over the cloud.*

For example, at some point in the coding cycle in Figure 3-6, Jane will need a service that can handle a certain requirement for her app—perhaps applying an XSL style sheet transformation that was requested by an end user. "Under the covers" Bluemix pushes down a design pattern that is used to instantiate the respective piece of software. After it is ready, the necessary hooks and API connectors to the service are returned to Jane so that she can tie them into the new app that is being developed on top of the PaaS. When design patterns are correctly leveraged as part of a PaaS environment, the complexities of provisioning and looping in external services are made transparent to the developer. In other words, Jane doesn't need to worry about *how* it's achieved, Jane simply moves forward with the confidence that the underlying PaaS environment handles that for her all abstracted through an API. Ultimately, this translates into the frictionless and more productive experience that developers like Jane thrive on.

Composing the Fabric of Cloud Services: IBM Bluemix

The culture around modern apps and tools for delivering content is constantly changing and evolving. Five years ago, there was no such thing as Kickstarter, the global crowd-funding platform. Four years ago, Instagram did not exist. There are more mobile devices today than there are people on the planet. We are in the "app now," "want it now" era of technology. This shift isn't a millennial or generational phenomenon, it's a fundamental shift in the collective degree of impatience to get projects delivered faster and to get the things we want done faster. In many respects, this impatience is due to the general perception that the burdens of IT infrastructure are gone.

To be successful in this new culture, modern application developers and enterprises must adopt four key fundamental concepts:

- First is *deep* and *broad* integration. What people use apps for today encompasses more than one task. For example, today's shopper expects a seamless experience to a storefront across multiple devices with different modalities (some will require gesture interactions, whereas others will use taps and clicks).

- The second concept is *mobile*. Applications need a consistent layer of functionality to guarantee that no matter how you interact with the storefront (on your phone, a tablet, or a laptop), the experience feels the same but is still tailored to the device. Here we are talking about the functionality that has to be consistent (we've all been frustrated by apps where the mobile version can't do what the web version does), and for that to happen, the customer-facing endpoints need to be deeply integrated across all devices.

- Third, developers of these apps need to be *agile* and *iterative* in their approach to design. Delivery cycles are no longer set according to static points in time (a yearly release of your on-premise software, for example). Users expect continuous improvement and refinement of their services and apps, and code drops need to be frequent enough to keep up with this pace of change. After all, the cloud culture is so different: For example, clients can decide to keep their license on a monthly or even daily decision checkpoint. It's easy to go elsewhere. Continuous delivery has moved from initiative to imperative.

- Finally, the *ecosystem* that supports these apps must appeal to customer and developer communities. Business services and users want to be able to use an app without needing to build it and own it. Likewise, developers demand an environment that provides them with the necessary tools and infrastructure to get their apps off the ground and often have next-to-zero tolerance for roadblocks (like budget approvals, DBA permissions, and so on).

These expectations and requirements precisely fit into the concept of PaaS and building cloud-native apps. Put another way, this is exactly the kind of environment that IBM Bluemix promotes and delivers.

As previously mentioned, Bluemix provides a PaaS over the IBM Cloud (powered by SoftLayer and Cloud Foundry) to deliver a venue for testing and deploying your apps. At its core, Bluemix is an open standards compliant, cloud-based platform for building, managing, and running apps of all types, especially for smart devices, which are driving the new data economy. You can think of Bluemix as a catalog of composable services and run times that is powered by IBM, open source, or third-party vendor-built technologies running on top of a managed hardware infrastructure. The goal is to make the process of uploading and deploying applications to the cloud as seamless as possible so that development teams can hit the ground running and start programming from day one. Bluemix capabilities include a Java framework for mobile back-end development, application monitoring in a self-service environment, and a host of other capabilities...all delivered through an as-a-service model. Bluemix offers a services-rich portfolio without the burden of mundane infrastructure tasks. Its target audience—developers, enterprise line-of-business users—can say goodbye to the drudgery of installing software, configuring hardware and software, fulfilling middleware requirements, and wrestling with database architectures. Bluemix has you covered.

As previously mentioned, Bluemix offers a catalog of services, drawing from the strengths of the IBM portfolio around enterprise-grade security, web, database management, Big Data analytics, cross-services and platform integration, DevOps, and more. These are known quantities—things that clients have come to expect when doing business with IBM. One of the things that the Bluemix team found is that developers often identify themselves with the technology that they choose to use. With this in mind, IBM also wants to ensure that the Bluemix platform provides a choice of code base, language and API support, and an infrastructure that will attract developers from communities that IBM has not traditionally addressed in the past. For example, Bluemix supports Mongo-based apps. Quite simply, Bluemix eliminates entry barriers for these programmers and developers by offering a streamlined, cost-flexible, development and deployment platform.

Figure 3-7 offers a tiny glimpse at the Bluemix service catalog where developers can browse, explore, and provision services to power their apps. Being able to provide a full lifecycle of end-to-end DevOps is important, given the experimental, iterative, sandbox-like approach that we expect developers to bring to this platform.

The entire app lifecycle is cloud agile—from planning the app to monitoring and managing these services. All of these services are supported by the Bluemix platform right "out of the box." This ultimately enables developers to integrate their apps with a variety of systems, such as on-premise systems of record (think transactional databases) or other public and private services that are already running on the cloud, all through Bluemix APIs and services.

If you want other developers on Bluemix to tap into the potential of these systems, you can work with IBM to expose your APIs to the Bluemix audience by becoming a service partner. Consider the fundamental Bluemix initiatives that we outlined: Bluemix is a collaborative ecosystem that supports

Figure 3-7 *The Bluemix catalog of composable services comes from IBM, partner, and open source technologies that are enabled for the continuous, agile development of cloud apps.*

both developers and customers, and enabling our partners to integrate across these verticals is a key part of that initiative.

Parting Words on Platform as a Service

We dedicated much of this chapter to PaaS, a key anchor of the as-a-service model. PaaS is about more than simply giving developers a sandbox to work in. Platforms such as IBM Bluemix enable transparent integration among multiple environments "under the covers." What this means for our users is access to a myriad of services and tools, all through a single "pane of glass." Bluemix rapidly brings products and services to market at a lower cost, thanks to the flexibility and on-demand nature of cloud-based PaaS. The fact that PaaS is a low up-front investment vehicle for application development encourages experimentation and innovative development, without concern for software configuration and hardware provisioning, or the need for on-hand staff to manage the infrastructure. Furthermore, Bluemix's iterative nature encourages developers to continuously deliver new functionality to their applications. Bluemix is designed so that developers can iterate on their code and app functionality as rapidly and painlessly as possible. Bluemix extends a company's existing investments in IT infrastructure. Many clients have heterogeneous, complex, on-premise environments that must be linked to new born-on-the-cloud applications.

With an on-demand and services-based infrastructure, Bluemix enables developers to go from raw to fully baked apps in as short a time as possible. Clients are able to securely connect to their existing on-premise infrastructure to power these apps, ensuring that apps made in the cloud can effectively leverage the resources that these companies have on the ground. With DevOps, teams both large and small are able to automate the development and delivery of applications: Bluemix makes the process of continuous iteration simple and straightforward for both developers and line-of-business users.

Consuming Functionality Without the Stress: Software as a Service

If PaaS is oriented toward the developer who wants to code and build the next generation of applications in a frictionless environment, then software as a service (SaaS) is geared much more toward the line-of-business (LOB) user who needs to consume the capabilities of a service that is already built and ready to deploy. SaaS consumers span the breadth of multiple domains and interest groups: human resources, procurement officers, legal departments, city operations, marketing campaign support, demand-generation leads, political or business campaign analysis, agency collaboration, sales, customer care, technical support, and more. The variety of ways that business users can exploit SaaS is extraordinarily complex: It can be specific (to the extent that it requires tailored software to address the problem at hand), or it can require a broad and adaptable solution to address the needs of an entire industry.

Not every SaaS vendor can guarantee that their packaged software will satisfy every vertical and niche use case we've outlined here. Nor do all SaaS vendors offer a catalog of services that supports deep integration hooks and connectors for when you need to scale out your solution or roll in additional tools in support of your business end users. Figure 3-8 highlights the fact that SaaS can apply to anything, as long as it is provisioned and maintained as a service over the cloud.

What differentiates IBM's solution is that it offers the complete stack—from IaaS to PaaS to SaaS—in support of every possible customer use case. We would argue that IBM's portfolio stands alone in being able to offer both tailored and extensible SaaS deliverables to address the various dimensions of *consumable* and *composable* functionality that are required by enterprises today.

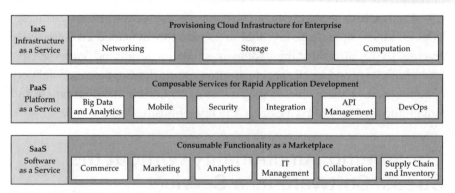

Figure 3-8   *SaaS delivers software that runs on the cloud, enabling you to consume functionality without having to manage software installation, upgrades, or other maintenance.*

And consider this: As developers build their apps on the Bluemix PaaS platform, they can seamlessly bring their solutions to a SaaS market and a sophisticated IBM Cloud Computing Marketplace (ibm.com/cloud-computing/us/en/marketplace.html), where new clients can consume them. Throughout this section, we explore SaaS and IBM's offerings in this space in more detail, but first, it is worth setting the stage by describing how cloud distributions are reshaping software.

The Cloud Bazaar: SaaS and the API Economy

In the marketplace today, there is a trend toward what many have called the *API economy*. The API economy is the ability to programmatically access anything through well-defined protocols and APIs. API economies enable developers and end users to easily and seamlessly integrate services with any new apps that they are building or consuming on the cloud. This is quite a departure from how things were done before. Many offerings that could historically be described as SaaS were driven by the user interface (UI). Today, companies such as Twitter and eBay leverage API integration into third-party services to drive revenue and traffic *far more* than they rely on a UI-driven strategy for attracting users.

At the most basic level, SaaS apps are software that is hosted and managed in the cloud. Salesforce.com is a well-known SaaS offering for customer relationship management (CRM). Instead of hosting your own CRM system on premise, the app resides on the cloud. Here's the stack: All software components are pre-installed (SaaS); the database and application server that support the app are already in place (PaaS); this all lives on top of a fully managed infrastructure layer (IaaS). As a client, you just interact with the app; there is no need to install or configure the software yourself. The key thing to remember is that although the app feels like a discrete piece of business logic, under the covers the SaaS model is more likely a collection of dozens (even hundreds or thousands) of APIs working in concert to provide the logic that powers the app.

Consider a service like Twitter. Its UI is minimal and straightforward: You have a timeline, 140 characters to compose your message, and a button to post your tweet. Under the covers, however, it calls a dizzying number of services through APIs. The real value of Twitter lies in its ability to seamlessly integrate with other apps. Have you ever bought something online and found an integrated tweet button for sharing your shopping experience? That vendor is leveraging Twitter's API to help you announce to the world that your new golf club is the solution to your slicing issues. When you tweet, underlying service authorizations can store your tweeted image in Flickr and leverage Google Maps to enrich the tweet with geospatial information visualizations. The API economy also lets you use that same tweet to tell all your Facebook friends how your golf game is set to improve. Such a neatly orchestrated set of transactions between distinct services is made possible and is done seamlessly by the API economy that drives today's cloud SaaS marketplace, as shown in Figure 3-9.

Having a well thought-out and architected API is crucial for developing an ecosystem around the functionality that you want to deliver through an as-a-service property. Remember, the key is designing an API for your services and software that plays well with others. Your API audience is not only people in your company, but partners and competitors too. Consumers of the SaaS API economy require instant access to that SaaS property (these services need to be always available and accessible), instant access to the API's documentation, and instant access to the API itself (so that developers can program and code against it). Furthermore, it is critical that the API architecture be extensible, with hooks and integration end points across multiple domains (Figure 3-9) to promote cooperation and connectivity with new services as they emerge.

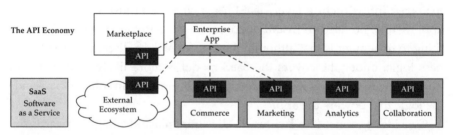

Figure 3-9 *IBM's "API economy" is made possible by a unified cloud architecture of well-defined integration end points between external ecosystems, cloud marketplaces, and IBM's SaaS portfolio.*

Demolishing the Barrier to Entry for Cloud-Ready Analytics: IBM's dashDB

In this section we want to talk about an analytics service from IBM called dashDB. As we went to press, the dashDB services were scheduled for release in both a PaaS model (for those composing apps that require analytics) and a SaaS model (for those that simply need a turnkey analytics service). What we describe in this section is the end goal; it might be the case that some of the things we talk about here aren't available when you first get this book, but they will come soon after. We are also going to talk about dashDB from a SaaS perspective.

Moving forward, you are going to see the IBM Information Management brand deliver capabilities on the cloud first in a much faster manner than with traditional models. This is in lockstep with the constant feature delivery and innovation users of the cloud expect from the services they consume there. For example, at its core, dashDB is the confluence of Netezza (Chapter 9) and BLU Acceleration (Chapter 8) technologies; it also includes some IBM DataWorks refinery services (Chapter 13), a Cognos visualization engine, and runs on SoftLayer.

What does continual integration look like? Netezza (also known as the IBM PureData System for Analytics) is famous for its deeply embedded IBM Netezza Analytics engine (INZA). Over time, more and more of the INZA capabilities will get deeply embedded into dashDB. The vision is that at some point you will be able to run all the same INZA algorithms that you can run in Netezza today directly on dashDB. The same can be said for the Netezza SQL API. IBM dashDB includes Oracle compatibility too, although this capability comes from another source (DB2 has a native execution layer for Oracle PL/SQL so that service is embedded in dashDB as well; you can see how the apps made of service components are the future). This continual feature delivery methodology empowers organizations with the ability to burst more and more analytics into the cloud from their Netezza appliances with less and less friction. At the same time, innovations that arrive in the cloud first will eventually find their way on premise. For example, the INZA capabilities being built into dashDB will be integrated into on-premise software instantiations of BLU Acceleration, like DB2.

So what is the difference when consuming dashDB as a PaaS or SaaS model? Developers can use PaaS to compose an app. They might want to surface the application in a SaaS model and charge for it down the road; IBM gives you that option as a service partner. That said, clients can use dashDB in a PaaS model for their own analytics needs—it's just not managed in the same way as a SaaS model. However, for customers who simply want to consume software without building and assembling it themselves, a ready-to-go and managed SaaS solution might be just the ticket. Remember, SaaS isn't for developers; it's for users and consumers who need to achieve new business outcomes rapidly and cost effectively.

You may see dashDB referred to as a data warehouse as a service (DWaaS)—which we think is best conceptualized as an added layer of classification atop the software as a service (SaaS) model. Fundamentally, DWaaS is very much a SaaS offering—clients consume the functionality of the service (in the case of dashDB, that functionality entails best-of-breed performance and analytics) without concern over provisioning or managing the software's lifecycle themselves.

IBM's portfolio of SaaS offerings is built on the same foundations of resiliency, availability, and security as the IaaS and Bluemix PaaS layers we talked about in this chapter. What differentiates dashDB from the pack are the three pillars that set DWaaS apart from the traditional on-premise data warehousing that has come before it: simplicity, agility, and performance. Let's take a moment to tease apart what each of these pillars offers clients that provision this service. *Simplicity*: dashDB is easy to deploy, easy to use, requires fewer resources to operate, and is truly "load and go" for any type of data you can throw at it. *Agility*: "train of thought" analytics are made possible by dashDB's integration across the IBM Big Data portfolio, making your apps faster and delivering actionable business insight sooner. *Performance*: dashDB delivers BLU Acceleration's signature, industry-leading performance at a price the market demands—all within a cloud-simple form factor. In ten words or less, dashDB gives faster actionable insight for unlocking data's true potential.

IBM dashDB is all about the shifting client values around how functionality is consumed and the explosive growth that we are witnessing in the delivery of SaaS on the cloud. Customers today are focused on assembling the components and services that they need to achieve their business outcomes. In terms of the marketplace, analytics are becoming increasingly valuable; in fact, we'd go so far as to say that in the modern marketplace, analytics are indispensable—like we said before, from initiative to imperative. Analytics are driving decisions about how skills are deployed across an organization, how resources and infrastructure are distributed in support of a business, and how clients access the mountains of data that they are actively creating or collecting.

One question being asked by many businesses is "How do we rapidly transition from data *collection* to data *discovery and insight* to drive decision making and growth strategies?" As companies move aggressively into this space, they quickly realize that the skills that are required to build the tools and perform data analysis are still pretty scarce; the combination of statistician and DBA guru in one individual is hard to come by! Cost becomes a major obstacle for companies that want to deploy or manage business analytics suites with an on-premise infrastructure and appliances. The future innovators in this space will be companies that enable their partners and customers to bypass the risk and costs that were previously associated with analytics. This is the drive behind SaaS delivery and in particular IBM's dashDB.

The idea of an analytics warehouse that can be consumed as a service is a product of powerful solutions and infrastructure emerging at just the right time…over the cloud. Speaking from our own firsthand interactions with clients, we can confidently say that the vast majority of IT and enterprise customers want to move at least part of their resources into a cloud environment. The trend is increasingly toward applications that are "born" in the cloud, developed and optimized for consumption over distributed systems. A key driver behind this momentum is centered on CAPEX containment, which is a SaaS product that scales elastically and can be "right-sized" for your business, translating into smaller up-front costs and greater flexibility down the road.

SaaS solutions are distinctly "cloud first." We believe that following best practices and architecting a software solution for the *cloud first* makes translating that asset into an on-premise solution much more straightforward and painless. In terms of the performance of on-premise and cloud deliverables, the laws of physics are ultimately going to win. With the cloud, there is the unavoidable fact that your data and instructions need to travel across a wire. In most cases, the latency in cloud deployments will be at least *slightly* greater (whether or not it is significant is another question). Being able to use in-memory analytic capabilities, perform data refinement, and ingest data for analysis in a real-time environment, all in the cloud, is propelling the industry toward new opportunities for actionable business insight. This is all being made possible through cloud-based SaaS. Don't forget—the cloud isn't so much about raw throughput performance as it is about agility and scale: how fast you can build, deploy, and iterate applications; how fast can you scale; or how fast you can attach (and tear down) add-on services such as analytic data marts.

Build More, Grow More, Know More: dashDB's Cloud SaaS

IBM dashDB can be provisioned as an expansion to the Cloudant NoSQL data layer, with purpose-built hooks for handling the ingestion and migration of data between Cloudant's JSON document and the dashDB analytics service. This is the kind of stuff we were referring to earlier in this chapter when we talked about integration of service points. For example, a mobile gaming app that stores information in Cloudant can back-end sync the JSON data into dashDB for light-speed analytics on collected information through a built-in facility.

The predecessor to dashDB on Bluemix is the Analytics Warehouse Service, which was solely based on BLU Acceleration technology. Over time, you will see users of this service migrate to dashDB, which provides a richer managed service and comes with the extended set of capabilities we outlined earlier.

IBM dashDB fits the pattern of whichever analytics use case your organization needs to fulfill. It can be procured as an integrated analytic warehouse that is embedded with Watson Analytics, coupled with Cloudant's NoSQL data stores, or integrated with services available in the IBM DataWorks data refinery catalog. Alternatively, dashDB can serve as a stand-alone analytics engine for clients looking to leverage the elasticity and flexibility of a DWaaS (remember: software as a service with added granularity specific to data warehousing) cloud deliverable. Again, for application developers working with IBM Bluemix, dashDB can form a vital piece in your composable fabric of services running atop IBM's managed PaaS.

The takeaway message for dashDB is as follows: It's a high-performance analytics service, it's delivered in a managed "cloud-easy" way (there is nothing for you to do but click and analyze), it has best-in-class simplicity in terms of provisioning and usage, and it comes with a rich set of built-in security features for enterprise customers. IBM dashDB enables you to build more, grow more, and know more.

We say build more because dashDB gives you the flexibility to get started without making costly CAPEX investments, which reduces risk and mitigates cost. The provisioning of this SaaS takes less than a dozen or so minutes for 1TB of data, and migration and performance have been tuned to delight users with their first experience. To support bursty workloads from on-premise infrastructures to dashDB in the cloud, a lot of effort has been put into data transfer rates. (Mileage is going to vary—remember that your network connection speed matters.) When these pain points are eliminated, LOB owners are free to experiment and pursue new insights that are born out of the cloud—in short, they can build more.

The beauty of the SaaS model is that capability enhancements can be delivered to your business *without* performance degradation or downtime to your customers. Consumption of its analytics capabilities becomes your only concern—that, and growing your business with your newfound insights, and this is why we say dashDB lets you grow more. Think about it: You can put personnel on discovering new insights and leveraging investigative techniques you could never apply before, or you can spend your time upgrading your on-premise investments.

IBM dashDB's in-database analytics also includes R integration for predictive modeling (alongside the INZA functionality that will continue to work its way into the service offering as dashDB iterates over time). R's deeply woven integration with dashDB delivers in-database functions that span the analytic gamut: linear regression, decision trees, regression trees, K-means, and data preparation. Other statistical showcases, such as support for geospatial analytics and developing analytics extensions through C++ UDX, will eventually round out dashDB's analytics portfolio.

From a security perspective, dashDB is Guardium-ready (covered in Chapter 12). Industry-leading data refinery services will add free (and some for fee) masking, transformation, and enrichment, as well as performance-enhancing operations, which we briefly discuss in the next section.

Refinery as a Service

Both Bluemix and Watson Analytics are platforms that consume and produce data; as such, they need governance and integration tools that fit into the SaaS model we've been describing in this chapter. IBM's engineering teams are taking its rich data governance capabilities and exposing them as a collection of rich composite and data refinery services known as DataWorks. Available at the time of writing are data load, masking, and data selection services that you can leverage in an integrated manner with your other services. We cover these capabilities in Part III of this book.

Wrapping It Up

Having well-performing and powerful analytics tools is critical to making data warehousing in the cloud a worthwhile endeavor. If you can get an answer in seconds rather than hours, you are more likely to think about the next step of analysis to probe your data even further. If you can set up a system in less than an hour instead of waiting months for budgetary approval and dealing with the numerous delays that get between loading dock and loading data, you can deliver business results sooner. This is why we say that dashDB and its BLU Acceleration technologies enable "train of thought" analytics: Having a high-performance analytics SaaS toolkit keeps business users hungry for more data-driven insight.

In this chapter, we implicitly touched on the four core elements that are central to IBM's brand and its cloud-first strategy. The first is *simplicity*: offering customers the ability to deploy, operate, and easily manage their apps and infrastructure. "Load and go" technology makes it possible to get off the ground and soar into the cloud quickly and cost effectively. *Agility* is next: If your business can deploy and iterate new applications faster, you will be positioned to adapt to a rapidly changing marketplace with ease. IBM's as-a-service portfolio (for infrastructure, development platforms, and software) makes that a reality. The third element (it's a big one) is *integration* with Big Data. Analytics that are being run in platforms such as Hadoop do *not* live in isolation from the type of questions and work that is being done in data warehousing. These technologies work in concert, and workflows between the two need to exist on a continuum for businesses to unlock the deep and actionable insight that is within reach. The fourth element in IBM's cloud vision is a *unified experience*. As we show in Figure 3-10, the integration hooks, interoperability, migration services, consistent and elastic infrastructure, and platform services layers that IBM's cloud solution has in place (and continues to develop) offer a truly holistic and unified experience for developers and enterprise customers alike.

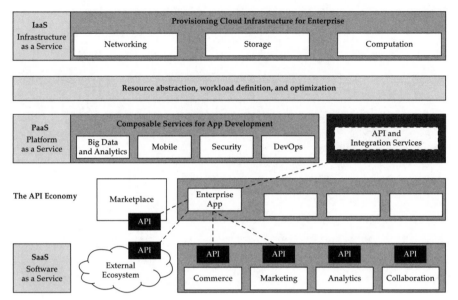

Figure 3-10 *IBM's cloud portfolio delivers a holistic approach to deeply integrated infrastructure, platform, and software as a service environments that is unrivalled in scalability, availability, and performance.*

No other competitor in the cloud space can offer an equally rich as-a-service environment with solutions that are designed for the enterprise, and still remain open to emerging technologies from partners and third-party vendors. *Cloud* used to be a term that was surrounded by hype, but over the years, the as-a-service model has transformed business challenges that had remained unsolved for decades into new sources of opportunity and revenues; quite simply, this proves that cloud is beyond the hype. As competitors race to stitch together their own offerings, IBM customers are already designing apps and composing solutions with a Bluemix fabric, consuming software as a service functionality on top of a SoftLayer infrastructure that lives in the cloud.

4

The Data Zones Model: A New Approach to Managing Data

The Big Data opportunity: Is it a shift, rift, lift, or cliff? We think it is a matter of time until you are using one (ideally two) of these words to describe the effect that Big Data has had on your organization and its outcomes. Study after study proves that those who invest in analytics outperform their peers across almost any financial indicator that you can think of: earnings, stock appreciation, and more. Big Data, along with new technologies introduced by the open source community and enhancements developed by various technology vendors, is driving a dramatic shift in how organizations manage their analytic assets. And when it's done right, it has the effect of lifting those organizations' Analytics IQ, our measure for how smart an organization is about analytics.

A common challenge to any organization investing in its Analytics IQ has been providing common access to data across the organization when the data is being generated in various divisional and functional silos. In a social-mobile-cloud world, this question hasn't changed, but its answer certainly has. Historically, the answer to this question was to make the enterprise data warehouse (EDW) the center of the universe. The process for doing this had become fairly standardized too. *If* companies want an EDW, they know what to do: Create a normalized data model to make information from different sources more consumable; extract required data from the operational systems into a staging area; map the data to a common data model; transform and move the data into a centralized EDW; and create views, aggregates, tiers, and marts for the various reporting requirements.

Over time, various challenges to this approach have given rise to some variations. For example, some organizations have attempted to move their data transformation and normalization processes into the warehouse, in other words, shifting from extract, transform, and load (ETL) to extract, load, and transform (ELT). Some organizations invested more heavily in operational data stores (ODSs) for more immediate reporting on recent operational and transaction-level data.

As organizations began to do more predictive analytics and modeling, they became interested in data that was not necessarily in the EDW: data sets whose volumes are too large to fit in the EDW, or untouched raw data in its most granular form. For example, consider a typical telecommunications (telco) EDW. Perhaps the most granular data in a telco is the call detail record (CDR). The CDR contains subscriber data, information about the quality of the signal, who was called, the length of the call, geographic details (location before, during, and at the end of the call), and more. Because this data is so voluminous—we're talking terabytes per day here—it can't possibly reside in the EDW. The data that ends up in the EDW is typically aggregated, which removes the finer details that a data scientist might require. This data is also likely to be range-managed; perhaps only six to nine months of the data is kept in the EDW, and then it's "rolled out" of the repository on some scheduled basis to make room for new data. As you can imagine, this approach makes it tough to do long-term historical analysis.

Analytics teams respond to such challenges by pulling down data directly from both operational systems and the data warehouse to their desktops to build and test their predictive models. At many organizations, this has created a completely separate path for data that is used for analytics, as opposed to data that is used for enterprise reporting and performance management.

With data center consolidation efforts, we've seen some organizations that make use of a specific vendor's warehousing technology load their EDWs with as much raw source system data as they can and then use the warehouse mostly for data preparation (this is where the ELT we mentioned earlier is used). As you can imagine, if an EDW is to be a trusted and highly responsive repository of information, saddling it with data preparation tasks and stale data drives up costs. In fact, we've seen some clients appropriate up to 60 percent of these systems' resources to simply manage cold untouched data or data transformation work. Figure 4-1 summarizes such a traditional architecture for enterprise data management.

EDWs didn't become problematic overnight. These shifts have been a gradual evolution. The high-level architecture and the overall approach to EDWs have been fairly constant…until recently, that is, when Big Data changed things. To synergize and optimize a modern-era analytics architecture, you have to think in *zones*—separate areas for storing, processing, and accessing your information based on their particular characteristics and purposes. These zones foundationally sit on the polyglot environment discussed in Chapter 2, but they also need data refinery services and governance, real-time processing, and more. What's more, they need to be able to access the foundation (or leverage capabilities) off premise in the cloud, on premise, and more likely in a hybrid environment that includes both, with the capability to burst into the cloud as needed. If you're familiar with The Zone diet, which advocates balance with respect to the source of your daily caloric intake in the form of carbohydrates, proteins, and fats, it's the same kind of thing. The data zones model that we talk about in this chapter is designed to deliver a balanced calibration of the right technology, economic cost curves, and data preparation whose confluence boosts your organization's Analytics IQ.

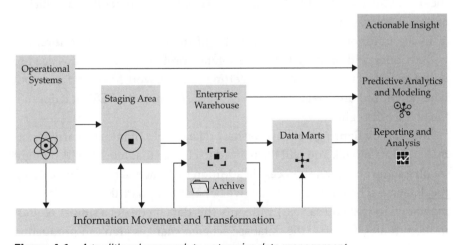

Figure 4-1   *A traditional approach to enterprise data management*

Challenges with the Traditional Approach

The biggest challenges that organizations are facing with the traditional EDW approach can be placed into three categories: *agility, cost,* and *depth of insight.*

Agility

Agility matters. It's critical in sports, politics, organizational effectiveness, and more. Agility is really a measurement of the ability to adapt or change direction in an efficient and effective manner to achieve a targeted goal. In fact, agility is so important that almost every role-playing game (RPG) has some sort of key performance indicator to measure a character's ability to carry out or evade an attack or to negotiate uneven terrain. Organizations are discovering that with traditional EDW approaches, it takes too long to make information available to the business. A common complaint from most business users is that any time they make a request for some additional data, the standard response is that it will take at least "several months" and "more than a million dollars"…and that's even *before* they share their specific requirements! But if you think about what it takes to make new information available in this kind of environment, responses like this are actually not as unreasonable as they might initially sound. At this point, we are beginning to feel a little sorry for operational teams because they really do get it from both ends: Developers don't want to wait on them (Chapter 2) and neither does the line of business (LOB). We think that IT ops is like parenthood, which is often a thankless job.

In the traditional "EDW is the center of the universe" architecture, if a LOB requires additional data to investigate a problem, several steps need to be taken. Of course, before even getting started, you have to figure out whether the required data already exists somewhere in the EDW. If it doesn't, the real work begins.

You start by figuring out how the new data should fit into the current normalized data model. You will likely need to change that model, which might involve some governance process in addition to the actual tasks of modifying the database schema. The next step (we hope) is to update the system's documentation so that you can easily identify this data if you get a similar request in the future. Of course, the database schema changes aren't in production yet; they are in some testing process to ensure that the required changes didn't break anything. After you are confident that you can deliver on the LOB's request, you need to schedule these changes in production so that they don't impact any business-critical processes. What about total time? It depends on your environment, but traditionally, this isn't an hour or days measurement; in fact, weeks would be remarkably good. Our scenario assumes you have all the data lined up and ready to go—and that might not even be the case.

After you've taken care of the "where the data will go" part, you have to figure out where and how to get the data. This typically involves multiple discussions and negotiations with the source system owners to get the data feeds set up and scheduled based on the frequency and timeliness requirements of the business. You can then start working on how to map the source data to your new target model, after which you have to start building or updating your data integration jobs.

After all this is done, your new data is *finally* available. Only at this point can you start building queries, updating reports, or developing analytic models to actually leverage the new data. Tired yet? Sound familiar? What we are talking about used to be the status quo: The zones model this chapter introduces you to is about turning the status quo on its head, in the name of agility, insights, and economies of scale.

This is a major reason why organizations continue to see new databases pop up across various LOBs and continue to experience data sprawl challenges even after investing in the ideal EDW. Remember, just like developers, business users require agility too. If IT ops doesn't deliver it to them, they will go and seek it elsewhere. Agility is one of the reasons that investing in a data zones model is a great idea.

Cost

No one ever suggested that EDWs are cheap. In fact, an EDW is one of the most expensive environments for managing data. But this is typically a conscious decision, usually made for very good reasons (think back to the gold miner discussion we had in Chapter 1). High-end hardware and storage, along with more advanced, feature-rich commercial software, are used to provide the workload management and performance characteristics needed to support the various applications and business users that leverage this platform. These investments are part of a concerted effort to maintain the reliability and resilience that are required for the critical, enterprise-level data that you have decided to manage in the EDW. In addition, as mentioned earlier, ensuring that you provide the consistent, trusted information that is expected from this investment drives up the effort and costs to manage this environment. Although EDWs are important, they are but a single technology within a polyglot environment.

Another thing about the "EDW is the center of the universe" approach is that organizations continuously have to add more and more capacity as the amount of data they are capturing and maintaining continues to rise and as they deliver additional reporting and analytic solutions that leverage that data. Companies are starting to realize that they will need to set aside significant amounts of additional capital budget every year just to support the current needs of the business, let alone the additional reporting or analytical requirements that continue to arise. Often, there isn't a clear understanding of the impact of the new applications and analytics that are being developed by the LOB. As a result, organizations can unexpectedly run into capacity issues that impact the business and drive the need for "emergency" capital expenditures, which are usually more costly and don't provide the flexibility to accommodate alternative approaches.

The cost issues all come down to this question: "Do you need to incur these high costs for *all* of your data, or are there more cost-effective ways to manage and leverage information across the enterprise?"

Depth of Insight

The third category of challenges that organizations face with the traditional EDW approach is related to the maturity and adoption of current approaches to enterprise data management. Initially, the organizations that invested in aggregating data for analysis and establishing an enterprise view of their business were able to drive competitive advantage. They were able to generate new insights about their customers and their operations, which provided significant business value. However, the early adopters are starting to see diminishing returns on these investments as their peers catch up.

Organizations are looking for new ways to deliver deeper, faster, and more accurate insights. They want to incorporate larger volumes of data into their analyses. They want to be able to leverage different types of information that are not necessarily structured or suited for a typical relational database. And they want to be able to generate insights much more quickly, often in real time. The world simply doesn't fit into neat and tidy rows and columns anymore—in fact, it never did! There's a great deal of semistructured and unstructured data out there, waiting to be harvested, that can take an organization's Analytics IQ to the next level.

Unfortunately, the historic approach to managing enterprise information has not lent itself to addressing most of these requirements. And those that could potentially be addressed by current systems cannot usually be addressed cost effectively. In some cases, costs grow because IT tries to manage unstructured data as though it were structured data, essentially trying to push a square peg into a round hole.

While many organizations have tried to make the EDW the center of the universe, forward-looking, data-driven organizations are now starting to realize that this might no longer be the right approach, given business requirements for more rapid response times, the growing volumes and complexity of data, and competitive demands. A shift toward purpose-built components is required to more effectively manage costs and compete in today's market.

Next-Generation Information Management Architectures

Next-generation (NextGen) architectures for managing information and generating insight are not about a single technology. Despite what some people think, Big Data *does not* equal Hadoop. Hadoop does play a major role in NextGen architectures, but it's a player on a team. There are various technologies, along with alternative approaches to managing and analyzing information, that enable organizations to address the challenges we have discussed and to drive a whole new level of value from their information.

The most significant transformation affects how data is maintained and used in different zones, each supporting a specific set of functions or workloads and each leveraging a specific set of technologies. When you have these zones working together with data refinery services and information integration and governance frameworks, you'll have a *data reservoir*.

Prepare for Touchdown: The Landing Zone

One of the most critical zones in a NextGen analytics architecture is the "landing" zone. It is fair to say that most organizations have already put in place some type of staging or landing area for their data, but it is the Next-Gen approach that is going to dramatically change your business. In the past, data from operational systems was copied to a "dumb" staging area, which was often an FTP server. These files had to be extracted, transformed, and loaded into some structured data repository before the data could be accessed or used. An alternative attempt to streamline this rigid process involved putting the data files directly into a database. But this approach still required an understanding of the existing source schema and configuration efforts in the target database to match that schema.

The landing zone is an area where Hadoop can play a central role. Organizations are beginning to discover that by landing all of the data from their operational systems in Hadoop, they can just "dump" the data as is, without having to understand the schema in advance or to set up any table structures, but still maintain the ability to access and work with the data. So, in essence, Hadoop is enabling companies to create smarter, more functional landing zones.

Some organizations are leveraging this enhanced capability to transform the way they respond to requests for more data from the business. They are shifting from selectively extracting specific data from operational systems to copying *all* of the data from their operational systems to this new Hadoop-based landing zone. Then, when the business asks for additional data, they point directly to the landing zone to provide more immediate access to the data. When you know exactly what data is needed to address the specific business problem in question, the data can be transformed and moved into a more refined state or repository. For example, perhaps a raw data set was "discovered" in the refinery. A LOB user could "massage" this data and chose to transform it, leveraging parts of the IBM DataWorks catalog. At this point she could then spin up a dashDB analytics service in the cloud in minutes and start to investigate the data. This type of approach requires sophisticated exploration capabilities, as well as on premise and off premise modality.

If all data lands in Hadoop, the data in its rawest form can be made available to those groups of users who were becoming frustrated at being provided with only aggregated data related to their problem domain—which is the focus of the next section.

Into the Unknown: The Exploration Zone

Landing data in Hadoop is powerful—and it is not just because of the economic benefits. Hadoop provides the ability to actually do something with the data prior to it being transformed or structured. This is a key aspect of Hadoop. It also happens to be a key value proposition in IBM's Big Data and Analytics platform: Hadoop *is also* for discovery and analytics. Most vendors in the Hadoop space agree with this concept; however, there are two notable traditional warehouse vendors that go to great lengths to portray Hadoop solely as a data preparation platform and mostly ignore its potential as a platform to accelerate discovery and analytics.

Right after data lands in Hadoop, you can make the data accessible and start generating some value prior to defining a schema. (This is why Hadoop is generally classified as a *schema-later* paradigm, whereas the relational world is generally classified as a *schema-first* paradigm; see Chapter 2 for more details.) Because Hadoop easily accommodates any data shape you can think of, the analytics performed in Hadoop can be very broad and rich. For example, imagine being able to merge system-of-record (SoR) order details with system-of-engagement (SoE) data that includes free-form text (such as call center notes and description fields), or customer contact emails, web logs, call recordings, client-initiated video uploads for diagnostics, and so on. A customer care worker who has access to all of these assets is in a much better position to deliver effective client service and address the problem at hand—we call this a *360-degree view* of the client. Think about that telco example we referenced earlier. Data scientists want to reach deep into the data in an attempt to discover correlations or insights, build prediction models, and so on. A typical telco stores about nine months of rolling data in their EDW—and it's not at the granularity of the CDR either. It's typically some aggregated higher-level obscure data; this type of zone enables users to explore the raw data in its truest form—and that is why we call it the exploration zone.

Organizations are starting to discover that there is a lot of data that straddles the line between the structured and unstructured worlds. There is a lot of data flowing through organizations that consists of elements that, by themselves, might be considered structured, but are combined in semistructured containers, often in key/value (K/V) pairs in delimited text files, such as JSON, XML, or other similar formats. Some examples include log files, clickstream sessionization details, machine- and sensor-generated data, third-party data feeds, and so on. And when you have all of this information available, you can start enabling knowledge workers to explore and navigate that data directly in a zone. This is where initial exploration often begins and is typically the best place for LOB analysts to discover what data is actually out there and might be available for further analysis.

You can start to see how a zone architecture that is polyglot based can help boost an organization's Analytics IQ. Traditional relational reporting sees a structure built to store the data—the reporting is often repeatable. In contrast, in this zone, activity is interactive and exploratory and the data is the structure. In fact, you may not even know what you are looking for; in other words, you don't even have a hypothesis to test. This is the methodology strongly associated with the RDBMS world. In this zone, data leads the way; you explore it all at will, and hope to discover or identify correlations you may have never even thought of before.

For example, Figure 4-2 shows clickstream data that can be used to perform sessionization analysis to better understand shopping cart abandonment.

You can see how the clickstream data in Figure 4-2 has some structure, yet this kind of data is perfect for Hadoop exploration. This figure shows how the Hadoop MapReduce framework can be used to categorize the web clicks for each visitor and also study those visitors who populated a shopping cart, waited a certain amount of time, and then abandoned it. Note how rich the data is—not only does it include the breadcrumb trail on the vendor's web

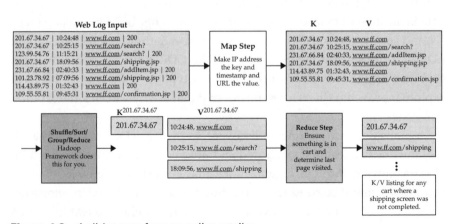

Figure 4-2   *A clickstream from an online retailer*

site, but it has spatial information (IP addresses) and temporal information (time stamps). Understanding data like this, across millions of users, could enable an organization to zoom in on why potential customers abandon their carts at the shipping calculation phase of their purchase. We've all been there—we thought we got a great online deal only to find that shipping was four times the price. Perhaps this organization could offer extra discount promotions. For example, it could give a point-in-time offer for free shipping if you spend $100 or more today.

However, the greater value comes when you start combining all of these different types of data and when you start linking your customer's transactions to their path through your web site—this is called *pathing*. Data includes comments from call center notes or emails, insights from linking the daily output of different production facilities to the condition of production equipment, machine sensor data, and environmental data from weather feeds. When you consider that our example shows only a small portion of the input data available for analysis, you will understand where Big Data gets its name. You have *volume*, you have *variety*, and you have *velocity* (clickstreams are typically measured in terabytes per day).

The landing zone should really be the place where you capture and store the raw data coming from various sources. But what do you do with the metadata and other information extracted from your unstructured data? And where do you create these linkages and maintain some type of structure that is required for any real analysis? Guess what? Metadata is cool again! It's how you understand the provenance of your data; it's how you announce data assets to the community (those data sets that are refined, and those left raw for exploration). We cover this in Chapter 13.

A separate set of "exploration" zones is emerging to provide the aforementioned capabilities, enabling different groups of users across the organization to combine data in different ways and to organize the data to fit their specific business needs. It also provides a separate environment to test different hypotheses or discover patterns, correlations, or outliers. Such an environment lets the data lead the way. We call it a *sandbox*.

These sandboxes become virtualized and agile testing and learning environments where you can experiment with data from the landing zone in various combinations and schemas, incorporating additional information that has been generated from the less structured data. These data sets can be more fluid and temporary in nature. Sandboxes provide a place where various groups of users can easily create and modify data sets that can be removed when they are no longer needed.

We are great proponents of sandboxes because they encourage us to fail, and fail fast. That caught you off-guard, right? Much can be learned from failure, and in yesterday's environments, because it cost so much to fail, we've become afraid of it. Some of the world's greatest accomplishments came after tremendous failures. Thomas Edison developed more than 10,000 prototypes of the lightbulb. James Dyson's iconic vacuum cleaner made it to market after 5,126 prototypes. And Steven Spielberg was rejected by the University of Southern California three times until he changed direction and started to make movies! Hadoop and cloud computing have changed the consequences of failure and afford new opportunities to learn and discover. This is why it's called a *sandbox*—go on and play, and if you find something, explore!

When leveraging Hadoop to host an exploration zone, the zone might be just another set of files that sits on the same cluster as the landing zone, or you can create different data sets for different user communities or LOBs. But you could also establish exploration zones on different clusters to ensure that the activities of one group do not impact those of another. What's more, you could leverage IBM BigInsights for Hadoop's multitenant capabilities that were designed for this very purpose (details in Chapter 6).

Of course, Hadoop *is not* the only place for doing exploration. Although Hadoop can be attractive from a cost and data preparation perspective, it might not provide the required performance characteristics, especially for deeper analytics. In-memory columnar technologies such as IBM's BLU Acceleration (learn about BLU in Chapter 8) are key instruments in any exploration architecture. Discovery via a managed service is key to a NextGen architecture since it provides an agile delivery method with LOB-like consumption—IBM Watson Analytics and dashDB are services we wholly expect to be part of such an architecture. Finally, there is an opportunity to leverage other fit-for-purpose environments and technologies, such as analytic appliances, instead of setting up exploration in the more expensive EDW counterparts.

Into the Deep: The Deep Analytic Zone

The need to go beyond Hadoop is even more important when you get into more complex analytical workloads that require higher performance. The exploration zone is a great place to do your initial, high-level analysis. But when you want to take things to the next level, developing complex models and performing more advanced analytics, you will want to continue to leverage RDBMS technologies as part of your analytics architecture. That said, you should consider offloading these processes from your EDW to flatten the associated cost curves, optimize performance, and minimize the impact on other enterprise reporting and performance management applications that have been the bread and butter of the warehouse.

Different systems are proving to be more suited for these types of analytic workloads. Analytic appliances, such as the IBM PureData System for Analytics (powered by Netezza technologies), dashDB, and so on were designed from the *ground up* for analytics rather than standard query and reporting needs. These appliances typically provide alternative approaches to indexing data, such as not creating indexes at all! Not only do they store data in a way that is more suited to parallel processing, they deeply embed analytical functions into the core of their processing engines. They also often provide various accelerators, sometimes hardware based, to decompress and process queries in a manner that dramatically improves performance.

These appliances eliminate DBA activities that are typically required to optimize performance and simplify installation and upgrade processes, thereby reducing the overall cost of ownership. The cloud is having an impact here too: Clients want to be able to burst some of their analytical functions into the cloud or host some of this data off premise. IBM's dashDB is all about offering on premise, off premise, or hybrid round-trip analytics functionality for this very purpose. We think IBM is significantly ahead of the marketplace in this critical area. We know of no other vendor that enables you to seamlessly burst into the cloud and leverage round-trip APIs and interfaces for data that resides on premise or off premise.

Curtain Call: The New Staging Zone

Before the advent of NextGen information management architectures, landing and staging areas were more or less identical because they were simply a place to put data that was captured from source systems prior to being transformed or loaded into an EDW. However, with the added capabilities of Hadoop-based systems, much more is possible.

To make data from your different source systems available for reporting and analysis, you need to define a target data model and transform the data into the appropriate structure. In the past, a typical data transformation process involved one of two approaches. The first approach was to extract the data from where it had landed into a separate system to perform the transformation processes and then to deliver the transformed data to the target system, usually a data warehouse or mart. When a large volume of data is involved and many transformations are required, this process can take a long time, create a complex and fragile stack of dependencies, and more. Many companies have become challenged by the long batch processing times that are associated with this approach. In some cases, the available batch windows are exceeded; in other cases, the required transformations are not complete before the next day's processing is set to begin.

The other approach was to move the required data into the target data warehouse or mart and then to leverage the "in-database" processing capabilities to perform the transformations—this is sometimes appealing to clients whose transformation logic is SQL-rich since an RDBMS is very good at parallelizing data. Although this initially helps to speed up some data transformations, it can often increase the complexity and cost. It drives up the data storage and processing requirements of the data warehouse environment and impacts the performance of other critical EDW applications. Because of the drain on capacity, many companies have found themselves once again faced with challenges around processing times. Finally, when you consider IBM's Big SQL standalone MPP query engine for Hadoop (Chapter 6), you can see that, for the most part, the future of transformation is not in the EDW; it's too expensive and consumes too many high-investment resources.

Our point is that there are different classes (or tiers) of analytical processing requirements. Tiers that deliver the most performance are likely to cost more than those that can't meet speed-of-thought response times or stringent service level agreements (SLAs). If you are investing in a platinum analytics tier that provides the fastest performance for your organization, then we suggest you keep it focused on those tasks. Having a platinum tier prepare data or having it house data that is seldom queried isn't going to yield the best return on your investment. Keep in mind that the more transformation work you place in the EDW, the slower it will be for those LOB users who think they are leveraging a platinum-rated service.

Organizations are finding that they can include Hadoop in their architecture to assist with data transformation jobs. Instead of having to extract data from where it has landed to perform the transformations, Hadoop enables the data to be transformed where it is. And because they leverage the parallel processing capabilities of Hadoop (more on that in a bit), such transformations can often be performed faster than when they are done within the EDW. This provides companies with the opportunity to reduce their required batch window time frames and offload processing from a platinum-tiered system. Faster processing *and* reduced costs…that's a *potential* win-win scenario!

We want to say a couple of things here with respect to Hadoop as a data preparation platform and why we just said the word potential—you can think of this as an appetizer for Chapter 13. We aren't proposing that you toss out your integration tools. In fact, Gartner has been very public about Hadoop on its own being used as a data integration platform and how such an approach demands custom code, requires specialized skills and effort, and is likely to cost more. And the famous Dr. Ralph Kimball (the godfather of data warehousing) noted in a Cloudera web cast that Hadoop *is not* an ETL tool. Our own personal experience with a pharmaceutical client saw a mere two days of effort to compose a complex transformation with a set of integration services, compared to 30 days for a roll-your-own, hand-coding Hadoop effort—and the two-day effort ran faster too! So, here's the point: Data integration isn't just about the run time; it's about a graphical data flow interface, reusability, maintainability, documentation, metadata, and more. Make no mistake about it, the data integration tool that you select must be able to work with data in Hadoop's distributed file system (HDFS) as though it were any other data source and even be able to leverage its scalable parallel processing framework. But here's the thing: We've seen other parallel frameworks vastly outperform MapReduce for data transformation. And if the transformation is heavy on the SQL side, it actually might make sense to do the transformation in the EDW itself or in a separate, dedicated, parallel-processing data integration engine (not always, but sometimes). The IBM Information Server platform (and its associated as-a-service IBM DataWorks capabilities) is this kind of integration tool. It enables you to *compose and document transformations once* and then run them across a wide range of parallel processing frameworks, choosing the one that makes the most sense—Hadoop, a relational database, a NoSQL database, or within its own processing framework. Hadoop is indeed a great contributor to data preparation, but it's just part of the solution.

Can you see the flow between zones at this point? Data from source systems finds its way into your organization through a "landing" zone, some of the information is combined in an "exploration" zone (i.e., sandboxes), and the information required for enterprise reporting and performance management is then transformed into the target data model and put into a "staging" zone, from which it can be loaded directly into the data warehouse or mart (or surfaced through Hadoop to the LOB). This staging zone is typically maintained in the same Hadoop system where the data has landed, but it has a structure that matches the target system rather than the source systems, like in the landing zone.

Having a lower-cost environment where data can be effectively processed and put into its target model provides substantial benefits. Not only does it streamline and lower the cost of transforming data, it also opens the door to new analytic possibilities.

You Have Questions? We Have Answers! The Queryable Archive Zone

Hadoop is also a great archiving area. And if all your data is staged in Hadoop as described earlier, you are effectively creating a *day zero archive*. Rolling data out of a traditional EDW requires effort. If all data in the EDW has been initially staged in Hadoop (and you maintain effective metadata), you can simply purge stale data from the EDW.

Pop quiz—what is one of the most popular features being requested for NoSQL data stores such as Hadoop? Full SQL access! To be fair, NoSQL today is really meant to convey the idea of "not only" SQL, but the majority of these systems still rely on low-level query or programming languages. They do not support the significant investments that most organizations have made in standards-based SQL skills and tool sets.

From a Hadoop perspective, organizations initially started leveraging the very basic SQL capabilities that are available through Apache Hive, and this enabled them to start querying Hadoop data by using commercial off-the-shelf (COTS) tools. Most of them found the performance and level of SQL support to be inadequate. An initiative codenamed "Stinger" was intended to make Hive faster and more SQL-complete, but it still has significant limitations.

There is also a movement by multiple vendors to create various SQL processing engines for Hadoop. IBM's offering is called *Big SQL*. We cover this capability in Chapter 6, but will say here that there is no other solution in the Hadoop space whose SQL support is as complete or as compatible with existing, standards-based interfaces. In fact, the IBM Big SQL technology was able to run *all* 22 TPC-H and *all* 99 TPC-DS queries without changes or workarounds. These are open data warehousing benchmarks that various Hadoop vendors are using as proof points for scalability and SQL compatibility. If you're looking into this space, you will find that no other vendor can match what IBM has done. Performance is even significantly better than other SQL solutions for Hadoop. IBM has been in the SQL parallelization and optimization game for almost half a century; in fact, IBM invented SQL!

The queryable archive zone was initially envisioned for the ability to find economies of scale and cost savings by leveraging the same reports and interfaces in Hadoop that you already have in place on the EDW (assuming that the data is in the same structure and data model). The initial interest in a queryable archive undoubtedly was because of the costs associated with the EDW and the sheer volume of data that needed to be maintained.

Before Hadoop, organizations took various steps to reducing these costs, such as archiving older data that is less frequently accessed. Such "cold" data is often put on lower-tier storage or removed from the system. Although such data can usually be restored if it is needed in the future, this typically is not a straightforward process, and it is often the case that organizations won't bother with it unless it becomes absolutely necessary. But with the ability to store data in a much less expensive environment where it can be accessed through standard SQL interfaces, the historical and detail-level data that accounts for the largest data volumes can now be offloaded from the EDW without requiring it to be "restored" whenever someone wants to access it.

Although SQL access to Hadoop plays a role in querying older data, it's also a rich and powerful interface for querying *any* data, in any zone, and that's where we are seeing the most traction. Hadoop gives you a lot of options!

Of course, the performance of queries running in Hadoop isn't likely to be equal to the performance of the same queries running in a relational store; however, for less frequently accessed data, this might be an acceptable compromise, given the cost savings. It all comes down to your SLA.

There are two ways to establish a queryable archive in Hadoop. The first approach is to follow standard archiving procedures, archiving the data into Hadoop instead of some alternative storage medium. Considering all the data storage cost models that are associated with Hadoop, we'll often refer to Hadoop as "the new tape." If you follow this approach, you can leverage your established processes for moving data to lower-cost storage. And because the data can easily be accessed with SQL, you can move data off the EDW much more aggressively. For example, instead of archiving only data that is older than seven years, you can archive data that is older than two years. And maybe you can start moving detail-level data even sooner. The IBM InfoSphere Optim product suite has been enhanced with Hadoop as a key repository for the archiving process, supporting HDFS as a repository for archived files. We discuss archiving, Hadoop, and information lifecycle management in Chapter 13.

The second approach for establishing a queryable archive in Hadoop involves creating the aforementioned *day zero archive*. Consider all the zones we've introduced so far. If you were to transform your overall data architecture to establish landing and staging zones, your staging zone could actually become a queryable archive zone. In other words, you could create your archive on day zero! If you create a load-ready staging zone, where the data structure and model matches, or can easily be mapped to the structure and model of your EDW, you essentially have a copy of most of the data in your EDW already in Hadoop—and in a queryable format. You can maintain that data there instead of archiving data from the EDW. You can then just delete unneeded older data from the EDW. The data will still reside in the Hadoop staging zone, which now is also your queryable archive zone. Even if you choose not to instantiate a mirror data model of the EDW, the data is still captured, and you can use metadata and SQL to retrieve it as needed.

Most organizations do not build their EDW from scratch, nor are they just getting started in this space. We have found that, in most cases, it is a gradual process and culture shift to get to a day zero archive architecture. We recommend starting small and learning "the ropes." Perhaps choose a limited subject area and perform an initial archiving of the data from your existing EDW. Most organizations already have multiple data transformation processes in place and cannot begin using new landing and staging zones, as outlined here, right away. But having a set of integration tools and services that works with HDFS as well as it works with an RDBMS enables you to change the execution engine for the transformations without rewriting thousands of lines of code. You might prefer to start with the first approach outlined earlier (following standard archiving procedures), but moving toward the second approach (creating a day zero archive) should be part of your longer-term plan.

In Big Data We Trust: The Trusted Data Zone

As you have likely figured out by now, there are many opportunities to offload data and processes from the EDW, and these options can dramatically reduce costs and provide greater agility. An EDW should not be forced to do things that it wasn't designed to do efficiently. We'll go so far as to say that the suggestions we outline in this chapter free the EDW to do what it was really designed to do: provide a "trusted data" zone for your most critical enterprise information.

Although these other "zones" and technologies will help you to reduce costs and provide greater agility to your business, you still need a reliable, robust, well-performing environment where you can establish a harvested, consolidated view of information from across the enterprise. Whether it is to address regulatory compliance reporting, understand and report on the financial performance of your business, or make strategic decisions about where to invest your resources, there are always going to be certain aspects of an organization that rely on absolute truths and that require reliable and quick responses. This is why we believe our zone architecture enables EDWs to return to what they were truly designed for and what they do best.

So, as organizations evolve their architectures and put in place fit-for-purpose zones to address the different functional and nonfunctional requirements of various business needs, it will be important to have a "trusted data" zone. And this zone is best served by the more traditional EDW offerings that have been evolving over the past several decades.

A Zone for Business Reporting

One thing that will remain the same is the need to create different data structures and reports to support the specific needs of different business and functional units across an organization. Although there is value in creating an enterprise view, each unit needs to understand its operations and performance on its own terms. Companies have historically addressed this by creating different data marts or separate views on the EDW to support these different business-reporting requirements.

This requirement will not go away, and the approach will remain fairly similar. Organizations will continue to maintain "business reporting" zones and will, at least for the immediate future, continue to rely on relational databases. The biggest advancement in this area is likely to be the use of in-memory technologies to improve query performance. Many business users have complained about the time it takes to run reports and get information about their business operations. To address this, some organizations are starting to leverage in-memory technologies as part of their operational systems so that they can report on those systems without impacting core operational processes. Others are starting to leverage in-memory databases for their actual data marts and improving response times, especially when reviewing business performance across multiple dimensions.

This is where the BLU Acceleration technology and the IBM managed dashDB service play such a crucial role in business reporting. They are designed from the ground up to be fast, to deliver incredible compression ratios so that more data can be loaded into memory, to be agile, and to be nearly DBA-free. With BLU Acceleration, you don't spend time creating performance-tuning objects such as indexes or materialized views; you load the data and go. This keeps things agile and suits LOB reporting just fine.

Finally, for data maintained on premise, the addition of BLU Acceleration *shadow tables* in the DB2 Cancun Release further extends the reporting capabilities on operational data by enabling the creation of in-memory reporting structures over live transactional data without impacting transactional performance. This latest enhancement reinforces the theme of this chapter: There are multiple technologies and techniques to help you deliver an effective analytics architecture to your organization.

From Forecast to Nowcast: The Real-Time Processing and Analytics Zone

The need to process and analyze data in real time is not something new, and products for performing real-time analytics, such as the many complex event processing (CEP) engines that are offered by various vendors, have been available for a while. However, the costs, complexity, and limitations that are often associated with "real-time" capabilities have often restricted the application of vanilla CEP technologies to the fringe use cases where the effort and investment required could be justified.

Big Data, along with some of its related evolving technologies, is now driving both the demand and the opportunity to extend these capabilities to a much broader set of mainstream use cases. As data volumes explode and organizations start dealing with more semistructured and unstructured data, some organizations are discovering that they can no longer afford to keep and store everything. And some organizations that used to just discard entire data sets are realizing that they might be able to get value from some of the information buried in those data sets. The data might be clickstreams generated from constantly growing web traffic, machine-generated data from device and equipment sensors being driven by the Internet of Things, or even system log files that are typically maintained for short periods of time and then purged.

New capabilities have emerged to address this need, enabling companies to process this data as it is generated and to extract the specific information required without having to copy or land all of the unneeded data or "noise" that might have been included in those feeds. And by incorporating analytic capabilities, organizations can derive true real-time insights that can be acted upon immediately. In addition, because there is so much focus on harvesting analytics from data at rest, people often miss the opportunity to perform additional analytics on the data in motion from what you learned through analytics on the data at rest. Both of these potential game changers underscore the need for a real-time processing and analytics zone.

The real-time processing and analytics zone, unlike some of the other zones, is not a place where data is maintained, but is more of a processing zone where data is analyzed or transformed as it is generated from various sources. Some organizations use this zone to apply transformations to data as it hits their doorsteps to build aggregated data structures on the fly. Whereas the raw data that is generated by those sources is the input, the output can be either a filtered set of that data, which has been extracted, or new data that was generated through analytics: in short, insight. This data can be put into one of the other zones for further analysis and reporting, or it can be acted upon immediately. Actions could be triggered directly from logic in the real-time processing and analytics zone or from a separate decision management application. This powerful zone is powered by IBM's InfoSphere Streams technology, which we cover in Chapter 7.

Ladies and Gentlemen, Presenting... "The Data Zones Model"

In this chapter, we covered a NextGen information management architecture that we believe sets the bar for a more cost-efficient and impactful analytics infrastructure. We explained the zones, piece by piece, and show you the result in Figure 4-3. A good recipe has multiple components and steps. When these components are brought together in harmony and balance, their confluence is delightful to the palate. We have given you the various ingredients so that you can create your own dish. You might need a little more of one zone and less of another; each use case will be different, and not all of them will be to your taste. Analytics is a dish that can be served cold or hot—depending on your organization's needs—so begin your journey. There's no reason to wait.

As you can see, this zone architecture leverages both open source and proprietary technologies. Each has strengths and key benefits that it can deliver to the business as a whole for data-driven decision making. This new approach to managing data is not about rejecting all of the technologies and approaches that have been used in the past. It is more about evolving to use existing capabilities in a more purpose-driven, cost-effective manner, while taking advantage of new capabilities and techniques that make new approaches to analytics possible.

Although these technologies can provide a lot of new value, they can't possibly address all of your data processing, management, and analytics

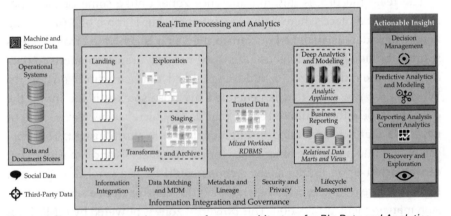

Figure 4-3 *A next-generation zones reference architecture for Big Data and Analytics*

needs, and a mission to completely replace all of your existing platforms or tools is not a good idea. It is important to emphasize that the evolution of these different zones for processing, managing, and analyzing data makes the need for information integration and governance capabilities even more critical. Some companies thought that the key to establishing trusted information is to put all the data in a single place—the EDW. But recently, organizations have begun to realize not only that data will continue to exist in different pockets across the organization, but that you can actually get more value at a lower cost by leveraging different zones and technologies. However, this makes it even more important to understand where your data is and where it came from. Your tools for integrating and securing data will need to work across multiple platforms and environments—this includes Hadoop, NoSQL, and SQL repositories. And there will be new challenges to match and link related data. This is where the concept of a *data reservoir* comes in.

With the data zones architecture, you have data and workloads assigned to platforms that are appropriate for the tasks at hand. Taken together, you can see all the data zones as the different repositories of your data reservoir. To manage the data in the reservoir (access control, data transformation, audit, and more), IBM provides a suite of information governance and integration tools and services that are designed to work with the data zones we've described in this chapter. These tools and services can be procured via traditional on-premise software—the IBM InfoSphere brand—and through a cloud service via the IBM DataWorks catalog.)

These services set the data reservoir architecture apart from a data lake, which we often hear discussed in Hadoop circles. It's easy to load Hadoop clusters with terabytes of data from many sources, but without proper management, any potential value quickly evaporates—sometimes we call that a data swamp. As we've discussed, Hadoop offers tremendous value as part of the data zone architecture, but by itself it does not have the capabilities needed to address all of your data processing, reporting and analytic needs, let alone ensure proper data governance. Taking the reservoir analogy a little further, IBM's data governance and integration capabilities are being made available as refinery services. In essence, you can filter your data as it pours into and travels through your reservoir through the appropriate refineries. IBM's refinery services are being provided as part of a deliberate strategic shift to ensure this architecture can work in cloud, on premise, or hybrid cloud environments. The IBM DataWorks refinery services and principles of data governance are the focus of Part III of this book.

In addition, there will be continued focus on streaming capabilities, in-memory analytics, and other related capabilities to improve performance and enable greater handling of real-time data and analytic requirements. And, of course, expect advances in workload management capabilities as companies attempt to bring more types of workloads to lower-cost environments.

Part II

Watson Foundations

5

Starting Out with a Solid Base: A Tour of Watson Foundations

It's a frightening thing to wake up one morning and realize that your business is data-rich but knowledge-poor. It seems that while the world spent the last few years collecting data 24/7, it neglected to put the same effort into decisioning that data—transforming it into something we like to call *actionable* insight. This concept might seem counterintuitive. You're likely thinking, "I have petabytes of data on my customers. Why can't I make predictions about where my business is heading?" But we are seeing an epiphany across enterprises and businesses. Companies have spent decades amassing mountains of data on their businesses, customers, and workforces, but now they are asking "What do we *do* with that data?" and "How do we transform data points into actionable insight?"

Elsewhere in this book we talk about the concept of a *data economy*, comparing data analytics to the transformation of crude oil into refined petroleum. Data is bountiful and can take on a variety of forms: structured, semistructured, unstructured, at rest, or in motion. Data generates insights…but…only when backed by understanding. If you have the tools to help you understand the bigger picture that your Big Data is painting, then the notion of mountains of data is no longer a frightening prospect; it becomes an opportunity for further discovery and insight. This chapter introduces the rich portfolio of services IBM offers in both on-premise and public off-premise cloud delivery mechanisms that empower your business to understand the bigger picture of your Big Data.

Overview of Watson Foundations

IBM Watson Foundations enables businesses to turn raw data into refined resources for analytically charged competitive advantage. Watson Foundations draws from the IBM Big Data and Analytics portfolio and was shaped from the manifesto we described in Chapter 1. Its sole purpose is to deliver a more vivid picture of your business and the critical points of impact that shape it, all done in real time with real-world insights.

The Watson Foundations name implies a relationship to IBM's groundbreaking cognitive technology, Watson. Watson is unprecedented in terms of volume of information stored and its ability to quickly understand and answer questions in natural languages. The game *Jeopardy!* provided a great freshman challenge for Watson because the game's clues involve analyzing subtle meanings, irony, riddles, and other complexities in which humans excel and computers traditionally do not. One of Watson's predecessors—Deep Blue—is an IBM machine that defeated the reigning world chess champion in 1997. Watson is yet another major leap forward from Deep Blue in the ability of IT systems to identify patterns, gain critical insight, and enhance decision making (despite daunting complexities). Although Deep Blue was an amazing achievement, it is an example of applying compute power to a computationally well-defined game. Watson, on the other hand, faces a challenge that is open-ended, quite unlike the well-bounded mathematical formulations of a game like chess. Watson has to operate in the nearly limitless, ambiguous, and highly contextual domain of human language and knowledge. And today, Watson is no longer a freshman; it's a senior! You can see this type of natural language interaction, critical to insights for the masses, work its way across the IBM portfolio. For example, Watson Analytics is a breakthrough natural language-based cognitive service that gives business professionals, of any skill level or industry, instant access to powerful predictive and visualization tools.

Now think about how this iconic game show is played: You have to answer a question, based on a category, within three seconds (and in the form of a question, of course)! The technology that is used by Watson to analyze and return answers was a precursor to the IBM InfoSphere Streams (Streams) technology; in fact, Streams was developed because the technology originally being used in Watson was not fast enough for some of the data in-motion requirements we detail in Chapter 7.

Jeopardy! questions are not straightforward either; they employ language or logical tricks to ante up the stakes. Some of the text analytic technology and the natural language processing that is used by Watson is found in Watson Foundations. Watson's big breakthrough came to fruition when the research team began using machine learning techniques to enhance its ability to think and learn. These capabilities are included in Watson Foundations—including a declarative R-like language, which puts machine learning into the hands of "the many" through high-performance SQL-like access to Hadoop. Watson needed access to a heck of a lot of data, as well as the ability to return answers within seconds. Technologies within the Watson Foundations stack—such as Apache Lucene and Apache Hadoop, among others—were used to load and index more than 200 million pages of data for the game show. Watson also had to build its corpus from data that existed in structured repositories such as a relational database, it had to search, it had to understand the data—all of these capabilities are part of Watson Foundations (of whose name should now be obvious).

Watson Foundations isn't just about exposing key Watson technologies—they have to work together as a platform—not everyone has the world's largest commercial research organization at their fingertips. In the case of text analytics and machine learning, IBM had to make them easier to consume so their Watson Foundations instantiations include a declarative language front end that make it SQL-like. This foundational platform is so well integrated that when you discover textual insights at rest, you can package the extractors and deploy them to analyze data in motion with mere taps, swipes, pinches, or clicks. The IBM Watson Foundations platform is shown in Figure 5-1.

Moving forward, there will always be a direct linkage between Watson and its inspired services—Watson Analytics and Watson Foundations—which together encompass the broader IBM Big Data and Analytics portfolio.

Today's organizations are investing heavily in different types of analytics for different types of data. IBM's strategy is to leverage Watson Foundations and its broad portfolio of capabilities to complement Watson's cognitive innovations, thereby creating trust and confidence in the data upon which business decisions can be made. This strategy both addresses the breadth of different analytic styles demanded by the market today and exploits the

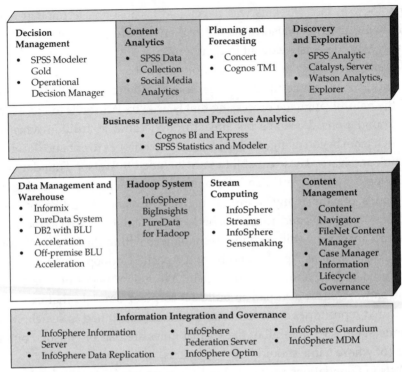

Figure 5-1 *The IBM Watson Foundations portfolio—leveraging the breadth of services and software available from IBM's Big Data and Analytics platform*

incredible advances in cognitive computing that IBM is pioneering. The solution is not "either-or": Companies that are investing in IBM do not need to choose a Big Data path *or* an analytics solution *or* Watson Cognitive suites—they are all connected.

A Continuum of Analytics Capabilities: Foundations for Watson

Watson Foundations opens up the corpus of all types of data (structured, semistructured, unstructured, at rest, and in motion) to the cognitive capabilities of IBM Watson. Clients love that Watson understands you, that it gives answers you can trust, and that it actively learns. You don't program Watson; you teach it. Linkages with Watson—such as the Watson Discovery Advisor for medical research pattern discovery, Watson for financial services, and Watson's API—are open to the Watson Foundations family of services. Watson Foundations provides the core capabilities that are going to fuel cognitive computing.

In Part II of this book, we will discuss further the components of the Watson Foundations portfolio that you see in the lower half of Figure 5-1. Keep in mind that many of these offerings are available via platform as a service (PaaS) and software as a service (SaaS) models for even greater value (see Chapter 3 if you need a refresher), and you can bring your own license (BYOL) to the IBM Cloud too. In fact, as we discussed earlier in this book, you will be exposed to new features and capabilities in the Watson Foundation stack through public cloud services before they are surfaced to traditional on-premise appliances and software offerings.

Watson Analytics, for example, brings cloud-based solutions for line-of-business users who want to explore and gain new insights into their data. No advanced statistics degree or analytics training is required! Business users are able to quickly interpret and understand their data with rich visualizations that are driven by Watson Analytics using the power of natural language. The IBM dashDB analytics service provides organizations with a turnkey in-memory data warehousing and analytics platform where provisioning is measured in minutes (we cover the BLU Acceleration technology behind dashDB in Chapter 8). The takeaway message here is that the entire Watson Foundations portfolio exists in a *continuum* with Watson's cognitive abilities; together, these solutions enable IBM's customers to ask train-of-thought questions about their data for smarter and actionable business insight.

The remaining chapters in this section give a more rigorous introduction to some of Watson Foundations' components. You will see how Watson Foundations is a Big Data and Analytics platform that taps into all relevant data, regardless of source or type, to provide fresh insights in real time and give you the confidence to act upon them. As part of the IBM Big Data and Analytics portfolio, Watson Foundations supports all types of analytics, including discovery, reporting, and analysis, as well as predictive and cognitive capabilities. It offers an enterprise-class open source Apache Hadoop, workload-optimized distribution, analytics on streaming data, text and content analytics, and many more capabilities so that organizations can infuse analytics into every decision, every business process, and every system of engagement. It's also a foundation to bring veracity to your Big Data—be it via IBM DataWorks cloud services or through on-premise software deployment with the IBM InfoSphere suite of products. With the governance, privacy, and security you need, this platform is open, modular, and integrated so that you can start small and scale at your own pace.

InfoSphere BigInsights for Hadoop brings the power of open source Apache Hadoop to the enterprise with application accelerators, analytics, visualization, development tools, performance, security features, and more—we cover this in Chapter 6.

InfoSphere Streams efficiently delivers real-time analytic processing on data in motion and enables descriptive and predictive analytics to support real-time decisions. Capture and analyze all data, all the time, just in time. With stream computing, your organization stores less, analyzes more, and makes better decisions faster—you learn about this in Chapter 7.

Watson Foundations has data management and warehouse services as well. Use these services to achieve industry-leading database performance across multiple workloads while lowering administration, storage, development, and server costs. Technologies in this segment include DB2 with BLU Acceleration (the technology behind IBM's dashDB), PureData System for Analytics, powered by Netezza technology and more; all are detailed in Chapters 8 and 9. In addition, the social-mobile-cloud world has ignited the need for agile NoSQL databases that store data in an accessible, schema-flexible manner—this is covered in Chapter 10.

Finally, Part III of this book (Chapters 11 through 14) is dedicated to the products illustrated by the bottom half of Figure 5-1 (the truly *foundational* component of Watson Foundations): using information integration and governance to build confidence in Big Data by integrating, understanding, managing, and governing data appropriately across its entire lifecycle.

Clients will find themselves using different styles to bring trust to their Big Data repositories. IBM DataWorks empowers organizations to use cloud services to refine and cleanse data through a set of rich and capable refinery services (we talked about this in Chapter 4 and detail them in Part III) inspired by capabilities in the IBM Information Management Optim and Guardium on-premise software offerings. For example, perhaps there is a large data set that needs some transformations and that work is bursted into the public cloud where these operations are performed as a service using IBM DataWorks—with a utility-like cost curve. The cleansed data is subsequently returned to land on premise. It could also be the case that a data set with unknown value is loaded into a dashDB instance that took minutes to create. With a billing rate at a per terabyte per minute that obliterates the cost of curiosity, the end user leverages IBM DataWorks to manipulate the data and, upon discovery of some insights, moves that data on premise (or stores it in the cloud). This hybrid model is not just empowered by the Watson Foundation stacks—it's embraced.

6

Landing Your Data in Style with Blue Suit Hadoop: InfoSphere BigInsights

One of the funny things about working in IT is watching new technologies get overhyped and then quickly slide into irrelevance. Hadoop is a notable exception. At the time of writing, Hadoop is just over eight years old, and interest in it has only grown. Venture capitalists and established IT firms have been falling over themselves to invest hundreds of millions of dollars in Hadoop startups with hope that they'll derive downstream profits that aren't there yet. Why?

For the most part, traditional data storage and analytics tools haven't been cutting it when dealing with a number of Big Data challenges. Many tools start being impractical solutions when thresholds in the dozens or hundreds of terabytes are exceeded. Sometimes, "impractical" means that the technology simply won't scale any further or that a tipping point is reached in terms of how much time it takes to transfer a data set over the network for processing. And other times, impractical means that although the technology can scale, the licensing, administrative, and hardware costs associated with the increased volume become unpalatable. In addition, traditional analytic tools tended to work well only with structured data, which represents, at most, 20 percent of the data in the world today.

We've witnessed a prominent change across the IT landscape in the last half-decade: a shift from spending money to *save* money to spending money to *make* money. Hadoop has drawn so much interest because it's a practical solution to save money *and* make money. For example, Hadoop enables large volumes of data to be stored on lower-tier storage with (relatively speaking) lower software licensing costs (saving money), *and* it enables users to perform analysis activities that weren't possible before because of past limitations around data volumes or variety (making money). We almost sound like an infomercial here—Hadoop provides the best of both worlds. But as we discussed in Chapter 4, while Hadoop is a major part of an information architecture, conversations about Big Data can't just be about Hadoop. In practice, what our successful clients have typically found is that they start by inserting Hadoop into their architecture to save money, and as their sophistication around the technology grows, they extend it to make money.

Considering the pressing need for technologies that can overcome the volume and variety challenges for data at rest, it's no wonder business magazines and online tech forums alike are still buzzing about Hadoop. And it's not all talk either. IT departments in almost all Fortune 500 companies have done some level of experimentation with Hadoop. The problem is that many of these initiatives have stagnated in the "science project" phase or have not been able to expand their scope. The challenges are common. It's easy and exciting to start dumping data into these repositories; the hard part comes with what to do next. Meaningful analysis of data stored in Hadoop requires highly specialized programming skills—and for many algorithms, it can be challenging to put them into a parallelizable form so that they can run properly in Hadoop. And what about information governance concerns, such as security and data lifecycle management, where new technologies like Hadoop don't have a complete story?

IBM sees the tremendous potential for technologies such as Hadoop to have a transformative impact on businesses. This is why IBM has scores of researchers, developers, and support staff continually building out a platform for Hadoop, called IBM InfoSphere BigInsights for Hadoop (BigInsights). BigInsights was released in October 2010 with a relatively straightforward goal: to maintain an open source Hadoop distribution that can be made enterprise-ready. In this chapter, we describe five aspects of enterprise readiness:

- **Analytics ease**   Enable different classes of analysts to use skills they already have (like SQL or R) to get value out of data that is stored in BigInsights. This avoids the need to pass requirements over the fence to Hadoop programmers or buy expensive consulting hours to procure custom Hadoop applications that no one in your organization understands. Think consumability!

- **Application development lifecycle**   Just like the database world, we see Hadoop evolving to the point where end users in organizations will need recurring reports and other interfaces to their Hadoop data. This requires apps, and BigInsights includes an integrated set of tooling that enables all activities in the application lifecycle: from development to deployment on an "App store"–style interface that lets end users consume these applications.

- **Cluster management**   Once people in your organization start depending on Hadoop, you will need to apply security policies, manage the competing requests for processing resources, ensure availability, and maintain current backups, among other tasks. BigInsights includes tooling for all these needs.

- **Integration**   If your business is analyzing data that's stored in Hadoop, you'll need to ensure that your Hadoop system integrates with the rest of your IT infrastructure.

- **Deployment flexibility**   We're seeing incredible variation in what our customers are doing with Hadoop, so there's no way a one-size-fits-all deployment model will work. With this in mind, BigInsights has been architected to work with a wide spectrum of hardware platforms (Intel, Power, and even System z), deployment models (on premise or off premise in a managed cloud), and services.

Before we describe the optional enterprise hardening and consumability IBM BigInsights for Hadoop extensions, you'll need to understand what Hadoop is in the first place.

Where Do Elephants Come From: What Is Hadoop?

At a very high level, Hadoop is a distributed file system and data processing engine that's designed to handle extremely high volumes of data in any structure. In simpler terms, just imagine that you have dozens or even hundreds (or thousands!) of individual computers racked and networked together.

Each computer (often referred to as a *node* in Hadoop-speak) has its own processors and a dozen or so 3TB or 4TB hard disk drives. All of these nodes are running software that unifies them into a single cluster, where, instead of seeing the individual computers, you see an extremely large bucket where you can put your data. The beauty of this Hadoop system is that you can store anything there: millions of digital image scans of mortgage contracts, weeks of security camera footage, trillions of sensor-generated log records, or all of the operator transcription notes from a call center. Basically, if the data is born into the Internet of Things (IoT), Hadoop is where we think it should land. This ingestion of data, without worrying about the data model, is actually a key tenet of the NoSQL movement (this is referred to as "schema later"), which we talked about in Chapter 2. In contrast, the traditional SQL and relational database world depends on the opposite approach ("schema now"), where the data model is of utmost concern upon data ingest. This is where the flexibility of Hadoop is even more apparent, because you can store data using both schema later and schema now approaches. There are Hadoop-based databases where you can store records in a variety of models: relational, columnar, and key/value. In other words, with data in Hadoop, you can go from completely unstructured to fully relational, and any point in between. The data storage system that we describe here is known as Hadoop's distributed file system (HDFS).

Let's go back to this imaginary Hadoop cluster with many individual nodes. Suppose your business uses this cluster to store all of the clickstream log records for its web site. Your Hadoop cluster is using the IBM BigInsights for Hadoop distribution, and you and your fellow analysts decide to run some of the sessionization analytics against this data to isolate common patterns for customers who abandon their shopping carts. When you run this application, Hadoop sends copies of your application logic to each individual computer in the cluster to be run against data that's local to each computer. So, instead of moving data to a central computer for processing (bringing data to the function), it's the application that gets moved to all of the locations where the data is stored (bringing function to the data). Having a cluster of independent computers working together to run applications is known as *distributed processing.*

One of the main benefits of bringing application code to the target data distributed across a cluster of computers is to avoid the high cost of transferring all the data to be processed to a single central point. Another way of putting this is that computing systems have to respect the laws of physics; shipping massive amounts of data to a central computer (data to function) is highly impractical when you start needing to process data at a terabyte (or higher) scale. Not only will it take a long time to transfer, but the central computer doing the processing will likely not have enough memory or disk space to support the workload.

An important aspect of Hadoop is the redundancy that's built into its environment. Not only is data redundantly stored in multiple places across the cluster, but the programming model is designed to *expect* failures, which are resolved automatically by running portions of the program on various servers in the cluster. Because of this redundancy, it's possible to distribute the data and programming across a large cluster of commodity components, like the cluster we discussed earlier. It's well known that commodity hardware components will fail (especially when you have many of them), but this redundancy provides fault tolerance and the capability for the Hadoop cluster to heal itself. This enables Hadoop to scale workloads across large clusters of inexpensive machines to work on Big Data problems.

A Brief History of Hadoop

Now that you have a high-level sense of what Hadoop is, we can get into why it's revolutionizing IT. To begin to understand this, let's take a quick look at Hadoop's origins.

Hadoop was inspired by Google's work on its distributed file system (called GFS) and the MapReduce programming model. Shortly after Google published papers describing GFS and MapReduce (in 2003 and 2004, respectively), people in the open source community applied these tools to the Apache Nutch web crawler and search engine. It became quickly apparent that the distributed file system and MapReduce modules together had applications beyond just the search world. It was in early 2006 that these software components became their own Apache project, called Hadoop.

Much of the early work in building Hadoop was done by Yahoo!, and it's no coincidence that the bulk of the inspiration for Hadoop has come out of the search engine industry. Hadoop was a necessary innovation for both Yahoo! and Google, as Internet-scale data processing became increasingly impractical on large centralized servers. The only alternative was to scale out and distribute storage and processing on clusters of thousands of nodes. As of June 2014, Yahoo! reportedly has more than 30,000 nodes spanning its Hadoop clusters, storing more than 365PB of data.

For the first seven years of Hadoop's existence, MapReduce was the primary distributed processing model for Hadoop. MapReduce is very good at a few specific kinds of *batch* processing, but with the IT world eager to take advantage of Hadoop's flexibility with data and inexpensive storage, this wasn't sufficient. So in October 2013, Hadoop 2 was released with a new component called YARN (Yet Another Resource Negotiator—the Yet Another part is a cultural naming thing developers do, dating back to the late 1970s). YARN may have a silly name, but there's nothing trivial about the impact it's had on Hadoop. YARN is a general-purpose resource manager for Hadoop, which enables applications from other processing frameworks to run on a Hadoop cluster in a distributed manner.

The most popular new processing framework for Hadoop is *Apache Spark*. In contrast to MapReduce, Spark is a far more general-purpose framework, featuring in-memory processing, and enabling programmers to define their own patterns for distributed processing. (MapReduce restricts programmers to *map* and *reduce* phases, so if you need to write a complex application, you'd have to string together map/reduce phases even where they normally don't make sense—this is highly inefficient, both for programmers and for application performance.) YARN and Spark are both supported in the IBM BigInsights for Hadoop distribution.

Unlike transactional systems, Hadoop is designed to scan through large data sets and to generate its results through a highly scalable, distributed *batch* processing system. Hadoop is not about speed-of-thought response times, real-time warehousing, or blazing transactional speeds; however, Hadoop *is* about discovery and making the once nearly impossible possible from a scalability and analytics perspective.

Components of Hadoop and Related Projects

As mentioned earlier, Hadoop is generally seen as having two main parts: a file system (HDFS) and a processing infrastructure (as of Hadoop 2, that's YARN—this includes the MapReduce framework as well). These are both part of the Apache Software Foundation (ASF). There are many other Apache projects that work with Hadoop; the following is a list of some of the more important ones (all of which, and more, are supported in BigInsights):

- **Apache Avro**   A data serialization framework (translates data from different formats into a binary form for consistent processing)

- **Apache Flume**   Collects and aggregates data and stores it in Hadoop

- **Apache HBase**   Real-time read and write database (this is a BigTable-style database—see Chapter 2 for more about BigTable)

- **Apache Hive**   Facility for cataloging data sets stored in Hadoop and processing SQL-like queries against them

- **Apache Lucene/Solr**   Indexing and search facility

- **Apache Oozie**   Workflow and job scheduling engine

- **Apache Pig**   A high-level data flow language and execution framework

- **Apache Sqoop**   Data transfer between Hadoop and relational databases

- **Apache Spark**   A flexible data processing framework

- **Apache Zookeeper**   Monitors the availability of key Hadoop services and manages failovers so the Hadoop system can remain functional

We'd love to get into more depth and describe how HDFS and YARN work, not to mention the additional projects in the Apache Hadoop ecosystem; however, unlike a Hadoop cluster, a limiting factor for a book is space. To learn about Hadoop in greater detail, visit BigDataUniversity.com where you can find a number of quality online courses for free! You may also want to get *Hadoop for Dummies* (Wiley, 2014), another book written by some of this same author team.

Open Source...and Proud of It

The open source community has been a major driving force for innovation in Big Data technologies, especially Hadoop. So far in this chapter, you'll have noticed that Hadoop itself and the supporting projects we just listed all have the word *Apache* as part of their full names. These technologies are all part of the Apache Software Foundation, which represents the gold standard for open source software.

Fully Open Source or Only Skin Deep?

There are two vitally important elements for open source software: licensing and development. The Apache license is a commercially (and user) friendly licensing model, which means anyone can use or even modify the code as long as they attribute where it comes from. The ASF has a rigorous set of procedures and standards ensuring that Apache software projects are run in an open and democratic manner for the benefit of the project's community. The idea is to prevent individuals or corporate agendas from taking over a project. So when people describe a software offering as being open source, investigate whether it's just the licensing or the development model as well. For example, Cloudera Impala is often touted as an open source project but is open source only from a licensing perspective. Cloudera engineers are the only people contributing code to this project. An open source license is well and good, but from a business perspective, that's not where the real benefits of open source code lie. (This isn't to besmirch Cloudera Impala; we think the IBM Big SQL technology does that on its own. Rather, it's to give you a framework to understand when something is open source and when something isn't. Both IBM and Cloudera have tremendous contributions to open source as well as their own proprietary technology.)

Apache Hadoop, for example, has contributions from hundreds of developers from dozens of different companies, all working together in a public manner. This has resulted in rapid innovation and the satisfaction of requirements from many different corners of the community. That's the real value of open source for businesses.

IBM's Commitment to Open Source

Sometimes we field questions about IBM's commitment to open source. This catches us off-guard, not because the question is hard—on the contrary, we're caught off-guard because we realize that perhaps IBM hasn't done a good enough job of evangelizing the many things it does in this space. For the record, IBM provides extensive support for many open source projects, including those in the Apache Hadoop community.

IBM has a long history of inventing technologies and donating them to the open source community as well. Examples include Apache Derby, Apache Geronimo, Apache Jakarta, DRDA, and XERCES; the list goes on and on. The leading open source integrated development environment (IDE) for Linux-based programming, Eclipse, came from IBM (this is the ubiquitous IDE in the open source community). IBM is also a major contributor to the original Apache project, the Apache web server, and Apache Lucene (search technology that was showcased in the winning Watson technology on the television program *Jeopardy!*). IBM also has provided major contributions and leadership on the Apache CouchDB project, the NoSQL document store you learned about in Chapter 2.

No discussion of IBM's open source support is complete without mentioning Linux. IBM has invested over a billion dollars in development effort to help grow Linux and in building Linux support into all its hardware and software offerings. IBM is actually the third-most prolific contributor to the Linux code base after only Red Hat and Intel. This is an especially important point, given that Hadoop runs on Linux.

Dozens of IBM engineers contribute code to the Apache Hadoop project and its associated ecosystem. The BigInsights development team includes a set of *committers* to these projects. (In Apache projects, the designation of "committer" is specially assigned to developers who are recognized as leaders in a project's community and are quality developers.) These committers contribute to the leadership of various open source projects and have the task of donating IBM code to the open source code base. By having committers on the BigInsights for Hadoop development team, IBM is involved with and a strong proponent of the continuing evolution of open source Hadoop. Committers also enable IBM to find and fix bugs in the open source code faster than would otherwise be possible. With open source Hadoop, even though the companies involved are sometimes competitors, there is a shared interest in making Hadoop better. In fact, while you'll often hear the marketing and sales initiatives of the competing Hadoop distribution companies "go at it," there is a fair amount of cooperation behind the scenes when it comes to the core Hadoop distribution.

Embrace and Extend: IBM's Hadoop Business Model

Fork or spoon? It's not just a question about which utensil you'd rather use but about how to add value to Hadoop. For all its power, Apache Hadoop is still a relatively young project. While it does provide a scalable and reliable solution for Big Data, most enterprises will find that they'll need tools and interfaces to take full advantage of it. Hence, technology solution providers, including IBM, are making efforts to bridge the gap and make Apache Hadoop easier for enterprise adoption.

IBM's approach to helping organizations use Hadoop is to *embrace* the open source Hadoop projects and *extend* them with technologies IBM is good at (this is exactly what Cloudera is attempting to do—only it's fair to note that IBM has a much larger portfolio of assets to build on Hadoop). Embracing the Hadoop projects means to include the open source Apache Hadoop components as is, without modifying the code base. BigInsights for Hadoop is the IBM-certified distribution of Apache Hadoop, and its accompanying Hadoop community projects are unmodified and surrounded with value-added, optional components that IBM believes augment and enrich the open source base. This enables IBM to quickly adopt any innovations or changes to the open source projects in its Hadoop distribution. It also makes it easy for IBM to certify third-party technologies that integrate with Apache Hadoop. This open source compatibility has enabled IBM to amass more than 1,000 partners, including hundreds of software vendors, for BigInsights. Simply put, if a software vendor uses the libraries and interfaces for open source Hadoop, they'll work with BigInsights as well.

In contrast, there are some software providers that are adding value to Hadoop by modifying the original open source code. For example, one Hadoop vendor has rewritten HBase to work with its proprietary file system. In software development parlance, this process is known as *forking*. Vendors adopting this approach effectively create a vendor-specific proprietary Hadoop distribution that's somewhat closed and makes interoperability with other complementary technologies much more difficult. In addition, forking open source code makes it difficult to incorporate innovations and improvements that are being applied to the open source components by the community. With each new release of open source code, the community improvements need to be applied to the forked code base—and where the real costs start piling up is recoding the forks to ensure they still work with the new code additions.

So again, we have to ask: fork or spoon? We've already explained the fork part of this analogy—spooning is another word for hugging someone. For open source software like Hadoop, the answer is clear. IBM has taken the smart road by spooning the open source Hadoop projects.

Open Source Integration and Testing

With each release of BigInsights, updates to both the open source components and IBM components go through a series of testing cycles to ensure they work together. That's another special point that we want to clarify:

You can't just drop new code into production. In our experience, backward-compatibility issues are always present in open source projects. BigInsights pretty much takes away all of the risk and guesswork that's associated with typical open source projects for your Hadoop components.

When you install BigInsights, you also have the assurance that every line of code from open source and from IBM has been tested using the same rigorous test cases, which cover the following aspects and more:

- Security in all code paths

- Performance

- Scalability (we have a Hadoop cluster that's well over 1000 nodes in our development lab where we test petabyte-scale workloads)

- Integration with other software components (such as Java drivers and operating systems)

- Hardware compatibility (our development lab clusters feature dozens of different brands and models of switches, motherboards, CPUs, and HDDs)

In short, BigInsights goes through the same rigorous regression and quality assurance testing processes used for all IBM software. So, ask yourself this: Would you rather be your own systems integrator, repeatedly testing all of the Hadoop components to ensure compatibility? Or would you rather let IBM find a stable stack that you can deploy without worry?

Making Analytics on Hadoop Easy

The biggest challenge facing organizations that have adopted Hadoop is how to quickly and easily derive value from the data that's stored in their clusters. There are many factors to consider here: the difficulty of parallelizing many analytics algorithms, making data stored in Hadoop accessible for business analysts and data scientists, and dealing with really messy data, among others. BigInsights delivers a set of integrated tools and services to address these issues through an integrated platform-based approach across its various components. The stuff we talk about in this section is central to any Big Data conversations you want to have beyond the hype.

As an analytics platform for Hadoop, BigInsights supports three classes of analytic users: line-of-business (LOB) analysts, data scientists, and application developers. In addition, the analytics and development components of BigInsights (which we cover later in this chapter) feature lifecycle management tooling—this enables developers to easily deploy analytic applications to LOB users and data scientists.

The Real Deal for SQL on Hadoop: Big SQL

The hottest topic in Big Data for the past few years has been native SQL access for data stored in Hadoop. This is a real testament to Hadoop's rapidly increasing adoption and acceptance as an established component in today's data centers, as well as a cry for help from organizations that want to derive value from these invested projects. After all, SQL is the preeminent interface for querying and analyzing data and has become a table stakes requirement for any organization serious about storing data in Hadoop. We'd go so far as to say that native SQL access to data in Hadoop is the single most important technology to make the data zones model, from Chapter 4, not just a vision but a reality that delivers impact and value to the business. It's that important. IBM has invested heavily in this area with its Big SQL technology, which offers industry differentiated native SQL access to data stored in BigInsights.

There are more than a dozen different SQL on Hadoop offerings from various vendors, which all claim their solution is superior. But, of course, they can't all be the best. We obviously think Big SQL is the winner here, but we don't want you to just take our word for it. In this section, we're going to look at different criteria for what makes an elite SQL on Hadoop solution and how the IBM Big SQL technology measures up. We think these are some of the things you will want to keep in mind when you talk about Big Data.

Architecture

The SQL on Hadoop solutions available in today's marketplace can be broken down quite neatly into three distinct categories (going from least effective to most):

- **Remote query facility** The approach taken by many of the established relational database management system (RDBMS) vendors—*except* IBM—such as Oracle, Teradata, and Microsoft, where the RDBMS remains the center of activity. Users submit SQL to the front-end RDBMS, which catalogs data on the separate Hadoop cluster as external tables. In this architecture, the database then sends the query to Hadoop, where some of the query work would be pushed down. Result sets are returned to the RDBMS, which then finishes any query processing work and returns the result to the user application. This approach does provide good ANSI SQL standard support, but performance is dependent on the network load and the database system itself; after all, you can't escape the law of physics—data has to flow over the wire. Altogether, we deem this approach to be the least effective overall, because it is the most disconnected from Hadoop itself and causes reliance on two significant systems (Hadoop and the RDBMS) for the single task of querying Hadoop data. The only parties benefiting from this approach are the RDBMS vendors who want to extract additional RDBMS license revenue from it.

- **Full relational database system on Hadoop**   The approach taken by some players in the RDBMS market such as Pivotal (formerly Greenplum), HP Vertica, and Actian. Here, these vendors have replatformed their RDBMSs to run on Hadoop, including the storage layer. It's well and good to run on Hadoop, but we don't really see the point because these systems don't openly integrate with the other Hadoop subsystems, like Sqoop, Hive's metadata catalog, and HDFS. The latter point is the most significant hit against these kinds of solutions because data stored in them is effectively locked into a proprietary format. For example, Pivotal announced such an architecture for the Hadoop SQL solution: HAWQ. The Pivotal HAWQ SQL engine actually runs against the Greenplum database and its tables. When you peel back the marketing veneer, all that's been done is a switch of the underlying storage mechanism for the Greenplum database. It's still the proprietary Greenplum database file (.gdb) only now it's on HDFS, and no other tools or software can access it. As a result, if you want to run a Pig script to do an experimental transform of the data, you can't. This approach attempts to capitalize on the hype of Hadoop, but we feel it falls short of being truly integrated with Hadoop.

- **SQL query engine running on Hadoop**   The approach taken by IBM with Big SQL, Cloudera Impala, and Hortonworks with the Stinger initiative for improving Hive. We feel (along with most of the Hadoop community) that this is the superior architecture for enabling SQL over

Hadoop. We will be blunt: No RDBMS is required. These solutions each feature a massively parallel processing (MPP) SQL query engine, which integrates deeply with Hadoop's components and projects. They operate directly against files stored in HDFS in common Hadoop data formats and use a common metadata repository (Hive's HCatalog). In other words, these are not full database stacks that happen to run on Hadoop, but they are relational query engines that are an integrated part of the Hadoop ecosystem.

Figure 6-1 shows Big SQL's architecture. A master node runs the Big SQL coordinator service, which handles all client requests and distributes them to the worker services that run on the Hadoop slave nodes. As we mentioned earlier, the data that's cataloged by Big SQL lives in HDFS files that can be read by any other Hadoop applications. In addition to the Hive catalog, Big SQL has a special catalog that gathers statistics on the cataloged HDFS data to enable the Big SQL optimizer to make more informed decisions.

As the Big SQL coordinator processes a SQL query, it is passed through a cost-based optimizer that determines the most efficient access plan for the query, and then this query is compiled. The compiled query is then passed to the Big SQL worker processes, which are each an implementation of the distributed Big SQL run time. When the Big SQL worker nodes are finished running, the result set is assembled and passed back to the client application.

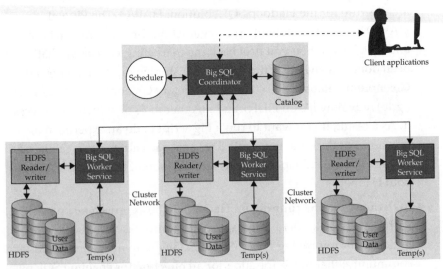

Figure 6-1 *Big SQL architecture*

Code Base Maturity

We talked earlier about how Hadoop is still a young project, having had its first release in 2006. Hive is the oldest SQL on Hadoop project, having started in 2008. Even though at the time of writing Hive is six years old, there are still major areas of the ANSI SQL 1992 standard that aren't supported, such as full support for subqueries. Developing optimized query engines is hard work and takes large teams of seasoned developers years to refine, and while we don't have any doubt that all the players are working on it, there is a lot that goes into this problem domain. We think analyst Curt Monash hit this point home when he blogged about the subject of SQL on Hadoop. He notes:

> *The cardinal rules of DBMS development. Rule 1: Developing a good DBMS requires 5–7 years and then of millions of dollars (that's if things go extremely well). Rule 2: You aren't an exception to Rule 1. DBMSs with Hadoop under-pinnings aren't exceptions to the cardinal rules of DBMS development. This applies to Impala (Cloudera), Stinger (Hortonworks), and Hadapt.*

IBM engineers have been gaining expertise and developing intellectual property assets in MPP SQL technologies for decades; after all, IBM invented SQL almost half a century ago! There have been hundreds of developers, countless patents, and decades of sustained attention and continual improvement to SQL processing systems. Add to this decades-old refinement iterations through thousands of customer engagements; it's in these interactive cycles where query performance issues would arise, and IBM development teams resolved them with tweaks and feature improvements to the SQL language, optimizer, compiler, and run-time component. The same IBM team is also bringing Netezza SQL support to dashDB and BLU Acceleration. They also created native Oracle PL/SQL compatibility, which you can find in dashDB and DB2. Not only is this capability available in Big SQL too, but these examples all speak to the breadth of expertise the IBM dev teams have with SQL processing engines. After all, getting someone else's SQL dialect to natively run, and run well for that matter, requires some "SQL chops."

This codebase maturity is a major benefit for Big SQL. Instead of building an MPP relational query engine for Hadoop from scratch (which is extremely expensive and difficult), IBM engineers took existing relational intellectual property and know-how and ported them to Hadoop so they would work with HDFS data.

ANSI SQL Standard Compliance

In our view, the biggest benefit of Big SQL's code base maturity is its unmatched support for the ANSI SQL standards. For all the applicable areas, Big SQL is ANSI SQL 2011 compliant. Of all the SQL query engines running natively on Hadoop, from what we can tell as of the time this book was written, Big SQL is the only solution that can claim this full support.

IBM engineers have been running internal performance benchmark tests using the TPC-DS and TPC-H queries and data sets. The first runs featured Big SQL, which ran all 22 TPC-H queries and all 99 TPC-DS queries *without modification*. In publicly blogged comparison runs featuring Cloudera Impala and Hive, many queries needed modifications in order to run cleanly. For some queries, no modifications were even possible to maintain an equivalent.

SQL compatibility is often glossed over by the marketing folks from other Hadoop vendors, but in our work with customers, who are beyond the hype and trying to get work done, SQL compatibility is a big deal. For many, it's been a deal breaker. After all, the whole point of SQL on Hadoop is to use a familiar language and interface.

Big SQL's query support goes beyond just the ANSI standard—as anyone who's worked with multiple database offerings knows, there are many SQL dialects. IBM has a long initiative of building SQL syntax compatibility into its relational query engine, and so Big SQL has full support for queries in the DB2 *and very strong support for* Oracle dialects. For other vendors such as Teradata, Big SQL has partial compatibility; for example, there are wrapper functions in Big SQL for many corresponding function signatures in Teradata.

Native Hadoop Data Format Support

One subthread in the SQL on Hadoop story has been the development of more efficient data formats that are optimized for SQL on Hadoop engines. Hortonworks has been heavily backing the ORC format, and Cloudera has been backing the Parquet format. Both formats have a lot in common, featuring columnar storage and optimizations for relational query engines. Big SQL supports both of these formats, as well as the older (but still commonly found) formats like RCFile. Obviously, native Hadoop formats such as sequence files and raw text files with delimited data are supported as well. If you have your own custom data format, you could write your own Hadoop serializer/deserializer (SerDe) to enable Big SQL (or other standard Hadoop tools like Hive or Pig) to read your data. For example, BigInsights ships a built-in SerDe that takes a JSON-encoded social feed (such as Twitter) and turns it into a "vanilla" structure that is Big SQL queryable. This is an additional example of how Big SQL is a first-class citizen, native to Hadoop.

Security

Setting aside the increase in Hadoop adoption rates, security as a foundational topic is more important than ever because it seems we can't go a month without realizing our data isn't as safeguarded as it should be. This is a great example of how IBM's experience in hardening enterprises for operations has come to benefit Hadoop. In the relational world, fine-grained access control (FGAC) and row column access control (RCAC) are well-known methods for implementing *application-transparent* security controls on data. These are capabilities available in BigInsights for Hadoop. This is a great example of where Big SQL's code maturity comes into play because IBM engineers have built these kinds of regulatory-compliant security features deep into the Big SQL architecture. Other SQL on Hadoop engines in the market simply offer access control at the database, view, or table level; but using these facilities, Big SQL can restrict access at the row or column level using SQL statements that any DBA would be comfortable with. Big SQL also includes an audit facility that can be used independently or integrates seamlessly with leading audit facilities such as InfoSphere Guardium (covered in Chapter 12).

Federation with Other Relational Sources

Integration is critical for almost any scenario involving the storage of relational data in Hadoop. Thinking back to the data landing zone model from Chapter 4, there are many situations where it would be useful to have the ability to run a federated query against data stored in Hadoop and other relational systems. Big SQL includes a federation engine that supports a number of data sources: DB2, PureData System for Analytics, PureData System for Operational Analytics, Oracle, and Teradata, among others. Once databases on a federated source are cataloged, you can query them from Big SQL.

Machine Learning for the Masses: Big R and SystemML

By now you've probably noticed that everything in BigInsights is, well, big. As such, the statistics capabilities for BigInsights are called Big R. While R has been around for a while, momentum around it has been growing steadily for some time, to the point where today's generation of statisticians and data scientists mostly favor R as their statistical platform of choice. And why not—it's open source, there's a huge public library of statistical models and applications coded in R (through the Comprehensive R Archive Network—CRAN—a network of FTP and web servers around the world that store identical, up-to-date versions of code and documentation for R), and there are a number of great R tools for development and visualization (like RStudio). Taken altogether, the R ecosystem provides a complete set of capabilities for data exploration, transformation, visualization, and modeling.

So, you'd think that R and Hadoop would be made for each other, right? Sadly, this isn't the case. While Hadoop is a parallel execution environment, R is not. R runs beautifully on a single computer with lots of memory, but it's not designed to run in a distributed environment like Hadoop. This is where Big R comes in—it enables R applications to be run against large Hadoop data sets. For data scientists and statisticians, this means they can use their native tools to do analysis on Hadoop data in a highly performant manner, without having to learn new languages or programming approaches (such as parallel programming).

At its core, Big R is simply an R package, and you can install it in your R client of choice (like RStudio). It's also installed on each node in the BigInsights cluster. When you use Big R, you have access to the entire dataset that's residing in Hadoop, but there is minimal data movement between the BigInsights cluster and the client. What makes Big R special is that you can use it to push down your R code to be executed on the BigInsights Hadoop cluster. This could be your own custom code or preexisting R library code from CRAN.

IBM's Big R also includes a unique machine learning facility that enables statistics algorithms to be run in parallel on a BigInsights cluster. We're not sure if our marketing teams will end up swizzling the name into something else, but for now, we'll refer to it by its research name: SystemML. (If you've followed IBM innovations, you'll note their projects get prefixed with the word *System*, for example, System R for relational databases, SystemT for text analysis, System S for streaming, and SystemML for machine learning.)

SystemML is an ecosystem for distributed machine learning that provides the ability to run machine learning models on the BigInsights cluster at a massive scale. SystemML includes a number of prebuilt algorithms for machine learning and descriptive statistics. For cases where you need to write your own custom algorithms, SystemML includes a high-level declarative language, which is syntactically similar to R (remember the consumability attribute we talked about earlier, declarative languages make technology consumable). This machine learning code is then compiled and optimized for excellent Hadoop performance. Underneath the covers, the SystemML compiler handles automatic parallelization and optimization wherever possible. Quite simply, it's difficult to write parallel programs—IBM has delivered a declarative language to open up the building of parallel-driven statistical applications in the same manner that it did for relational databases when it invented SQL. As opposed to a library of hand-coded MapReduce functions, the SystemML algorithms are optimized by the compiler and tailored to the task at hand, which gives them a significant performance advantage. SystemML is designed to run optimally at any scale. The SystemML run time decides whether it is more efficient to run a set of operations in-memory on a single node, or in distributed memory on multiple nodes using MapReduce.

You can call SystemML algorithms using a special R API. This means you can call these scalable algorithms from within your existing R tools, just like Big R. Also like Big R, all the complexity of Hadoop is hidden from the R developer. (Nice!)

Alternatives in the Hadoop community today are fairly limited. For example, the Apache Mahout project does feature a library of machine learning models written for Hadoop, but they lack automatic performance optimization and there is no integration with standard R tools. A typical data science workflow involves extracting data, doing some transformations and other preparations, applying machine learning models or descriptive statistics, and then visualizing the data. The traditional R ecosystem covers this whole workflow. Big R and SystemML fit into this workflow beautifully. You can use standard R code with Big R to do the extraction and preparation operations. And for the more heavy-duty descriptive statistics and machine learning methods, you can call SystemML. This can all be done from within your R client. In short, data scientists don't need to be Java programmers and Hadoop experts; they can use their existing tools and skills against data in BigInsights—they can be data scientists.

The Advanced Text Analytics Toolkit

The approach in trying to get value from text data is to parse it, find the elements that are being searched for, understand their meaning, and extract them in a structured form for use in other applications. We can tell you from experience that manually developing this workflow for Hadoop would require a great deal of tedious hand-coding. IBM has decades of text analytics experience (think about the natural language processing capabilities in Watson Analytics we talked about in Chapter 1) and includes in BigInsights an Advanced Text Analytics Toolkit. While the BigInsights analytics components all connect to this toolkit, it's also integrated into IBM InfoSphere Streams (covered in Chapter 7). This means the text extractors that you write for your organization's data can be deployed on data at rest (through BigInsights) or data in motion (through Streams). For example, you can expose a set of extractors as an app (see the later section "Hadoop Apps for the Masses: Easy Deployment and Execution of Custom Applications"), or you can apply it to a column of data in a BigSheets sheet (see the next section).

The biggest challenge in text analysis is to ensure the *accuracy of results*. To keep things simple, we will define accuracy of results through two components, precision and recall:

- **Precision**   A measure of exactness, the percentage of items in the result set that are relevant: "Are the results you're getting valid?" For example, if you wanted to extract all the references to publicly traded companies from news stories, and 20 of the 80 passages identified as referring to these companies weren't about them at all, your precision would be 75 percent. In summary, precision describes how many passages are correctly identified.

- **Recall**   A measure of completeness, the percentage of relevant results that are retrieved from the text; in other words, are all the valid strings from the original text showing up? For example, if you wanted to extract all of the references to publicly traded companies from news stories, and got 80 out of 100 that would be found by a human expert, your recall would be 80 percent, because your application missed 20 percent of references. In summary, recall is how many matching passages are found out of the total number of actual matching passages.

As analysts develop their extractors and applications, they iteratively make refinements to tune their precision and recall rates. The development of extractors is really about adding more rules and knowledge to the extractor itself; in short, it's about getting more powerful with each iteration.

The Text Analytics Toolkit has two interfaces: a web-based GUI designed for business users to quickly and simply design text extractors (see Figure 6-2)

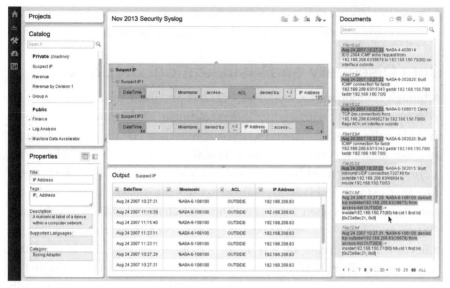

Figure 6-2 *The text extraction GUI for business users*

and a rich developer ecosystem included as an Eclipse plug-in, featuring development, testing, and deployment GUIs.

What's special about these tools is their approach to text extraction: To ensure high accuracy (precision) and full coverage (recall), the solution builds many specific rules. These rules are expressed in a declarative language (think consumability again) for text analysis that IBM researchers built, called the Annotator Query Language (AQL). AQL enables you to aggregate many rules to represent an individual extractor. For example, an extractor for telephone numbers can contain literally hundreds of rules to match the many ways that people around the world express this concept (dashes or decimals separating numbers, brackets for area codes, how many digits in a phone number, and so on). In addition, AQL is a fully declarative language, which means that all these overlapping rules get distilled and optimized into a highly efficient access path (similar to an SQL compiler for relational databases, where IBM researchers first developed this declarative concept), while the complexity of the underlying system is abstracted from the end user. Quite simply, when you write extraction logic in AQL, you tell the IBM Big Data platform *what* to extract, and the platform figures out *how* to extract it.

While AQL and the run-time engine make flexible and high-speed text analytics possible, the tool set for developing the text extractors makes this simple. With such a rich tool set, your business users are shielded from AQL code and only see visual representations of the extractions.

Data Discovery and Visualization: BigSheets

Although Hadoop makes analyzing Big Data possible, you pretty much need to be a programmer with a good understanding of the MapReduce paradigm to explore the data. We've seen what happens when you try to explain parallel programming concepts to nontechnical people, so clearly there's a big barrier that keeps most business analysts from being able to make sense of data that's stored in Hadoop. BigInsights has the answer: a browser-based visualization tool called BigSheets. This tool enables LOB users to harness the power of Hadoop using a familiar spreadsheet interface. (We can hear the collective sigh of relief of any LOB personnel reading this book. Don't worry—you still get to stay in your decades-old spreadsheet love affair). BigSheets requires *no programming* or special administration (it automatically generates Hadoop Pig code underneath the covers). If you can use a spreadsheet (pivot, slice, dice, and so on), you can use BigSheets to perform analysis on vast amounts of data, in any structure.

Three easy steps are involved in using BigSheets to perform Big Data analysis:

1. *Collect data.* You can collect data from multiple sources, using apps that are deployed in BigInsights to crawl the web, social sites such as Twitter, local files, or files on your network. Multiple protocols and formats are supported, including HTTP, HDFS, Amazon S3 Native File System (S3n), Amazon S3 Block File System (S3), and more. You can also generate sheets based on data from Big SQL queries. If that's not enough, there's a facility to extend BigSheets with custom plug-ins for importing data. For example, you could build a plug-in to harvest data from your favorite RSS feeds and include it in your BigSheets collections.

2. *Extract and analyze data.* After you have collected the data, you can see a sample of it in the spreadsheet interface, such as that shown in Figure 6-3. At this point, you can manipulate your data by using the spreadsheet-type tools that are available in BigSheets. For example, you can combine columns from different collections, run

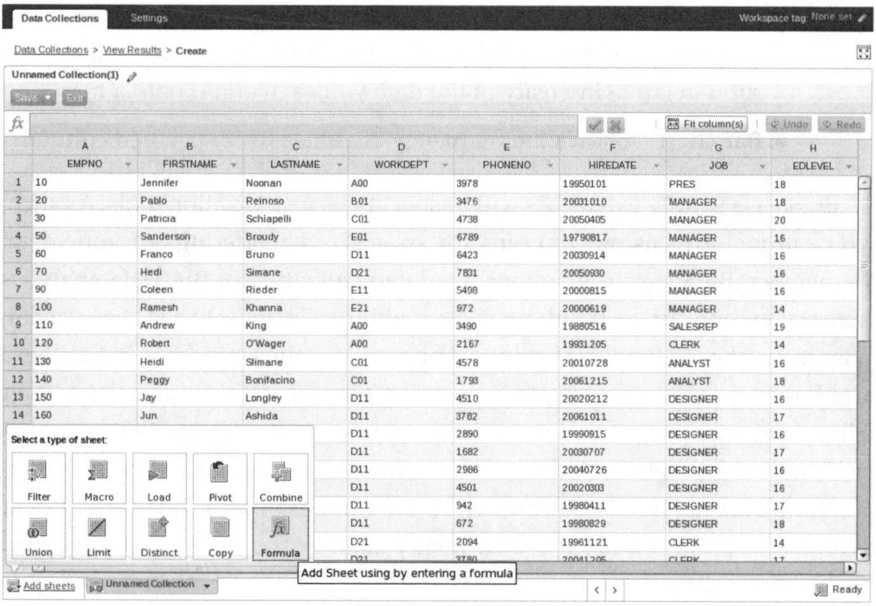

	Data Collections	Settings					Workspace tag: None set

Data Collections > View Results > Create

Unnamed Collection(1)

fx   Fit column(s)   Undo Redo

	A	B	C	D	E	F	G	H
	EMPNO	FIRSTNAME	LASTNAME	WORKDEPT	PHONENO	HIREDATE	JOB	EDLEVEL
1	10	Jennifer	Noonan	A00	3978	19950101	PRES	18
2	20	Pablo	Reinoso	B01	3476	20031010	MANAGER	18
3	30	Patricia	Schiapelli	C01	4738	20050405	MANAGER	20
4	50	Sanderson	Broudy	E01	6789	19790817	MANAGER	16
5	60	Franco	Bruno	D11	6423	20030914	MANAGER	16
6	70	Hedi	Simane	D21	7831	20050930	MANAGER	16
7	90	Coleen	Rieder	E11	5498	20000815	MANAGER	16
8	100	Ramesh	Khanna	E21	972	20000619	MANAGER	14
9	110	Andrew	King	A00	3490	19880516	SALESREP	19
10	120	Robert	O'Wager	A00	2167	19931205	CLERK	14
11	130	Heidi	Slimane	C01	4578	20010728	ANALYST	16
12	140	Peggy	Bonifacino	C01	1793	20061215	ANALYST	18
13	150	Jay	Longley	D11	4510	20020212	DESIGNER	16
14	160	Jun	Ashida	D11	3782	20061011	DESIGNER	17
				D11	2890	19990915	DESIGNER	16
				D11	1682	20030707	DESIGNER	17
				D11	2986	20040726	DESIGNER	16
				D11	4501	20020303	DESIGNER	16
				D11	942	19980411	DESIGNER	17
				D11	672	19980829	DESIGNER	18
				D21	2094	19961121	CLERK	14
				D21	3780	20041205	CLERK	17

Select a type of sheet:

Filter	Macro	Load	Pivot	Combine
Union	Limit	Distinct	Copy	Formula

Add Sheet using by entering a formula

Add sheets   Unnamed Collection ▾   < >   Ready

Figure 6-3   *The BigSheets spreadsheet-like interface*

formulas pivot, filter data, and so on. You can also deploy custom macros for BigSheets. For example, you can deploy a text extractor that you built with the BigInsights development tools as a BigSheets macro. As you build your sheets and refine your analysis, you can see the interim results in the sample data. It's only when you click the Run button that your analysis is applied to the complete data collection. Because your data could range from gigabytes to terabytes to petabytes in size, working iteratively with a small data set is the best approach.

3. *Explore and visualize data.* After running the analysis from your sheets against the data, you can apply visualizations to help you make sense of your data. BigSheets provides a number of traditional and new age Big Data visualizations, including the following:

- **Tag cloud**   Shows word frequencies; the larger the letters, the more occurrences of data referencing that term were found.

- **Pie chart**   Shows proportional relationships, where the relative size of the slice represents its proportion of the data.

- **Map**   Shows data values overlaid onto maps for specific geographies. This can be represented as a heat map as well to show relative intensity of the data values overlaid onto a map.

- **Bar chart**   Shows the frequency of values for a specified column.

BigSheets is fully extensible with respect to its visualization tools. As such, you can include custom plug-ins for specialized renderings of your data. Remember, BigSheets is all about the democratization of Big Data analytics across your enterprise. It's about consumability. The tool set has been used in a large number of Big Data projects. For example, the University of Southern California (USC) Annenburg's School of Communications used it for their Film Forecaster project that made national news in the United States. In that news coverage, it was noted "the Film Forecaster sounds like a big undertaking for USC, but it really came down to one communications masters student who learned Big Sheets in a day, then pulled in the tweets and analyzed them." Enough said.

Spatiotemporal Analytics

Much of the data we see flowing into Hadoop clusters today comes from IoT applications, where some kind of status or activity is logged with a time code and a geocode. To make it easier to get value out of this data in BigInsights, IBM has included a spatiotemporal analytics library with BigInsights. This is actually the same spatiotemporal analytics library that's included in the Geospatial toolkit for InfoSphere Streams, which further shows IBM's commitment to a unified analytics experience across the Big Data stack.

The spatiotemporal analytics library consists of a number of functions such as interpreting bounding boxes and points in space/time; calculating area, distances, and intersections; and converting geohash codes. The beauty of the integration of these functions in BigInsights is that they're surfaced in BigSheets. This means nonprogrammers can apply a rich set of powerful spatiotemporal functions using a GUI tool. Moreover, since this is in BigSheets, it means other analytics tools in BigInsights can consume them; for example, you can query a BigSheets sheet with the spatiotemporal functions using a Big SQL query.

Finding Needles in Haystacks of Needles: Indexing and Search in BigInsights

So far in this chapter we've talked about the various ways to derive insights from data in Hadoop; however, we've yet to talk about how to find the data. As it turns out, most organizations are guilty of not knowing what they could already know. In other words, an easy approach for deriving insights from data is a simple search. BigInsights comes with two options for providing enterprise search capability for data in your cluster: Apache Solr and Watson Explorer.

Solr is an indexing and search facility that's part of the Apache Lucene project. Solr works well in a Hadoop setting, and in fact, generating indexes for Solr and Lucene was one of the earliest use cases for Hadoop.

Watson Explorer is an indexing and search facility that's designed to provide a "single pane of glass" view of data across multiple enterprise-sources, including Hadoop clusters. Watson Explorer is bundled with BigInsights, and you can use it to index as much data in a BigInsights Hadoop cluster as you want (to index data volumes from other data sources, you'll need extra Watson Explorer licenses). You can also build intelligent search-driven applications in Watson Explorer, which can leverage apps you've deployed on BigInsights. One additional appealing feature in Watson Explorer is that it integrates with other technologies in the IBM Big Data portfolio, such as Streams (see Chapter 7), Big Match (see Chapter 14), and the Advanced Text Analytics Toolkit, which we discuss earlier in this chapter.

It's important to note that between Solr and Watson Explorer you get the choice of two distinct approaches for enterprise indexing and searching. Solr is an in-Hadoop solution in this case that runs on the BigInsights cluster and is focused only on data in the cluster. Watson Explorer is installed on a separate cluster from BigInsights and can work with data from multiple sources, including BigInsights.

Cradle-to-Grave Application Development Support

In 2008, Steve Ballmer made YouTube history with his infamous "Developers… Developers… Developers…" speech. Search for it, and you'll quickly find him on the stage in a passionate frenzy, repeating the word "Developers!" with increasing intensity. While this might make you question your own sanity in choosing a career in IT, we can't help but agree that Steve Ballmer was onto something important here: developers. (Refer to our discussion on this topic in Chapter 2 for more details.) If you want your platform to succeed, you had better make it easy for your developers to write applications for it. It's with this thought in mind that IBM built a rich set of developer tools for BigInsights. The ultimate goal is to minimize the barrier between analysts and developers so that apps can quickly be developed and tested with the BigInsights cluster and be easily consumed. This section describes the BigInsights developer tool set.

The BigInsights Integrated Development Environment

One of the main components of BigInsights is a set of Eclipse plug-ins that provides a rich development environment for creating BigInsights applications. This includes all of the usability features that you'd typically associate with an integrated development environment, namely, content completion, context-sensitive assistance, design-time assistance and error detection, a breakpoint and debugging console, code editors, workflow assistants, testing tools, a deployment tool, and more.

You can use the BigInsights Development Environment to develop text extractors, SQL queries (including for Big SQL and Hive and also more specialized HBase expressions), and Big Data applications (for example, Pig and MapReduce). The BigInsights Development Environment provides you with an enriched experience when you use any of these languages. In the Eclipse editor, you see code highlighting and syntax error checking. There are also templates and integrated help for the supported languages to get you started more quickly.

In addition to the query and application development tooling in the BigInsights Development Environment, there is a graphical workflow editor for easy development of Oozie workflows (see Figure 6-4). This is otherwise a painstaking process, involving the manual editing of an XML file based on the Oozie schema. Using this workflow editor, you simply drag and drop Oozie elements (`Start`, `End`, `Kill`, `Action`, `Fork`, `Join`, and `Decision`) to compose a workflow. There is also a code editor (featuring code highlighting, syntax error detection, and so on), where you can edit the generated Oozie XML.

To speed up application deployment, you can configure the BigInsights Development Environment to be aware of your BigInsights cluster so that pushing application code to the cluster is as easy as clicking a button.

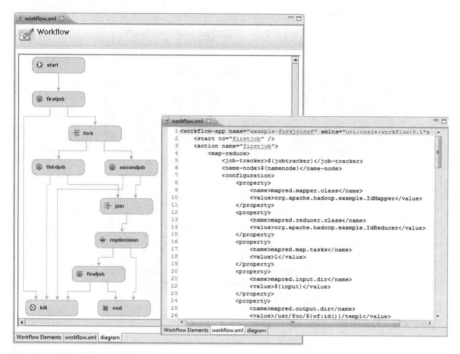

Figure 6-4   *Oozie workflow graphical interface*

The fact is that the population of specialized programmers for Hadoop is quite small, but the number of developers who know Eclipse, or SQL, is very large. Think about consumability as you start any Big Data project, and from proof of concept to enterprise production, you will move from a handful of developers to a full development, architecture, and QA team—potentially hundreds of developers. The BigInsights Development Environment has been designed to cater to the skill set of an average developer. So if your business is making the jump to BigInsights, you have integrated tooling that will help your development team get up to speed more quickly.

The BigInsights Application Lifecycle

Now that we've covered the analysis and application development tools in BigInsights, let's step back and see how the big picture of application lifecycle management has been baked into BigInsights (see Figure 6-5).

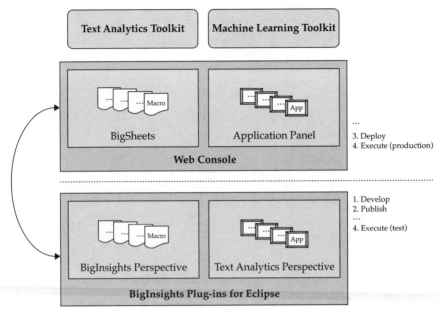

Figure 6-5   *The BigInsights application lifecycle*

The following details the lifecycle steps and their impacted components:

- **Develop**   Using the BigInsights development tools for Eclipse, you can, for example, create text extractors to isolate connection failures in your web server logs.

- **Publish**   From Eclipse, you can push your text extractor to be available in the Web Console as either an app (through the Applications panel) or a macro for BigSheets.

- **Deploy**   From the Web Console, someone with the Application Administrator role can deploy and configure an application for execution on the BigInsights cluster.

- **Execute**   An end user can run the text extractor in the console (either as an app or as a macro, depending on how it was published). Alternatively, a developer can run the app from the Web Console and download the results for testing in the Text Analytics debugging tool.

These are all steps that an IT organization needs to take to develop and deploy applications in a Hadoop context. In BigInsights, IBM has provided extensive automation and orchestration to make this process much faster, simpler, and more reliable. Without this tooling, not only would you have to manually move files around and set configurations, you would also have to develop wrappers and interfaces for your applications so that your users can execute them.

An App Store for Hadoop: Easy Deployment and Execution of Custom Applications

The BigInsights Web Console has a tab called Applications, where you can see a number of apps that are ready for you to run. IBM has modeled this panel after the "app store" concept that is common today for mobile devices. Running these apps takes a simple common approach: Click the app, enter the path from which the data to be analyzed will be read, enter another path where you want the results to be stored (and any of the app's additional fields), and you're ready to run the application. You don't have to spend precious budgets on app deployment with installers and such—just click and run.

BigInsights ships with a number of apps, which you can use to test the cluster and to get an idea of the kinds of apps you can build. In fact, the code to write every app that's shipped with BigInsights can be downloaded from the console as an Eclipse BigInsights project, so you have a ready-made starting point for your own app projects! Another nice thing about this feature is that you can use it as a front-end scheduler for end users to run Big Data apps distributed in your enterprise.

Your business analysts and data scientists can also leverage existing apps as building blocks to create new apps. Users can do this by using a graphical drag-and-drop tool to chain existing apps together in a workflow. You can easily direct the outputs from one app into the inputs of the next app in the chain. This type of capability has the direct effect of accelerating the Big Data journey that organizations start. Why? Think about it. If you're not Yahoo! or Facebook, you don't have a massive number of development teams. With such a framework, you can have a small group of hard-core Hadoop developers build discrete pieces of logic and expose them as building blocks for nonprogrammers to compose their apps by tying together these "widgets" into a rich application. Pretty powerful stuff.

The emphasis on security in BigInsights shows through here, because someone with an Application Administrator role can determine which users are to be authorized to run specific apps. Given that there are data sources or services where security credentials are required, the app's interface lets you leverage the BigInsights credentials store, enabling you to securely pass authentication information to the data source or service to which you're connecting.

Keeping the Sandbox Tidy: Sharing and Managing Hadoop

Real production installations of Hadoop rarely involve just one use case or a single data set. Once an organization adopts Hadoop, the best way to get value out of it is to load as much data as possible and realize the landing zone vision we talk about in Chapter 4. But with multiple users and multiple data sets come challenges. Even though a larger Hadoop cluster will have a great deal of processing capability, it's still finite, and those finite resources need to be managed for the applications and users competing for them. Also, with multiple users needing access to the Hadoop cluster, questions about security become important: You can't just isolate your cluster on the network. IBM has a deep understanding of enterprise requirements like this and has applied IT management expertise to BigInsights. This section describes the admin tooling, IBM's GPFS-FPO file system (an optional alternative to HDFS), and Adaptive MapReduce—an optional, more efficient and flexible job scheduler and resource manager for Hadoop.

The BigInsights Web Console

One of the nice features BigInsights brings to Hadoop is a rich interface called the BigInsights Web Console (see Figure 6-6). Whether you're running on a public cloud instance in a cluster halfway across the world or on a 1,000-node cluster in your company's server farm, this console is the focal point of the entire cluster because all administration, application deployment, and application execution activities are performed there.

What you're able to see in the console depends on your level of access as a BigInsights user. For example, if you have an administrator account, you can see the administrative dashboards, such as Application Status and Cluster Status. And if you have a user account, you'll only be able to see the dashboards that are applicable to browsing files, running applications, and doing analysis work, namely, the File Explorer, the Application Dashboard, and the BigSheets interface.

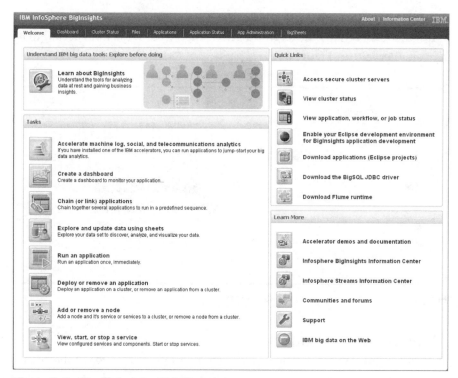

Figure 6-6   *The BigInsights Web Console*

Monitoring the Aspects of Your Cluster

To aid in the administration of your cluster, the BigInsights Web Console provides a real-time, interactive view of your cluster's components. The BigInsights Web Console includes graphical tools for examining the health of your BigInsights environment, including the nodes in your cluster, the Hadoop and BigInsights services, HDFS metadata, MapReduce metrics, the status of your jobs (applications), and more.

Monitoring the Cluster

BigInsights features a rich monitoring dashboard that enables you to tailor your view of administrative key performance indicators (KPIs). There are predefined dashboards for the following areas: System (covering CPU utilization and load average), Cluster, HDFS (covering total files and corrupted blocks), MapReduce (covering map and reduce tasks running and tasks failed), and more. Each dashboard contains monitoring widgets that you can configure to a high degree of granularity, ranging from the time period to its refresh interval (see Figure 6-7).

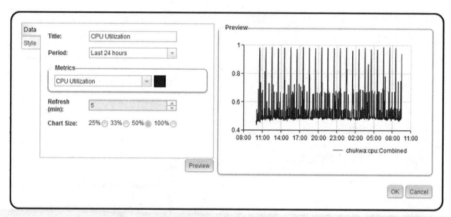

Figure 6-7 *Customizing monitoring widgets*

Monitoring Applications

The BigInsights Web Console provides context-sensitive views of the cluster so that people see only what they need to see based on their role. For example, if someone with the role of "user" runs an application, they see only their own statistics in the Application History view. This particular view is optimized to show a high level of application status information, hiding the lower-level workflow and job information.

People with administrator roles can see the state of all apps in the Application History view and the Application Status monitoring dashboard; additionally, they're able to drill into individual workflows and jobs for debugging or performance testing reasons. The Application Status pane has views for Workflows and Jobs, which list every active and completed workflow and job in the cluster. You can drill into each workflow or job to get further details and from there also see related elements.

Securing the BigInsights for Hadoop Cluster

Security is an important concern for enterprise software, and in the case of open source Hadoop, there are limitations to consider before moving to production. The good news is that BigInsights addresses these issues by reducing the security surface area through securing access to the administrative interfaces, key Hadoop services, lockdown of open ports, role-based security, integration into InfoSphere Guardium (Guardium), and more.

The BigInsights Web Console has been structured to act as a gateway to the cluster. It features enhanced security by supporting Lightweight Directory Access Protocol (LDAP) and Kerberos authentication protocols. Secure authentication and reverse-proxy support help administrators restrict access to authorized users. In addition, clients outside of the cluster must use secured REST interfaces to gain access to the cluster through the gateway. In contrast, Apache Hadoop has open ports on every node in the cluster. The more ports you need to have open (and there are a lot of them in open source Hadoop), the less secure the environment and the more likely you won't pass internal audit scans.

BigInsights can be configured to communicate with an LDAP credentials server or Kerberos key distribution center (KDC) for authentication. In the case of LDAP, all communication between the console and the LDAP server occurs using LDAP (by default) or both LDAP and LDAPS (LDAP over HTTPS). The BigInsights installer helps you to define mappings between your LDAP/Kerberos users and groups and the four BigInsights roles (System Administrator, Data Administrator, Application Administrator, and User). After BigInsights has been installed, you can add or remove users from the LDAP groups to grant or revoke access to various console functions.

BigInsights also supports alternative authentication options such as Linux pluggable authentication modules (PAMs). You can use this to deploy biometric authentication and other custom protocols.

Putting the cluster behind the Web Console's software firewall and establishing user roles can help lock down BigInsights and its data, but a complete security story has to include auditing, encryption, data masking and redaction, and enhanced role-based access. In Chapter 12, the Guardium and Optim solutions that provide on-premise and off-premise (for IBM Data-Works) governance and integration services are described in detail. Earlier in this chapter we describe Big SQL, which features fine-grained and label-based access controls for data at the row or column level.

Adaptive MapReduce

BigInsights includes enhanced workload management and scheduling capabilities to improve the resilience and flexibility of Hadoop, called Adaptive

MapReduce. This low-latency scheduling solution supports sophisticated workload management capabilities beyond those of standard Hadoop MapReduce. BigInsights Adaptive MapReduce uses the highly optimized IBM Platform Symphony scheduling engine, and provides full API compatibility with open source MapReduce so that Hadoop applications run without modification.

In order to measure the performance advantage of Adaptive MapReduce over open source Hadoop, IBM engaged an independent organization called STAC Research to undertake an audited benchmark. The STAC auditors chose the SWIM (Statistical Workload Injection for MapReduce) benchmark, which was developed at the University of California at Berkeley to simulate real industry workloads. For example, the SWIM benchmark includes a workload featuring a 24-hour window of traces contributed by Facebook from their production cluster. In the audited result, BigInsights with Adaptive MapReduce was found to deliver, on average, four times the performance of open source MapReduce running the Facebook workloads.

Hadoop has limited prioritization features, whereas the adaptive MapReduce component has thousands of priority levels and multiple options that you can configure to manage resource sharing. This sophisticated resource sharing allows you to prioritize for interactive workloads in a manner not possible in a traditional Hadoop environment. For example, with the Adaptive MapReduce component, you can start multiple Hadoop jobs and associate those jobs with a consumer definition. Within that consumer, jobs can dynamically share resources based on individual priorities. Adaptive MapReduce supports extremely fast job preemption and proportional resource allocation so that critical jobs can get instant access to needed resources. Clients with more sophisticated requirements can license IBM Platform Symphony Advanced Edition and build a true multitenant infrastructure that isn't possible with open source Hadoop.

A Flexible File System for Hadoop: GPFS-FPO

The General Parallel File System (GPFS) was developed by IBM Research in the 1990s for high-performance computing (HPC) applications. Since its first release in 1998, GPFS has been used in many of the world's fastest supercomputers, including IBM Sequoia, Blue Gene, and Watson (the *Jeopardy!* supercomputer). In addition to HPC, GPFS is commonly found in thousands of other mission-critical installations worldwide. Needless to say, GPFS has earned an enterprise-grade reputation and pedigree for extreme scalability, high performance, and reliability.

The design principles behind HDFS were defined by use cases that assumed Hadoop workloads would involve sequential reads of very large file sets, and no random writes to files already in the cluster—just appends. In contrast, GPFS has been designed for a wide variety of workloads and for a multitude of uses.

Extending GPFS for Hadoop: GPFS File Placement Optimization

GPFS was originally available only as a storage area network (SAN) file system, which typically isn't suitable for a Hadoop cluster, because MapReduce jobs perform better when data is stored on the node where it's processed (which requires locality awareness for the data). In a SAN, the location of the data is transparent, which requires a high degree of network bandwidth and disk I/O, especially in clusters with many nodes. In 2009, IBM extended GPFS to work with Hadoop, and this work is known as GPFS-FPO (File Placement Optimization).

By storing your Hadoop data in GPFS-FPO, you are free from the design-based restrictions that are inherent in HDFS. You can take advantage of GPFS-FPO's pedigree as a multipurpose file system in your Hadoop cluster, which gives you tremendous flexibility. A significant architectural difference between GPFS-FPO and HDFS is that GPFS-FPO is a kernel-level file system, whereas HDFS runs on top of the operating system. Many limitations in HDFS stem from the fact that it's not fully POSIX compliant. On the other hand, GPFS-FPO is 100 percent POSIX compliant, which can give you significant flexibility.

Because GPFS is POSIX compliant, files that are stored in GPFS-FPO are visible to all applications, just like any other files stored on a computer. For example, when copying files, any authorized user can use traditional operating system commands to list, copy, and move files in GPFS-FPO. This isn't the case in HDFS, where users need to log into Hadoop to see the files in the cluster. Because Hadoop and non-Hadoop applications can share the same files, customers can avoid copying data in and out of Hadoop file systems, accelerating workflows and avoiding unnecessary replication. In fact, some customers who deployed GPFS-FPO in place of HDFS have found that they can reduce their total storage footprint by as much as one third, helping reduce infrastructure costs and their data center footprint.

The full POSIX compliance of GPFS-FPO enables you to manage your Hadoop storage just as you would any other servers in your IT shop. That's going to give you economies of scale when it comes to building Hadoop skills and just make life easier. Many Hadoop people seem to take it for granted that they can't do anything but delete or append to files in HDFS—in GPFS-FPO, you're free to edit your files! Also, your traditional file administration utilities will work, as will your backup and restore tooling and procedures. This is actually a big deal—imagine you need to quickly look for differences between two data sets. In Linux, you'd simply use the diff command, but in Hadoop you'd have to write your own diff application.

GPFS includes a rich replication facility called Active File Management (AFM), which supports a range of high availability options. With AFM you can create associations to additional BigInsights clusters within your data center, or in other geographic locations. AFM will asynchronously replicate data between the clusters, enabling you to have a single namespace, spanning multiple data centers, even in different countries. You can configure active-active or active-passive configurations for the associated BigInsights clusters. In the case of disasters, AFM supports online recovery. This goes light years beyond what HDFS is capable of.

GPFS-FPO enables you to safely manage multitenant Hadoop clusters with a robust separation-of-concern (SoC) infrastructure, allowing other applications to share the cluster resources. This isn't possible in HDFS. This also helps from a capacity planning perspective because without GPFS-FPO, you would need to design the disk space that is dedicated to the Hadoop cluster up front. If fact, not only do you have to estimate how much data you need to store in HDFS, but you're also going to have to guess how much storage you'll need for the output of MapReduce jobs, which can vary widely by workload. Finally, don't forget that you need to account for space that will be taken up by log files created by the Hadoop system too! With GPFS-FPO, you only need to worry about the disks themselves filling up; there's no need to dedicate storage for Hadoop.

All of the characteristics that make GPFS the file system of choice for large-scale, mission-critical IT installations are applicable to GPFS-FPO. After all, this is still GPFS, but with Hadoop-friendly extensions. You get the same stability, flexibility, and performance in GPFS-FPO, as well as all of the utilities that you're used to. GPFS-FPO also provides hierarchical storage management (HSM) capabilities—another favorite of ours—whereby it can manage and use disk drives with different retrieval speeds efficiently. This enables you to manage multitemperature data, keeping "hot" data on your best-performing hardware.

GPFS-FPO also features extensive security and governance capabilities, which you can configure as automatically deployed policies. For a particular data set, you can define an expiration date (for defensible disposal), a replication policy (for example, you may only want to replicate mission-critical data off site), specific access controls, mutability (whether people can edit, append, or delete files), compression, or encryption. That last point about encryption is worth an extra bit of attention: the GPFS-FPO encryption is NIST SP 800-131A compliant. And even better, this is file system–based encryption that doesn't require extra tools or expense. In addition, GPFS-FPO includes a secure erase facility that ensures hard disk drives in the cluster won't include traces of deleted data.

GPFS-FPO is such a game changer that it won the prestigious Supercomputing Storage Challenge award in 2010 for being the "most innovative storage solution" submitted to this competition.

Playing Nice: Integration with Other Data Center Systems

A key value of IBM's vision for Big Data is the importance of integrating data from a variety sources. Hadoop is not a one-size-fits-all solution to meet all your storage and processing needs, so you'll continue to have other repositories in the enterprise, as discussed in Chapter 4. But once you make the commitment to add a Hadoop cluster to your IT infrastructure, it's inevitable that some of these other systems will need access to it. It's with this in mind that IBM has developed Big SQL, a native SQL interface for data in BigInsights. With the standard open source Hadoop interfaces and Big SQL, BigInsights supports integration with a large number of other data management–related software offerings—both from IBM and from other enterprise software vendors. This section describes some of the unique integrations BigInsights has with other key IBM data management software offerings. In addition, there's a section on integration with software from other vendors.

IBM InfoSphere System z Connector for Hadoop

Companies using the System z mainframe do so for three main reasons: rock-solid reliability, virtualization, and airtight security. However, there are many cases where they may need to analyze their mainframe data using Big Data technologies like Hadoop; they need to do so in a secure manner and without having to make large investments in new skills. The System z Connector for Hadoop scratches this itch, enabling mainframe admins to transfer data from the mainframe to a BigInsights cluster. This connector works in the following stages:

1. Using a simple GUI, mainframe administrators choose mainframe data sets from multiple System z sources. This connector uses existing metadata from DB2 and IMS catalogs and uses COBOL copybooks to build a menu of data sets to choose from.

2. The connector takes advantage of parallel streaming technologies and quickly transfers the data to the designated BigInsights cluster. There is a small System z footprint here to minimize MIPS impact.

3. Data is placed in the BigInsights cluster with secure access controls.

4. Selected data sets are converted from mainframe formats for consumption in BigInsights. This is done in BigInsights, where data processing is inexpensive.

This solution is designed to make it as easy as possible—and as secure as possible—for mainframe users to take advantage of BigInsights. The installation of this tool is designed to take hours, not days. Once data is transferred into a BigInsights cluster, authorized users can start using tools such as BigSheets and Big SQL immediately. Also, prebuilt System z log formats included will enable customers to rapidly analyze their own mainframe utilization and performance characteristics for operational optimization.

IBM PureData System for Analytics

You can exchange data between BigInsights and IBM PureData System for Analytics (or earlier versions of Netezza) in two ways: from your database server or from your BigInsights cluster. These IBM database technologies can both connect and interact with BigInsights through a set of user-defined functions (UDFs) that can be installed on the database server. BigInsights can connect to the IBM PureData System for Analytics and Netezza through a special high-speed adapter.

The IBM PureData System for Analytics Adapter

BigInsights includes a connector that enables data exchange between a BigInsights cluster and IBM PureData System for Analytics (and its earlier incarnation, the Netezza appliance). This adapter supports splitting tables (a concept similar to splitting files). This entails partitioning the table and assigning each divided portion to a specific mapper. This way, your SQL statements can be processed in parallel.

The adapter leverages the Netezza technology's external table feature, which you can think of as a materialized external UNIX pipe. External tables use JDBC. In this scenario, each mapper acts as a database client. Basically, a mapper (as a client) will connect to the database and start a read from a UNIX file that's created by the IBM PureData System's infrastructure.

InfoSphere Streams for Data in Motion

As you'll discover in Chapter 7, Streams is the IBM solution for real-time analytics on streaming data. Streams includes a sink adapter for BigInsights, which lets you store streaming data directly into your BigInsights cluster. Streams also includes a source adapter for BigInsights, which lets Streams applications read data from the cluster. The integration between BigInsights and Streams raises a number of interesting possibilities. At a high level, you can create an infrastructure to respond to changes detected in data in real time (as the data is being processed in-motion by Streams), while using a wealth of existing data (stored and analyzed at rest by BigInsights) to inform the response. You could also use Streams as a large-scale data ingest engine to filter, decorate, or otherwise manipulate a stream of data to be stored in the BigInsights cluster.

A Streams application can write a control file to the BigInsights cluster, and BigInsights can be configured to respond to the appearance of such a file so that it would trigger a deeper analytics operation to be run in the cluster. For more advanced scenarios, the trigger file from Streams could also contain query parameters to customize the analysis in BigInsights. There are other integration points we've alluded to earlier in this chapter. For example, we already talked about how the Text Analytics Toolkit allows you to orchestrate text extraction across both product, the spatiotemporal support is the same, and more. Both the PureData System for Analytics and BigInsights include some entitlement to the Streams product.

InfoSphere Information Server for Data Integration

Increasingly, we're seeing Hadoop being leveraged as a dynamic ETL engine, especially for unstructured data. ETL is not just about the transformation, though. Orchestration, debugging, lifecycle management, and data lineage are but a few important considerations. Information Server for Data Integration and the rest of the InfoSphere Information Server platform provide the means to deal with all these items and more. Expanding its role as a data integration agent, Information Server for Data Integration has been extended to work with BigInsights and includes a connector to push and pull data to and from BigInsights clusters. The real power comes from the deep integration of these connectors with BigInsights, taking advantage of the clustered architecture so that any bulk writes to the same file are done in parallel. The result of this integration is that BigInsights can quickly exchange data with any other software product able to connect with Information Server for Data Integration.

Data transformation is where many ETL projects in Hadoop have failed because of their complexity. Analysts have gone so far as to say that Hadoop should not be an ETL engine because of the difficulty of programming ETL stages on Hadoop and the lack of mature metadata management and staging orchestration facilities. Information Server for Data Integration integrates with the processing infrastructure in BigInsights, enabling transformation logic generated by ETL architects to be run natively on data residing in a BigInsights cluster. You can find further details on InfoSphere Server integration with BigInsights, and how these capabilities are also exposed as a service via IBM DataWorks, in Chapter 13.

Matching at Scale with Big Match

In Chapter 4 we talked about the data zones model as an architectural overview of a next-generation analytics platform. Hadoop is an excellent technology for landing data from multiple repositories across an organization in this architecture. But what happens when the rubber hits the road and analysts want to explore this data from different sources and make correlations? Without a matching facility, this exploration becomes a tedious exercise. To solve this problem, IBM has taken its probabilistic matching engine from the master data management offering and ported it to Hadoop with the new name: Big Match. (Yes, everything with BigInsights is big. We're not a creative bunch when it comes to naming, but we like to think we are foreshadowing the results.) For more about Big Match, see Chapter 14.

Securing Hadoop with Guardium and Optim

IBM's Guardium solutions for auditing data and encrypting data are industry leaders in the security segment and bring the vitally important aspect of regulatory compliance to BigInsights. After all, if you can't meet regulatory guidelines such as ensuring that your administrators aren't able to manipulate audit logs to hide their own tracks or providing deep encryption capabilities for your data, Hadoop won't be an option for you.

For years, the IBM Optim brand has been providing databases with the ability to restrict the visibility of data. This ability is now available for BigInsights as well, because the Optim Data Privacy and Optim Test Data Management offerings have been rearchitected to exploit Hadoop. With Optim, you can automatically find sensitive data and then either mask it or redact it when users access it. When you're developing applications, one of the more difficult tasks is finding realistic test data that doesn't have sensitive information. Optim Test Data Management automates the testing process and ensures testers aren't exposed to sensitive data, while ensuring the application is properly exercised. In line with the recurring theme throughout this book, these capabilities are also available as a service in a cloud environment. more on the Guardium and Optim security capabilities in a Hadoop world, see Chapter 12.

Broad Integration Support

We recognize that most IT shops use software from many vendors. IBM wants to provide value to as many organizations as possible, so it's worked hard to build partnerships with as many software vendors as possible—large and small, and even some of our bitter competitors! We call this "coopetition."

Enterprise software can be a tricky business; on one hand, we may be competing with another vendor for a database offering, an ETL tool, or an analytics offering, and on the other hand, our customers need BigInsights to work with these other offerings. Here's a sampling list of software offerings from other vendors that are certified to work with BigInsights: Datameer, Informatica Power Center, MicroStrategy Analytics Enterprise, SAS Visual Analytics, SAS LASR Analytic Server and SAS Enterprise Data Integration Server, Splunk, and Tableau, among others.

We're sure there are some IBMers who will be annoyed with us for publishing this, but we're realistic—we want you to be able to take Big Data conversations beyond the hype and include a realization of heterogeneous environments. In the same manner that Big Data doesn't not equal Hadoop alone, a Big Data project doesn't have to equal IBM alone either (though we sure like the sound of that). For a more complete list of the software vendor business partners IBM has, check out this link: http://ibm.co/WyW5MU.

Deployment Flexibility

When people deploy Hadoop today, there is a fairly limited set of options available out of the box. What if you want to run Hadoop on noncommodity (that is, non-Intel) hardware for some different use cases? Cloud computing is all the rage now, but how many cloud services for Hadoop can boast baremetal hardware deployments with hardware that's optimized for Hadoop? Bottom line, we recognize that what different organizations need from Hadoop is varied, and to best serve these different needs, IBM has provided a number of varied deployment options for BigInsights.

BigInsights Editions: Free, Low-Cost, and Premium Offerings

BigInsights comes in three flavors: a free offering (Quick Start Edition), an entry-level offering (Standard Edition), and a premium offering (Enterprise Edition). The for-fee offerings feature a perpetual software license and IBM's legendary 24/7 global technical support lines, which offers considerable value as compared to the annual licenses offered by most of the other Hadoop vendors in the market. You pay for BigInsights on a per-node basis. There's also a cloud-friendly option, where you pay the BigInsights license fee only for the time you use it.

Quick Start Edition

BigInsights Quick Start Edition gives you free access to most of IBM's enterprise-grade extensions for Hadoop. This edition is free for as long as you want, for as much data as you want; the only restriction is that you can't use it in production. As such, all the features we mention in this chapter are included, except the production-oriented ones. Specifically, this includes the two accelerators (for social and machine data), GPFS-FPO support, Adaptive MapReduce, and the additional licenses for related IBM analytics technologies (see the "Enterprise Edition" section for more on this). But if you want to try the other software offerings, they have free trial licenses as well.

Since the Quick Start Edition of BigInsights is intended to get you to try it for yourself, we've included a number of hands-on tutorials to truly give you a "quick start" for whatever you want to try. It comes in two formats: a VMware instance you can start running as soon as you've finished downloading it or an installable image you can deploy on your own hardware, virtual nodes, or cloud-based nodes. You can download this from the Try It tab at the HadoopsDev site: https://ibm.biz/hadoopdev.

Standard Edition

BigInsights Standard Edition is designed to help you get your feet wet with BigInsights in a budget-friendly way. It has Big SQL, Big Sheets, development tools, security features, administration console, and, of course, the same open source Hadoop foundation as the Enterprise Edition. It's the enterprise features (Big R, the analytic accelerators, Text Analytics Toolkit, GPFS-FPO support, Adaptive MapReduce, and the additional software license) that are exclusive to the Enterprise Edition. However, to provide additional value, both Big SQL and BigSheets are included in the Standard Edition.

Enterprise Edition

BigInsights Enterprise Edition includes all of the features described in this chapter. In addition, you get a number of software licenses for other data analytics offerings from IBM:

- **InfoSphere Streams** A streaming data analysis engine; we describe this in Chapter 7. This license entitles you to run streaming data jobs in conjunction with your data-at-rest processing using BigInsights.

- **Watson Explorer** A scalable enterprise indexing and search solution. This license entitles you to index all the data stored in your BigInsights cluster.

- **Cognos BI** This license entitles you to have five authorized users of Cognos BI.

To reflect different kinds of deployments, BigInsights Enterprise Edition also has nonproduction and developer licenses.

A Low-Cost Way to Get Started: Running BigInsights on the Cloud

With the rise of virtualization technologies, the cloud has become a popular platform for businesses to leverage IT resources. Given the significant work involved in procuring and building a moderately sized Hadoop cluster, the cloud (as you learned in Chapter 3) can be a convenient means for short-term testing or an ad hoc project.

Let's say you're interested in seeing what BigInsights can do for your business. You have a large data set, and you have analysts and developers ready to experiment with it. If you're considering an on-site experimental Hadoop installation, it could take weeks, if not months, for your organization's procurement process to run its course and for the hardware to finally be installed. On the other hand, you could have a made-to-order, cloud-based BigInsights cluster up and running within hours. Let's take this scenario a little further and imagine that your data is loaded on this cloud-based cluster and that your analysts are working away. If some aspect of performance is poor, no problem! Additional compute resources (memory, data nodes, CPU) can be added dynamically to your cluster. This is another reason why the cloud is such a great option for trial deployments: there's no need to spend a lot of time ironing out reference architecture details. With the cloud, if it doesn't work, make adjustments in real time.

Like other components in the IBM Big Data platform, BigInsights works well in cloud deployments. From a technology perspective, BigInsights supports virtualization, which is a must in cloud environments. BigInsights also has an excellent security story, whereby the entire cluster can be isolated behind a single point of access through the Web Console. From a licensing perspective, it couldn't be easier because you can pay for BigInsights based on how much time you need.

BigInsights supports two flexible cloud options: bring your own license (BYOL) to whatever cloud provider you want or provision a powerful and secure bare-metal deployment on the IBM Cloud. BigInsights is also available as a platform as a service component in IBM Bluemix (for more, see Chapter 3).

Bring Your Own License

With your BigInsights license, you can deploy your cluster wherever you want. BigInsights has been successfully deployed on some of the most notable cloud providers, such as SoftLayer, Amazon EC2, and RackSpace. IBM regularly delivers trials for BigInsights and several other IBM products on both public clouds and private clouds.

The Flexibility of Cloud, the Reliability of Bare Metal

The IBM Cloud is underpinned by IBM's 2013 acquisition of SoftLayer, one of the world's leading cloud computing providers. Since then, at the time of writing, IBM has doubled the number of SoftLayer data centers worldwide, greatly increasing cloud capacity. As you learn about in Chapter 3, one of SoftLayer's unique offerings is its bare-metal servers, where you can provision compute resources by reserving actual servers that only you have access to—there's no virtualization or resource sharing! So, you get the best of both the on-premise and cloud worlds, by having the stability and performance of a server in your own data center and the convenience of having someone else provision and manage this server for you in the cloud. BigInsights has a bare-metal deployment option on SoftLayer, where you can order whatever hardware you need using a handy GUI, and it's provisioned for you.

As anyone who's worked with Hadoop knows, much of the effort in tuning Hadoop's performance is in getting the right hardware components and configuring them properly. BigInsights performance engineers from our development teams have been working with the SoftLayer team to ensure that the hardware options you choose for your BigInsights cluster are suitable for Hadoop, and when they're provisioned, their settings are tuned for optimal Hadoop performance. Figure 6-8 shows the handy BigInsights cluster provisioning tool, which enables you to quickly order a cluster that's tuned to your needs.

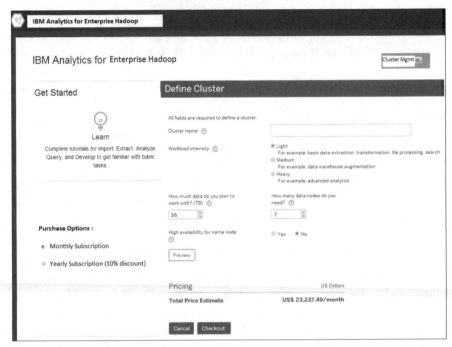

Figure 6-8   *Provisioning BigInsights over the cloud and getting it right.*

There are many cases where the cloud is appealing if you just need to try something and performance doesn't matter. But when reliable performance does matter and you don't have the time or desire to provision your own Hadoop cluster, this Hadoop-optimized SoftLayer bare-metal option is a winner.

Higher-Class Hardware: Power and System z Support

Although commodity hardware deployments have been the norm for Hadoop clusters up to this point, we're seeing some alternatives. IBM provides two compelling options: support for BigInsights on Power or System z hardware.

BigInsights on Power

One of the most significant benefits of Power hardware is reliability, which makes it well suited to be deployed as master nodes in your cluster. If you need higher-energy efficiency or need to concentrate data nodes to fewer tiles or simply need more processing power, Power can most definitely be a great way to go. In 2011, the IBM Watson system beat the two greatest champions of the American quiz show *Jeopardy!*—Linux on Power was the underlying platform for Watson, which also leveraged Hadoop for some of its subsystems. During the development of the IBM PowerLinux Solution for Big Data, customizations and lessons learned from the Watson project were applied to this offering for both on-premise and off-premise deployments.

BigInsights on System z

Nothing says uptime and rock-solid stability like the mainframe. The next time you talk to a System z admin, ask her about the last outage—planned or unplanned. It's likely that it was many years ago. Also, System z has an extremely secure architecture and access control regime. Not everyone wants to run Hadoop on commodity hardware, and a number of IBM's mainframe customers have been asking for the flexibility of Hadoop. So, to provide that flexibility, BigInsights can be installed on Linux on System z.

Get Started Quickly!

We hope this chapter has gotten you excited enough to try BigInsights for yourself. To get going, try the InfoSphere BigInsights Quick Start Edition for free (as either an installable package or preinstalled on a VMware image). You can download this from the Try It tab at the HadoopDev site: https://ibm.biz/hadoopdev. There's also other helpful material on HadoopDev, such as tutorials, articles, and sample code.

Wrapping It Up

We said it earlier in this book, but it's really important to understand that Big Data conversations do not solely equal Hadoop conversations. Hadoop is but one of multiple data processing engines you will need to address today's challenges (and the ones you don't yet know about yet). For this reason, IBM has been long committed to Hadoop, with code contributions to open source and continual engineering around the ecosystem. With its long history of enterprise-grade infrastructure and optimization, IBM has taken this experience and applied it to Hadoop through BigInsights. BigInsights includes open source Hadoop and adds some operational excellence features such as

Big Data–optimized compression, workload management, scheduling capabilities, and even an app development and deployment ecosystem.

While operational excellence delivers economics of scale and infrastructure trust, the true potential of Hadoop lies in the analytic capabilities—more accurately, the consumability of the analytic capabilities. For this reason, BigInsights includes toolkits, accelerators, and tools such as Big SQL, which seek to democratize the use of Big Data so it isn't bottled up in deeply skilled tech departments that require an army of Java programmers to monetize the data. In addition, BigInsights provides an end-to-end text extraction framework. Quite simply, IBM builds a high-value stack that treats Hadoop as a first-class citizen and integrates it across the IBM Big Data platform.

7

"In the Moment" Analytics: InfoSphere Streams

In business climates where success or failure depends on how quickly you react to conditions and trends, analysis of *data in motion* is critical. This is where InfoSphere Streams (Streams) shines as one of the most industry-differentiated Big Data services within the IBM Watson Foundations platform. Its design lets you leverage massively parallel processing (MPP) techniques to analyze data *while it is streaming by* so you can understand what's happening in real time and optionally take action, make better decisions, and improve outcomes. While some vendors suggest *real time* means fast analytics on data that has to "land" in a repository, Streams sets the definition—the bar if you will—of what real-time analytics is all about.

Introducing Streaming Data Analysis

For people used to traditional "at-rest" data processing and analysis, dealing with data in motion is a radically different concept. To help you get your feet wet, we'll start you off with a story from the healthcare industry.

Emory University Hospital is using IBM InfoSphere Streams software and Excel Medical Electronics (EME) devices to pioneer new methods in creating advanced, predictive medical care for critical patients through real-time streaming analytics. Emory's new system can identify patterns in physiological data and instantly alert clinicians to danger signs in patients. In a typical intensive-care unit (ICU), a dozen different streams of medical data light up the monitors at a patient's bedside, including markers for heart physiology,

179

respiration, brain waves, and blood pressure, among others. This constant feed of vital signs is transmitted as waves and numbers and routinely displayed on computer screens at every bedside. Currently, it's up to doctors and nurses to rapidly process and analyze all this information in order to make medical decisions.

Emory aims to enable clinicians to acquire, analyze, and correlate medical data at a volume and velocity that was never before possible. IBM Streams and EME's bedside monitors work together to provide a data aggregation and analytics application that collects and analyzes more than 100,000 real-time data points per patient per second. Think about how bedside monitoring is handled today. A nurse comes and records charting information every half-hour or so; if there are no major changes, the nurse is apt to just record the same number. Throughout this book we keep talking about how our Big Data world involves 24/7 data collection (in a single hour, a bedside monitor could produce a whopping 360 million data points). The problem here is captured perfectly by the *"enterprise amnesia"* we talked about in Chapter 1. Many potentially interesting patterns could be found in those 360 million data points, but current hospital practices use just a few dozen.

The software developed by Emory identifies patterns that could indicate serious complications such as sepsis, heart failure, or pneumonia, aiming to provide real-time medical insights to clinicians. Tim Buchman, MD, PhD, director of critical care at Emory University Hospital, speaks to the potential of analyzing those missing 359,999,999,998 records when he notes, "Accessing and drawing insights from real-time data can mean life and death for a patient." He further notes how IBM Streams can help because it empowers Emory to "...analyze thousands of streaming data points and act on those insights to make better decisions about which patient needs our immediate attention and how to treat that patient. It's making us much smarter in our approach to critical care." For example, patients with a common heart disorder called atrial fibrillation (A-fib) often show no symptoms, but it is a common and serious condition that can be associated with congestive heart failure and strokes. Using the new research system, Emory clinicians can view a real-time digital visualization of the patient's analyzed heart rhythm and spot A-fib in its earliest stages.

In short, we say it's advancing the ICU of the future. In fact, we saw this work pioneered by Dr. Caroyln McGregor from the University of Ontario

Institute of Technology (UOIT) and her work in the neonatal ICU (NICU) at Toronto's Sick Kids hospital—search the Internet for "IBM data baby" and learn about this incredible story.

A variety of industries have adopted information technology innovations to transform everything, from forecasting the weather to studying fraud, and from homeland security to call center analytics—even predicting the outcomes of presidential elections. Emory's vision of the "ICU of the future" is based on the notion that the same predictive capabilities possible in banking, air travel, online commerce, oil and gas exploration, and other industries can also apply in medicine. With this in mind, let's take a look at the IBM Watson Foundations software that allows you to take data at rest and apply it to analytics for data in motion.

How InfoSphere Streams Works

IBM Streams is a powerful analytic computing software platform that continuously analyzes and transforms data in memory *before* it is stored on disk. Instead of gathering large quantities of data, manipulating and storing it on disk, and then analyzing it, as is the case with other analytic approaches, Streams enables you to apply the analytics directly on data in motion. When you analyze data in motion with Streams, you get the fastest possible results, huge potential hardware savings, and the highest throughput.

With all these advantages, you might ask, "What's the catch?" There is no catch, but it's also important to understand that Streams represents a different approach to analytics, where you're dealing with data the instant it hits your network (Streams actually expands your fields of vision from when the data is landed to when the data event happens). Streams components operate either on one event at a time or on "windows" of data that are maintained in memory. A window of data can be configured to represent the last few seconds to the last few days (or more) of data, where the size of the window is limited by the amount of memory in the system and data flow rates (for example, the more memory you have, the longer history you can maintain in your windows). This "in-the-moment data" can be enriched with context that has been accumulated during processing and with data from an at-rest engine, such as Hadoop or a relational database management system (RDBMS), a content store, or virtually any other data source.

A Simple Streams Application

A *stream* of data is a continuous sequence of data items (or packets). (Before we continue, note the distinction between *Streams*, which is the InfoSphere Streams product for streaming data analysis, and *stream*, which is a stream of data in motion.) The individual data packets in a stream are known as *tuples*. In an RDBMS sense, you can think of a tuple as being similar to a row of data (in fact, RDBMS purists calls rows tuples; others call them records). Each element in the tuple contains the value for that attribute, which can be a character string, a number, a date, or even some sort of binary object, such as a video frame. For applications with semistructured data, it is common for Streams applications to start with tuples that consist of a small amount of metadata coupled with an unstructured payload in each tuple, with subsequent operators progressively extracting more information from the unstructured payload.

A Streams application can be viewed as a *graph of nodes with directed connections (edges)*. Each node in the graph is an *operator* that processes the data from a stream. Operators have zero or more inputs and zero or more outputs. The output (or outputs) from one operator connects to the input (or inputs) of another operator (or operators). The edges of the graph that join the nodes together represent the stream of data moving between the operators. Each output of an operator defines a new stream, and other operators can connect to the stream. Operators occurring early in a pipeline can even connect to a stream that is produced by "downstream" operators, enabling control flows to change the computation of upstream operators as new insights are uncovered. Figure 7-1 represents a simple stream graph that reads data from a file, sends the data to an operator known as a *Functor* (this operator transforms incoming data in some programmatic manner), and then feeds that data to a *Split operator*, which then feeds data to either a file or a database (depending on the logic inside the split operator).

Operators that don't perform windowing work on one tuple at a time. These operators can filter a tuple based on characteristics of its attributes, extract additional information from the tuple, and transform the tuple before sending data to an output stream. Because a stream consists of a never-ending sequence of tuples, how can you correlate across different streams, sort tuples, or compute aggregates? The answer is *windows*. A window is a finite

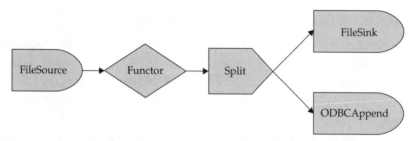

Figure 7-1   *A simple data stream that applies a transformation to data and splits it into two possible outputs based on predefined logic*

sequence of tuples and looks a lot like a database view. Windows are continuously updated as new data arrives, by eliminating the oldest tuples and adding the newest tuples. Windows can be easily configured in many ways. For example, the window size can be defined by the number of tuples or an aging attribute such as the number of seconds. Windows can be advanced in many ways, including one tuple at a time, or by replacing an entire window at once. Each time the window is updated, you can think of it as a temporarily frozen view. It's easy to correlate a frozen view with another window of data from a different stream, or you can compute aggregates using similar techniques for aggregates and joins in relational databases. The windowing libraries in Streams provide incredible productivity for building applications. *Windowing* is an important concept to understand because Streams *is not* just about manipulating one tuple at a time, but rather analyzing large sets of data in real time and gaining insight from analytics across multiple tuples, streams, and context data.

Streams also has the concept of *composite operators.* A composite operator consists of a reusable and configurable Streams subgraph. Technically, all Streams applications contain at least one composite (the main composite for the application), but they can include more than one composite (composites can also be nested). A composite defines zero or more input streams and zero or more output streams. Streams can be passed to the inputs of the composite and are connected to inputs in the internal subgraph. Outputs from the internal subgraph are similarly connected to the composite outputs. A composite can expose parameters that are used to customize its behavior. This is all technical-speak for saying you can nest flows of Streams logic within other flows of Streams logic—which makes for a powerful composition paradigm.

Recommended Uses for Streams

We generally recommend Streams for the following use cases: identifying events in real time, such as determining when customer sentiment in social media is becoming more negative; correlating and combining events that are closely related in time, such as a warning in a log file followed by a system outage or a certain kind of network attack; and continuously calculating grouped aggregates, such as price trends per symbol per industry in the stock market.

We don't recommend Streams for analytics that require multiple passes over a large data set, so developing a regression model is not possible, and this should be done using InfoSphere BigInsights for Hadoop (BigInsights, covered in Chapter 6) or one of the purpose-built IBM analytic data warehousing engines with data at rest (we talk about these in Chapters 8 and 9). This all said, Streams can take advantage of rich historical context by using models built by BigInsights, the IBM PureData System for Operational Analytics (formerly known as the IBM Smart Analytics System), the IBM Pure-Data System for Analytics that's powered by Netezza technology, or other analytic tools, such as SPSS, SAS, R frameworks, and more.

How Is Streams Different from CEP Systems?

If you're already familiar with Complex Event Processing (CEP) systems, you might see some similarities in Streams. However, Streams is designed to be much more scalable and dynamic, to enable more complex analytics, and to support a much higher data flow rate than other systems. Many CEP or stream-processing systems, including new open source projects such as Apache Storm, advertise a few *hundred thousand* events per second within a whole *cluster*. In contrast, the IBM Streams technology has been demonstrated to handle a *few million* events per second on a single *server*—it is *fast*. (Don't forget, you can deploy Streams in a cluster with near-linear scalability.) In addition, it's fair to note that Streams comes with a CEP toolkit for that "style" of real-time analytics. Specifically, the CEP toolkit enables the detection of complex events based on the occurrence of a sequence of events or a time-correlated set of events. The main point we are trying to make is that CEP isn't designed for massive scalability (or unstructured data for that matter).

Stream Processing Modes: Preserve Currency or Preserve Each Record

Streams applications generally fall into one of two types. The first keeps up with the most current data no matter what happens, even if it means dropping older data. For these applications, *now* is more important than processing every bit of data. Examples of applications that need to keep up with the most current data include detecting and responding to denial-of-service and cyber-attacks, making buy-and-sell decisions on the stock market, or monitoring a person's vital signs. For these applications, you need to make decisions based on the most current data. Streams supports these types of applications by delivering scalability and high throughput, allowing operators to intelligently drop tuples (load shedding) when necessary, and maintaining system-level high availability to keep applications running.

The second type of application requires every bit of data to be processed, no matter what. These applications typically used database technology in the past, but for reasons of efficiency, timeliness, or the inability to keep up, a portion of the application has been moved to Streams. One example of this type of application is processing call detail records (CDRs) for the telecommunications industry. For compliance and business reasons, these CDRs need to be de-duplicated, transformed, and stitched together without losing a single record—in the telco industry, they call this mediation. By moving processing to Streams while the CDRs are still in motion, significant efficiency gains are realized, and new business opportunities arise. For these kinds of applications, the inherently high throughput coupled with system-level high availability and application patterns make Streams an excellent choice.

Flexibility in being able to choose between two very different processing modes is a *major* differentiator for Streams. For example, some of the emerging Hadoop-related streaming projects such as Spark Streaming are limited to having to process each individual record. For some use cases, this approach is useful, but it falls apart when it comes to applications where maintaining a current view of incoming data is the highest priority.

High Availability

Large, massively parallel jobs have unique availability requirements because in a large cluster there are bound to be failures; massively parallel technologies such as Streams have to plan for when things fail in a cluster by expecting failures (Hadoop's architecture embraced this notion as well). Streams has built-in availability protocols that take this into account. Coupled with application monitoring, Streams enables you to keep management costs low and the reputation of your business high.

When you build a streaming application, the operators that make up the graph are compiled into processing elements (PEs). PEs can contain one or more operators, which are often "fused" together inside a single PE for performance reasons. (You can think of a PE as a unit of physical deployment in the Streams run time.) PEs from the same application can run on multiple hosts in a network, as well as exchange tuples across the network. In the event of a PE failure, Streams automatically detects the failure and chooses from among a large number of possible remedial actions. For example, if the PE is restartable and relocatable, the Streams run-time engine automatically picks an available host in the cluster on which to run the PE, starts the PE on that host, and automatically "rewires" inputs and outputs to other PEs, as appropriate. However, if the PE continues to fail over and over again and exceeds a retry threshold (perhaps because of a recurring underlying hardware issue), the PE is placed into a stopped state and requires manual intervention to resolve the issue. If the PE is restartable but has been defined as not relocatable (for example, the PE is a sink that requires it to be run on a specific host where it intends to deposit output of the stream after some operation), the Streams run-time engine automatically attempts to restart the PE on the same host, if it is available. Similarly, if a management host fails, you can have the management function restarted elsewhere. In this case, the recovery metadata has the necessary information to restart any management tasks on another server in the cluster. As you can see, Streams wasn't just designed to recover from multiple failures; it was designed to expect them. Large scale-out clusters have more components, which means the probability of an individual component failing goes up.

Data processing is guaranteed in Streams when there are no host, network, or PE failures. You might be wondering what happens to the data in the event of one of these failures. When a PE (or its network or host) does fail, the data in the PE's buffers (and data that appears while a PE is being restarted) can be lost without special precautions. With the most sensitive applications requiring very high performance, it is appropriate to deploy two or more parallel instances of the streaming application on different servers in the cluster—that way, if a PE in one instance of a graph fails, the other parallel instance is already actively processing all of the data and can continue while the failed graph is being restored. There are other strategies that can be used, depending on the needs of the application. Streams is often deployed in production environments in which the processing of every single bit of data with high performance is essential, and these high-availability strategies and mechanisms have been critical to successful Streams deployments. The fact that Streams is hardened for enterprise deployments helped one customer recover from a serious business emergency that was caused by an electrical outage—if only everything were as reliable as Streams!

Dynamically Distributed Processing

When you're ready to deploy your streaming application, Streams autonomically decides, at run time, where to run the PEs based on real-time cluster-based load balancing and availability metrics. Streams also gives you fine-grained control over the placement of one or more operators by programmatically specifying which operators run on which servers and which operators should run together or separately.

This autonomic streaming and customizable platform enables you to increase the number of servers performing analysis on the stream simply by adding servers and assigning operators to run on those servers without concern for the underlying cluster. The Streams infrastructure ensures that the data flows successfully from one operator to another, whether the operators are running on distinct servers or on the same server. Not only can you add or remove servers, but you can also dynamically add applications that will automatically connect to running applications and that can be reconfigured programmatically. Of course, you can also remove applications on the fly, which enables you to change priorities and improve analysis over time. These features provide a high degree of agility and flexibility to let you start small and grow the platform as needed.

InfoSphere Streams Platform Components

Streams is a full-featured platform for streaming data analytics. At its core, Streams features a powerful engine to run distributed streaming data applications. As a platform, Streams includes a declarative flow language and an Eclipse-based integrated development environment (IDE) plug-in to build these applications, toolkits with special-purpose prebuilt code, and a management environment. This section describes these Streams platform components.

The Streams Console

The Streams Console is a web-based tool that provides management services and a wealth of information about a Streams instance. You can quickly see the health and status of your Streams instance; manage and monitor servers, services, and applications in your cluster; and control overall settings for the instance (such as security). Additionally, you can configure views for operators in your applications that sample and buffer data for live export from Streams to visualization tools. What's more, you can configure charts to visualize data directly in the Streams Console.

The bottom of Figure 7-2 shows how the Streams Console can be used for host (server) management. The console includes a sortable and filterable

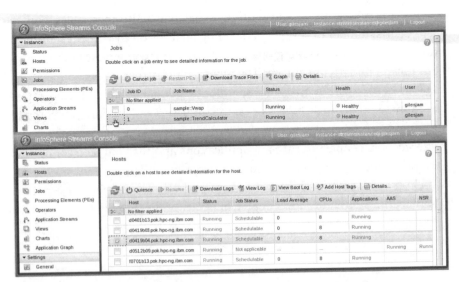

Figure 7-2 *The management of jobs and hosts in the Streams Console*

view that shows each available host in a Streams cluster. At a glance, you can see host health in the `Status` field. You can also see the status of services on each host, whether the host is available for running applications, metrics for the host, including load average and number of CPU cores when metrics collection is enabled, and so on. Tags, such as *IngestServer*, can be added to hosts to facilitate optimal application placement in the cluster. When something goes wrong with a host, you can view or download logs with the click of a button for problem determination. It's also possible to quiesce workloads on a server so that it can be taken out of service for maintenance. Similar features for jobs, operators, and processing elements are available as well; for example, the top of Figure 7-2 shows the console's jobs view.

Operations Visualized

A great feature in the Streams Console is the ability to monitor results of Streams applications in a natural way, using graphs. The Application Graph service displays all running applications and run-time metrics from a Streams instance in an interactive and customizable window.

For example, Figure 7-3 illustrates two running financial services applications, one calculating trend metrics and one calculating the volume-weighted average price (VWAP) for every stock symbol on a tick-by-tick basis. At the top of Figure 7-3 you can see that the graph is configured to continuously update the color of the operator based on the tuple rate. The thickness of the lines is also updated to be proportional to the data flow rate to give you a quick visual cue as to how much data is flowing through the system. The bottom of Figure 7-3 illustrates a different view—one in which the operators are grouped by job. By clicking an operator in the TrendCalculator application, additional information, such as tuples processed by the operator, is displayed. Clicking other objects, such as ports or a stream, also provides significant detail.

A Picture Is Worth a Thousand Words: Visualizing Streams Data

The Streams Console also enables *data visualization*, which is key in making your in-motion analytics come alive. In addition to making live data available for external visualization tools such as Cognos or Tableau, live streaming data can be visualized directly in the Streams Console. Tables and graphs

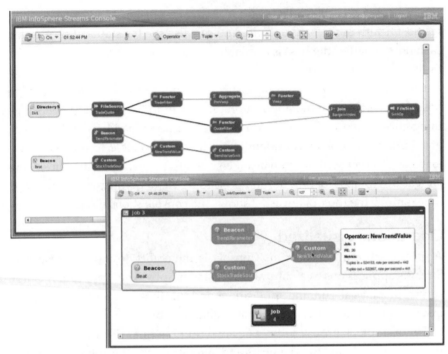

Figure 7-3 *The Streams Console showing the Application Graph service with two running jobs at the top and a grouping by jobs showing details about the NewTrendValue custom operator at the bottom*

can be extensively configured by selecting and rearranging attributes from the tuples, as well as filtering. Figure 7-4 shows a chart for a stock and its ticker data with VWAP, Min Price, Max Price, and Average Price.

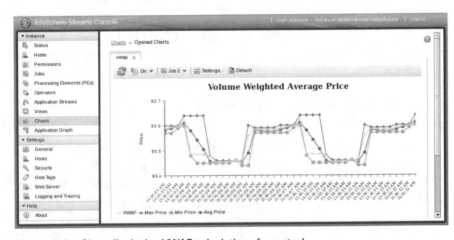

Figure 7-4 *Chart displaying VWAP calculations for a stock*

An Integrated Development Environment for Streams: Streams Studio

As previously mentioned, Streams includes an IDE that provides a rich drag-and-drop work-as-you-think programming experience, operational and data visualizations, and analytic toolkits designed to take the programming out of developing a Streams application. Not every company can hire waves of new programmers, and this is why conversations about Big Data that include consumability are just as important as capability conversations when it comes to getting beyond the hype and into value delivery.

Streams Studio is an interactive tool set that's used for creating and deploying Streams applications. It's a typical IDE, so if you have experience in application development, you will love what you're getting here: content assist, design-time assistance, contextual help, templates, design-time validation, drag-and-drop palettes, and more. Besides gestured application construction and editors, Streams Studio can configure and manage Streams instances. The first thing you will notice when starting Streams Studio is a Task Launcher view with a list of First Steps as well as broader tasks. The Task Launcher guides you through everything from conceptual design to deployment, and all tasks in between, when building a Streams application. The inspiration behind these helpers came from observing what our Streams experts did when personally working with our clients; we sometimes refer to this stuff as "Nagui in the box" after an IBM Fellow who was one of this product's founders. (Disclaimer: Nagui Halim isn't actually included in the product's licensing terms, but his codified ideas to simplify your experience are.)

As mentioned, you don't need to be a coder to build Streams applications. There is a drag-and-drop application development tool called the *Streams Graphical Editor*. With this tool, it's possible to create and deploy Streams applications without writing a single line of code! Recognizing that applications often start by sketching a graph on paper, Streams Studio lets users sketch an application flow in the Streams Graphical Editor without necessarily choosing operator implementations—it's the work-as-you-think paradigm we keep talking about. Generic operators can subsequently be connected and manipulated until the flow is right. The operators and graphs can also be annotated with the functions that should be performed. Other users, or developers, can later choose and configure the remaining operator implementations, creating new operators if they don't already exist in one of the extensive toolkits.

For example, Figure 7-5 shows a simple sketched application with operators labeled Reader, Filter, and Writer. The implementation for Reader is already known to be a FileSource (a built-in operator for reading data from files). The Filter and Writer operators are generic operators that serve as placeholders until an implementation is chosen. In this example, an architect has annotated the graph, indicating that the generic Filter placeholder should be implemented using the Streams standard toolkit Filter operator, with filtering based on ticker symbol. The figure also shows a user searching for operators starting with fil and subsequently dragging (the squared icon hovering over the operator) the standard toolkit Filter operator onto the graph to provide an implementation for the Filter placeholder. If the

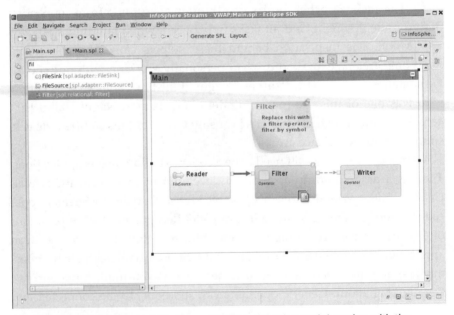

Figure 7-5   *Application building is as simple as dragging and dropping with the Streams Graphical Editor.*

implementation needs to be changed to another operator later, it can be over-written in the same way. After choosing an operator for the `Writer` place-holder and configuring the properties, a complete application is ready to run.

Extending existing applications is also a snap. Figure 7-6 shows the volume-weighted average price (VWAP) sample application that comes with Streams. In this example, a user extended the sample application so that the `QuoteFilter` stream is written to a file. This is one of the greatest benefits associated with all of the samples that are shipped with Streams: You can extend and customize them to build your application.

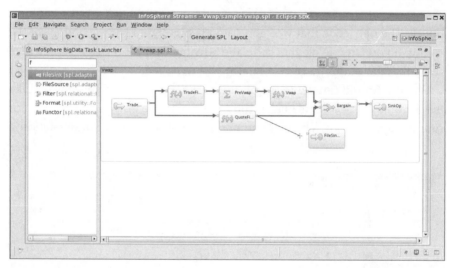

Figure 7-6 *Extending the VWAP sample to write tuples from QuoteFilter to a file*

In this example, a user simply dragged a `FileSink` operator from the Streams standard toolkit onto the palette and connected the `QuoteFilter` stream to the new `FileSink` operator. The `FileSink` operator was renamed to `QuoteWriter`, and the `file` property was set to the `QuoteFile.txt` file. After running the new application, we see that by default the tuple attri-butes are written one row at a time to `QuoteFile.txt` in a comma-separated value (CSV) form, such as the one shown here:

```
80.43,83.49,10,(1135711808,117000000,0),"XYZ"
83.43,83.46,10,(1135711813,283000000,0),"XYZ"
83.42,83.46,10,(1135711813,718000000,0),"XYZ"
81.42,83.45,3,(1135711815,751000000,0),"XYZ"
```

Even though applications can be built completely within the Streams Graphical Editor, this tool set also provides a powerful round-trip linkage with the Streams Processing Language (SPL) editor—we introduce you to this declarative language that simplifies Streams development in the next section—so that advanced developers can further customize applications.

For example, this integration gives you the ability to implement custom operators, which didn't initially exist in the Streams toolkits. Streams application builders often find it convenient to start with the Streams Graphical Editor and switch back and forth between it and the SPL editor after the initial application has been sketched. Figure 7-7 shows the SPL editor with the new `QuoteWriter` operator that was added using the Streams Graphical Editor. The new code that was generated is highlighted at the bottom of the listing. If you later delete that code, the Streams Graphical Editor would also show that the `QuoteWriter` operator was removed.

Streams Studio can deploy applications and run them on the cluster. Like the Streams Console, Streams Studio can display the graphs and metrics for running applications. There are numerous other features for understanding

Figure 7-7 *The Streams Graphical Editor and SPL editor are linked for round-trip updates.*

applications, such as the ability to color or group a graph based on jobs, hosts, and flow rates. It is also possible to quickly gather and display logs from the cluster if an application is not behaving as expected. For example, Streams Studio applies colorization to a job and its operators, and even to the PE containing the operator, so that different PEs have different colors.

Additionally, by clicking any operator, it is possible to highlight upstream or downstream operators to understand provenance (the origin of the data and any changes applied to it in the stream). The ability to quickly visualize the upstream operators is extremely useful for debugging large applications when an operator is not receiving the data that is expected. For example, if an operator is not receiving data, by highlighting upstream operators, you can quickly trace back to the problem in the application.

One of the most useful features in Streams Studio for debugging applications is the ability to click a stream in an Instance Graph to display the data that is flowing on that stream. The live data that is flowing on the stream is displayed in a tabular form that can be filtered and manipulated. Figure 7-8 shows a user selecting *Show Data* for the NewTrendValue stream. It also shows the live data from the stream after the user runs through an assistant that helps to configure the optimized attributes and filters that should be applied. Data in the table can be paused for closer examination without impacting the running applications; after updates are resumed, the latest data in the view buffer is displayed. Because you can quickly see the data elements as they pass by in the stream, it is much easier to extend and debug applications.

The Streams Processing Language

With the Streams Graphical Editor, many applications can be created without looking at any source code. However, under every Streams application is the Streams Processing Language. SPL is a structured application development language that can be used to build Streams applications. It's supported by both the Streams Graphical Editor and the Streams Processing Language editor in Eclipse, which are integrated with "round-trip ability" so that it's possible to go back and forth between both editors.

SPL is also a declarative language. It provides a higher level of abstraction for building Streams applications than using lower-level languages or

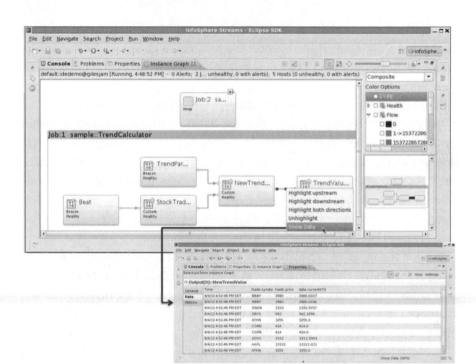

Figure 7-8 *Display live data being fed from the NewTrendValue stream by clicking the Instance Graph.*

application programming interfaces (APIs), in the same way that SQL makes it easy to pull desired data sets out of database tables instead of hand-coding C or Java applications. In fact, Dr. Alex Philp, founder and CTO of Adelos, Inc., noted that his developers can "deliver applications 45 percent faster due to the agility of [the] Streams Processing Language." We think that Bó Thide, a professor at Sweden's top-ranked Uppsala University, said it best when referring to SPL: "Streams allows me to again be a space physicist instead of a computer scientist." After all, technology is great, but if you can't quickly apply it to the business need at hand, what's the point?

Streams-based applications built with the Streams Graphical Editor or written in SPL are compiled using the Streams compiler, which turns them into C++ code and invokes the C++ compiler to create binary executable code—this executable code runs in the Streams environment to accomplish tasks on the various servers in the cluster. An SPL program is a text-based representation of the graph that we discussed in the preceding section. It defines the sources, sinks, and operators, as well as the way in which they are interconnected with a stream. For example, the following SPL code reads data from a file line by line into tuples, converts each line to uppercase, and then writes each line to standard output:

```
composite toUpper {
   graph
      stream<rstring line> LineStream = FileSource() {
         param   file                : "input_file";
                 format              : line;
      }
      stream<LineStream> upperedTxt = Functor(LineStream) {
         output upperedTxt           : line = upper(line);
      }
      () as Sink = FileSink(upperedTxt) {
      param   file     : "/dev/stdout";
      format           : line;
      }
}
```

In this SPL snippet, the built-in `FileSource` operator reads data from the specified file one line at a time and puts it into a stream called `LineStream` that has a single tuple attribute called `line`. The built-in `Functor` operator consumes the `LineStream` stream, converts the `line` attribute from each streamed tuple to uppercase text, and creates a new output stream called `upperedTxt` using the same tuple type as `LineStream`. The `Sink` operator then reads the `upperedTxt` stream of data and sends the tuples to standard output (`stdout`). Notice that the application is wrapped in a composite operator that encapsulates the function, as described in the previous sections.

This snippet represents the simplest graph with a single source, a single operation, and a single sink. The flexibility of Streams lies in the fact that you can combine simple and complex operations to do whatever you want against a huge variety of data streams. And, of course, the power of Streams is that it can run massively parallel jobs across large clusters of servers, where each operator, or a group of operators, can be running on a separate server. But before we get into the enterprise-class capabilities of Streams, let's look at what gives Streams its great flexibility: the adapters, operators, and toolkits you can use to piece together your applications.

Source and Sink Adapters

It goes without saying that in order to perform analysis on streaming data, the data has to enter the application. Of course, a stream of results has to go somewhere when the analysis is done. Let's look at the most basic source adapters available to ingest data along with the most basic sink adapters through which data can be sent to the outside world. Perhaps the most powerful adapters we describe are Import and Export; these operators provide dynamic connections for jobs that can be configured at deployment time and at run time.

FileSource and FileSink

As the names imply, FileSource and FileSink are standard built-in adapters that are used to read from or write to a file. You use parameters to specify the name and location of the file that is to be used for the read or write operation, the file's format, and a number of other optional parameters that can be used to specify column separators, end-of-line markers, compression, and more.

TCPSource/UDPSource and TCPSink/UDPSink

The TCPSource and TCPSink adapters are the basic TCP adapters used in Streams to read from and write to a TCP socket. When you use these adapters, you specify the IP address (using either IPv4 or IPv6) along with the port, and the adapter will read from the socket and generate tuples into the stream. The UDPSource and UDPSink adapters read from and write to a UDP socket in the same manner as the TCP-based adapters.

Export and Import

The Export and Import adapters work together to connect jobs within a Streams instance. An Export adapter can be used to make data from a job available to other jobs that are already deployed or that might be deployed in the future. You can export data using the Export adapter and assign properties to the exported stream consisting of arbitrary name/value pairs that characterize the stream.

After the stream is assigned these export properties, any other Streams applications that are deployed to the same Streams instance can import this data using an Import operator and a subscription expression that matches the export properties—assuming the application is authorized to access the exported data stream. Using built-in APIs, both export properties and import subscriptions can be changed dynamically at run time. This means that applications can be built to evolve in powerful ways over time, depending on the jobs that are submitted and the processing that is being done. For example, a sentiment analysis job might subscribe to all streams with the property `textForSentimentAnalysis=true`. There might be jobs processing email and blog text that export a stream with that property. At some time in the future, if you decide to process instant messaging text for sentiment, you just need to deploy the job to process the instant messages and export a stream with the property `textForSentimentAnalysis=true`; it will automatically be connected in an efficient point-to-point way to the sentiment analysis job. Using `Export` and `Import` is a powerful way to dynamically stream data between applications running under the same Streams instance.

MetricsSink

The `MetricsSink` adapter is an interesting and useful sink adapter because it enables you to set up a *named* metric, which is updated whenever a tuple arrives at the sink. You can think of these metrics as a gauge that you can monitor using Streams Studio or other tools. If you've ever driven over one of those traffic counters (those black rubber hoses that lie across an intersection or road), you have the right idea. While a traffic counter measures the flow of traffic through a point of interest, a `MetricsSink` can be used to monitor the volume and velocity of data flowing out of your data stream.

Analytical Operators

Operators are at the heart of the Streams analytical engine. They take data from upstream adapters or other operators, manipulate that data, and create a new stream and new tuples (possibly pass-through) to send to downstream operators. In addition to tuples from an input stream, operators have access to metrics that can be used to change the behavior of the operator, for example, during periods of high load. In this section, we discuss some of the more common Streams operators that can be strung together to build a Streams application.

Filter

The `Filter` operator is similar to a filter in an actual water stream or in your furnace or car: Its purpose is to allow only some of the streaming contents to pass. A Streams `Filter` operator removes tuples from a data stream based on a user-defined condition specified as a parameter to the operator. After you've specified a condition, the first output port defined in the operator will send out any tuples that satisfy that condition. You can optionally specify a second output port to send any tuples that did not satisfy the specified condition. (If you're familiar with extract, transform, and load [ETL] flows, this is similar to a `match` and `discard` operation.)

Functor

The `Functor` operator reads from an input stream, transforms tuples in flexible ways, and sends new tuples to an output stream. The transformations can manipulate or perform calculations on any of the attributes in the tuple. For example, if you need to keep a running tally of the number of seconds a patient's oxygen saturation level is below 90 percent, you could extract the applicable data element out of the patient's data stream and output the running total for every tuple.

Punctor

The `Punctor` operator adds punctuation into the stream, which can then be used downstream to separate the stream into multiple windows. For example, suppose a stream reads a contact directory listing and processes the data flowing through that stream. You can keep a running count of last names in the contact directory by using the `Punctor` operator to add a punctuation mark into the stream any time your application observes a changed last name in the stream. You could then use this punctuation mark downstream in an aggregation `Functor` operator that sends out the running total for the current name, to reset the count to zero and start counting occurrences of the next name. Other operators can also insert punctuation markers, but for the `Punctor` that is its only role in life.

Sort

The aptly named `Sort` operator outputs the tuples that it receives, but in a specified sorted order. This operator uses a window on the input stream. Think about it for a moment: If a stream represents an infinite flow of data, how can you sort that data? You don't know whether the next tuple to arrive will need to be sorted with the first tuple to be sent as output. To overcome this issue, Streams enables you to specify a window on which to operate. You can specify a window of tuples in the following ways:

- **count** The number of tuples to include in the window

- **delta** Waiting until a given attribute of an element in the stream has changed by a specified delta amount

- **time** The amount of time, in seconds, to allow the window to fill up

- **punctuation** The punctuation used to delimit the window (inserted by a Punctor or some other upstream operator)

In addition to specifying the window, you must specify an expression that defines how you want the data to be sorted (for example, sort by a given attribute in the stream). After the window fills up, the sort operator will sort the tuples based on the element that you specified and then send those tuples to the output port in sorted order. Then the window fills up again. By default, Streams sorts in ascending order, but you can specify a sort in descending order.

Join

As you've likely guessed, the Join operator takes two streams, matches the tuples on a specified condition, and then sends the matches to an output stream. When a row arrives on one input stream, the matching attribute is compared to the tuples that already exist in the operating window of the second input stream to try to find a match. Just as in a relational database, several types of joins can be used, including inner joins (in which only matches are passed on) and outer joins (which can pass on one of the stream tuples even without a match, in addition to matching tuples from both streams).

Aggregate

The aggregate operator can be used to sum up the values of a given attribute or set of attributes for the tuples in the window; this operator also relies on a windowing option to group together a set of tuples. An Aggregate operator enables groupBy and partitionBy parameters to divide up the tuples in a window and perform aggregation on those subsets of tuples. You can use the Aggregate operator to perform COUNT, SUM, AVERAGE, MAX, MIN, and other forms of aggregation.

Beacon

The Beacon is a useful operator because it's used to create tuples on the fly. For example, you can set up a Beacon to send tuples into a stream, optionally rate-limited by a time period (send a tuple every n tenths of a second) or limited to a number of iterations (send out n tuples and then stop), or both. The Beacon operator can be useful for testing and debugging your Streams applications.

Throttle and Delay

Two other useful operators can help you to manipulate the timing and flow of a given stream: Throttle and Delay. The Throttle operator helps you to set the "pace" of the data flowing through a stream by slowing it down. For example, tuples that are read in bursts from a file or a socket can be sent to the output of the Throttle operator at a specified rate (defined by tuples per second). Similarly, the Delay operator can be used to change the timing of the stream with respect to another stream. A Delay operator can be set up to output tuples after a specific time interval.

Split and Union

The Split operator takes one input stream and, as the name suggests, splits that stream into multiple output streams. This operator takes a parameterized list of values for a given attribute in the tuple and matches the tuple's attribute with this list to determine on which output stream the tuple will be sent. The Union operator acts in reverse: It takes multiple input streams and combines all of the tuples that are found in those input streams into one output stream.

Streams Toolkits

In addition to the adapters and operators that are described in the previous sections, Streams ships with a number of toolkits that enable even faster application development. These toolkits enable you to connect to specific data sources and manipulate the data that is commonly found in databases or Hadoop, perform signal processing on time series data, extract information from text using advanced text analytics, score data mining models in real time, process financial markets data, and much more. Because the Streams toolkits can dramatically accelerate your time to analysis with Streams, we cover the Messaging, Database, Big Data, Text, and Mining

Toolkits in more detail here. There are many more toolkits available as part of the product, such as the TimeSeries, Geospatial, Financial Services, Messaging, SPSS, R-project, Complex Event Processing, Internet, and IBM InfoSphere Information Server for Data Integration toolkits. There are also toolkits freely downloadable from GitHub (https://github.com/IBMStreams), such as the MongoDB and JSON toolkits.

The Messaging Toolkit: Operators for MQ Telemetry Transport

The Messaging Toolkit enables a stream to receive or send messages using Message Queue Telemetry Transport (MQTT), which is a protocol used in Internet of Things applications. The IBM Connected Car demo (http://tinyurl.com/mmldq2w) is a great example of how Streams uses MQTT to receive constant updates from an entire city's cars detailing their status and local conditions, analyze that information in real time, and send notifications of changing conditions.

The Database Toolkit: Operators for Relational Databases

The Database Toolkit enables a stream to read from or write to an ODBC database. Moreover, it provides high-performance parallel operators to write to DB2, any of the IBM PureData systems, BigInsights for Hadoop's Big SQL, and HP Vertica data stores, among others. This toolkit enables a stream to query an external database to add data or to verify data in the stream for further analysis.

The Big Data Toolkit: Operators for Integration with BigInsights

The Big Data Toolkit has operators for connecting to Hadoop's distributed file system (HDFS). This toolkit is essential for applications where Streams and BigInsights work together. It enables high-speed parallel writing to the HDFS for the fastest possible data exchange.

The Text Toolkit: Operators for Text Analytics

The Text Toolkit lets your applications take advantage of the same powerful text analytics functions that you use with BigInsights for Hadoop. The TextExtract operator uses an Annotated Query Language (AQL) specification and processes incoming text documents and sends the results to downstream operators. Imagine you're looking for occurrences of a specific group of people's phone numbers. Using AQL rules, you can cast a net into the stream of data where matching names and numbers would be extracted. Advanced Text Analytics is important for many use cases, including social data analysis (the Text Toolkit is used heavily by the Accelerator for Social Data Analysis), log analytics where log lines need to be parsed to extract meaning, and cyber-security where message contents are analyzed as part of deep packet inspection, among others. The nice thing about this toolkit is that it can be used with BigInsights for Hadoop. This means you can build your textual extractions and insights at rest in Hadoop and then run them in real time as data is generated, thereby harvesting analytical insights found at rest and deploying them in motion. We talked about BigInsights for Hadoop and text analytics in Chapter 6.

The Mining Toolkit: Operators for Scoring Data Mining Models

The Mining Toolkit has operators to score several different types of data mining models in real time. Although data mining software such as SPSS requires multiple passes over data to build models, scoring can often be done on a record-by-record basis. The Data Mining Toolkit can score data mining models that are defined by the Predictive Model Markup Language (PMML) standard. This toolkit includes the following kinds of operators:

- **Classification**   Examples include support for Decision Trees, Naïve Bayes, and Logistic Regression algorithms that are used to classify tuples

- **Clustering**   Examples include support for Demographic Clustering and Kohonen Clustering algorithms that are used to assign tuples to a related group

- **Regression**   Examples include support for Linear Regression, Polynomial Regression, and Transform Regression algorithms that are used for predictive analytics

- **Associations**   Examples include support for association rules for predicting cause-and-effect relationships

In addition to scoring PMML models, Streams can score a wide range of algorithms that are exported by the SPSS Modeler Solution Publisher and Watson Analytics.

Solution Accelerators

IBM has also surfaced the most popular streaming data use cases as solution accelerators. For example, IBM provides a customizable solution accelerator known as the IBM Accelerator for Telecommunications Event Data Analytics, which uses Streams to process call detail records (CDRs) for telecommunications. A customizable solution accelerator known as the IBM Accelerator for Social Data provides analytics for lead generation and brand management based on social media.

Use Cases

To give you some insight into how Streams can fit into your environment, in this section we'll provide a few examples of use cases where Streams has provided transformative results. Obviously, we can't cover every industry in such a short book, but we think this section will get you thinking and excited about the breadth of possibilities that Streams technology can offer your environment.

In telecommunications companies, the quantity of CDRs their IT departments need to manage is staggering. Not only is this information useful for providing accurate customer billing, but a wealth of information can be gleaned from CDR analysis performed in near real time. For example, CDR analysis can help to prevent customer loss by analyzing the access patterns of "group leaders" in their social networks. These group leaders are people who might be in a position to affect the tendencies of their contacts to move from one service provider to another. Through a combination of traditional and social media analysis, Streams can help you to identify these individuals, the networks to which they belong, and on whom they have influence.

Streams can also be used to power up a real-time analytics processing (RTAP) campaign management solution to help boost campaign effectiveness, deliver a shorter time to market for new promotions and soft bundles, help to find new revenue streams, and enrich churn analysis. For example, Globe Telecom leverages information gathered from its handsets to identify the optimal service promotion for each customer and the best time to deliver it, which has had profound effects on its business. Globe Telecom reduced from 10 months to 40 days the time to market for new services, increased sales significantly through real-time promotional engines, and more.

Streams provides a huge opportunity for improved law enforcement and increased security and offers unlimited potential when it comes to the kinds of applications that can be built in this space, such as real-time situational awareness applications, multimodal surveillance, cyber-security detection, legal wire taps, video surveillance, and face recognition. Aelos, Inc., uses Streams to provide covert sensor surveillance systems that enable companies with sensitive facilities to detect intruders before they even get near the buildings or other sensitive installations. They've been the recipients of a number of awards for their technology (the Frost and Sullivan Award for Innovative Product of the Year for their Fiber Optic Sensor System Boarder Application, among others). Corporations can also leverage streaming analytics to detect and prevent cyber-attacks by streaming network logs and other system logs to stop intrusions or detect malicious activity anywhere in their networks. To this end, IBM has delivered industry-leading security solutions using its QRadar Security Intelligence Platform in tandem with Streams.

The financial services sector (FSS) and its suboperations are a prime example of how the analysis of streaming data can provide a competitive advantage (as well as regulatory oversight, depending on your business). The ability to analyze high volumes of trading and market data, at ultra-low latencies and across multiple markets and countries simultaneously, offers companies the microsecond reaction times that can make the difference between profit and loss through arbitrage trading and book of business risk analysis. For example, Algo(rithmic) Trading supports average throughput rates of about 12.7 million option market messages per second on a few servers and generates trade recommendations for its customers with a latency of 50 microseconds.

The amount of data being generated in the utilities industry is growing rapidly. Smart meters and sensors throughout modern energy grids are sending real-time information back to the utility companies at a staggering rate. The massive parallelism built into Streams enables this data to be analyzed in real time so that energy generators and distributors are able to modify the capacity of their electrical grids based on the changing demands of consumers. In addition, companies can include data on natural systems (such as weather or water management data) in the analytics stream to enable energy traders to predict consumption requirements and meet client demand. This approach can deliver competitive advantages and maximize company profits.

From smarter grids to Internet of Things to "Who's Talking to Whom?" analysis, and more, Streams use cases are nearly limitless.

Get Started Quickly!

We hope this chapter has gotten you excited enough to try Streams for yourself. To get going, try the InfoSphere Steams Quick Start Edition for free (either an installable package or pre-installed on a VMware Image). You can download this from the Downloads tab at the StreamsDev site: http://ibm .co/streamsdev. There are also other helpful materials on StreamsDev, such as tutorials, articles, and sample code.

Wrapping It Up

IBM InfoSphere Streams is an advanced analytic platform that allows user-developed applications to quickly ingest, analyze, and correlate information as it arrives from thousands of real-time sources. The solution can handle very high data throughput rates, up to millions of events or messages per second. InfoSphere Streams helps you to do the following:

- **Analyze data in motion**   Provides submillisecond response times, allowing you to view information and events as they unfold

- **Simplify development of streaming applications**   Uses an Eclipse-based integrated development environment (IDE), coupled with a declarative language, to provide a flexible and easy framework for developing applications; for non-programmers, there is a web-based drag and drop interface for building Streams applications

- **Extend the value of existing systems**   Integrates with your applications and supports both structured and unstructured data sources

In this chapter, we introduced you to the concept of data in motion and InfoSphere Streams, the world's fastest and most flexible platform for streaming data. The key value proposition of Streams is the ability to get analytics to the frontier of the business—transforming the typical forecast into a now-cast. We're starting to hear more buzz about streaming data of late, but the other offerings in this space are limited by capability and capacity and are often highly immature (one can create a storm of problems with data loss issues at high volumes). Streams is a proven technology with a large number of successful deployments that have helped transform businesses into leaders in their peer groups. In a Big Data conversation that seeks to go beyond the hype, Streams can help you overcome the speed and variety of the data arriving at your organization's doorstep—and just as important, you'll be able to easily develop applications to understand the data.

8

700 Million Times Faster Than the Blink of an Eye: BLU Acceleration

When you're thinking of market-disruptive technology buzz words, next to Hadoop, Internet of Things, and Big Data, in-memory columnar databases have to come to mind. BLU Acceleration from IBM is a next generation in-memory computing engine that does not require massive data sets to wholly fit into RAM in order to process the query. This feature makes the system more agile as data sets continue to grow in a Big Data world, but is surprisingly missing from many competing solutions available today. BLU Acceleration uses innovative and leading-edge technologies to optimize the underlying hardware stack of your on-premise or cloud hosted or managed resources and squarely addresses many of the shortcomings of existing columnar in-memory solutions. We call these technologies "big ideas" and discuss them later in this chapter. For example, BLU Acceleration can operate directly on compressed data, and it can intelligently and effortlessly skip data that is not relevant to the query—on disk, in memory, or even in the CPU!

BLU Acceleration is simple. We've seen clients engage with this easy-to-use technology and within hours achieve significant performance and compression results. For example, the University of Toronto experienced 106 times faster admission and enrollment workloads in its Cognos environment—from download to downright amazing in less than three hours! The university estimates that it has saved 42 days a year in hand-tuning exercises. Add load-and-go capabilities that make it easy to meet new end-user reporting needs, provision it on or off premise, and you have an in-memory computing technology that is fast, simple, and agile—you have what we would call a NextGen database technology—you have BLU Acceleration.

The first question we always get asked about BLU Acceleration is "What does BLU stand for?" The answer: nothing. We are sure it's somewhat related to IBM's "Big Blue" nickname, and we like that, because it is suggestive of big ideas and leading-edge solutions like Watson. The IBM research project behind BLU was called Blink Ultra, so perhaps that is it. With that in mind, you might also be wondering what IBM dashDB stands for, since BLU Acceleration and SoftLayer play a big role behind the scenes for this managed analytics cloud service. Don't let trying to figure out the acronyms keep you up at night; these technologies are going to let you sleep…like a baby.

The one thing we want you to understand about BLU Acceleration is that it is a technology and not a product. You are going to find this technology behind a number of IBM offerings—be they cloud-based services (such as dashDB) or on premise. For example, making BLU Acceleration technology available in the cloud is fundamental to empowering organizations to find more agile, cost-effective ways to deploy analytics.

GigaOM Research, in its May 2013 ditty on the future of cloud computing, noted that 75 percent of organizations are reporting some sort of cloud platform usage. Make no mistake about it: cloud adoption is happening now. We think that the coming years will be defined by the hybrid cloud; sure private clouds exist today, but so do public ones—ultimately, clients are going to demand that they cohesively work together in a hybrid cloud. Gartner does too. In its report last year on the breakdown of IT expenditures, it predicted that half of all large enterprises would have a hybrid cloud deployment by the end of 2017. It's simple: BLU Acceleration is readily available off premise; it's also available through a public cloud platform as a service (PaaS) offering aimed at developers (Bluemix) and eventually as a managed service in a software as a service (SaaS) model. BLU skies and billowy clouds sound like a perfect analytics forecast to us!

BLU Acceleration is the DNA behind the IBM Bluemix dashDB service (formerly known as the Analytics Warehouse service on Bluemix). It enables you to start analyzing your data right away with familiar tools—in minutes. The official IBM announcement notes that Bluemix is a PaaS offering based on the Cloud Foundry open source project that delivers enterprise-level features and services that are easy to integrate into cloud applications. We like to say that Bluemix is a PaaS platform where developers can act like kids in a sandbox, except that this box is enterprise-grade. You can get started with this service (along with hundreds of other IBM, non-IBM, and open source services that let you build and compose apps in no time at all) *for free* at https://bluemix.net.

Earlier we alluded to the fact that BLU Acceleration will also be found as part of a SaaS-based offering. You will often hear this type of usage referred to as a database as a service (DBaaS) offering or a data warehouse as a service offering (DWaaS). We envision dashDB being available in the future in multiple tiers through a DBaaS/DWaaS offering where you contract services that relate to the characteristics of the run time and how much control you have over them, their availability commitments, and so on, in a tiered service format. No matter what you call it, a DBaaS/DWaaS would deliver a *managed* (not just hosted like others in this space) turnkey analytical database service.

This service is cloud agile: It can be deployed in minutes with rapid cloud provisioning, it supports a hybrid cloud model, and there is zero infrastructure investment required. IBM dashDB is also simple like an appliance—without the loading dock and floorspace. It is just "load and go," and there is *no tuning required* (you will see why later in this chapter).

The data that you store in a data repository, enriched by BLU Acceleration, is memory and columnar optimized for incredible performance. And more importantly, when you are talking off premise, the data is enterprise secure. IBM's SoftLayer-backed as a service offerings exceed compliance standards and come with advanced compliance reporting, patching, and alerting capabilities that put the "Ops" into DevOps. They also provide the option for single-tenant operations where you can isolate yourself from the "noisy neighbor" effect. We cover dashDB, Bluemix, noisy neighbors, and other cloud computing concepts in Chapter 3.

BLU Acceleration technology is available on premise too. This is fundamental to IBM's *ground to cloud* strategy. We think that this is unique to IBM. The seamless manner in which it can take some workloads and burst them onto the cloud without changing the application (and this list of workloads is ever expanding) is going to be a lynchpin capability behind any organization that surges ahead of its peers. For example, suppose that an organization's quarter-end report stresses the on-premise infrastructure to such an extent that certain critical daily reports cannot finish on time. For 85 percent of the year, this organization's existing capital investment is more than enough, but for 15 percent of the year, they need double that amount! What would an IT-savvy organization do here? Would they double their capacity and try to do something with it during the majority off-peak times? We think that the smartest organizations would burst the extra processing to a managed public cloud service such as dashDB during those eight weeks in the year when the current investment isn't enough, transfer CAPEX costs to OPEX costs, and invest the rest in new insights.

If what goes up must come down, it is worth noting that there are going to be times when data is landed in the cloud and you want to ground it on premise. There could be many reasons for this. Perhaps it's a regulatory compliance issue, or perhaps you use the cloud to burst discovery, and when key insights are found, you land the data in the zone architecture that we talk about in Chapter 4. For example, you might be storing mobile data in IBM's Cloudant SaaS offering, the same technology that underpins the Cloudant NoSQL DB services on Bluemix. Now imagine having the ability to take the data that resides in this repository and being able to seamlessly populate an on-premise database such as DB2 with BLU Acceleration. You don't have to imagine this—you can do this today. You can also keep the data in the cloud and use an integrated service to populate a dashDB service and run analytics on the data there.

As previously mentioned, BLU Acceleration technology can be found on premise too. For example, BLU Acceleration is buried deep within the IBM Informix technology that accelerates warehousing, within its time series capabilities for solutions such as meter data management, and more. BLU Acceleration's first deeply embedded, but fully exposed, debut was in the DB2 10.5 release. Unlike other technologies where BLU Acceleration was helping but you didn't know it, DB2 10.5 was when BLU Acceleration stepped into the spotlight, like a "new" pop star who spent years writing hits for other people before finally taking center stage under their own name.

BLU Acceleration is deeply integrated with its host delivery vehicle (be it dashDB or DB2) and works in synergy with that software. You can see the undeniable value proposition and relief that DB2 with BLU Acceleration has offered on the SAP BW marketplace and harvested analytical reporting structures. DB2 recently debuted its DB2 Cancun Release 10.5.0.4 (we will just refer to it as the DB2 Cancun release), which introduces the concept of *shadow tables*. This innovation leverages BLU Acceleration technology directly on top of OLTP environments, which enables a single database to fulfill both reporting and transactional requirements—very cool stuff! The DB2 Cancun release also includes the ability to set up BLU Acceleration in an on-premise deployment by using DB2's High Availability and Disaster Recovery (HADR) integrated clustering software. In this chapter, we don't dive deeply into the use of BLU Acceleration in DB2 or dashDB—we talk about the BLU Acceleration technology and what makes it so special. Both Informix and DB2 technologies, and a whole lot more of the IBM Information Management portfolio, are available through IBM's PaaS and SaaS offerings and can also be deployed in IaaS environments.

Now think back to the application developers we talked about in Chapter 2—their quest for agility and how they want continuous feature delivery because the consumers of their apps demand it. In that same style, you will see most BLU Acceleration enhancements show up in dashDB before they are available in a traditional on-premise solution. This is all part of a *cloud-first* strategy that is born "agile" and drives IBM's ability to more quickly deliver Big Data analytic capabilities to the marketplace.

For example, the IBM PureData System for Analytics, powered by Netezza technology includes a suite of algorithms referred to as IBM Netezza Analytics—INZA. Over time you are going to see these deeply embedded statistical algorithms appear in the BLU Acceleration technology. In the dashDB public cloud service offerings, these kinds of new capabilities can be delivered more quickly and in a more continuous fashion when compared to traditional on-premise release vehicles. Perhaps it's the case that a number of phases are used to quickly deliver new capabilities. Netezza SQL compatibility with dashDB is also an example of a capability that could be continually delivered in this manner. We're not going to further discuss this topic in this chapter, although we do cover the INZA capabilities in Chapter 9. The point we are making is that a cloud delivery model allows your analytics service to get more capable on a continuum as opposed to traditional software release schedules. You can see the benefit for line of business (LOB) here: if the service is managed, you aren't applying code or maintenance upgrades; you are simply getting access to a continually evolving set of analytic capabilities through a service to empower your business to do new things and make better decisions.

This chapter introduces you to the BLU Acceleration technology. For the most part, we remain agnostic with respect to the delivery vehicle, whether you are composing analytic applications in the cloud on Bluemix or running on premise within DB2. We discuss BLU Acceleration from a business value perspective, covering the benefits our clients are seeing and also what we've personally observed. That said, we don't skip over how we got here. There are a number of ideas—really big ideas—that you need to be aware of to fully appreciate just how market-advanced BLU Acceleration really is, so we discuss those from a technical perspective as well.

What Is BLU Acceleration?

BLU Acceleration is all about capturing unrealized (or deriving new) value for your business from existing (and future) analytics-focused hardware, software, and human capital investments. BLU Acceleration is also about letting you ask questions and do things that you have not been able to do in the past. If you asked us to sum up all of the BLU Acceleration value propositions that we cover in this chapter by placing them into just three buckets (that we call *pillars*), they'd be named Next Generation (NextGen) Database Service for Analytics, Seamlessly Integrated, and Hardware Optimized.

What Does a Next Generation Database Service for Analytics Look Like?

The value that is associated with this first pillar was identified by a self-challenge for IBM research and development to define what technologies or attributes would be worthy of a service bucket list called Next Generation Database for Analytics. For example, you hear a lot these days about in-memory analytics, a proven mechanism to drive higher levels of performance. BLU Acceleration is about dynamic in-memory optimized analytics—its optimizations extend well beyond system memory so that, unlike some alternative technologies, all of the data that is required by a query doesn't have to fit into system memory to avoid massive performance issues. Some technologies return query errors if the data can't fit into memory, which isn't the case with BLU Acceleration; others are worse! BLU Acceleration uses in-memory processing to provide support for the dynamic movement of data from storage with intelligent prefetching. After all, we're in a Big Data era; if the cost of memory drops by X percent every year but the amount of data we're trying to store and analyze increases by Y percent (>X percent), a nondynamic, memory-only solution isn't going to cut it—you're going to come up short. This is why a NextGen technology needs to avoid the rigid requirement that all of the query's data has to fit into memory to experience super-easy, super-fast analytics. Of course, better compression can help to get more data into memory, but NextGen analytics can't be bound by memory alone; it needs to *understand* I/O. For this reason, we like to say that "BLU Acceleration is in-memory optimized *not* system memory constrained."

Although there is a lot of talk about just how fast in-memory databases are, this talk always centers around system memory (the memory area that some vendors demand your query data is not to exceed) compared to disk. System memory compared to disk is faster—it is way faster, even faster than solid-state disk (SSD) access. How much faster? About 166,666 times faster! But today's CPUs have memory too—various hierarchies of memory—referred to as L1, L2, and so on. The IBM Power 8 CPU, the nucleus of the OpenPower Foundation, leads all processor architectures in levels of CPU cache and size. CPU memory areas are even faster than system memory! How fast? If L1 cache were a fighter jet rocketing through the skies, system memory would be a cheetah in full stride. Not much of a race, is it? A Next-Gen database has to have prefetch and data placement protocols that are designed for CPU memory, include system memory, and also have provisions for SSD and plain old spinning disk; it has to make use of all of these tiers, move data between them with knowledge, purpose, optimization, and more. BLU Acceleration does this—be it in the cloud through the dashDB service or in a roll-your-own on-premise software deployment such as DB2. In fact, BLU Acceleration was built from the ground up to understand and make these very decisions in its optimizations.

Columnar processing has been around for a while and is attracting renewed interest, but it has some drawbacks that a NextGen platform must address. BLU Acceleration is about enhanced columnar storage techniques, and has the ability to support the coexistence of row-organized and column-organized tables.

A NextGen database should have what IBM refers to as *actionable compression*. BLU Acceleration has patented compression techniques that preserve order such that the technology almost always works on compressed data without having to decompress it first. Our research leads us to believe that no other database can match the breadth of operations that BLU Acceleration technology can perform on compressed data, which include (but are not limited to) equality processing (=, <>), range processing (BETWEEN, <=, <, =>, >), grouping, joins, and more.

A NextGen database that is geared toward analytics must find new and innovative ways to optimize storage that not only find disk space savings, but also optimize the I/O pipe and more. Although it is fair to note that the power and cooling costs that are associated with database storage have experienced double-digit compounded annual growth rates over the last few years and mitigation of these costs is an imperative in our Big Data world, that is not the whole story. Finding higher and higher compression ratios enables you to get more data into memory—effectively driving up in-memory yields because more data is in the memory-optimized part of the analytics server. BLU Acceleration does this too.

Making things easy to use and consume is a requirement for any NextGen technology. In our Big Data world, companies are facing steep learning curves to adopt new technologies (something that IBM is aggressively addressing with its toolkits and accelerators, but that's outside of the scope of this book). You want to get all of the benefits of a NextGen analytics engine with minimum disruption, and that's going to mean ensuring that impressive NextGen technology is consumable and simple to use, while delivering amazing performance and incredible compression ratios. We cover this topic in the next section.

A NextGen database also has to understand how IT assets are being consumed today and in the future. In consideration of this point, such a database has to be offered as an analytics service from an infrastructure as a service (IaaS), platform as a service (PaaS), and a fully managed software as a service (SaaS) such as IBM dashDB.

To sum up, a NextGen database needs to deliver out-of-the-box high performance for complex queries, groundbreaking storage savings, and ultimately flatten the cost of the analytics curve with an unapologetic focus on consumability. We also think that a NextGen database has to deliver quantum benefits without interfering with your operations. We're sure that by the time you are done reading this chapter, you will agree that BLU Acceleration is a NextGen analytics database.

Seamlessly Integrated

A NextGen in-memory database technology must be simple to use and must seamlessly integrate with your environment. In fact, on premise or off premise, BLU Acceleration comes with Cognos software to help you get going faster.

When it comes to DB2, the BLU Acceleration technology is not bolted on; it has been deeply integrated and is actually part of the product. BLU Acceleration is in DB2's DNA: This is not only going to give you administrative efficiencies and economies of scale, but risk mitigation as well. Seamless integration means that the SQL language interfaces that are surfaced to your applications are the same no matter how the table is organized. It means that backup and restore strategies and utilities such as LOAD and EXPORT are consistent. Consider that in DB2, BLU Acceleration is exposed to you as a simple table object—it is not a new engine, and that's why we say it is not bolted on. It is simply a new format for storing table data. Do not overlook that when you use DB2 with BLU Acceleration, it looks and feels just like the DB2 you have known for years, except that a lot of the complexity around tuning your analytic workloads has disappeared. If you compare DB2 with BLU Acceleration with some other vendor offerings, we are sure that you will quickly get a sense of how easy it is to use and why it doesn't leave DBAs "seeing red." We should mention that BLU Acceleration even supports some of the Oracle PL/SQL protocols and data types, which would make porting applications to any database that surfaces this technology easier too!

Another compelling fact that resonates with clients (and makes our competitors jealous) is that you don't have to rip and replace on-premise hardware investments to get all the benefits of BLU Acceleration. Some vendors are suggesting that there is no risk involved in upgrading your applications, swapping in a new database, retraining your DBAs, and tossing out your existing hardware to buy very specific servers that are "certified" for their software. Although some of this might not matter in the cloud, it all matters on the ground.

Hardware Optimized

The degree to which BLU Acceleration technology is optimized for the entire hardware stack is a very strong, industry-leading value proposition, which matters on or off premise. BLU Acceleration takes advantage of the latest processing technologies, such as parallel vector processing, which we detail later in this chapter. If you think about the traditional approaches to performance tuning, you're likely to focus on three areas: memory, CPU, and I/O. We don't know of any other vendor that has put as much engineering effort into optimizing all three hardware-provisioned computing resources for their in-memory database technology as IBM has done with BLU Acceleration.

Sure, there are other products in the marketplace that have an in-memory analytics solution, but our experience (and that of the clients we have been talking to) is that as soon as the data exceeds the memory allocation by a few bytes, those products keel over from a performance perspective, some "error out," and others do even worse! We've seen other database systems that claim they are I/O optimized; however, as more and more data is placed into memory, their advantage is mitigated. The point is that if your solution is focused on optimizing a single performance factor, you're going to end up with limitations and trade-offs.

BLU Acceleration optimizes the entire hardware stack, and it seeks every opportunity (memory, CPU, and I/O) to squeeze all that it can out of your hardware investment. As an analogy, think about your home computer, laptop, or even your smart phone. They all have multicore processing capabilities. Now ask yourself, "How much of the software that I've paid for has been developed from the ground up to fully exploit those cores?" If you have ever bought a new laptop with double the cores and memory of your old one, yet the application that you use all the time still runs at the same pace, you get the idea of where we are coming from. BLU Acceleration is designed to fully exploit all the computing resources that have been provisioned to the software (we detail this in the section "How BLU Acceleration Came to Be: Seven Big Ideas" later in the chapter).

Convince Me to Take BLU Acceleration for a Test Drive

In this section, we share our clients' experiences, which serve to illustrate just how disruptive (in a good way) the BLU Acceleration technology really is.

Pedal to the Floor: How Fast Is BLU Acceleration?

It is fast. Remember this motto: Super analytics, super easy. In both our internal and client performance tests, we have seen anywhere from single-digit to quadruple-digit performance speedups. Although your results are subject to a lot of variance (depending on your workload, your data, what server you are running on, on premise or off premise, and other things that you can imagine our lawyers want us to list here), you are going to hear about—and likely experience for yourself—headshaking performance speedups with minimal effort.

One member of the Blue Cross Blue Shield (BCBS) Association (a North American health insurance organization that has been in business for more than 80 years) had their DBA team with their SAS actuaries to offer them a different way to perform their analytics—they gave them BLU Acceleration. The result? They experienced incredible speedups in their analyses: One report ran 640 times faster, and another ran 1,200 times faster! At this point, our lawyers are really getting concerned, and although there are many clients experiencing triple- to quadruple-digit performance increases with their toughest analytic challenges, we will simply tell you that on average (we will define this soon) things are likely going to get faster with BLU Acceleration… a lot faster!

Ruel Gonzalez at DataProxy LLC (a technology provider for a nameplate auto manufacturer) loaded up one of his systems in BLU Acceleration and said, "Wow, unbelievable speedup in query run times! We saw a speedup of 273 times in our Vehicle Tracking report, taking its run time from 10 minutes to 2.2 seconds. That adds value to our business; our end users are going to be ecstatic!"

There is more. Taikang Life's Cognos reporting workloads improved 30-fold on average; Triton saw a 45-fold performance boost; Mindray, 50-fold; YonYou ERP accounting software ran 40 times faster, and TMW Systems saw a 128-fold performance improvement on average and one query ran 1552 times faster!

How fast will your queries run? A politician's answer: It depends. With that said, we are personally pretty comfortable suggesting that if you use BLU Acceleration for the right analytical workloads, you should expect to see, *on average*, a 25-fold performance improvement—or better—for your queries. That's a number that we feel will pacify our legal team, but prepare to be amazed.

Let's clarify what we mean by "average"—some clients witness mind-blowing quadruple performance speedups for single (typically their most difficult) queries, but we think it is most important to appreciate the average speedup of the query set, which is what we are referring to here.

Finally, keep this in mind: If a query that is running fast and within your service level agreement (SLA) runs faster, that is a nice benefit. However, it is the query that you have never been able to run before where the real value resides. We are convinced that you are going to find some of these with BLU Acceleration. The toughest queries are going to see the most benefit and are going to give you that jaw-dropping triple to quadruple performance boost. The same BCBS member that we mentioned earlier had an analyst drop a research hypothesis because the query that was used to test the hypothesis ran for three hours and seemed to run "forever" so he just stopped it. When the same query was loaded into BLU Acceleration, it completed in 10 seconds—that is 1,080 times faster!

From Minimized to Minuscule: BLU Acceleration Compression Ratios

You are going to hear a lot about the NextGen columnar technology that is being used in BLU Acceleration, and you'll likely correlate that with storage savings. Indeed, column organization can greatly reduce the database foot-print for the right kinds of tables, but there is more to it than that. BLU Acceleration is as much about what you do *not* get (or have to do) as what you get.

With BLU Acceleration, you do not get to create and experiment with various performance objects such as indexes or multidimensional clustering tables—almost all the storage that would have been required for secondary performance structures is no longer needed. In fact, if your trusted extract, transform, and load (ETL) processes have validated the uniqueness of your data, you do not even need to use storage to enforce uniqueness because BLU Acceleration includes informational uniqueness constraints. These constraints enable you to inform BLU Acceleration about the uniqueness of a row without persisting a secondary table object to strictly enforce that uniqueness. The bottom line is that all of these objects take up space, and because you are not going to need these objects when you use BLU Acceleration (and you are not enforcing uniqueness because a reliable ETL process has cleansed and validated the data), you are going to save lots of space. That said, if you want BLU Acceleration to enforce uniqueness, you can still create uniqueness constraints and primary keys on BLU Acceleration tables.

Just like performance results, compression ratios will vary. Our personal experiences lead us to believe that you will see, on average, about a 10-fold compression savings with BLU Acceleration (our lawyers hate it when we convey compression savings just like performance results). Later in this chapter we talk about how BLU Acceleration can achieve amazing compression ratios, but for now, let's share a couple of client experiences. Andrew Juarez, Lead SAP Basis and DBA at Coca-Cola Bottling Consolidated (CCBC), told us that "in our mixed environment (it includes both row- and column-organized tables in the same database), we realized an amazing 10- to 25-fold reduction in the storage requirements for the database when taking into account the compression ratios, along with all the things I no longer need to worry about: indexes, aggregates, and so on." So although baseline compression with BLU Acceleration was 10-fold, when the CCBC team took into account all the storage savings from the things that they no longer have to do (create indexes and so on), they found savings of up to 25-fold!

Just a word or two on compression ratios: The term *raw data* is used to describe the amount of data that is loaded into a performance warehouse; think of it mostly as the input files. The 10-fold compression that CCBC realized was on raw data. When you ask most people how large their warehouses or data marts are, they will tell you a number that includes performance tuning objects such as indexes. This is not raw data; we call this *fully loaded data*. The compression ratios that we discuss in this chapter are based on raw data (unless otherwise noted, such as the 25-fold savings achieved by CCBC). Because the difference between raw and fully loaded data can be quite astounding (sometimes double the raw data amount or more), ensure that you clarify what's being talked about whenever having discussions about the size of a database for any purpose, not just compression bragging rights.

Mike Petkau is the director of database architecture and administration at TMW Systems—an industry-leading provider of enterprise management software for the surface transportation services industry, including logistics, freight, trucking, and heavy-duty repair and maintenance. His team loaded one of TMW Systems' largest customer databases into BLU Acceleration and found that it produced "astounding compression results." TMW Systems found compression savings ranging from 7- to 20-fold when compared with its uncompressed tables. In fact, one of its largest and most critical operations tables saw a compression rate of 11-fold, and these measurements are only on raw data; in other words, they do not even account for the performance-tuning objects that they no longer need. We like how Mike summed up his BLU Acceleration experience: "These amazing results will save us a great deal of space on disk and memory."

Don't forget: BLU Acceleration has a wide spectrum of run-time optimizations for your analytics environment, and it has a holistic approach that we have yet to see any other vendor adopt. For example, the more concurrency you need for your analytic database, the more temporary (temp) space you're going to need. If a table spills into temp storage, BLU Acceleration might choose to automatically compress it if it's beneficial to the query. What's more, if BLU Acceleration anticipates that it will need to reference that large temp table again, it might compress it as well. So, although temp space is a definite requirement in an analytics environment, we want you to know that those unique benefits are not even accounted for in the experience of our clients. We don't know of another in-memory database technology that can intelligently autocompress temp space—a key factor in analytic performance.

Where Will I Use BLU Acceleration?

As enterprises begin to see the limits of their current enterprise data warehouse (EDW) and data mart technologies that are used to drive decision making, they are desperately looking for solutions. Typical challenges include latency, synchronization or concurrency problems, and scalability or availability issues. The offloading of or bursting data that supports online analytical processing (OLAP) from an EDW into an analytics mart (either through a managed service over the cloud or on premise) is an excellent opportunity to remedy these types of problems through the power of BLU Acceleration and your commercial off-the-shelf (COTS) analytics tool set.

Considering the value proposition that we shared with you in the last couple of sections, we're sure that you're eager to see what BLU Acceleration can do for you on or off premise. What's more, for your on-premise needs, since the DB2 Cancun Release 10.5.0.4 and its BLU Acceleration shadow tables became generally available, you can have a single database for both your OLTP and OLAP queries, making the decision to use DB2 with BLU Acceleration for on premise more compelling than ever!

BLU Acceleration simplifies and accelerates the analysis of data in support of business decisions because it empowers database administrators (DBAs) to effortlessly transform poorly performing analytic databases into super-performing ones, while at the same time insulating the business from front-end application and tool set changes. From a DBA's perspective, it is an instant performance boost—just load up the data in BLU Acceleration and go...analyze. Of course it empowers LOB (the future buyers of IT) to self-serve their BI, spinning up analytic data marts with swipes and gestures in minutes through the managed dashDB service. And don't forget how Bluemix offers developers the ability to effortlessly stitch in analytic services into their apps—no DBA required!

When the BLU Acceleration technology first made its debut, one of our early adopters, who works for one of the largest freight railroad networks in North America, told the press "...I thought my database had abended because a multimillion-row query was processed so fast." Think of that impact on your end users. BLU Acceleration makes your business agile too. Typical data marts require architectural changes, capacity planning, storage choices, tooling decisions, optimization, and index tuning; with BLU Acceleration, the simplicity of create, load, and go becomes a reality—it's not a dream.

There's been a lot of integration work with Cognos Business Intelligence (Cognos BI) and BLU Acceleration. For example, deploying a Cognos-based front end is done by simply modeling business and dimensional characteristics of the database and then deploying them for consumption by using Cognos BI's interactive exploration, dashboards, and managed reporting. BLU Acceleration technology flattens the time-to-value curve for Cognos BI (or any analytics tool sets for that matter) by decreasing the complexity of loading, massaging, and managing the data at the data mart level. This is one of the reasons why you will find BLU Acceleration behind the IBM Watson Anlaytics cloud service that we talked about in Chapter 1. We think that perhaps one of the most attractive features in BLU Acceleration and Cognos is that the Cognos engine looks at a BLU Acceleration database just like it does a row-organized database. Because they are both just tables in a data service to Cognos, a Cognos power user can convert underlying row-organized tables to BLU Acceleration without changing anything in the Cognos definitions; that's very cool!

Almost all LOBs find that although transactional data systems are sufficient to support the business, the data from these online transaction processing (OLTP) or enterprise resource planning (ERP) systems is not quickly surfaced to their units as actionable information; the data is "mysterious" because it is just not organized in a way that would suit an analytical workload. This quandary gives way to a second popular use case: creating local logical or separate physical marts directly off transactional databases for fast LOB reporting. Because BLU Acceleration is so simple to use, DBAs to LOBs can effortlessly spin up analytics-oriented data marts to rapidly react to business requirements. For example, consider a division's CMO who is sponsoring a certain marketing promotion. She wants to know how it is progressing and to analyze the information in a timely manner. BLU Acceleration empowers this use case: Data does not need to be indexed and organized to support business queries. As well, the data mart can now contain and handle the historical data that's continuously being spawned out of a system of record, such as a transactional database.

As you can see, BLU Acceleration is designed for data mart–like analytic workloads that are characterized by activities such as grouping, aggregation, range scans, and so on. These workloads typically process more than 1 percent of the active data and access less than 25 percent of the table's columns in a single query when it comes to traditional on-premise repositories—but BLU Acceleration isn't just limited to this sweet spot. A lot of these environments are characterized by star and snowflake schemas and will likely be top candidates to move to BLU Acceleration, but these structures are not required to benefit from this technology.

With the DB2 Cancun release and its shadow tables, you no longer need to spin off physical data marts, unless you want to, of course—and there are still really good reasons to do so—more on that in a bit. Be careful not to overlook the incredible opportunity if you are an on-premise BLU Acceleration user. You really do have the best of both worlds with this offering. BLU Acceleration shadow tables enable you to have your operational queries routed seamlessly to your collocated row-organized tables and your analytical queries routed to your collocated logical marts through shadow tables in the same database!

There aren't many compromises to be made here: Keep your industry-leading OLTP performance and get world-class OLAP analytic performance in the same database when deploying DB2 with BLU Acceleration! Piqued your interest? You'll learn more about shadow tables a bit later in this chapter.

How BLU Acceleration Came to Be: Seven Big Ideas

The number seven is pretty special in almost any domain. If you're a numbers person, it is a base and double Mersenne prime, a factorial prime, and a safe prime. If you study the Christian bible, you will find the seven days of Genesis, the seven Seals of Revelation, and more. Art aficionado? The Group of Seven means something to you. Mythologists have their seven heavens, and if you are a music lover and fan of Queen, you have undoubtedly heard their hit song "Seven Seas of Rhye." There also happen to be seven "big ideas" that served as guiding principles behind the BLU Acceleration design points, which we cover in this section.

Big Idea #1: KISS It!

Although we are sure that you are going to want to kiss the people behind BLU Acceleration when you get a chance to take it for a test drive, this big idea was to ensure that our dev teams gave it a KISS—"Keep it simple, Sweetie." (We might have used a different word than Sweetie in our instructions to the teams, but we will leave it at that.) The point was to keep BLU Acceleration super easy to use; we didn't want dozens of parameter controls, required application changes, forklift migration of existing skills, mandated hardware investments, or for DBAs to have to decide what data is hot and partition that data to fit into memory, and so on. We also wanted the technology to be modular, in that it wasn't tied to a particular offering. Finally, it had to be cloud-ready and cloud-consumable.

Keeping it simple was the key behind the "Super Analytics, Super Easy" BLU Acceleration tagline. In fact, the simplicity of BLU Acceleration is one of its key value propositions. If you were to have a conversation with us about the administration of the BLU Acceleration technology in an on-premise deployment, you would find that we spend more time telling you what you do not have to do instead of what you have to do. How cool is that? First, there's no physical design tuning to be done. In addition, operational memory and storage attributes are automatically configured for you. Think about the kinds of things that typically reside in a DBA's toolkit when it comes to performance tuning and maintenance. These are the things you are not going to do with BLU Acceleration, even if you are not using it through a hosted managed service such as dashDB. You are not going to spend time creating indexes, creating aggregates, figuring out what columns are hot, implementing partitioning to get the hot data into memory, reclaiming space, collecting statistics, and more. This is why BLU Acceleration is so appealing. None of this is needed to derive instant value from the BLU Acceleration technology— be it on premise or off premise. From a DBA's perspective, you "load and go" and instantly start enjoying performance gains, compression savings, and the ability to do things that you could never do before. Now compare that to some of our competitors that make you face design decisions like the ones we just outlined.

Big Idea #2: Actionable Compression and Computer-Friendly Encoding

The second big idea behind BLU Acceleration pertains to how it encodes and compresses data and the way that it "packs" the CPU registers. Quite simply, BLU Acceleration has the ability to operate on the data while it's still compressed (yes, you read that right). There's more to this idea that isn't obvious—the encoding has a trick or two up its sleeve and we will give you some insights here.

Why would you want to do this, and more so, why is this a big idea? First, if the data is smaller, you can put more of it into memory. However, if you can save the most space on the data that is repeated the most, you are going to expend even fewer computing resources to work on the data that you use the most. Now, since we know that BLU Acceleration can operate on data while it is still compressed, not only will the on-premise or off-premise run times realize more memory savings, but it will also save on all those CPU cycles that would have gone into decompressing the data just to perform predicate evaluations, among other operations that we outlined earlier in this chapter. For example, BLU Acceleration technology can apply equality and inequality predicates on compressed data *without* spending CPU cycles to decompress that data on disk or in memory; as you can imagine, this is valuable for range queries (for example, "Give me the run rate percentage and year-over-year dollar growth of revenue for Canada between 2012 and 2014").

The way that BLU Acceleration is able to work on compressed data comes from the way it encodes the data—*both* on disk and in memory. BLU Acceleration's fundamental approach to compression is a variation of Huffman encoding. Huffman encoding looks for the symbols that occur most frequently and gives them a shorter representation. Think of it this way: Something that appears many times should be compressed more than other things that do not appear as often, regardless of its size. This encoding method yields impressive compression ratios. Using approximate Huffman encoding as its base, BLU Acceleration adds several other compression methods to eke out a supertight form factor for its data.

Consider a compressed `Last_Name` column in a table that tracks complaints for a certain airline carrier. The name of a frequent complainer (with four registered complaints), Zikopoulos, has ten characters in it, but as you can see on the left side of Figure 8-1, it's using a smaller encoding scheme than Huras, which has only five characters and two registered complaints. Notice that Lightstone is the same length as Zikopoulos, but since this traveler has only one complaint, it has the largest bit-encoded representation of them all.

This encoding is dynamic in nature. This is a really important point: Data values in BLU Acceleration are compressed and said to be *order preserving*, which means they can be compared to each other *while they are still compressed*. For example, assume the value `50000` compresses to a symbol like `10` (for simplicity's sake) and `20000` compresses to `01`. These two values are

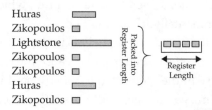

Figure 8-1 *A representation of how BLU Acceleration encodes and packs the CPU register for optimal performance and compression*

said to be ordered (`01` is less than `10` because `20000` is less than `50000`). As a result, the BLU Acceleration query engine can perform a lot of predicate evaluations without decompressing the data. A query such as `select * ...` `where C1 < 50000` using this example becomes `select * ... where C1` `< 10`. In our example, BLU Acceleration would filter out the values that are greater than `50000` *without* having to decompress (materialize) the data. Quite simply, the fact that BLU Acceleration has to decompress only qualifying rows is a tremendous performance boost. Specifically, note how instead of decompressing all the data to see whether it matches the predicate (`<` `50000`), which could potentially require decompressing billions of values, BLU Acceleration will simply compress the predicate into the encoding space of the column. In other words, it compresses `50,000` to `10` and then performs the comparisons on the compressed data—using smaller numbers (such as `10` compared to `50000`) results in faster performance for comparison operations, among others. That's just cool!

The final tenet of this big idea pertains to how the data is handled on the CPU: BLU Acceleration takes the symbols' bits and packs them as tightly as possible into *vectors*, which are collections of bits that match (as closely as possible) the width of the CPU register; this is what you see on the right side of Figure 8-1 (although the figure is intentionally oversimplified and intended to not reveal all of our secrets, we think you will get the gist of what the technology is doing). This is a big deal because it enables BLU Acceleration to flow the data (in its compressed form) into the CPU with *maximum* efficiency. It's like a construction yard filling a dump truck with dirt that is bound for some landfill—in this case the dirt is the data and the landfill is a data mart. Is it more efficient to send the dump truck away loaded to the brim with dirt or to load it halfway and send it on its way? You'd be shocked at how many of the competing technologies send trucks half full, which is not only inefficient, it's not environmentally friendly either.

To sum up, all of the big idea components in this section will yield a synergistic combination of effects: better I/O because the data is smaller, which leads to more density in the memory (*no matter* what hierarchy of memory you are using), optimized storage, and more efficient CPU because data is being operated on without decompressing it *and* it is packed in the CPU "register aligned." This is all going to result in much better—we say *blistering*—performance gains for the right workloads.

Big Idea #3: Multiplying the Power of the CPU

The third big idea has its genesis in the exploitation of a leading-edge CPU technology found in today's modern processors: single-instruction multiple data (SIMD). SIMD instructions are low-level CPU instructions that enable you to perform the same operation on multiple data points at the same time. If you have a relatively new processor in your laptop or home computer, chances are it is SIMD enabled, because this technology was an inflection point for driving rich multimedia applications.

BLU Acceleration will autodetect whether it is running on an SIMD-enabled CPU (for example, a qualifying Power or Intel chip) and *automatically* exploit SIMD to effectively multiply the power of the CPU. Automation is a recurring theme in BLU Acceleration; it automatically detects and senses its environment and dynamically optimizes the run time accordingly. Because SIMD instructions are low-level specific CPU instructions, BLU Acceleration can use a single SIMD instruction to get results from multiple data elements (perform equality predicate processing, for example) as long as they are in the same register. For example, imagine the performance benefit of being able to put 128 bits or more into an SIMD register and evaluate all of that data with a single instruction! This is why this big idea is so important: Being able to compress data as much as possible, compress the most commonly occurring data, and then optimally pack it at register widths (big idea #2) reveals the synergy that lies at the core of this big idea. From what we know, IBM Power 8 processors have the widest CPU registers in the market today, so you can really see pronounced benefits of this big idea on those servers; however, all CPU manufacturers are pushing the width of their registers, so you will experience benefits everywhere. It's also worth noting that for some processor architectures that don't have SIMD capabilities (such as Power 6 chips), BLU Acceleration will emulate SIMD operations using software to boost its performance on these architectures. What a contrast to "rip and replace" forced hardware migrations—BLU Acceleration lets you exploit even older generation hardware to stretch the return on your IT investments to the limit!

Figure 8-2 illustrates the power of SIMD using a scan operation that involves a predicate evaluation. Although Figure 8-2 shows a predicate evaluation, we want you to be aware that SIMD exploitation can be used for join operations, arithmetic, and more—it's not just a scan optimization. This is yet another differentiator between BLU Acceleration and some other in-memory database technologies that are available in today's marketplace. On the right side of this figure, we show four column values being processed at one time. Keep in mind this is only for illustration purposes because it is quite possible to have more than four data elements processed by a single instruction with this technology.

Contrast the left side (without SIMD) of Figure 8-2 with the right side (with SIMD), which shows an example of how predicate evaluation processing would work if BLU Acceleration were not engineered to automatically detect, exploit, and optimize SIMD technology, or implement big idea #2 to optimally encode and pack the CPU register with data. In such an environment, instead of optimally packing the register width, things just happen the way they do in so many competing technologies: Each value is loaded one at a time into its own register for predicate evaluation. As you can see on the left side of Figure 8-2, other data elements queue up for predicate evaluation, each requiring distinct processing cycles that waste resources by having to schedule the execution of that work on the CPU, context switches, and so on.

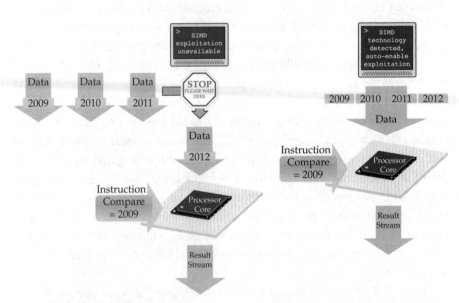

Figure 8-2 *Comparing predicate evaluations with and without SIMD in a CPU packing-optimized processing environment such as BLU Acceleration*

In summary, big idea #3 is about multiplying the power of the CPU for the key operations that are typically associated with analytic query processing, such as scanning, joining, grouping, and arithmetic. By exploiting low-level instructions that are available on modern CPUs and matching that with optimizations for how the data is encoded and packed on the CPU's registers (big idea #2), BLU Acceleration literally multiplies the power of the CPU: A single instruction can get results on multiple data elements with relatively little run-time processing. The big ideas discussed so far compress and encode the data and then pack it into a set of vectors that matches the width of the CPU register as closely as possible. This gives you the biggest "bang" for every CPU "buck" (cycles that the on-premise or off-premise servers on which the technology is running consume). BLU Acceleration literally squeezes out every last drop of CPU that it can wherever it is running.

Big Idea #4: Parallel Vector Processing

Multicore parallelism and operating on vectors of data with extremely efficient memory access is a powerful idea that delivers on something in which you have already invested for a long time: exploiting the growing number of processing cores on a server's socket. Central to this big idea is that BLU Acceleration was designed to be extraordinarily diligent in leveraging the processing cores that are available to it. Where should data be placed in a cache that will be revisited? Should this data flush out of a CPU cache into system memory, or will it be needed again...soon? How should work be shipped across sockets? These are just a couple of examples of the optimization considerations that are baked into BLU Acceleration algorithms and that work behind the scenes to astonish its users.

This big idea is about BLU Acceleration using the "Kill It with Iron" (KIWI) technique to optimize its on-premise or off-premise run times. KIWI starts with the fact that we all know that the CPU core counts on today's (and tomorrow's) servers are going to continue to increase. While other vendors are talking about in-memory databases, the BLU Acceleration value proposition declares that memory is too darn slow! System memory access is something to be avoided (we get it: This message is completely different from what you are hearing from other vendors today).

BLU Acceleration is designed to access data on disk rarely, access RAM (the area that the majority of in-memory database providers focus on) occasionally, and attempt to do the overwhelming bulk of its processing on data and instructions that reside in a CPU cache. This is the race between the F14 fighter jet (L1 cache) and the cheetah (system RAM) we touched on earlier in this chapter.

BLU Acceleration has been engineered to pay careful attention to CPU cache affinity and memory management so that the majority of memory access occurs in a CPU cache and not by accessing data from system RAM over and over again. By operating in a manner that almost exclusively tries to keep data in a CPU cache and not in RAM, BLU Acceleration minimizes the "latency" and is able to keep the server CPUs on which it runs busy. We've seen a lot of benefit from the work that we've done in this area and have personally seen excellent scalability between 32- and 64-way parallelism—where even a single query can exploit 64 cores of shared memory with almost perfect scalability. Parallelizing a single query 64 ways is impossible for most database technologies.

In summary, big idea #4 recognizes that servers have an increasingly larger number of cores with more and more levels of cache and memory. BLU Acceleration is designed from the ground up to take advantage of the cores that you have and to always drive multicore parallelism for your queries. Its focus on efficient parallel processing with memory-conscious algorithms enables you to fully utilize the power of multiple CPU cores along with their respective memory areas. In fact, we feel our marketing teams may have erred in classifying BLU Acceleration as an in-memory database, but we get it—it's a market segment. If it were up to us, we would have called BLU Acceleration an in-CPU-cache database.

Big Idea #5: Get Organized...by Column

Big idea #5 reminds us of a pocket square for a men's suit. It's a trendy concept of late, despite being around for a long time: *column store*. From the database world to the Hadoop world, the columnar storage format is excellent for certain kinds of data. That said, test after test demonstrates the *inefficiency* of current columnar formats for high-volume transactional processing. (We are definitely aware of some vendor claims out there; but we've seen the details of clients that have tested these claims and the performance issues that arise when transactional activity occurs on their columnar storage format.)

Essentially, this big idea for BLU Acceleration is to bring all of the typical benefits of columnar stores (such as I/O minimization through elimination, improved memory density, scan-based optimizations, compelling compression ratios, and so on) to modern-era analytics. What makes BLU Acceleration so special is not just that it is a column store; indeed, many claim to be and are...just that. Rather, it is how the BLU Acceleration technology is implemented with the other big ideas detailed in this chapter.

With all the focus on columnar these days, we took a leap of faith and assume that you have the gist of what a column-organized table is, so we won't spend too much time describing it here. To ensure that we are all on the same page, however, Figure 8-3 shows a simplified view of a row-organized table (on the left) and a column-organized table (on the right). As you can see, a column-organized table stores its data by column instead of by row. This technique is well suited to warehousing and analytics scenarios.

With a columnar format, a single page stores the values of just a single column, which means that when a database engine performs I/O to retrieve data, it performs I/O for only the columns that satisfy the query. This can save a lot of resources when processing certain kinds of queries, as well as sparse or highly repeating data sets.

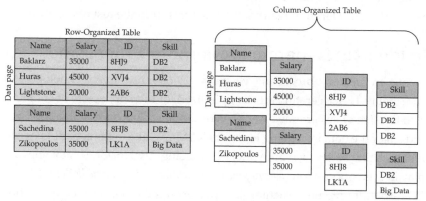

Figure 8-3 *Comparing row-organized and column-organized tables*

Columnar Is Good: BLU Acceleration Engineering Makes It Better

BLU Acceleration uses columnar technology to store data on disk *and* in memory—not all vendors do the in-memory part. However, by combining that with all the big ideas detailed so far, we think it gives BLU Acceleration big advantages over our competitors. By using a column store with encoding, BLU Acceleration is able to get an additional level of compression that leads to even more downstream I/O minimization. In addition, recall that BLU Acceleration is able to perform predicate evaluation (among other operations) without having to decompress the data by using its actionable compression capabilities, and that even further reduces the amount of I/O and processing that needs to be performed. What's more, with this technology, the rows are not accessed or even "stitched" back together until absolutely necessary—and at the latest possible moment in a query's processing lifecycle for that matter. This process of combining the columns as late as possible is called *late materialization*.

To sum up, column store is *a part of* BLU Acceleration, and it is leveraged to help minimize I/O (performing I/O only on those columns and values that satisfy the query) and delivers better memory density (columnar data is kept compressed in memory in the same format) and extreme compression. However, it is only when you understand how it is mixed with other big ideas, such as packing the data into scan-friendly structures and order preserving encoding techniques (among others), that you truly start to appreciate how BLU Acceleration really sets itself apart from the rest of the industry.

Big Idea #6: Dynamic In-Memory Processing

Dynamic in-memory processing covers a set of innovative technologies to ensure that BLU Acceleration is truly optimized for memory access but not limited to the size of system memory (RAM)—because, let's face it, in a Big Data world, all of the data isn't going to fit into RAM. We like to think of BLU Acceleration as being better than in-memory processing. Two major technologies are at play in this concept: *scan-friendly memory caching* and *dynamic list prefetching*.

Scan-friendly memory caching is a powerful idea that, to the best of our knowledge, is unique to BLU Acceleration. Effectively caching data in memory has historically been difficult for systems that have more data than memory. With BLU Acceleration, not only can the data be larger than allocated RAM, the technology is *very* effective at keeping the data in memory, which allows for efficient reuse and minimizing I/O; this is true even in cases where the working set and individual scans are larger than the available memory. BLU Acceleration's scan-friendly memory caching is an automatically triggered cache-replacement algorithm that provides egalitarian access, and it is something new and powerful for analytics. How that translates for your business users who don't really care about technology details is that performance won't "fall off the cliff" when a query's data requirements are bigger than the amount of memory that is available on the provisioned server—be it on the ground or in the cloud.

The *analytics-optimized page replacement* algorithm that is associated with BLU Acceleration assumes that the data is going to be highly compressed and will require columnar access and that it is likely the case that all of this active data (or at least 70 to 80 percent of it) is going to be put into memory. When surveying our clients, we found that the most common memory-to-disk ratios was about 15 to 50 percent. Assuming a conservative 10-fold compression rate, there is still a high probability that you are going to be able to land most (if not all) of your active data in memory when you use a data store with BLU Acceleration technology. However, although we expect most, if not all, of the active data to fit in memory for the majority of environments, we don't require it, unlike the technology sold by a certain ERP vendor-turned-database provider. When DB2 accesses column-organized data, it will automatically use its scan-friendly memory-caching algorithm to decide which pages should stay in memory to minimize I/O, as opposed to using the ubiquitous least recently used (LRU) algorithm, which is good for OLTP but not optimized for analytics.

The second aspect of dynamic in-memory processing is a new prefetch technology called *dynamic list prefetching.* You will find that the prefetching algorithms for BLU Acceleration have been designed from scratch for its columnar parallel vector-processing engine.

These algorithms take a different approach because BLU Acceleration does not have indexes to tell it what pages are interesting to the query (list prefetching), which would be a common case with a traditional database technology. Of course, almost any database could simply prefetch every page of every column that appears in a query, but that would be wasteful. BLU Acceleration addresses this challenge with an innovative strategy to prefetch only a subset of pages that are interesting (from a query perspective), *without* the ability to know far in advance what they are. We call this *dynamic list prefetching* because the specific list of pages cannot be known in advance through an index.

To sum up, remember that one of the special benefits of BLU Acceleration in comparison to traditional in-memory columnar technologies is that performance doesn't "fall off the cliff" if your data sets are so large that they won't fit into memory. If all of your data *does* fit into memory, it is going to benefit you, but in a Big Data world, that is not always going to be the case, and this important BLU Acceleration benefit should not be overlooked. Dynamic memory optimization and the additional focus on CPU cache exploitation truly do separate BLU Acceleration from its peers.

Big Idea #7: Data Skipping

The seventh (but not final because we are sure more ideas are coming as we enhance this technology in subsequent releases) big idea that inspired BLU Acceleration is *data skipping.* The idea is simple: We wanted BLU Acceleration to be able to skip over data that is of no interest to the active query workload, automatically, without any effort. For example, if a query is to calculate the sum of last month's sales, there is no need to look at any data that is older than last month. With data-skipping technology, BLU Acceleration can *automatically* skip over the nonqualifying data because it keeps metadata that describes the minimum and maximum range of data values on "chunks" of the data that translates to how the data is stored…anywhere, disk or memory.

This idea enables BLU Acceleration to automatically detect large sections of data that simply are not needed by the query and effectively ignore all that data *without* having to process it. Data skipping can deliver an order of magnitude in savings across compute resources (CPU, RAM, and I/O). Of course, in keeping with the *Super Easy* part of the BLU Acceleration mantra we have been chanting throughout this book, this metadata is automatically maintained during data ingestion operations such as load, insert, update, and delete, so you don't have to worry about defining or maintaining it.

BLU Acceleration's data skipping is conceptually similar to the ZoneMap technology that is found in the PureData System for Analytics (powered by

Netezza technology) that we cover in Chapter 9. We say similar because unlike ZoneMaps, this metadata is not tied to any particular page or extent boundary—it is tied to a certain "chunk" of data records (about 1,000). Because data skipping enables a query to skip over ranges of uninteresting data, BLU Acceleration is able to avoid touching this data, *whether it is on disk or in memory*, during query execution. Data-skipping metadata is actually kept in a tiny column-organized table called a *synopsis table*, which is automatically maintained, loaded, and persisted into memory when needed. This metadata is extremely valuable because it empowers BLU Acceleration to save precious compute resources by enabling the database engine to intelligently and accurately skip over data that is not needed; this saves I/O and keeps the system's memory filled with useful active data rather than data that the query doesn't actually need. Of course, all this means is that more memory is available for more of the important data that you really want to analyze.

How Seven Big Ideas Optimize the Hardware Stack

If you have spent any amount of time performance tuning a database, you know that there are three things you always care about: memory, CPU, and I/O. You iterate through various approaches to remove bottlenecks in any of these hardware attributes to find higher and higher levels of performance. The driving force behind many of the amazing results coming from the BLU Acceleration technology was a relentless focus on hardware exploitation. Figure 8-4 summarizes the seven big ideas from the perspective of squeezing every last ounce of compute resources from the supporting hardware stack. This is important, whether you deploy in an on-premise CAPEX-focused environment or an off-premise OPEX-focused one. For example, in an IaaS environment, such as the one that is provisioned by IBM SoftLayer, you want to get the best bang for your buck. But even in a managed service environment such as dashDB, you'd like to think that absolutely everything is being done to optimize provisioned compute resources by that managed service provider to deliver the best performance for the money you are spending; Figure 8-4 shows this.

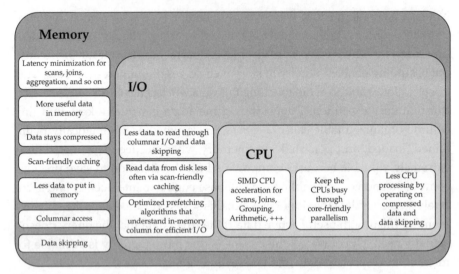

Figure 8-4 *Looking at BLU Acceleration's seven big ideas from a compute resources perspective: the hardware stack*

The Sum of All Big Ideas: BLU Acceleration in Action

Now it is time to bring all of the big ideas together and experience how they have been integrated into an exceptional analytics engine by working through a typical example in analytics processing. As always, "your mileage will vary," depending on the kind of data you're storing, your server, the queries you're running, and so on.

To be honest, LOB workers and data scientists likely don't know or care about BLU Acceleration; when these folks hear "column," they think Excel as opposed to a database storage format and wonder why the data isn't local on their laptop in the first place. The analyst has questions, and he or she only cares about getting the answers fast. If you're trying to empower an analyst, consider this experience.

We started with the assumption that you have provisioned a 32-core server and you have a corpus of 10 years of data (2004 to 2013) that is ready to be loaded into a relatively wide (100-column) table. Before loading the data, the on-disk *raw* footprint of this data is 10TB. An analyst wants to run a simple query that counts all of the new customers that were added to the company's loyalty program through various client profile acquisition campaigns (web, mailings, and so on) that were run in a specific year. Using a favorite tool or service and without any idea what BLU Acceleration is, the analyst composes the following query: `select count(*) from LOYALTYCLIENTS where year = '2012'`.

The BLU Acceleration goal is to provide the analyst with subsecond response times from this single nonpartitioned, 32-core server *without* creating any indexes or aggregates, partitioning the data, and so on. When we tabled this scenario to a group of LOB users (without mentioning the BLU Acceleration technology), they laughed at us. We did the same thing in front of a seasoned DBA with one of our biggest clients, and she told us, "Impossible, not without an index!" Figure 8-5 shows how the seven big ideas worked together to take an incredible opportunity and turn it into something truly special.

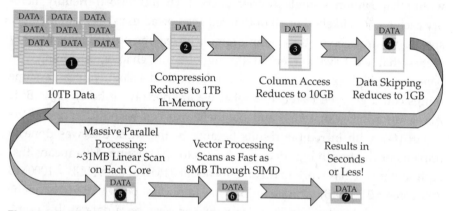

Figure 8-5 *How some of the seven big BLU Acceleration ideas manifest into incredible performance opportunities*

The example starts with 10TB of *raw* data (❶) that is sitting on a file system waiting to be loaded into an analytics repository with BLU Acceleration. Although we have shared with you higher compression ratio experiences from our clients, this example uses the average order of magnitude (10-fold) reduction in the raw data storage requirements that most achieve with BLU Acceleration's encoding and compression techniques. This leaves 1TB (❷) of data. Note that there are not any indexes or summary tables here. In a typical data warehouse, 10TB of raw data is going to turn into a 15- to 30-TB footprint by the time these traditional kinds of performance objects are taken into account. In this example, the 10TB of data is *raw* data. It is the size before the data is aggregated, indexed, and so on. When it is loaded into a BLU Acceleration table, that 10TB becomes 1TB.

The analyst's query is looking only for loyalty members acquired in 2012. YEAR is just one column in the 100-column LOYALTYCLIENTS table. Because BLU Acceleration needs to access only a single column in this table, you can divide the 1TB of loaded data by 100. Now the data set is down to 10GB (❸) of data that needs to be processed. However, BLU Acceleration is not finished applying its seven big ideas yet! While it is accessing this 10GB of data using its columnar algorithms, it also applies the data-skipping big idea to skip over the other nine years of data in the YEAR column. At this point, BLU Acceleration skips over the nonqualifying data without any decompression or evaluation processing. There is now 1GB (❹) of data that needs to be worked on: BLU Acceleration is left looking at a single column of data and, within that column, a single discrete interval. Thanks to scan-friendly memory caching, it is likely that all of that data can be accessed at main memory speeds (we are keeping the example simple by leaving out the CPU memory caches that we have referenced throughout this chapter; assuming you believe that high-speed bullet trains are faster than a sloth, you can assume things could go even faster than what we are portraying here). Now BLU Acceleration takes that 1GB and parallelizes it across the 32 cores on the server (❺), with incredible results because of the work that was done to implement the fourth big idea: parallel vector processing. This means that each server core has work to do on only about 31MB of data (1GB = 1000MB / 32 cores = 31.25MB). Don't overlook this important point that might not be obvious: BLU Acceleration is *still operating on compressed* data at this point, and nothing has been materialized. It is really important to remember this, because all of the CPU, memory density, and I/O benefits *still* apply.

BLU Acceleration now applies the other big ideas, namely, actionable compression (operating on the compressed data, carefully organized as vectors that automatch the register width of the CPU wherever the technology is running) and leveraging SIMD optimization (❻). These big ideas take the required scanning activity to be performed on the remaining 32MB of data and make it run several times faster than on traditional systems. How fast? We think you already know the answer to that one—*it depends*. The combined benefits of actionable compression and SIMD can be profound. For the sake of this example, you can assume that the speedup over traditional row-based systems is four times faster per byte (we think it is often much higher, but we are being conservative—or rather, being told to be). With this in mind, the server that is empowered by BLU Acceleration has to scan only about 8MB (32MB / 4 speedup factor = 8MB) of data compared to a traditional system. Think about that for a moment. Eight megabytes is about the size of a high-quality digital image that you can capture with your smartphone. A modern CPU can chew through that amount of data in less than a second... no problem. The end result? BLU Acceleration took a seemingly impossible challenge on 10TB of raw data and was able to run a typical analytic query on it in less than a second by using the application of seven big ideas and BLU Acceleration technology (❼).

DB2 with BLU Acceleration Shadow Tables: When OLTP + OLAP = 1 DB

Up until this point, we have discussed all the cool things that make up BLU Acceleration. Now we take you through a scenario where we use BLU Acceleration to give you performance advantages on OLAP queries while still maintaining your on-premise OLTP performance in the same database. We call this *enhancement DB2 shadow tables*.

The concept behind this innovation is keeping your transactional data in place and running analytics in the same environment. This is often done by carving off a data mart (and that is not always a bad thing). With DB2 shadow tables, you have the ability (as of DB2 10.5.0.4) to keep a single database environment and get the best of both worlds.

What Lurks in These Shadows Isn't Anything to Be Scared of: Operational Reporting

Analytics on transactional data environments (often referred to as OLTP environments) are those in which both transactional and analytical SQL execution occur on the *same database*. (Analytical requirements are often referred to as OLAP workloads to keep things simple; however, when we use this term in this chapter, we are referring to reporting as well as other operations that fall within the analytics domain.) Traditionally, most are reluctant to use this approach because there are unacceptable performance trade-offs; what's typically lurking in this shadow is a broken SLA and that is scary. For example, a highly indexed OLTP database that is being used for analytics is going to incur a lot of overhead when rows are inserted, updated, or deleted because all of the supporting analytical indexes have to be maintained. Of course, if you did not have those indexes, then reporting requirements would result in full-table scans and kill the performance of your analytic workloads and put at risk the OLTP transactions that require seconds-or-less performance.

Because of these trade-offs, IT shops typically take data from their transactional system and extract, transform, and load that data into some kind of analytical reporting system that is exposed to the LOB. The disadvantage of this approach is that it can often require a complex ETL setup and massive data movement between different systems. There are data time lags (different degrees of freshness of the data on the OLAP system as compared to the real-time OLTP system), and the complexity of managing multiple systems can be a nightmare.

Figure 8-6 shows a simplified high-level architectural view of a traditional analytical environment. You can see in this figure that an OLAP database is

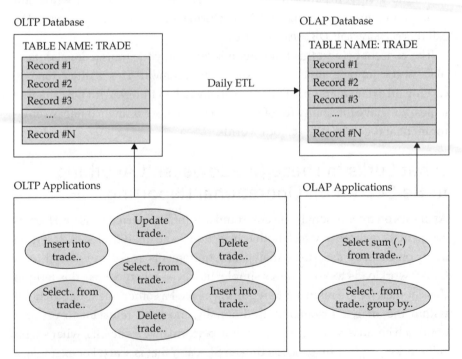

Figure 8-6   *A traditional analytic environment where data from a transactional source is moved to another database for reporting and analytics purposes*

sourced from an OLTP database and has periodic refresh cycles to bring the reporting and analytics data up to date.

Although this common approach is effective, having different data in two systems and needing to refresh the data daily has its disadvantages, as mentioned earlier. You can see how this environment could get wildly complex if we expanded the OLAP database to tens if not hundreds of marts (quite typical in a large enterprise) for LOB reporting. Suppose there is a schema change in the OLTP database; that would create an enormous trickle-down change from the ETL scripts and processes to the OLAP database schema and into the reports, which would require effort and introduce risk.

Clients have been trying to figure out ways to offer reporting and analytics on OLTP databases without the risk profile or trade-offs of the past. We believe that the "right" answer is the BLU Acceleration shadow tables that had their debut in the DB2 Cancun release.

Before we introduce you to shadow tables, we want to note that you will likely need both approaches for LOB reporting and analytics. Think about the challenge at hand: How does IT provision deep analytical reporting environments with historical data to LOB but at the same time give them access to the real-time data for real-time reporting? And in a self-service manner too?

Reporting on a single transactional system is great for operational reporting. But think about the kinds of data that you need to explore higher-level domain analytics versus "What is the run-rate of our inventory levels hour to hour?" If you want to empower LOB for tactical or strategic work, you are more than likely going to want to work with a 360-degree view of the problem domain, and that's likely to require bringing together data from multiple sources. The point we are trying to make is that acquiring the ability to get real-time operational reports has been frustrating IT for years, and BLU Acceleration on premise has a solution for that. But the coordination of subject domains from across the business is not going away either because you are not going to keep all the data in your OLTP system, as some of our competitors (who ironically have data warehousing solutions) are suggesting.

Shadow tables deliver operational reporting capabilities to your transactional environment from a single database, which addresses the shortcomings of most current environments. As of the time that this book was published, this capability was available only for DB2 with BLU Acceleration; if you are leveraging BLU Acceleration off premise, it is not available...yet.

A shadow table is a BLU Acceleration copy of a row-organized table that includes all columns or a subset of columns from a base table that's a critical part of your OLTP database. We say a subset because for OLAP queries, you might not need to query all columns in your OLTP table. Shadow tables are *automatically* maintained for you by the host database: *Super Analytics, Super Easy.*

By using shadow tables, you get the performance benefits of BLU Acceleration for analytic queries in first rate transactional processing environment. Analytic queries against transactional row-organized tables are automatically routed to BLU Acceleration shadow tables if the optimizer determines that such rerouting will be beneficial from a performance perspective *and* if the data in the shadow tables complies with a set of business rules that define the acceptable degree of freshness of the data that is being retrieved. Combine this enhanced performance for complex analytic queries with the efficiency of row-organized tables for OLTP, and you have an on-premise best of "both worlds" environment in a single database that is blazingly fast.

DB2 Database with BLU Acceleration Shadow Tables

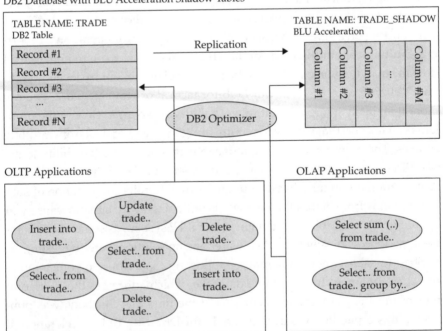

Figure 8-7 *A high-level look at how BLU Acceleration shadow tables operate in an on-premise DB2 environment*

Shadow tables are maintained by a set of services that are part of the DB2 offering. These services asynchronously replicate SQL change activities that were applied to the source table (where the transactional workload is running) to the BLU Acceleration shadow table (where the analytics are running). By default, all applications access the source transactional tables. Queries are transparently routed to either the source table or the shadow table, depending on the workload and certain business rules that you apply to the analytics environment. Figure 8-7 shows an example of DB2 with BLU Acceleration shadow tables.

The DB2 optimizer decides at query optimization time, on which table to execute the SQL workload: the DB2 table or the BLU Acceleration shadow table. This decision is based on two factors: the cost of the SQL statement and the business-defined latency rules. Although an administrator might set up a shadow table to refresh its data at specific intervals, it is the business' defined latency that determines whether the shadow table is used.

You can define a latency-based business rule that is used to prevent applications from accessing the shadow tables when the actual latency is beyond the user-defined limit. This enables you to effectively control the "freshness" of the data that your analytical workloads will access. You can imagine how beneficial these governance rules are. Perhaps a report calculates the run-rate costs that are associated with a manufacturing line's reject ratio KPI; such a calculation might need to be performed on data that is not older than a certain number of seconds. For example, it could be the case that data that is older than 10 seconds is considered too stale for this KPI as defined by the LOB. If the shadow table's required data was refreshed within the last 10 seconds when the SQL statement executes, the optimizer transparently routes the query to the shadow table.

Let's assume that the acceptable latency was set to 5 seconds and the data was last updated 10 seconds ago. In this case, the query will be routed to the row store to access the freshest data for the report. If a report hits the row table, you have access to all the services and capabilities of that technology to manage the query. For example, the time-sensitive query could "waterfall" its resource consumption such that it gets 30 seconds of exclusive access to unlimited resources; then for the next 30 seconds, it gradually is forced to decrease its consumption of the various compute resources available on the system until the query completes. Remember, this is all transparent to the end user.

As previously noted, you can set these business rules at the connection level, but you can granularly set them at the statement level too. For example, perhaps the same reporting application also maintains a dashboard with a KPI that measures the mechanical fluid level on the production line; the data behind this KPI might have business relevance that is measured in minutes or even hours.

We have mentioned the transparency of this solution. From an application point of view, this transparency is key. Both transaction workloads and analytical queries will reference the *same* base row-organized table names. There is no change to the application, nor to the SQL statements. The database determines and handles query routing as described earlier. This makes using BLU Acceleration shadow tables easy for existing DB2 environments. The advantage here is that OLTP queries get the great DB2 OLTP performance, and analytical queries get the great BLU Acceleration performance. *Super Analytics, Super Easy.*

Wrapping It Up

In this chapter, we introduced you to one of the "crown jewels" in the IBM Information Management portfolio: BLU Acceleration. We talked about seven big ideas that are the inspirations behind the BLU Acceleration technology. We took some time to articulate how BLU Acceleration is a technology that can be provisioned as a service off premise (hosted or managed as a Bluemix service or in dashDB) or on premise. We also talked about how this technology can be found deeply embedded but not exposed within IBM technologies such as Informix, as well as deeply embedded and surfaced, such as in DB2. Finally, we introduced you to the latest BLU Acceleration innovation, shadow tables, which you can find in the DB2 Cancun Release 10.5.0.4.

Many clients have noticed the transformative opportunity that BLU Acceleration technology can have on their business. For example, LIS.TEC's Joachim Klassen observed one of the key benefits of BLU Acceleration when he noted, "Even if your data does not completely fit into memory, you still have great performance gains. In the tests we ran we were seeing queries run up to 100 times faster with BLU Acceleration." It's a very different approach than what's been taken by some other vendors. After all, if the price of memory drops by about 30 percent every 18 months yet the amount of data grows by 50 percent, and in a Big Data world data is being used to move from transactions to interactions, you're not going to be able to fit all your data in memory—and that's why BLU Acceleration is so different.

We shared the experiences of only a few of the clients who are delighted by the BLU Acceleration technology from a performance, simplicity, compression, and, most of all, opportunity perspective. Handelsbanken, one of the more secure and profitable banks in the world, saw some of its risk insight queries speed up 100-fold with no tuning, and were actively seeing the effect that BLU Acceleration had on its queries within six hours of downloading the technology!

Paul Peters is the lead DBA at VSN Systemen BV—a builder of high-density, high-volume telecom and datacom applications. VSN Systemen first started using BLU Acceleration when it debuted two years ago and was quite pleased with the 10-fold performance improvements and 10-fold compression ratios. As part of a set of clients who jumped on to the DB2 Cancun release and its BLU Acceleration shadow tables, VSN Systemen was pleased with the ability "to allow our clients to run reports directly on top of transactional tables. The results are delighting my end users, and we don't see any impact to our transactional performance," according to Peters.

Ruel Gonzalez from DataProxy LLC notes that in the "DB2 Cancun Release 10.5.0.4, shadow tables were easily integrated into our system. This allows our transactional and analytic workloads to coexist in one database, with no effect on our transactional workloads. We get the extreme performance of BLU Acceleration while maintaining our key transactional execution!"

You are going to hear a lot of chest thumping in the marketplace around in-memory columnar databases, some claiming the ability to run OLTP or OLAP applications, and more. Although there is no question that we did some chest thumping of our own in this chapter, we want to invite you to ask every vendor (including IBM) to put their money where their mouth is. We invite you to try it for yourself. It won't take long; you just load and go! In fact, things are even easier than that... just dashDB, load, and go!

9

An Expert Integrated System for Deep Analytics

Organizations have deployed data warehouses to provide broader access to information, help them react to it faster, and facilitate quicker decisions. Indeed, the language used to describe the size of data warehouses has changed over the last decade: from gigabytes to terabytes and petabytes. Workloads have evolved from being primarily reporting to increasingly analytical, and the number of reports and queries run per day on data warehouses has grown from hundreds to hundreds of thousands and into the millions. These changes create a realization for many that the traditional approaches to data warehousing can no longer efficiently address the broader information and analytic demands they now face.

Organizations expect that when they need critical information urgently, the platform that delivers it should be the last thing on their minds and, quite frankly, should not matter. After all, when you turn on the lights at your house, do you consider the wiring and circuitry that makes it happen? Obviously not. You expect to be able to consume what you need to get the job done without effort (well, you have to flip the light switch, but you get the point). When you make toast for breakfast, you don't think about it, you just push a lever; after all, when was the last time you read your toaster's manual? To support the escalating complexity, throughput, data and user volumes, and variety of workloads, organizations need different platforms. And they are requiring greater simplicity and reliability to handle the more analytic-oriented workloads, without impacting standard business reporting and performance management applications or being burdened by the administration, processes, and rigidity typically enforced around enterprise data warehouses.

As organizations begin pursuing the next generation information management architecture we outlined in Chapter 4, they are recognizing the need to have separate fit-for-purpose components; they are recognizing the need for separate environments that nurture deeper and more complex analytics and that a different set of technologies may be more appropriate to support these workloads. Indeed, this recognition is a conscious effort to move the conversation beyond the hype and into value-driven commitments to the business.

The first generation of data warehouse technologies was modeled after OLTP-based databases running on large symmetric multiprocessing (SMP) machines. These machines had inherent architectural limitations that prevented them from becoming a viable platform for analytics. Subsequent iterations tried to incorporate parallel processing techniques and distributed storage subsystems into the architecture. The resulting complexity of operation (various kinds of indexes, indexes on indexes, aggregates, optimization hints, and the like) made these systems extremely complex to operate and expensive to maintain. This is one of the reasons that a traditional approach to achieve consistent performance against increasing data volumes and diverse workloads without a significant increase in total cost of ownership (TCO) has always been the biggest challenge in data warehousing implementations. Invariably, the biggest bottleneck across all data warehouse operations was the speed at which the database engine could read from and write data from a storage tier, known as *I/O bottleneck*.

When warehouses were made up of piece-parts, various providers delivered a number of I/O innovations in an attempt to address this bottleneck; however, these innovations were brought to market independently and exhibited little synergy across warehouse tiers: the relational database management system (RDBMS), storage subsystem, and server technologies. For example, using caching in the storage subsystem, faster server network fabrics, and software optimizations (such as partitioning and indexing) are all optimizations that were brought to market to minimize I/O. And although they addressed the issues *locally* and that helped, these efforts weren't cohesively optimized to improve I/O. In addition, these optimization techniques relied on the data warehouse designers to guess query patterns and retrieval needs up front so that they could tune the system for performance. This not only impacted business agility in meeting new reporting and analytics requirements, but also required significant manual effort to set up, optimize, maintain, tune, and configure the data warehouse tiers. As a result, collectively, these systems became expensive to set up and manage and brutal to maintain.

The IBM PureData System for Analytics, powered by Netezza technology, was developed from the whiteboard to the motherboard to overcome these specific challenges. (Since this chapter talks about the history of the Netezza technology that is the genesis for the IBM PureData System for Analytics, we will refer to its form factor as an appliance and the technology as *Netezza* for most of this chapter.) In fact, it's fair to say that Netezza started what became the appliance revolution in data warehousing by integrating the database, processing, analytics, and storage components into a flexible, compact, purpose-built, and optimized system for analytical workloads. This innovative platform was built to deliver an industry-leading price-performance ratio with appliance simplicity. As a purpose-built appliance for high-speed Big Data analytics, its power comes not from the most powerful and expensive components available in the current marketplace (which would spike the slope of its cost-benefit curve) but from how the right components can be assembled to work together in perfect harmony to maximize performance. In short, the goal wasn't to build a supercomputer, but rather an elegantly designed system to address commonplace bottlenecks with the unequalled ability to perform complex analytics on *all* of your data. Netezza did this by combining massively parallel processing (MPP) scalability techniques, highly intelligent software, and multicore CPUs with Netezza's unique hardware acceleration (we refer to this as Netezza's secret sauce) to minimize I/O bottlenecks and deliver performance that much more expensive systems could never match or even approach—all without the need for any tuning.

Netezza didn't try to catch up to the pace of analytics-based appliance innovation—it set it. Unlike some Exa-branded offerings in the marketplace that take an old system with known analytic shortcomings and attempt to balance it with a separate storage tier that requires further database licensing and maintenance, the Netezza technology was not inspired by the "bolt-on" approach. Netezza was built from the ground up, specifically for running complex analytics on large volumes of structured data. As an easy-to-use appliance, the system delivers its phenomenal results out of the box, pretty much no indexing, aggregates, or tuning required. Appliance simplicity enables rapid innovation and the ability to bring high-performance analytics to the widest range of users and processes. For users and their organizations, it means the best intelligence to all who seek it, even as demands escalate from all directions.

Looking back at the history of Netezza and today's Big Data era, we think it's safe to assert that Netezza took the CFO/CIO discussion from "spending money to save money" and added to it the benefit of "spending money to make money." It handed businesses, both large and small, the ability to democratize deep analytics, while flattening the cost curve that was once associated with this domain. It did this by enabling organizations to process queries and generate insights dramatically faster than they were able to in the past, sometimes even enabling queries that never finished before, which in turn provided entirely new opportunities to deliver business value.

Netezza has had an inflection-point effect on the mainframe too. The IBM DB2 Analytics Accelerator (IDAA) is a high-performant appliance that packages the IBM Netezza technology we outline in this chapter with IBM zEnterprise technologies via DB2 for z/OS. In the same manner that Netezza can help you query data at high speeds, extend capabilities, and lower operating costs, IDAA can do the same for this platform using the very same technologies we outline in this chapter.

In this chapter we want to introduce you to the Netezza technology behind the IBM Pure Data System for Analytics and the IBM DB2 Analytics Accelerator and specifically the secret sauce that made the spark that started the data warehouse appliance evolution and what makes it so special. We are going to be a little more detail oriented with respect to the "How did you do that?" conversation compared to other chapters because we think it brings clarity to what we mean by "secret sauce."

Before We Begin: Bursting into the Cloud

In Chapter 3 we introduced you to cloud computing and the impact it's having on the IT landscape. The clients we talk to want the flexibility to explore analytics in the cloud. IBM's dashDB (based on the BLU Acceleration technology we talked about in Chapter 8) is such an offering. Work is being done to make it as seamless as possible to burst analytic workloads into the cloud from a Netezza system. For example, Netezza includes a suite of algorithms referred to as IBM Netezza Analytics that truly makes it an embedded, purpose-built, advanced analytics platform that enables analytics to run where the data resides—delivered free with every IBM Netezza appliance. As you will learn later in this chapter, these capabilities appear in the BLU Acceleration technology (in public cloud dashDB offerings first). This will streamline the ability to burst grounded on-premise Netezza workloads (among others) into compatible public cloud services such as IBM dashDB and still leverage the same analytics. You are also going to see more and more SQL compatibility in the dashDB service, thereby creating a true hybrid model.

Clients also want to explore the analysis of data in the cloud and later solidify the results of that analysis on premise in an analytic data mart such as Netezza—you will find capabilities driven into this ecosystem from that perspective too. Finally, leveraging data refinery services such as masking and transforming data, assisted in the cloud, is also on the wish list for the clients we talk to. Solutions for this are provided by the IBM DataWorks service catalog and Netezza integrates with these capabilities too. In addition, the IBM DataWorks refinery components will be made available to dashDB (in fact, some come with it) to help integrate with on-premise solutions such as Netezza or software installations of BLU Acceleration.

Starting on the Whiteboard: Netezza's Design Principles

Netezza's approach to data analysis is patented and proven. Its goal has always been to minimize data movement while processing data at "physics speed" in parallel and on a massive scale—all delivered within an easy-to-use appliance form factor at a low cost. From the point in time when Netezza was its own company to its IBM acquisition and evolution into the IBM Pure-Data System for Analytics (PDA), *its architecture has always stayed true to a core set of design principles*. These design principles have been a hallmark of Netezza's price-performance leadership in the industry, and we will cover them in this section.

Appliance Simplicity: Minimize the Human Effort

It's a fact: Enterprises are spending more and more money on human capital to manage their analytic systems. Now consider this fact in a world where cheaper labor is presumably so readily available through outsourcing, and you can see that the required amount of human effort to manage many of today's systems is a problem. Quite simply, as the cost of labor as a percentage of overall IT costs should be going down, it is actually going up—because of the human effort and complexity associated with traditional solutions.

Appliances are dedicated devices that are optimized for a specific purpose (like the toaster we referred to earlier). They are self-contained and ready to go. They are fast to install and easy to operate. They have standard interfaces that enable other systems to interoperate with them. All of these characteristics make appliances an elegant vehicle for delivering IT solutions. In certain areas, such as network and storage solutions, appliances are the preferred means for delivering specific capabilities.

Netezza pioneered the concept of appliances in the data warehousing and analytics realm. All of its technologies are delivered in an appliance form, shielding end users from the underlying complexity of the platform and its components. Simplicity rules whenever there is a design trade-off with any other aspect of this appliance. Unlike other solutions, appliances just run, handling demanding queries and mixed workloads at blistering speeds. Even normally time-consuming tasks, such as installing products, upgrading them, and ensuring high availability and business continuity, are built into the appliance and are vastly simplified, saving precious time and resources and mitigating operational risk.

Process Analytics Closer to the Data Store

Netezza's architecture is based on a fundamental principle of computer science: When operating on large data sets, don't move data unless you absolutely must. Moving large data sets from physical storage units to compute nodes increases latency and affects performance. Netezza minimizes data movement by sending the processing to the data and using innovative hardware acceleration. It uses field-programmable gate arrays (FPGAs) to filter out extraneous data as early in the data stream as possible and basically as fast as data can be streamed off the disks. This process of data elimination close to the data source removes I/O bottlenecks and keeps downstream components, such as the CPU, memory, and network, from having to process superfluous data; this produces a significant multiplier effect on system performance.

The NYSE Euronext is a Euro-American corporation that operates multiple securities exchanges around the world, most notably the New York Stock Exchange (NYSE) and Euronext. Its analysts track the value of a listed company, perform trend analysis, and search for evidence of fraudulent activity. As you can imagine, their algorithms perform market surveillance and analyze every transaction from a trading day, which translates into full table scans on massive volumes of data. As is the case with many enterprises, NYSE Euronext's traditional data warehouse was moving data back and forth between storage systems and its analytic engine; it took more than 26 hours to complete certain types of processing! How did the company address this challenge? It chose Netezza technology and reduced the time needed to access business-critical data from 26 hours to 2 minutes because analytics were getting processed closer to the source.

Balanced + MPP = Linear Scalability

Every component of Netezza's architecture, including the processor, FPGA, memory, and network, is carefully selected and optimized to service data as fast as the physics of the disks allow, while minimizing cost and power consumption. The Netezza software orchestrates these components to operate concurrently on the data streaming from disk in a pipeline fashion, maximizing utilization and extracting the utmost throughput from each MPP node. Although the use of open, blade-based components enables Netezza to incorporate technology enhancements quickly, the turbo-charger effect of the FPGA, a balanced hardware configuration, and tightly coupled intelligent software combine to deliver overall performance gains far greater than those of the individual elements. In fact, Netezza has typically delivered more than fourfold performance improvements every two years since its introduction, far outpacing other well-established vendors.

Modular Design: Support Flexible Configurations and Extreme Scalability

One of the key concerns with traditional appliance-based architectures has been their ability to scale after data volumes outgrow the physical capacity of the appliance. Netezza addresses this concern with a modular appliance design that simply scales from a few hundred gigabytes to petabytes of user data for query. In fact, the system has been designed to be highly adaptable and to serve the needs of different segments of the data warehouse and analytics market. For example, aside from being a dedicated deep analytics appliance, Netezza can execute in-database MapReduce routines (the original programming framework for Hadoop that we covered in Chapter 6) right in the database—allowing you to leverage skills across the information management architecture we introduced you to in Chapter 4.

T-Mobile is a terrific example that illustrates the scalability of Netezza technology. Every day it processes 17+ billion events, including phone calls, text messages, and data traffic, over its networks. This translates to upward of 2PB of data that needs to be crunched. T-Mobile needed a Big Data solution that could store and analyze multiple years of call detail records (CDRs) containing switch, billing, and network event data for its millions of subscribers. T-Mobile wanted to identify and address call network bottlenecks and to ensure that quality and capacity would be provisioned when and where they are needed.

Netezza proved to be the right technology for T-Mobile to manage its massive growth in data. More than 1,200 users access its Netezza system to analyze these events and perform network quality of experience (QoE) analytics, traffic engineering, churn analysis, and dropped session analytics, as well as voice and data session analytics. Since deploying Netezza, T-Mobile has realized a near evaporation in data warehouse administrative activities compared to its previous solution, which had ironically redlined, and has also been able to reduce tax and call-routing fees by using the greater volume of granular data to defend against false claims. To top it off, T-Mobile has been able to increase call network availability by identifying and fixing bottlenecks and congestion issues whenever and wherever they arise.

What's in the Box? The Netezza Appliance Architecture Overview

Netezza's architecture is based on an asymmetric massively parallel processing (AMPP) methodology that combines the best elements of symmetric multiprocessing (SMP) and MPP to create a purpose-built appliance for running blazingly fast analytics on petabytes of data.

Figure 9-1 shows a single-rack Netezza system. As you can see, it has two high-end rack-mounted servers called *hosts*, which function both as the external interface to the Netezza appliance and the controller for the MPP infrastructure. The hosts are connected through an internal network fabric to a set of *snippet blades* (we'll often refer to them simply as *S-blades*), where the bulk of the data processing is performed. The S-blades are connected through a high-speed interconnect to a set of disk enclosures where the data is stored in a highly compressed format.

If any component fails, be it the host, disk, or S-blade, recovery is automatic. Thus, the full range of automatic failure detection and recovery options demonstrates the advantages of an appliance approach. Netezza has built-in component and operational redundancy, and the system responds automatically and seamlessly to the failure of critical components.

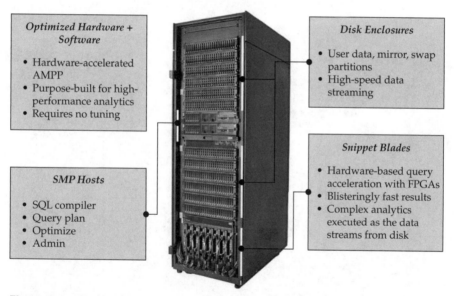

Figure 9-1   *The IBM Netezza appliance (now known as the IBM PureData System for Analytics)*

A Look Inside a Netezza Box

Every component of Netezza's AMPP architecture, including the processor, FPGA, disk drives, memory, and network, is carefully selected and integrated to create a harmonized overall system. In addition to raw performance, this balanced architecture can deliver linear scalability to more than 1,000 processing streams executing in parallel, while offering industry-leading TCO. These parallel streams work together to "divide and conquer" the workload. Figure 9-2 illustrates the key components of a Netezza system.

The *host* is the primary interface to the system. Netezza hosts are high-performant Linux servers that are set up in an active-passive configuration for high availability (note that Figure 9-2 has two of them stacked on top of each other). The host compiles SQL queries into executable code segments called *snippets*, creates optimized query plans, and distributes the snippets to the MPP nodes (S-blades) for execution. The active host presents a standardized interface to external tools and applications, such as business intelligence reporting tools, data integration and ETL tools, advanced analytics packages, backup and recovery tools, and so on. These external applications use ubiquitous protocols (for example, JDBC) to interface with the Netezza host.

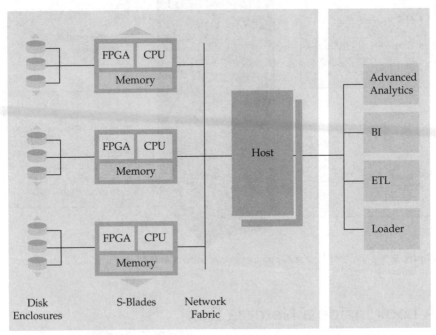

IBM Netezza data warehouse appliance
(IBM PureData System for Analytics)

External Applications

Figure 9-2   *The IBM Netezza AMPP architecture*

Hosts run both high-availability clustering software and mirroring technology. All write operations to the active host are mirrored to the standby host, preparing it to take over system processing at any moment if a failure should occur. The standby host monitors the active host through Ethernet links and assumes the primary role should the active host fail.

S-blades are intelligent processing nodes that make up the MPP engine of the Netezza appliance. Each S-blade is an independent server that contains powerful multicore CPUs, multiengine FPGAs, and gigabytes of RAM, all balanced and working concurrently to deliver peak performance. Netezza protects against S-blade failures as well. The system management software continuously monitors each S-blade; if a failure is detected, the S-blade is taken out of service, and its processing load is automatically transferred among the other S-blades. Monitoring of the S-blade includes error correction code (ECC) checking on the blade memory. If the system management software detects that ECC errors have exceeded a failure threshold, it takes the S-blade out of service.

Note that the PureData System for Analytics was designed to run at peak performance with one less S-blade per rack than delivered in the system—IBM ships all systems with an extra S-blade. However, to optimize performance and minimize the time to take over if a failure should occur, all the S-blades are active. If a failure occurs, the drives logically attached to the failed S-blade are mounted onto the surviving S-blades and processing continues.

You can see the *disk enclosures* in Figure 9-2. A Netezza system's disk enclosures (which each contain slices of a table's data) contain high-density, high-performance disks that are mirrored for data protection. Disk enclosures are connected to the S-blades through high-speed interconnects that enable the disks in Netezza to simultaneously stream data to the S-blades at the maximum rate possible. There are at least two independent data paths from each S-blade in the chassis to each disk for redundancy. The data on each drive is mirrored to another drive in the system. In the event of a disk failure, processing is completed on the mirror without any interruption of service. I/O is simply redirected to the mirror drive by the storage subsystem. Spare drives are included in each appliance so that it can transparently self-heal by selecting a spare to take the place of the failed drive and regenerating its contents to restore redundancy.

A *network fabric* is the "central nervous system" of a Netezza solution—it gets all the body parts connected. Internode communication across Netezza's MPP grid occurs on a network fabric running a customized IP-based protocol that fully utilizes the total cross-sectional bandwidth of the fabric and eliminates congestion even under sustained, bursty network traffic. The network is optimized to scale to more than 1,000 nodes, while allowing each node to initiate a large data transfer to every other node simultaneously.

Netezza's custom network protocol is designed specifically for the data volumes and traffic patterns that are associated with high-volume data warehousing and analytics. It ensures maximum utilization of the network bandwidth without overloading it, thereby allowing predictable performance close to the data transmission speed of the network. The Netezza network fabric infrastructure has the same level of redundancy as the other major components. This is achieved by *multipathing*—which means that every component within the appliance has at least two paths to reach another component. An example of multipathing is Netezza's redundant fabric network switches. Each switch connects to the hosts and the SPUs. Therefore, the loss of one switch can be overcome by rerouting to the alternative switch. The data network is not only redundant but also physically distinct from the separate management network, enabling the system to assess the health of its components even if the data network experiences problems.

The "Not So Secret" Sauce: FPGA-Accelerated Analytics

We suppose it is not much of a secret if we are writing about how it works, but the FPGA is a special piece of the Netezza architecture. The FPGA is a critical enabler of the price-performance advantages Netezza still enjoys over other vendors that followed the path of Netezza. An FPGA is a semiconductor chip equipped with a large number of internal gates that can be programmed to implement almost any logical function. After an FPGA is programmed, it operates more like special-built hardware than a general-purpose processor, giving it optimum performance for narrowly defined tasks. FPGAs are particularly effective at managing special-purpose stream processing tasks and are extensively used in such applications as digital signal processing, medical imaging, and speech recognition. In fact, it is likely the case that you have an FPGA in your house and didn't even know it! Do you watch DVDs or Blu-ray Discs? An FPGA is likely behind the scenes, facilitating reads of high-quality compressed digital data off the spinning disc without the jitters. An FPGA is tiny in size (about 1 inch by 1 inch of square silicon) but performs programmed tasks with enormous efficiency, drawing little power and generating little heat.

A dedicated high-speed interconnect from the storage array enables data to be delivered to Netezza memory as quickly as it can stream off the disk. Compressed data is cached in memory using a smart algorithm, which ensures that the most commonly accessed data is served right out of memory instead of requiring disk access.

Each FPGA contains embedded engines that perform compression, filtering, and transformation functions on the data stream. These engines are dynamically reconfigurable (enabling them to be modified or extended through software), are customized for *every snippet* through instructions provided during query execution, and act on the data stream at extremely high speeds. They all run in parallel and deliver the net effect of decompressing and filtering out 95 to 98 percent of table data at *physics speed,* thereby keeping only the data that's relevant to the query. The process described here is repeated on about 100 of these parallel snippet processors running in the appliance. On a 10-rack system, this would represent up to 1,000 parallel snippet processors, with performance that exceeds that of much more expensive systems by orders of magnitude.

How a Query Runs in Netezza

There are a whole bunch of optimization steps that go on when Netezza executes a query. For example, when joining multiple small tables to a large fact table, the optimizer can choose to broadcast the small tables in their entirety to each S-blade, while keeping the large table distributed across all snippet processors. This approach minimizes data movement while taking advantage of the AMPP architecture to parallelize the join. Netezza will also rewrite a query if it could have been written better (think of it as a word processing grammar checker—only for SQL).

Ultimately, a compiler turns the auto-optimized query plan into executable code segments, called *snippets.* Snippet processors execute query segments in parallel across all of the data streams in the appliance. Each snippet has two elements: compiled code that's executed by individual CPU cores and a set of FPGA parameters that customize the embedded engines' filtering for that particular snippet. This snippet-by-snippet customization enables

Netezza to provide, in effect, a hardware configuration that is optimized on the fly for individual queries. We call this *bespoke* optimization because the system literally writes new code for the FPGAs that contain the specific query-tuned instructions on how best to fetch the needed data each and every time. There is a smart cache here too, so a query plan looking for NAME='Marc' can leverage the same compiled code as NAME='PAUL'.

When the code snippets execute, *ZoneMap* acceleration exploits the natural ordering of rows in a data warehouse to accelerate performance by orders of magnitude. This technique avoids scanning rows with column values outside the start and end range of the query. For example, if a table contains two years of weekly records (approximately 100 weeks) and a query is looking for data for only one week, ZoneMap acceleration can improve performance up to 100 times. Unlike typical indexes associated with optimizations in traditional data warehousing technology, ZoneMaps are automatically created and updated for each database table, without incurring any administrative overhead. In fact, ZoneMaps heavily influenced the data skipping capabilities of dashDB.

As you have learned, a key component of the Netezza technology is the way in which its streaming architecture processes data; it uses the FPGA as a turbocharger, which is a huge performance accelerator that not only allows the system to keep up with the data stream, but actually accelerates the data stream through decompression before processing it at line rates, ensuring no bottlenecks in the I/O path. FPGAs acting on the data stream have the effect of accelerating things four- to eightfold by decompressing the data stream at the transmission speed of the disk drives. Next, its embedded engines filter out any data (columns and rows outside the range) that's not relevant to the query. The resultant data at this stage is typically a tiny fraction (2 to 5 percent) of the original stream, greatly reducing the execution time that's required by the processor core. We think Figure 9-3 does a great job of illustrating the "FPGA effect."

You can think of the way that data streaming works in Netezza as similar to an assembly line; it has various stages of operations within the FPGA and the associated CPU cores. Each of these stages, along with the disk and network, operate concurrently, processing different chunks of the data stream at any given point in time. The concurrency within each data stream further increases performance relative to other architectures.

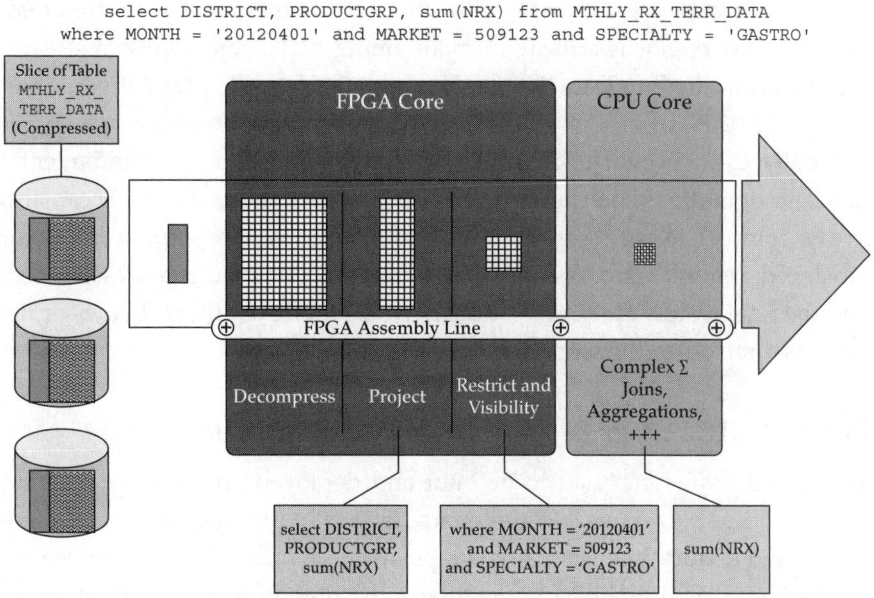

```
select DISTRICT, PRODUCTGRP, sum(NRX) from MTHLY_RX_TERR_DATA
 where MONTH = '20120401' and MARKET = 509123 and SPECIALTY = 'GASTRO'
```

Figure 9-3 *The FPGA role in a Netezza query run—The "FPGA effect"*

The first thing to note is that this system needs to read only a page of data and not the entire table (the solid block that makes its way from the disks to the FPGA assembly line in Figure 9-3—this is an initial qualifying row restriction) because storage ZoneMaps know what data values reside within each page and can completely skip data that is of no interest to the query. These pages contain compressed data that gets streamed from disk onto the assembly line at the fastest rate that the physics of the disk will allow (this is why you see the solid block expand and its pattern changes in the figure—it is now decompressed). Note that if data were already cached, it would be taken directly from memory.

The FPGA then uses its Project engine to apply any query projections in order to filter out any attributes (columns) based on parameters specified in the SELECT clause of the SQL query being processed, in this case, the DISTRICT, PRODUCTGRP, and NRX columns. Next, the assembly line applies any restrictions from the query using its Restrict engine. Here rows that do not qualify based on restrictions specified in the WHERE clause are removed. This phase includes a Visibility engine that feeds in additional parameters to the Restrict engine to filter out rows that should not be "seen" by a query; for example, perhaps there is a row with a transaction that is not yet committed. The Visibility engine is critical for maintaining ACID compliance at streaming speeds in the PureData System for Analytics (see Chapter 2 if you don't know what this is).

Finally, the processing core picks up the data and performs fundamental database operations such as sorts, joins, and aggregations. The CPU can also apply complex algorithms that are embedded in the snippet code for advanced analytics processing. All the intermediate results are assembled, and the final results are sent over the network fabric to other S-blades or the host, as directed by the snippet code.

How Netezza Is a Platform for Analytics

Traditionally, analytics had to be built and deployed on separate analytics servers. These servers would run computationally intensive analytical algorithms and extract data from a data repository, such as a data warehouse, on the back end. This architecture lengthens the time from model inception to deployment and requires data movement from the data repository to the analytics server. Not only does this process take too much time, but it is also inefficient, limits the data that can be used to derive insight, constrains the scope of the analytic modeling, and impedes the ability to experiment iteratively.

Netezza offers a distinctive and simple-to-use approach for serious analytics on structured data with IBM Netezza Analytics (INZA; you will often hear it referred to as "in-zaa"—which ironically makes it sound magical, which it is). INZA is an advanced analytics platform that's shipped *free* inside every Netezza appliance. With INZA, analytic activities such as data exploration, discovery, transformation, model building, and scoring can all be performed right where the data resides—in the data warehouse. This reduces the time it takes to build and deploy analytic models throughout an enterprise. By shrinking the time from model inception to deployment, companies can move to enterprisewide, fact-based decisions by infusing more of their decisions with insightful on-demand analytics. This also enables practitioners to experiment quickly and iterate through different analytical models to find the best fit. After a model is developed, it can seamlessly be executed against all of the relevant data in the enterprise. The prediction and scoring can be done right where the data resides, inside the data warehouse. Users can get the results of prediction scores in near real time, helping to operationalize advanced analytics and making it available throughout the enterprise.

There are over 200 analytical algorithms that have been deeply integrated into the Netezza system. For example, INZA includes ranging estimation models (regression tress, nearest neighbor analysis), simulations (matrix engine and Monte Carlo analysis), k-means cluster, Naïve Bayes classifier, and hundreds more we don't have the space to detail here. Through a planned number of phases, you're going to see these INZA capabilities get deeply embedded within the BLU Acceleration technology. As mentioned earlier in this book, IBM Information Management will iterate capabilities over the cloud first—in a manner that allows us to deliver capabilities much faster than traditional models. For example, you will eventually be able to run the same INZA statistical algorithms that you can run in Netezza on the dashDB service (powered by BLU Acceleration) in the cloud. This greatly empowers organizations with the ability to take bursty Netezza workloads into the cloud. This said, the INZA capabilities will also find their way into on-premise software instantiations of BLU Acceleration too; DB2 will eventually gain these capabilities as well.

IBM Netezza Analytics supports multiple tools, languages, and frameworks. It enables analytic applications, visualization tools, and business intelligence tools to harness parallelized advanced analytics through a variety of programming methods such as SQL, Java, MapReduce, Python, R, C, and C++, among others; all can be used to deliver powerful, insightful analytics. The following table summarizes the in-database analytics built into the Netezza technology:

Transformations	Execute in-database data transformations to realize significant performance gains.
Mathematical	Perform deep in-database mathematical calculations to leverage MPP processing.
Statistics	Calculate rich statistics without moving the data.
Time series	Create forecasts and identify trends using rich histories to improve model accuracy.
Data mining	Use more data, or all of the data, to discover new and emerging insights.
Predictive	Move from batch processing to near-real-time speed-of-thought analytics to predict with great accuracy and speed.
Geospatial	Implement location-based analytics on Big Data with immediate feedback.

Netezza also enables the integration of its robust set of built-in analytics with leading analytics tools from such vendors as Revolution Analytics (which ships a commercial version of R), open source R, SAS, IBM SPSS, Fuzzy Logix, and Zementis, among others. Additionally, you can develop new capabilities using the platform's user-defined extensions.

This comprehensive advanced analytics environment makes it easy to derive benefit from this platform, giving you the flexibility to use your preferred tools for ad hoc analysis, prototyping, and production deployment of advanced analytics. Do not overlook this INZA stuff—our clients are far outpacing their peer groups by latching onto these capabilities.

Wrapping It Up

The IBM PureData System for Analytics, powered by Netezza technology, is a simple data appliance for serious analytics. It simplifies and optimizes the performance of data services for analytic applications, enabling very complex algorithms to run in minutes and seconds, not hours. Clients often cite performance boosts that are 10–100x faster than traditional "roll-your-own" solutions. This system requires minimal tuning and administration since it is expert integrated and highly resilient. It also includes more than 200 in-database analytics functions, which support analysis where the data resides and effectively eliminate costly data movement, yielding industry-leading performance while hiding the complexity of parallel programming; collectively, this capability is known as INZA. In fact, the INZA algorithms serve as the base for the embedded analytic capabilities that will emerge within the BLU Acceleration technology over time—showing up in its as-a-service dashDB offering first.

In this chapter we referred to the IBM PureData System for Analytics as an appliance and by its ancestry name, Netezza. We did this because it made it simpler to explain the way it works. The truth is that the Netezza technology has evolved from an appliance into an expert integrated system since the technology was acquired by IBM. Expert integrated systems fundamentally change both the experience and economics of IT, and they are quite different from appliances.

Expert integrated systems are more than a static stack of self-tuned components—a server here, some database software there—serving a fixed application at the top. Instead, these systems have three attributes whose confluence is not only unique, but empowering.

The first is built-in expertise. Think of expert integrated systems as representing the collective knowledge of thousands of deployments, established best practices, innovative thinking, IT industry leadership, and the distilled expertise of business partners and solution providers—captured into the system in a deployable form from the base system infrastructure through the application. Indeed, some appliance vendors aren't packaging in expertise into the offering. While these offerings are better than the alternative in that they minimize deployment time, they aren't baking in the expertise in the form of patterns and so on.

The second is that expert integrated systems are integrated by design. All the hardware and software components are deeply integrated and tuned in the lab and packaged in the factory into a single ready-to-go system that is optimized for the workloads it will be running—all of the integration is done for you, by experts.

The third is that the entire experience is much simpler—from the moment you start designing what you need to the time you purchase—to setting up the system—to operating, maintaining, and upgrading it over time. We call it a simplified loading dock to loading data experience. In an expert integrated system, the management of the entire system of physical and virtual resources is integrated. And all this is done in an open manner, enabling participation by a broad ecosystem of partners to bring their industry-optimized solutions to bear. We think that when you look at the IBM PureData System for Analytics, or its mainframe cousin, the IDAA, you will find them to be true expert integrated systems.

10

Build More, Grow More, Sleep More: IBM Cloudant

More than ever, we live in a time in which the desire to consume functionality without having to manage and maintain the solution is the expectation, if not the norm. This is particularly true for cloud-based initiatives and "as a service" delivery models, such as infrastructure as a service (IaaS), platform as a service (PaaS), software as a service (SaaS), database as a service (DBaaS), database warehouse as a service (DWaaS), business process as a service (BPaaS), and any others that might have arisen since this book was written. Today's marketplace is bearing witness to an inflection point: There has been an explosion in new classes of middleware, infrastructure provisioning over the cloud, and applications (apps) that are offered as a service. The buyer of information technology (IT) is increasingly the chief marketing officer (CMO) and line-of-business (LOB) user. For example, in a recent report, Gartner suggested that corporate IT spending will come more from the CMO's office than it will from the chief information officer (CIO). "By 2016, 80% of new IT investments will directly involve LOB executives," Gartner notes. The as-a-service model is about six things that we want you to remember long after you're done reading this book: agility, agility, agility and simplicity, simplicity, simplicity.

With this in mind, it is our expectation that the cloud as a service delivery model is going to see a sprint (not a walk) of ever-growing adoption by established and emerging markets. If you think about it, this change was inevitable, a natural evolution. Social-mobile-cloud created so much friction that Big Data and Internet of Things (IoT) apps had no choice but to adopt this model. For businesses, developers, and the enterprise, the answer to delivering these new consumption models is simply "the cloud."

But is the cloud truly *simple?* Application developers for mobile devices and modern web apps are often challenged by their database management systems. Choosing your database solution intelligently and correctly from the outset is essential. Selecting an inappropriate data persistence model (a developer's way of referring to a database) or building apps on top of a poorly sized or misconfigured data layer can result in serious, even debilitating, issues with performance and scalability down the road. What's more, in a mobile-social-cloud world, the demand placed on database systems can change on a day-to-day basis.

No doubt you've heard about overnight Internet app sensations. Consider Hothead Games, an IBM Cloudant (Cloudant) client and maker of some of the most amazing mobile games you will find. Its published mission statement is "develop kick-ass mobile games or go bust." We're happy to say that it is doing quite well. In fact, as an example of just how well the company is doing, it leveraged a fully managed IBM NoSQL JSON data-layer service running Cloudant to grow its cluster 33-fold over the course of a year! (If you're thinking that JSON is the name of the guy in the "Friday the 13th" horror franchise, check out Chapter 2.) Hothead Games needed agility and simplicity from a managed data service so they could focus on gaming, not scaling the database. Hothead Games needed DBaaS (a type of SaaS). More specifically, its developers needed a solution that enabled them to accommodate fluctuations in load and use of their infrastructure. With growing demand for their games, they required a delivery model that could scale up without requiring a corresponding scaling up of the "administrative bench"—database administrators (DBAs) and operations (ops) teams, all of which bring added costs to an organization. Improper planning from day zero will saddle any app with performance, scalability, and availability issues that translate into higher costs for the business; Cloudant scopes these requirements for you and delivers a managed service to grow your data layer as needed.

Cloudant eliminates the aforementioned potential pitfalls by putting to rest the complexities of database management and growth. Startups and enterprises have traditionally needed to spend time on things that have nothing to do with their business: selecting what hardware to purchase, deciding on a database and then maintaining it, hiring DBAs, and so on. Cloudant is designed specifically to eliminate these stressors and to enable the developers of net-new mobile and "born on the web" apps to focus purely on building their next generation of apps. There's no need to manage database infrastructure or growth.

Cloudant is a *fully managed* NoSQL data layer service that is available both on and off premise (in cloud-speak, these deployment models are described as *on prem* and *off prem*). Cloudant guarantees its customers high availability, scalability, simplicity, and performance, all delivered through a fully hosted *and* managed DBaaS in the cloud, or through an on-premise implementation. Cloudant is also deeply integrated with IBM's PaaS offering called Bluemix, where it's known as Cloudant NoSQL DB. Cloudant's potential to interoperate between on-premise deployments and scalable cloud IaaS is key to IBM's cloud computing and Mobile First initiatives.

In this chapter, we'll introduce you to the Cloudant service and demonstrate how it offers greater agility for launching or rapidly evolving new products in response to an ever-changing market. In short, Cloudant gives you to the ability to *build more, grow more, and sleep more*, and who couldn't use more of all of these, especially the last one?

Cloudant: "White Glove" Database as a Service

Readying your teams and apps for the tumultuous world of the web and mobile is not only a matter of having the fastest code. In fact, in a social-mobile-cloud world, the speed of deployment and "change-agility" are what come to mind first when we hear the word *performance*. The database needs to robustly support usage requirements, be able to scale (and downsize) rapidly, and guarantee high availability for users across an increasingly global footprint. It is important that we point something out here in case we are not being explicit: When you go to the cloud, it's because you want agility. It does not necessarily mean you do not care about database infrastructure; in fact, the opposite might be true because database infrastructure is critical. Customers want other experts to spend their time on it so that developers can spend *their* time on what's most important—building your business and growing your client base.

Strategically planning for an infrastructure that is able to accommodate high throughput and consumer demand years into the future is prudent but also costly. It is difficult to justify significant capital expenditure (CAPEX) on hardware that your business *might* need, unless you can be certain that demand for your product will meet expectations. Most businesses want to trade CAPEX costs for operational expenditures (OPEX) in a manner not unlike the way you consume electricity. (You do not have your own power plant at home, do you?) If you are a small startup with a bright idea and aim to solicit a million dollars from a venture capital firm to get things going, and your proposal shows half of that investment being allocated to setting up a data center in support of your bright idea, our prediction is that your bright idea will get eclipsed by a not-so-bright idea—a CAPEX request.

The studios and startup developers building the apps that run today's (and tomorrow's) ecosystem of mobile and web services, although technically skilled, do not necessarily have on hand the database expertise necessary to scope out the requirements and manage the deployment of a database back end—nor do they want to, for that matter. For a game development studio, investing in DBA bench strength makes it more difficult to hire creative programmers and artists that the company needs to innovate and deliver better products. From the perspective of a company getting off the ground, which needs to rapidly provision a database on which to build its apps, what is the landscape of data-layer solutions that exists today? Figure 10-1 summarizes our assessment.

For businesses that are committed to managing in-house database solutions, there is the option of a "roll-your-own"(RYO) data layer. On paper, this option can appear cost effective: The price of licensing these databases, many of which are open source and available at little to no cost, starkly contrasts with priced offerings that deliver a database on top of the necessary infrastructure. For companies that have made hardware investments previously and have the necessary tooling on-site, a relatively inexpensive database license can be tempting. We ask you to consider again the hidden database administration costs that are associated with making an RYO solution viable: the expense of having a DBA on hand, the person-hours spent configuring and maintaining the solution, and the absolute necessity of correctly anticipating the infrastructure demands your app will experience months or even years into the future. Think back to the 33-fold growth of Hothead Games

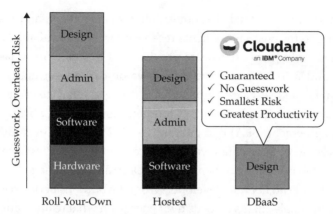

Figure 10-1 *The value of a fully managed DBaaS. Cloudant's customers are able to focus purely on the design of their apps, without having to manage the software or hardware provisioning or the administration of their data layer.*

and to the demands of that growth on its cluster. Collectively, this authoring team has more than a century of experience in IT, and we cannot imagine the turmoil that budget planning and execution for this kind of scaling demand would cause. Each of these factors imparts a hidden cost in addition to the investment your company will make into infrastructure and licensing; scoping any of these requirements incorrectly will impact your costs even further.

An alternative to the RYO approach is what's described as a *hosted* solution. We are a little disappointed in some database vendors who have taken this term and misleadingly marketed it as a catchall for managed databases. In reality, these "hosted" data layers are only one step removed from the RYO approach. Sure, the infrastructure layer is provisioned and set up by the vendor, but the remaining software administration, configuration, and maintenance responsibilities rest with the customer. These vendors openly market their offerings as a "managed database service." But, having only "delivered the car and its keys," it remains the sole responsibility of the client to drive the car. In fact, the client has to fill the tank with gas, change the oil, schedule time to comply with a recall on any defects, and more.

IBM Cloudant's distinguishing feature is the *risk-free delivery of a fully managed (not just hosted) data layer* through a cloud-distributed DBaaS solution. Unlike RYO solutions, which ask developers to handle everything from provisioning the hardware to database administration at the top of the stack,

DBaaS handles cloud database provisioning, management, and scaling as a paid service to the customer. Clients receive guaranteed availability and reliability for their business, hardware provisioning that can grow elastically as required, and a flattening of the time-to-value curve with undeniable risk mitigation. Hosted services simply cannot claim to offer the same degree of comprehensive services. In essence, Cloudant customers are purchasing a service level agreement (SLA) that guarantees 24/7/366 (yes, even during leap years) coverage of their data layer, as well as "white-glove" service management for database scaling, when needed. Only a fully managed service like IBM's Cloudant can liberate developers from the burdens of database administration and enable clients to focus their energy on what really matters: building the next generation of web and mobile apps that propel their businesses.

Consider the scenario discussed earlier of the small startup developer for tablet and web-browser apps that has a problem: the runaway success of its newest game. Companies like this are typically of modest size and equally modest budget. The opportunity starts when one of the company's creations gets named "featured app" on a myriad of app stores. Such unexpected success must be met with a rapid service scale-out to accommodate increasing demand for the application.

One Cloudant client had an interactive mobile game where you and your social circles participate in a guessing game. After the game was declared a featured app, the company went from nothing to double-digit million downloads in weeks, with a run rate of about two million downloads a day. Initially, they tried to run the data layer themselves on a NoSQL document store, and eventually, the app found itself at a standstill. The load on the inadequate database architecture was so great that the mobile game became unusable. Customers were unable to access the game they paid for, and the studio was powerless to remedy the situation with the infrastructure it had on hand. Despite their best efforts to prepare for scaling, including a soft launch of the game, no one on the team had ever faced such an onslaught of users. Demand for the product eclipsed even the most optimistic projections the studio had scoped for its infrastructure requirements. Negative customer reviews continued to pile up, and the company's ability to conduct business was gridlocked. Without experts in database administration on staff to support the strenuous demand for the app, the financial repercussions of this ongoing service outage proved disastrous.

To cope with the existing dilemma and avoid repeating the same mistakes, the design studio articulated five criteria that need to be satisfied before it is able to commit to a solution:

- The improved database back end needs to scale massively and elastically (up and down like a thermostat controls temperature) in response to fluctuating demand on the app vendor store.

- The solution needs to be highly available and deployable without downtime to the existing service so that the delivery of entertainment to users around the world is not interrupted.

- The solution needs to be up and running quickly, while the studio still has a chance to capitalize on early popularity and buzz around the game.

- The data layer needs to be managed. Hiring a large DBA team doesn't make sense for the company's long-term objectives of developing better games for its customers.

- The technology has to deliver improved tooling and techniques for data management. The messy and frustrating experience of managing a CouchDB instance (and the complexity of some RDBMS alternatives) is a contributing factor to the outage the company suffered.

Why would this studio come to use the IBM Cloudant DBaaS (as so many others have done)? As we've discussed, IBM Cloudant's database scales massively and elastically: As demand for an app grows or wanes (the mobile gaming marketplace is often described as a cyclical business of peaks and valleys), Cloudant database clusters can shrink and grow as needed. Moreover, the costs associated with Cloudant adjust accordingly to the size of your business (in fact, you can *get started for free* with a freemium plan). Customers do not require a big capital investment up front (no CAPEX) to get a massive database solution up and running ahead of time. If demand for your company's services inflates in the months and years ahead, the elastic scalability of Cloudant's data layer will be able to grow accordingly.

There is also the matter of guaranteed performance and uptimes. Cloudant has many unique capabilities for delivering customer access to data. Cloudant clients are not just buying database software; in addition to the technology, clients are buying the peace of mind that comes from an SLA that removes concerns over high availability and disaster recovery. If a data center goes down, Cloudant will reroute users to another replicate of the data. In this way, your data is guaranteed to remain highly available, even in the event of hardware failure, anywhere in the world, when and where you need it. You are likely thinking what we thought when we first met the team shortly after the IBM acquisition: Cloudant feels like an extension of its customers' development teams. They provide expert operational development for the data-layer back end, applying their expertise to growing apps and providing guidance on application architecture as you manage your business.

In this section, we used the gaming industry as an example of a domain that greatly benefits from the DBaaS service that Cloudant offers. It does not stand alone. You will find that the Cloudant value proposition has no industry boundaries. From Microsoft's Xbox One gaming platform to the Rosetta Stone language learning system to the Dropbox file-sharing solution—each of these products interacts and engages with IBM Cloudant's NoSQL document store database.

Where Did Cloudant Roll in From?

Before we delve into how Cloudant works and what makes it so special, we thought we'd take a moment and get you up to speed on where Cloudant came from, the Apache community it is part of, its contributions to that community, and more.

Cloudant's earliest incarnation was as a data management layer for one of the largest data-generating projects on Earth: the Large Hadron Collider (LHC), operated by the European Organization for Nuclear Research (CERN). Among the many hypotheses that particle physicists investigate with the LHC include the origin of the universe and replicating the conditions of the Big Bang theory, to name a few. Big Data such as this requires big solutions. You can imagine how rigorous and scalable a technology must be to make data generated by the LHC—on the order of petabytes *per day* when the collider is in operation—available to scientists and particle physicists across the globe. Cloudant emerged battle hardened as the solution of choice for CERN and the Large Hadron Collider, and is the same technology available from IBM today—whether or not you're in the business of discovering the origins of the universe!

The flexibility and on-demand consumption models for "as a service" solutions means that vendor lock-in is a huge concern for customers we see looking to make the jump to cloud-based technologies. The last thing you want is to invest in a solution that you expect to be "pick up and go" and then find yourself restricted to only products from the same vendor as you look to build out and extend your service. Many competing vendors in the cloud space follow these kinds of lock-in practices, offering an enticing entry service that scales dramatically in cost if you need to tack on additional functionality or services—and only from their own catalog of services, which might not be the best fit for your use case! We think you will agree that lock-in practices such as these run contrary to the type of open, low-risk, fast time to value environment promoted by as-a-service cloud offerings.

Open is key here: Cloudant maintains a 99 percent compatibility with open source Apache CouchDB (the foundation on which Cloudant was built), allowing Cloudant and CouchDB users to replicate between the two databases; query and perform create, read, update, and delete operations; and build secondary indices with MapReduce—all in a consistent way. A team of Cloudant engineers has made a number of significant contributions to the Apache CouchDB open source community from which it emerged, such as adding Cloudant's user-friendly dashboard to the latest iteration of CouchDB. In addition, a number of Cloudant engineers—Adam Kocoloski, Joan Touzet, Paul Davis, and Bob Newson—also serve as members of the Apache CouchDB Project Management Committee (PMC).

There are considerable advances that Cloudant has made atop CouchDB, of course: Cloudant has a different authorization model (by virtue of being a hosted service, which CouchDB is not); Dynamo-style database clustering is alien to CouchDB; Apache Lucene and GeoJSON geospatial querying do not extend from Cloudant to CouchDB; and so on. However, because Cloudant's API is deeply compatible with CouchDB, Cloudant frequently leverages the open source community for things like building libraries and promoting best practices for interacting with that shared API. Cloudant is a strong supporter of open standards—using JSON instead of a binary alternative that requires adding drivers just to interact with your data.

The motivation behind this is simple: native compatibility eases the pain points for CouchDB users making the move to a managed cloud service; opening the platform to external services and libraries (and not locking in users to a particular vendor) makes it easier to develop with Cloudant; and the ease of integration with existing platforms fosters the type of environment and culture that web and mobile developers cherish.

Cloudant or Hadoop?

A question we get a lot is "What NoSQL technology should I use, Cloudant or Hadoop?" Sometimes the answer is "both," applying each to the use cases for which it was designed. We covered the NoSQL landscape in Chapter 2, so you know that Cloudant is a purpose-built document database and Hadoop is an ecosystem of technologies that includes NoSQL technologies and more. Recall that Cloudant is best utilized as an operational data store rather than as a data warehouse or for ad hoc analytical queries. Cloudant is flexible enough to handle any type of work you could throw at it, but a jack-of-all-trades is a master of none, or so the saying goes. You will want to intelligently apply Cloudant where it can be most useful, namely, as the back-end data layer to systems of engagement (remember: web, mobile, social) because of the incremental index builds that support its query architecture.

We explore this in much more detail in the upcoming "For Techies" sections, but for now, just remember that with Cloudant, your indexes are rebuilt incrementally as the data that they index changes. This results in high-performing queries: Cloudant is fast because you perform searches against an index that has already done the heavy lifting of being built ahead of time. Index the fields that you want to query, send out the results to a Reduce job to consolidate your results (from the MapReduce framework you hear about in Hadoop so much), and format the output. These are the types of indexes that you can design with Cloudant, which then handles the work of ensuring that your searchable indexes are kept up to date as data streams in or is altered.

Imagine, however, that you are a data scientist who regularly changes the type of index you need to define or frequently tests new query patterns. Because Cloudant needs to rebuild an index every time the design document changes, it would be computationally demanding for your database to follow this kind of access pattern. Cloudant keeps pace with the work of building indexes across massive collections of data through Dynamo-style horizontal clustering and a masterless architecture. Nodes operate independently with no single host node governing the jobs that are running on other parts of the cluster. Each node is able to service requests made by the client, and requests that are delivered to an offline node can simply be rerouted to other hosts in the cluster. This contrasts starkly with a Hadoop-style master-slave architecture and ensures that Cloudant clusters achieve the highest degree of availability and uptime. The failure of any one of its masterless nodes does not result in any breakdown of job coordination among other nodes in the cluster. Should you need to scale your database for added nodes and computational power, Cloudant is able to move and divide existing partitions at the database level for rebalancing. The advantage for end users is that the high costs that would be associated with building indexes incrementally can be distributed among the masterless nodes of the cluster—divide and conquer!

Being Flexible: Schemas with JSON

One of the defining characteristics of Cloudant's NoSQL data layer is its use as a JavaScript Object Notation (JSON) document data store. We discussed JSON in Chapter 2. In a nutshell, JSON has become the de facto data interchange format on the web. This is attributable to JSON's lightweight, easily readable (by humans and machines alike) format and to the fact that every JSON document includes a self-describing schema. Data representation and structure can vary from document to document, and JSON's flexible schema enables you to describe nearly any object, regardless of whether the data is structured, semistructured, or unstructured.

Unlike tabular relational databases, which require tightly enforced schemas for insertion and deletion of data, every JSON document within a Cloudant database can have a unique schema. For this reason, Cloudant databases require no table locking, downtime, or intervention by DBAs to alter a single JSON document's schema. This schema flexibility is, of course, convenient to work with; however, its true value is apparent when your app needs to persist data from a variety of object types. The data of today's systems of engagement (web, mobile, social media) is highly variable and messy. Think of the kinds of games your kids are playing on Facebook in between having a Hangout on Google and posting photos of their lunch to Twitter. These are exactly the heterogeneous data sources that Cloudant's JSON can handle with ease. Customers who trust their data layer to Cloudant do not need to spend time migrating data and redesigning databases every time they need to change a schema. Cloudant facilitates faster and more agile development environments.

Cloudant Clustering: Scaling for the Cloud

You might be wondering "Why do developers seem to push for the migration of an RDBMS paradigm to a NoSQL paradigm?" And like with any relationship that has tension, the answer is "It's complicated." We attempted to outline the main reasons in Chapter 2. These developers might have run up against scalability limitations with their existing relational database, might be overwhelmed by having to constantly tune their databases to fit the data, or are looking for an alternative solution that offers more agility and rapid time to market. Developers who are building apps for mobile and web-connected devices need to place data as close to their users as possible. Lower latencies for reads and writes translate into better-performing apps and happier customers. Scalability, therefore, is essential—even at the cost of consistency (which we also talk about in Chapter 2).

One of Cloudant's major value propositions to clients is its ability to manage data over distributed clusters—across *both* bare-metal *and* virtualized data centers—to power apps and deliver content to mobile devices worldwide. Developers of mobile and web apps can host their businesses on a global network of service providers, including IBM SoftLayer, Rackspace, Microsoft Azure, and Amazon Web Services. Regardless of the service provider, Cloudant's data layer gives assurances that a company's underlying services are fully supported by a scalable and flexible NoSQL solution. For this reason, Cloudant typically attracts customer verticals in the areas of online gaming, mobile development, marketing analytics, SaaS companies, online education providers, social media, networking sites, and data analytics firms, among others. By the time we went to print, we counted almost 40 data centers around the world where the Cloudant service was being hosted. IBM Cloudant enables total flexibility in document and database design, as well as control over where that data is hosted. Cloudant is able to scale out these deployments by up to millions of databases. Furthermore, you can instantiate databases to isolate data on an individual database level. This combination of scaled development and deployment across data centers worldwide, as well as the partitioning of data across individual databases, enables you to isolate and tightly control how data is persisted on the network.

We alluded earlier that Cloudant is able to achieve this level of scalability because of a multimaster architecture that is designed for *Dynamo-style* horizontal clustering. This "masterless" framework ensures that Cloudant is able to scale and replicate across multiple systems, racks, data centers, and cloud operations; furthermore, it guarantees that any node can be leveraged to perform read-write capabilities in the event of hardware failure within your cluster. Cloudant's DBaaS is provisioned across multiple servers and maintains redundant copies throughout the cluster for durable and highly available storage. What looks like a logical database to the customer is something that's actually partitioned across machines.

Avoiding Mongo-Size Outages: Sleep Soundly with Cloudant Replication

Having examined how Cloudant's architecture leverages Dynamo-style quorum-based clustering to satisfy read and write requests, we can now go a little deeper into how data is replicated and synchronized across the nodes of a Cloudant cluster. Unlike most other vendors in this space who use master-slave architectures, Cloudant has no notion of a master node; it has a multimaster ("masterless") cluster architecture. A client who wants to write a document to a Cloudant database can have that write request land anywhere in the cluster. The request does not need to hit a node that actually hosts the document in question. The node that receives the request subsequently consults the partition table, performs a lookup to determine which nodes are hosting the requested document, and simultaneously submits requests to store it on three hosts (the default value for the replication parameter). After a quorum is reached, a response is delivered to the client to signify a successful write to disk.

The process of rebalancing a Cloudant cluster when adding a new node does not require splitting partitions. Instead, as new nodes are added to a cluster, the data layer employs a module inside the cluster that computes a set of moves to yield a balanced distribution of shard files. Many Cloudant clusters can be measured in *thousands* of partitions, so you can imagine how important it is to not just automate this process but also have it managed for you. During movement, new shards are copied while old shards remain online to perform lookups. When the process of replicating shards is complete, the shard mapping points to the newly replicated shards.

Note that indexes must be copied first (before the main database files) because if Cloudant detects an index that is out of step with the documents it is indexing, that index is considered to be corrupt and must be rebuilt. Although the process of rebalancing your cluster can be time consuming (particularly with large data sets), absolutely no downtime occurs as a result of the rebalancing procedures. This is a significant advantage over other solutions such as MongoDB (which we believe mandates downtime to perform rebalancing) and Couchbase (which does not offer a fully managed service to handle these operations for you).

We like to think that Cloudant is an equal-opportunity employer in how it distributes labor: If you are a node in a Cloudant cluster, you will be working. This design decision emerged from the need to ensure that all indexes remain available in the event of hardware failure. Cloudant passes any client-submitted request to all nodes in a cluster, which then work in parallel (and independently; remember that this is a masterless architecture) to satisfy the request. For example, if a database has four partitions and three replicas per partition, then there are at any given time 12 workers that are indexing that database. The work is being done in triplicate (if the replication factor is set to the default value of N=3) to ensure that the request can be satisfied if any of the worker nodes goes offline before the request can be satisfied. There is also some redundancy because each node is operating on its own independent copy of the data.

The concern for Cloudant engineers, however, is that if they defer or deprioritize construction of redundant copies of an index, the database runs the risk of having apps made unavailable from the loss of a single index replica. The coordinator follows a similar strategy in response to index queries that are submitted to the cluster. Unlike the quorum parameters for reads and writes that must be satisfied by a simple majority, the coordinator does not assemble answers from each response to an index query; rather, the first answer received by the coordinator is accepted as the correct response. If your data is replicated over three nodes with a shard count of four (N=3, Q=4) and a query is submitted to the secondary index, the coordinator passes that request to *all 12 partitions*. The first index query response to be received by the coordinator is returned to the client making the request, and all subsequent responses that follow from the other nodes are ignored. Cloudant sends a "cancel" response to those nodes that (as of the time the coordinator receives its answer) have not yet submitted a response. Doing so cancels streaming jobs that are running on those nodes but does not cancel background indexing tasks. It might seem that the work being done by these "redundant" nodes is for naught, but keep in mind that this extra effort provides some assurance of a timely response to the client. If one node is busy at the time of the request, one of the other two nodes should be able to respond in a timely manner.

Cloudant Sync Brings Data to a Mobile World

For developers who are building apps that are mobile-centric—thinking beyond just screen size and operating system and aspiring to deliver to platforms with semi-to-no connectivity—Cloudant Sync delivers local read, write, and index query access to data on your mobile devices. The result is incredibly well-performing apps that need to rely only on your local device to do the computations, instead of waiting for server-side calls and responses. Cloudant Sync is now available across two client libraries: one for iOS and one for Android. The Cloudant Sync service also works with web apps built to leverage PouchDB too—a portable, almost fully capable version of Apache CouchDB that runs natively in the browser.

Cloudant Sync shines in scenarios where you have high levels of write activity and, critically, where your application and device rely on connectivity. Imagine a shipping truck leaving a warehouse to make its deliveries. The more processing the operator can do on her tablet, the better the experience for both the driver and the customers along the route. You really want to "sync" only those moments that are novel and interesting. Cloudant can create very small JSON documents (for example, in the event of a car's deployed airbag), which subsequently trigger other apps on a very short turnaround, such as piping telematics data to an analytics or reporting tool. In this particular use case, Cloudant has the ability to shred JSON data and load it into the high-performance BLU Acceleration technology in the dashDB service or on premise in DB2 (we cover this in Chapter 8).

SQLite is a relational database that is ubiquitous across nearly every mobile phone and tablet. Furthermore, it is a data layer that is familiar to many of today's application developers, as well as a proven technology. The elegance of Cloudant's SQLite implementation is that it abstracts the migration process (through Cloudant Sync libraries) from the perspective of end users and developers. Cloudant's Sync libraries handle the mapping of JSON documents to SQLite's relational data store on your mobile devices, without intervention by the developer. Cloudant's SQLite-based "Sync" libraries follow a multiversion concurrency control (MVCC) data model (employed by databases such as Oracle and optionally on DB2) to build indexes locally on your mobile device. Replication is still handled by Cloudant, but during connectivity outages, the SQLite data layer manages local reads, writes, and indexing. When your device regains connectivity to the network, the Sync library handles pushing up that data to the Cloudant cluster. When your device's data hits the cluster, your edits are propagated through the traditional Cloudant replication and synchronization mechanisms to the rest of the nodes according to the quorum parameters that you defined earlier. As before, no additional libraries are required for Cloudant Sync to interact with your database cluster; all requests are passed over HTTP or HTTPS through Cloudant's RESTful API. You can see how this kind of robustness is critical for occasionally connected clients.

Make Data, Not War: Cloudant Versioning and Conflict Resolution

With distributed systems, there is always the potential that two clients are introducing different updates to the same document at the same time. When you think about it, use of a data layer that supports writing to a database on a device and a server simultaneously, or across clusters, further increases the likelihood of document conflict scenarios. Your database solution needs to be able to track all the edits being made to an individual document and needs to have easy-to-use and elegant mechanisms to reconcile these changes and persist them in some logical way.

Imagine two separate clusters of nodes: clusterA hosts the document llama01, and clusterB hosts the document llama02. Now for the sake of this example, let's stipulate that llama01 and llama02 have the same content. Each has a revision identifier value that reflects both the document's path (relative to the database) and a hash of the document's content. Although the *contents* of documents llama01 and llama02 are identical, the resulting hash value of the two documents will differ because of the unique paths these documents have with respect to their separate databases. Two documents with the same content in *different* databases will not generate a revision conflict, which seems sensible when you think about it—you would not want to run up against a situation where you cannot create a "Hello, World!" script on your database because others have identical "Hello, World!" documents on their databases. Hash values are injected at commit time to ensure that the edit history is deeply "baked" into the core of the database architecture. This is necessary for Cloudant to guarantee that replications are performed correctly and that data consistency is maintained. With Cloudant, the revision and hash history of every document is persisted internally as a B-tree structure and continues to be stored alongside the document as it is replicated across servers. Without this revision history, Cloudant would be unable to detect and repair divergences within a given cluster.

Recall that every node in a Cloudant cluster is "masterless" and therefore independent; in that context, you can think of the process of synchronization between two nodes as a matter of deterministically achieving the same state between nodes. A replication task can be submitted for one node, such that the contents of node X are replicated (either continuously or as a "snapshot" in time) to node Y. However, to maintain the same state across multiple nodes, it is necessary to instantiate replication in both directions; in other words, you need to establish bidirectional replication (as shown in Figure 10-2), which is a cornerstone of Cloudant's architecture.

With replication underway in both directions, each database deterministically agrees upon the contents and state of each node. The ballpark latency for achieving this is in the order of seconds. When you write a document into a database, the primary key index and the _changes feed are atomically updated. The _changes feed maintains a list of all documents that have changed since the last time you checked in. Cloudant uses incremental check-in to achieve this. Ultimately, the largest contributing factor to the time that it takes a write request to update the _changes feed and then trigger

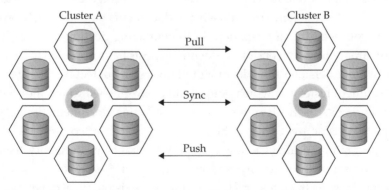

Figure 10-2 *Bidirectional synchronization between Cloudant clusters. Replication jobs between Cluster A and Cluster B are defined to establish this kind of "mega-cluster."*

responses such as replication and sync is the physical latency between your data centers.

Versioning and document conflicts will inevitably arise with any large distributed system, and although Cloudant employs numerous strategies to avoid document update conflicts—such as the requirement that all updates to documents include the document ID and the *latest* revision ID of the document—there must always be a contingency for resolving conflicts. In other words, expect the best, but always plan for the worst. Cloudant's solution is to never delete conflicts; instead, conflicting documents are both persisted inside the database and left for the application layer to deterministically resolve. Minimizing write contention is rule number one for avoiding conflicts. Requiring document updates to supply both the document ID and revision value certainly helps to reduce the number of conflicts that might arise. Cloudant recommends you treat your data as *immutable documents* and that you create new documents instead of updating existing ones as a strategy for further cutting down on the number of revision conflicts. This has some storage implications, but the benefits of having fewer document update conflicts and having a traceable document lineage are valuable to many Cloudant customer use cases.

The "right" version of a document is something that Cloudant deterministically returns for you by default. If you want to know about all existing conflicts, you must ask for them. The parameter `conflicts=true` returns a list of revision identifiers for siblings of the document that you specify. Today, Cloudant will not inform you as to the number of conflicts that exist in a document's metadata; however, you can easily leverage Cloudant's built-in MapReduce functionality to build a list of documents that have revision conflicts if you need this information. With conflicting documents, the cluster coordinator detects that one of the document hosts has responded to a request with an older version of the document. It does so by detecting divergence in the document history, at which point it can determine—through the conflicting document's hash history—how the conflicting document fits into the complete revision tree. This enables a developer to later commit that document programmatically. Cloudant actively leverages hash history technology to preserve the integrity and consistency of the cluster as a whole. Append, merge, drop, and pick the winning revision; as a developer, the choice is up to you. Conflicts are never automatically resolved within the database (which is to say, Cloudant will never take the leap of deleting data without your express permission); it is up to the developer to resolve them at the application layer.

Unlocking GIS Data with Cloudant Geospatial

How can Cloudant decrease the time needed to deliver data harvested from the web, embedded Internet of Things (IoT) systems, and Geographic Information Systems (GIS) systems to mobile phone and tablet endpoints? Shipping, logistics, governments, and land management, as well as oil and gas industries (among others), have all struggled to make this type of data available at the point of impact. Such data is typically persisted in relational databases, which have continued to serve as the persistence model of choice for GIS analysts. However, we have found that a plethora of companies vested in on-premise GIS systems experience difficulties when scaling this data across regions (horizontally across distributed systems) or are unable to leverage the data properly for consumer-driven apps.

Cloudant's replication and synchronization deliver the high availability and intelligent geoload balancing that your apps need to fully exploit GIS data for the modern era of cloud and mobile computing. Sharding of the data is key; your company's records might be government compliance bound, subject to privacy concerns, or might be unable to leave certain boundaries or national borders. This can be a security concern or a performance consideration. For example, you do not necessarily need oceanographic data from the South China Sea uploaded to a user who is surveying olive groves in Greece. It is a matter of delivering the correct data to the right user, with a minimal amount of latency for well-performing apps. Cloudant geospatial libraries enable the sharding and distribution of your data based on geospatial attributes and coordinates, all of which are available within your JSON document metadata!

To facilitate this granular level of control, Cloudant uses GeoJSON, a format for encoding a variety of geographic data structures, to describe geometries; it persists this data in geospatial indexes based on R*-trees (data structures that are used for spatial access methods, such as calculating the size of a bounded quadrilateral floodplain). The decision to use R*-trees instead of

R-trees is based on expense versus performance: R*-trees are computationally more expensive to generate but produce fewer overlapping regions on the resulting tree map. However, because Cloudant indexes need to be computed only once (until the data set being indexed changes) and the job of building these indexes is distributed across the cluster, much faster queries are possible after the index has been built, even on remote devices such as your phone or tablet.

Geospatial coordinates can be mapped and indexed as two-dimensional or three-dimensional coordinates, and they support all standard coordinate reference systems (UTMs, grids, variations of Mercator, and so on). You can run powerful queries with these indexes; Cloudant Geospatial supports searches against polygons (even hand-drawn maps), circles, ellipses, bounding boxes, and virtually any other geometrical shapes that come to mind. You can use these shapes to run inclusive-exclusive queries (as well as a myriad of other geospatial relations), such as a donut-shaped bounding area that includes all points within a circle except for the circular region in the center—very impressive stuff!

Queries are not limited to points on a map. Consider for a moment how virtually all data generated in today's social-mobile-cloud world is temporally and spatially enriched. Just take a quick look at a Twitter feed or Facebook wall, which includes information about when the entry was made, from where, and on what platform. Assuming that users do not opt to hide this information behind a privacy wall, this rich catalog of metadata is available for you to explore and discover. With Cloudant, developers can leverage this wealth of metadata to perform temporal (four-dimensional) searches with *time* as a metric, which enables predictive forecasting. This level of functionality is of great interest to shipping and logistics companies.

Additionally, you can combine your geospatial data with other secondary or search indexes to gain deeper insight into your business. For example, you could search a database of employee business cards to identify all the people who live within a five-kilometer radius of Toronto, Canada; who speak French; and who have Hadoop skills. There are also integration points between Cloudant and ESRI for further extending Cloudant's NoSQL document data with GIS relational database stores. Finally, because Cloudant Geospatial is deeply integrated within the database architecture, you can rest assured that your geospatial data remains interoperable across CouchDB, PouchDB, and, of course, Cloudant.

Cloudant Local

By the time we go to print, IBM will have a special offering, called Cloudant Local, which is designed for enterprise, healthcare, security, and other organizations that have privacy-related ordinances or government regulations that restrict their data to on-premise deployment models. Cloudant's dedicated team of engineers can fully support the deployment of your on-premise infrastructure, as well as make your on-premise data available on the cloud, if and when your business requires it.

Cloudant will provide support for the initial provisioning and system calibration of Cloudant Local; however, Cloudant Local will not carry the same level of ongoing managed support. After Cloudant Local begins its on-site residency, the further provisioning, management, and scaling of your database is up to you. Of course, you will interact with Cloudant Local through the same interfaces and APIs that you currently employ with traditional Cloudant (a dashboard GUI, the cURL command line, the RESTful HTTP- or HTTPS- based API, and so on).

We want to stress that the core strengths of Cloudant's functionality are preserved across both cloud and on-premise deployments. Cloudant Local offers superior agility for developers: a NoSQL data layer built on top of open source Apache CouchDB, with fully supported database replication and synchronization protocols. Cloudant's multimaster ("masterless") replication architecture, as well as mobile application sync capabilities for occasionally connected devices, are also available in Cloudant Local. Furthermore, Cloudant's powerful query suite—including geospatial, real-time indexing, incremental MapReduce, and Apache Lucene full-text search—is carried over to on-premise deployments.

We think you will leverage Cloudant Local to integrate directly with existing on-site NoSQL environments or infrastructures. But more importantly, because Cloudant Local maintains compatibility with traditional Cloudant, you can leverage the same API libraries to "burst" data to the cloud for additional capacity (for backups, disaster recovery, or high availability, for example) when and as needed. Even if your organization is not subject to regulatory requirements, it might make sense to start your deployment on premise and take "bursty" workloads into the cloud as needed—we refer to this as *hybrid* cloud computing.

Here on In: For Techies...

A key part of being an operational data store (instead of a parallelized analytics framework like Hadoop) has to do with indexing. For this reason, we want you to think of this section as the "How do you find things fast?" approach to database design. That said, the value of indexing reaches new levels when you expand the scope of this topic to include index maintenance and build times, which are just as important as search speed in the broader scheme of things. Cloudant has rich and flexible indexing services that make it exceptional at retrieving documents or document subcomponents that you specify, with techniques that go far beyond simple key lookups.

Cloudant supports multiple kinds of indexes: primary, secondary, search, and geospatial indexes. A key differentiator that makes Cloudant so appealing for transactional JSON-backed apps is that its indexes do not need to be completely rebuilt from scratch with every update, deletion, or creation of a new document; instead, an index can be incrementally updated "on the fly." This Cloudant feature makes it well suited for online data stores and for serving as the data layer for web apps and mobile devices.

In the remaining sections in this chapter we're going to take a peek at the Cloudant technology with a tech-head in mind (but still keep it at a high level—just a technical high level).

For Techies: Leveraging the Cloudant Primary Index

Cloudant provisions an out-of-the-box primary index, which is a B-tree index that is persisted at the database level and is the underlying fit-to-purpose mechanism for fast data retrieval. This primary index can be accessed through the Cloudant dashboard, through your web browser, or through the cURL command line at the `_all_docs` endpoint. By default, querying the index gives you a list of every document in your database, returning a key `_id` and a value `_rev`.

You can further refine your query by passing parameters to retrieve a specific document by its key, submit `include_docs=true` to return the entire document as the value, swap the order by setting `descending=false`, specify the start and end keys ranges, and more. The takeaway message here is that the primary index can be an extremely efficient tool when properly leveraged by your application layer. Cloudant supports the specification of customized document IDs (versus the autogenerated UUIDs that Cloudant supplies by default) to make it easier to locate documents and to perform searches against the primary index. Figure 10-3 illustrates how a simple JSON document can be written to or retrieved from a Cloudant document database endpoint using the HTTP-based API.

All interactions with a Cloudant database are made through a RESTful HTTP or HTTPS API. Queries against the primary index nicely demonstrate how a web-based API can be both intuitive and expressive to users. Any application that "speaks the language of the web" can interact with your Cloudant data layer through its RESTful API. Nearly every modern programming language and development environment you can imagine—Java, Python, .NET, Ruby, Node.js, and so on—cleanly integrates with the web; such languages can therefore just as easily interoperate with a Cloudant data layer. Developers can issue commands using verbs such as GET, PUT, POST, DELETE, and COPY to a set of logically organized URI endpoints. The hierarchy of endpoints that developers specify through this API is intuitive to any user of a modern web browser (and, in fact, the API *can* be accessed and queried through your favorite browser at any time). Cloudant's language-agnostic API is incredibly useful for developing apps for any platform or device that speaks a web language.

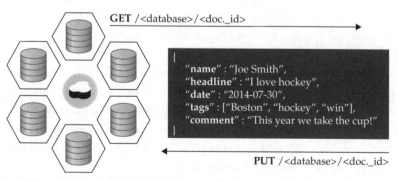

Figure 10-3 *Cloudant's RESTful API follows a logical set of URI endpoints to interact with your data layer through HTTP or HTTPS.*

Exploring Data with Cloudant's Secondary Index "Views"

For those of you who are coming from the world of RDBMS technologies, Cloudant's secondary indexes are called *views* because of how closely they follow the design pattern of materialized views in the SQL world. Secondary indexes (and search indexes, which we will explore shortly), unlike primary indexes, do not exist out of the box; they are defined using _design documents, a special class of JSON documents. All indexes that are defined by a design document are built in sequence, one after the other, so that deciding to define all indexes within the same design document will result in a slower index build than defining one index per design document. There is no limit on the number of secondary indexes that you can define and build. However, just like in the relational world, the more secondary indexes you have, the more rebuild work is required to maintain them across your cluster.

Cloudant uses an incremental MapReduce framework to generate secondary indexes, which demonstrates the ubiquity of this skill across your business. For example, you might have some developers building an IBM InfoSphere BigInsights for Hadoop solution cluster, and their MapReduce skills can be used to index Cloudant data. (These same skills can also be used to run in-database MapReduce programs within an IBM PureData for Analytics System—formerly known as Netezza.) The data ultimately lands in Hadoop for analytics, which can later be leveraged at your mobile device endpoints, thanks to Cloudant's synchronization and replication libraries. Cloudant's MapReduce indexing services follow the classic Map (and optional Reduce) paradigms for building indexes, enabling users to perform more advanced queries against one or more secondary fields in their documents. Unlike competing NoSQL vendors, Cloudant does not recommend placing all updates and sprawling lines of data into single documents, precisely because the secondary index enables you to "roll up" across multiple, smaller (individual) documents using the incremental MapReduce framework.

Just like in the relational world, designing an index requires that you recognize potentially high-value access patterns. A mandatory Map phase typically scans through every document in the database. Its sole purpose is to emit qualifying keys and corresponding values. In the case of a secondary index, the key might be *complex*, meaning it is defined by multiple fields.

(In the relational world, a *compound* key contains multiple columns.) This capability is extremely powerful when you consider that the resulting index, when queried, is automatically sorted by key. For example, you could retrieve a list of all books written about a specific topic, sorted by copyright date and version, by using a complex key.

Developers have the option to specify a Reduce job following the Map phase. Cloudant provides Reduce job boilerplates that are natively compiled in *Erlang*, a programming language that is designed specifically for engaging with and powering massively distributed apps. Erlang-compiled jobs are much more efficiently built on disk than custom Reduce functions. Cloudant also lets you define custom Reduce jobs in JavaScript, but these will perform slower than their Erlang counterparts. Recall that Cloudant is best applied as an operational data store precisely because it builds its query indexes incrementally in real time—it is not optimized for building indexes in batch. Cloudant does support the query parameter ?stale=ok, which enables prioritization of performance over consistency by giving Cloudant permission to query the last-built index rather than waiting for a currently running index job to finish rebuilding before processing the query. If you have a large production environment, we recommend you leverage ?stale=ok for improved query responses as a best practice.

Performing Ad Hoc Queries with the Cloudant Search Index

Cloudant has built-in support for Apache Lucene libraries (the same libraries that are used by open source Elasticsearch and Solr) for performing powerful ad hoc queries against any fields you choose to index. To query the search index, your application needs to reference the database, the _design doc, _search, and the name of the index. Developers can further augment their queries by using wildcard expressions, ranges, inclusive and exclusive parameters, fuzzy searches, search term boosting, Boolean operators, and more. If, like this team of authors, you too are prone to typos and slips of the finger, performing a fuzzy search for *bongo* will give the NoSQL results you were looking for. The fact that Lucene search is built into Cloudant, unlike other competing vendors, gives Cloudant a serious leg up in this space. Like secondary indexes, search indexes must be defined in your _design document as a function that parses the contents of the whole document. The resulting output creates an index of one or more fields that can be queried. These indexes are built as soon as you load the design document. Over time, any event that updates your documents will trigger a rebuild of your indexes, as well as subsequent replication of the indexes across the cluster.

Defining a search index requires supplying the key for the field that you want to index, as well as several optional parameters if you are feeling adventurous. One parameter that Cloudant practitioners often use in place of a custom identifier (which would be used for querying a field by name) is default; it enables you to submit a search against the index without knowing the name of the field. For example, you could perform an equivalent search to q=animalName:zebra by using q=zebra, without having to specify the field identifier. Cloudant's search index also supports more advanced types of queries, such as searches against geospatial coordinates, group searches, and faceting. Lucene supports sorting on a particular field. By default, it sorts based on the Lucene order number; however, if you want to have reliable sorts that are based on relevance, you can index by a particular field name.

Parameters That Govern a Logical Cloudant Database

Four key Cloudant parameters govern a Cloudant cluster and affect the way it operates from a scaling perspective, data safety perspective, consistency perspective, and more. If this were *Sesame Street*, these sections would be brought to you by the letters Q, N, W, and R.

Q Is for the Number of Shards

We are not quite sure how the letter Q came to mean the number of individual database partitions over which your data is distributed in a Cloudant cluster, but like so much around naming and labeling in the Apache world, mystery prevails. With that said, if your Cloudant database is configured with Q=4, it means that the cluster has four shards (shards is a NoSQL way of saying partitions). In such an environment, any document that is submitted to this database must pass through a consistent hashing function. The hashing function, like in the RDBMS world, determines where the complete (or "master") copy of the data will reside once it is placed across Q hosts.

If you have ever lined up at an amusement park to ride a roller coaster and have been placed into one of several lines waiting to fill the carts, then you have been part of a hashing function—what a rush! Determining where to distribute the document shards is a purely functional computation of the document ID; there is no lookup table that says "For this document ID 123, host on partition X." Instead, the location is determined as a pure hash function of the document ID to a segment in the hash key-space. The only state that Cloudant needs to maintain is the mapping of shards to nodes. This is persisted in a separate database that is continuously replicated to every node in the cluster. Each document is guaranteed to fall into the key-space of that hash function, where each key-space represents a shard. Selecting a good, consistent hashing function will generate an even distribution of the number of documents per shard across your key-space. By sharding (distributing) your data over multiple nodes, you are able to house within your database (and thus across your cluster) more data than could be persisted on just a single host. To ensure that these shards are stored durably and consistently, you need to calibrate the replication factor for each shard. This brings us to the letter N.

N Is for the Number of Copies

The N parameter determines the number of copies (replicas) of every data shard that will be generated across a Cloudant cluster—this parameter is mainly used to determine high-availability and redundancy levels. Typically, multitenant Cloudant clients would use $N=3$. Keeping with the example from the previous section, if a Cloudant service was configured such that $N=3$ and $Q=4$, there would be 12 ($N \times Q = 3 \times 4$) shards distributed across your cluster.

W Is for the Write Quorum

The Cloudant quorum parameter (W) specifies the number of nodes that need to acknowledge that they have successfully written data to disk before the write can be considered "durably" committed to the cluster. Only when this number is reached can Cloudant consider the client's write request (be it for document creation, insertion, deletion, or update) to have been successfully executed. For example, an application that submits a write operation to a six-node cluster will submit the request to each of nodes 1, 2, and 3; however, only a majority of these nodes needs to acknowledge the request (in a response to the client) for that write to be considered successful.

Consider the example shown in Figure 10-4. An operator would consider the write request successful if two out of the three nodes report a successful response code. Note that if N=3 for this cluster, an additional replica of the data being written will eventually be replicated to the third node, which did not report back because it was the last to respond or because of some error. The two-thirds majority is sufficient to guarantee a durable write to disk.

This scenario describes Cloudant's model of "eventual consistency," which is the premise that, given a sufficient amount of time, the replication state of the cluster and all views into the data will be consistent across the cluster.

One last point about write requests: Cloudant does not have the notion of a "rollback." Instead, write requests that don't satisfy the simple majority quorum requirement return a 202 status code. This signals to the application developer that although the write operation did not meet the quorum requirement, it was still committed to one of the nodes. You cannot roll back failed write requests via the database servicer, but you can design program logic to handle such cases after the fact.

R Is for the Return Read Requests

The R quorum parameter specifies the *number of nodes* that must return copies of data that "agree" (match) on the value of the data being returned to the requesting client. Included with the data will be the document's revision

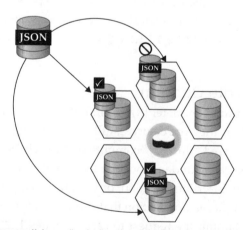

Figure 10-4 *Conceptualizing a "write" request from a client to a Cloudant cluster of six nodes with a write quorum of 2*

identifier, which is a combination of an incremental identifier (denoting the number of times the document has been revised) appended to the front of a string (generated by a hash function applied to a combination of the contents of the document and its path relative to the database). How do nodes in the cluster agree on the data value that a client receives when making a request to the database?

Similar to the W parameter, R, by default, is the simple majority of the total number of nodes in the cluster. If an insufficient number of nodes are able to return a replica of the requested data, the read request fails. In other words, if the cluster doesn't agree with R degree of certainty that this data is valid, it will not return the data. Let's clarify with the example shown in Figure 10-5.

In Figure 10-5, the read quorum is R=3 for a cluster of six nodes, with a shard factor of Q=3. For the sake of this example, let's assume the replication factor for these shards is 2 (N=2), such that there are two copies of every shard in the database. If this is the case, the coordinator can have its pick of which hosts to consult for the "read" request: There are six shards (N x Q = 2 x 3 = 6 hash key ranges) across the database cluster, only three nodes need to be consulted, and only a simple majority of two nodes is needed to produce a document that "agrees" to satisfy the client's request. There is a high probability, therefore, that this read will be successful, precisely because this cluster has been tuned to be highly available and durable. You'll note that one copy of the

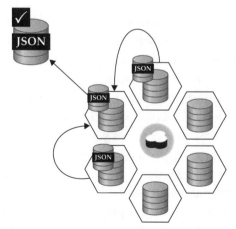

Figure 10-5 *Conceptualizing a "read" request from a client to a Cloudant cluster of six nodes*

data happens to reside on the coordinating node, and other host nodes in the cluster share two replicas. If these three replicas are in agreement and able to produce a version of the requested JSON document, then a quorum is reached, and the document is returned to the requesting application.

Remember! Cloudant Is DBaaS

Throughout this chapter we talk about how Cloudant is a fully managed database as a service solution. As part of your partnership with IBM, experienced Cloudant technical engineers work with you to select the optimal values for Q, N, W, and R (among other parameters that we are not detailing here). Changing the replication factor and sharding key are nontrivial tasks after a database is up and running, so it is vitally important to choose the optimal values up front because they govern the operational aspects of your Cloudant database. IBM and Cloudant help you do that—because the right configuration is as much an art form (experience matters) as it is a science.

Now consider some alternative NoSQL document stores. They require you to make some pretty big (almost hu*mongo*us) decisions with respect to the shard key, for example, all on your own. This is just one of so many reasons why the Cloudant model stands head and shoulders above alternative offerings. If you stop to consider the aggregate value of Cloudant's fully managed approach to database provisioning, configuration, and maintenance—supported by a master-master architecture and flexible tenancy options—we think the choice is apparent.

Let's close this section by illustrating why selection of the aforementioned parameters is so critical and how the backing of Cloudant artisans and technical experts (who are with you every step along that journey) means an end to sleepless nights for you as a customer.

As previously mentioned, one of the key considerations when selecting the shard count (Q) for your cluster is that indexes are constructed locally on individual partition files. This becomes very nuanced when you understand that only one copy of each partition is consulted to satisfy a single view query. Stated more accurately, it is the first copy that is given to the coordinator in response to the query request.

Therefore, there are two factors in play when you are selecting an optimal Q value. First, you want to keep the required throughput on a partition (the number of writes the partition must juggle) low enough so that the index can be computed fast enough to give a response with low latency. Second, you want to minimize the amount of network traffic that is generated across your cluster: If you are building an index that you expect will be queried against thousands of times per second, you need to consider that each of those (thousand) queries will be sent to every single partition. Cranking up the number of partitions significantly increases the load you place on both the CPUs that support your database and the network itself. If an application is read-heavy, the database should favor a lower number of shards. Conversely, if your application is write-heavy, you will want a higher number of shards to balance out and distribute the work of performing write operations. In general, the number of shards should be a multiple of the number of nodes in the cluster so that the shards can be distributed evenly.

Of course, "stuff happens." In the event of failure, Cloudant operators manage the restoration of a downed node by first returning this failed host to life in *maintenance mode*. The node accepts write operations and continues to perform internal replication tasks to bring it in step with the rest of the cluster, but it does not respond to *coordination requests*, which are read and write quorum acknowledgments in response to client requests.

When the node matches the replication state of the rest of the cluster, Cloudant operators turn off maintenance mode, and the node is available for servicing coordination tasks. Cloudant engages maintenance mode in the event of a node failure to preserve and minimize the consistency-related responses that you might get on secondary index queries. The bottom line is that your database solution partner (IBM) strives to keep you from having to wrestle with the underlying technology while delivering reliable uptime document store services—which is why you chose a managed service in the first place.

Wrapping It Up

In this chapter, we talked about how Cloudant eliminates complexity and risk when you build fast-growing web and mobile apps by providing *not* just a hosted, but a fully managed data-layer solution. With Cloudant, you receive a cloud service that enables your developers to focus on creating the next generation of apps without needing to manage their database infrastructure and growth. The flexibility of a NoSQL JSON persistence model ensures that you can work with nearly any type of data, structured or unstructured, on an architecture that is scalable, available, and distributed.

On top of this data layer, Cloudant adds a suite of advanced indexing and querying capabilities (for use with even multidimensional spatial data), including Cloudant Sync libraries to support local write, read, and indexing capabilities on occasionally connected or even disconnected mobile devices. Delivered from the cloud as a managed DBaaS that is unparalleled in the industry, Cloudant simplifies application development for a new class of systems of engagement. At the same time, Cloudant Local offers companies that are not ready (or unable because of regulations) the ability to leverage an off-premise environment while taking advantage of the many Cloudant advantages we outlined in this chapter. Cloudant Local maintains pure API compatibility with traditional cloud-based Cloudant deployments to enable hybrid apps that support bursty workloads.

Cloudant brings cloud-based scalability and continuous availability to empower application developers to build more, grow more, and sleep more. We think you will find IBM Cloudant to be the "do more" NoSQL layer that your business is looking for. Get started for free at https://cloudant.com/sign-up/.

Part III

Calming the Waters:
Big Data Governance

11

Guiding Principles for Data Governance

IBM has long been promoting the importance of data governance, both in word, by advising clients, and indeed, by building governance capabilities into our software. This part of the book discusses both, by first outlining key principles for data governance and, in the following chapters, by describing the on-premise and off-premise data governance tools that can be used to bring order to your Big Data challenges. Where the first two parts of this book are about understanding Big Data, blue sky thinking (industry trends, ideal architectures), and the latest tech (the Watson Foundations data storage and processing technologies), this is the parental guidance section. The chapters in this part of the book are critical to any Big Data project that aspires to transform an organization from the hype phase to a data decisioning one—there is no hype allowed here. We feel that this is an appropriate closing note for our book because as exciting as new technologies are, real success in analytics and data management comes from a properly deployed data governance strategy. In this chapter, we're going to lay out the IBM data governance maturity model as a set of directives, a modus operandi if you will. We'll use the remaining chapters in this book to explain their application in a Big Data setting. This is the sort of chapter you pick up and reread a few times a year to see how your organization measures up to data governance criteria.

The IBM Data Governance Council Maturity Model

The IBM Data Governance Council was formed in 2004, with the goal of growing a community around the discipline of data governance. The council wasn't started to be just an IBM thing: It's composed of companies spanning all industries, universities, and business partners. This council has expanded its scope and membership and now exists as the more global InfoGov community. You can join this community and participate in the dialogue at www .infogovcommunity.com.

In 2007, the council published the IBM Data Governance Council Maturity Model, which codified a number of key criteria capturing the breadth of the data governance domain. This document has stood the test of time and is just as important a resource today as it was when it was first published—even after major technical changes, such as service-oriented architectures, cloud computing, NoSQL, and Big Data, have evolved the data center. In fact, we would argue that the latest technical developments in IT have amplified the importance of the data governance principles in this model.

The following sections describe each of the 11 data governance principles from the IBM Data Governance Council Maturity Model and discuss their Big Data implications.

1. Organizational Structures and Awareness

Data centers and analytic tools exist to serve the organization that pays for them. The first step in developing a data governance plan is to document the nature of your organization and the key decision makers. There has to be an organizationwide understanding that data governance is a shared responsibility between the business side of the organization and IT. Specifically, business goals need to drive all aspects of data governance.

We personally make it a point to stress the importance of proper data governance in all of our customer engagements. Big Data technologies have been a catalyst for healthy strategic thinking about the role of data in organizations.

2. Stewardship

More often than not, we see discussions around stewardship begin and end with the question of which department should own certain data sets. A proper discussion on stewardship needs to go beyond control and should include details about how the people in control of the data will take care of it, nurture it, feel responsible for it, and instill a culture of responsibility across the population that consumes the organization's information supply chain—which should be everyone.

3. Policy

Most people find documenting policies boring, as do we, but without having the desired practices around your organization's data written in black and white, you're asking for trouble. We've seen this with many early Big Data projects, where teams went off and played with new technologies without having firm documented goals. More often than not, the lack of documented policies indicates a potential problem. Documented policies are like a Big Data constitution for your organization—they spell out expectations and ordinances in how data is to be handled—not to mention they come in handy if you're ever subjected to an audit. But step back for a moment and try to imagine any highly invested ecosystem for which you don't have a set of well-documented policies. Do you have a credit card? Ever rent a car? Gym membership? Policies state out the rules, regulations, and remediation actions for a service, so why shouldn't your data by governed by them?

4. Value Creation

Mature organizations tend to be good at identifying the value of their data assets. In the same way that analytics helps organizations to make better decisions, quantifying the importance that data assets have to an organization helps IT departments prioritize how they deal with these assets. For example, which data sets need to be hosted on tier-one storage and are subject to performance requirements (such as, a service level agreement)? Or which data sets are most important to cleanse? These questions are equally relevant to data sets that people call Big Data. For example, much of the data that is harvested from social sources is sparse and poorly identified, but there might be little value in applying the same quality techniques to this type of data that you would apply to relational data. The bottom line is that all data is not created equal: It doesn't all have to be as fast or as available or as cleansed, and it's not all going to have the same value. As kids, all the authors of this book collected hockey cards (yes, even the U.S. ones) and we recounted about how we would keep them in an ordered fashion that reflected their value. You should have value statements around your Big Data sources and they will dictate how the data is used, trusted, curated, invested in, and so on.

5. Data Risk Management and Compliance

Regulatory compliance issues dominate the agendas of IT department meetings, and this has not changed as Big Data trends have entered the mainstream. Data retention policies, audit readiness, separation of duties and concerns, access control, and privacy, among others, all need to be considered here. How long does the data have to be retained and is it subject to immutability (you can't change it) rules? When the data is no longer needed, is it subject to defensible destruction requirements? Does data need to be masked in test systems, does it need to be encrypted, or both? Conversations about these topics are covered in this part of the book.

6. Information Security and Privacy

Not a month goes by when some prominent company experiences an embarrassing and costly security breach. A commonality in all the data breach cases we hear about is that unauthorized people accessed highly valuable information. Security is one of the most obvious and important hallmarks of organizations that have mature governance strategies. Such strategies are important when the key levers of security (surface area restriction, separation of duties, separation of concerns, authentication, authorization, and encryption) are chosen for each data asset.

In a Big Data era, massive amounts of data that describe all aspects of people's lives are stored by organizations, and governments have been legislating tighter controls for customer data and other personally identifiable information (PII). One recent Eurozone trend is the "right to be forgotten," whereby an organization can be compelled to remove all traces of an individual's experience with it at the request of the person that is the subject of this data. Without first defining security and privacy policies for data and then acquiring tools that can track the lineage for someone's data, compliance with right-to-be-forgotten legislation becomes impossible. This is especially a concern with emerging technologies such as Hadoop. In Chapter 12, we describe IBM's data security solutions for Hadoop and relational data stores.

7. Data Architecture

Well-planned and well-documented data architectures might sound like an obvious part of a data governance model, but we've been in enough customer situations where architecture has been an afterthought. A lack of architectural thinking is especially common when IT teams face urgent new requirements and implement solutions that are quick and inexpensive. This often results in costly changes being needed in the future.

8. Data Quality Management

As the saying goes, quality is a habit. It's more than a habit really; it's a documented process where criteria are defined, applied to data, and then tested throughout the data lifecycle. Even in some Big Data scenarios where people might say "Quality doesn't matter," it does. It's just that the thresholds for quality might be different. Each threshold needs to be documented and associated with a policy. One aspect of data quality is having reliable reference data and a master data management (MDM) strategy. In Chapter 14 we talk about Big Match, a matching engine for Hadoop that can be used to generate quality reference data.

9. Classification and Metadata

Properly classified data—with a well-maintained business glossary and metadata store—is critical for any data consumers. On the one hand, this is essential for maintaining business continuity as people in your organization come and go. For the proverbial "hit by a bus" scenario (where someone is suddenly no longer at the company for whatever reason) where the person who understands the mappings between data elements and business concepts has left organization, how do you move forward? On the other hand, consider data scientist types, whose job it is to explore data and to look for new and valuable questions to ask. Properly classified data and current, complete metadata are critical for them to be productive.

The data zones model described in Chapter 4 is highly dependent on a shared metadata catalog. In Chapter 13, we describe the IBM Information Governance Catalog, which enables the storage and management of metadata so that it can be consumed by people exploring data sets.

10. Information Lifecycle Management

All data that is managed by an organization needs to have an associated lifecycle policy. The following questions are all vital in building a data lifecycle management policy: How is the data ingested or created? What cleansing work needs to be done? What transformations are done to the data? When does the data need to be archived? When does the data need to be destroyed? Are there defensible disposal considerations? In Chapter 14, we address many of these questions and the tools you can use to deploy data lifecycle policies.

Much of the marketing hype around Big Data (and we're guilty of this as well) talks about how inexpensive storage enables us to keep things longer and to ask more questions of it. But this should not be an excuse to avoid a retention policy; after all, the decision to keep something forever is a policy. What's needed is for this policy to be captured in metadata around the data in question.

11. Audit Information, Logging, and Reporting

There are many industry regulatory regimes that require data repositories to data accesses and provide a secure audit reporting facility. In short, for some industries, if you can't provide complete and secure audit reports for sensitive data, you're breaking the law. This needs to be a factor in your data architecture and in the kinds of data persistence technologies that you choose. If you think the material you need to get through a compliance audit is as simple as zipping up your log files, you're in for a surprise (and not a pleasant one). Auditing sensitive data is very much a part of data security; we cover the Guardium Audit services in Chapter 12.

Wrapping It Up

None of these principles of data governance should be looked at in isolation. This is an interrelated set of practices—when you deal with one principle, you need to consider the other ten principles as well. Good data governance is a cultural thing: The things we outlined in this chapter are the virtues of a strong culture. For example, no discussion of data risk management and compliance is complete without considering information lifecycle management.

Applying the principles of data governance becomes increasingly important as the complexity and volume of the data that is being managed continue to grow. This is not just about making life easier for analysts or DBAs, or even about saving money with cheaper data centers. The success—even survival—of organizations today hinges on the quality of their analytics, which demands a mature implementation of data governance principles. The remainder of this book focuses on tools and strategies to apply many of the data governance principles that we've looked at in this chapter. The chapters that follow aren't part of any hype conversations: They cover concepts that have been readily applied to the relational world for years. IBM has gone to great lengths to extend good governance capabilities, be it on premise or off premise via cloud services such as IBM DataWorks, to the Big Data world including NoSQL and Hadoop. Take your time through these chapters—you can save yourself a lot headaches in the future.

12

Security Is NOT an Afterthought

Data breach! Did the hair on the back of your neck stand up? Concerned about hackers, crackers, and spies, oh my? Take a breath and relax. This is a test. The authors are conducting a test of your built-in data breach fear system to see whether this concept still scares you. If it doesn't, do an Internet search on the topic to see what the last year or two has brought to the headlines. From retailers with credit card breaches to the personal profiles of productivity software users to gamers—three breaches alone impacted more than 250 million people, and that's more people than the population of every individual country in the world except for China, India, and the Unites States. Now consider what happens to a public company's market capitalization when they are associated with a headline breach. In this social-mobile-cloud world, more and more clients will give you their personal information for a deal or a better personalized marketing experience, but if you give them the impression that you have not done all that you can to protect their data, they will punish you…with their wallets.

There are two kinds of security breaches: those that have happened and those that are going to happen. So, let's start with the fact that no organization is immune to security breaches. We don't want you walking around thinking "It will never happen to us." Breaches can happen because of planned ill intent (from outside or within) or merely by accident. In short, we are telling you this: Where there is data, there is the potential for breaches and unauthorized access. The other thing to consider is that when it comes to hackers executing a successful security breach, they have to be successful only once. When your job is to protect sensitive data, you have to be successful all the time.

The best advice we can give you is that security can't be an afterthought—it should actually be the first one. When you jump into the car for a drive, the first thing you do is buckle up. Thrill seeker? We have yet to see a single person who doesn't check the safety device on that roller coaster before traveling over hills at 140 kilometers per hour—that would be dangerous. So, why operate like this with your—actually, other people's—data? Every sound security implementation begins with planning; you make choices to govern data up front, not after the fact.

Security Big Data: How It's Different

Why should storing data in a relational database management system (RDBMS) or in Hadoop's distributed file system (HDFS) be any different? If anything, security is even more critical when working with Big Data in Hadoop because there are a number of challenges that should be of concern to you. These challenges include the following:

- **Greater volumes of data than ever before**   If you don't have an effective security plan for the data that you have now, when those volumes explode, so too will the challenges.

- **The experimental and analytical usage of the data**   Delivering raw data from the privileged in your organization and democratizing it for the many is the path to unlock the value of Big Data and propel your organization beyond the hype; however, access to data that isn't trusted or governed properly can hurt your analytics too. Building trust into Big Data platform (lineage, ownership, and so on) is key for any successful Big Data project.

- **The nature and characteristics of Big Data**   It contains more sensitive personal details than ever before because it comes from multiple sources such as social media, machines, sensors, and call centers.

- **The adoption of technologies that are still maturing**   All things considered, Hadoop is relatively new—having had its first release in 2006. The point is that Hadoop (and much of the NoSQL world for that matter) doesn't have all of the enterprise hardening from a security perspective that's needed, and there's no doubt compromises are being made. Beyond helping technologies such as Hadoop mature into secure enterprise offerings, IBM offers a number of on-premise and off-premise composable services (under the IBM DataWorks catalog) that helps to lock down Hadoop—as well as traditional SQL and NoSQL data stores—and we cover those in this chapter.

At the start of this book, we said that Big Data is an opportunity—in fact, we described that opportunity as a shift, lift, rift, or cliff. We will let you guess which of those terms refers to Big Data without a sound data security plan.

We continue to talk to a large number of organizations across a diverse number of industries, including insurance, finance, manufacturing, retail, banking, automotive, and so on. The fact that Big Data in general—and Hadoop in particular—are such new technologies and the subject of so much attention means that we want you to ensure that the solutions you are responsible for are ready to support your business when it begins to adopt them. We wrote this chapter because we don't want you to "Go to jail. Go directly to jail. Do not pass Go. Do not collect $200"—a phrase from the popular game *Monopoly* that is often invoked in situations where there are only negative consequences and no choice. Indeed, a security breach can send the perpetrators to jail; but, in rare circumstances, it can also have dire consequences for those who were charged with protecting the data. We are just trying to make the point that running to a Big Data project without a governance process is like running with scissors.

When we see clients embrace Hadoop as a new data platform, we are always interested in getting their perspective on security, what types of data they are considering putting into Hadoop, and for what purpose. Inevitably, after the first hour of talking about Hadoop, HDFS, Pig, Spark, Yarn, Zoo-Keeper, Shark, Hive, or whatever other zany word the open source community has dreamed up, the discussion turns to *security*. For example, how will you apply *immutability rules* (ensuring that the data is not changed) to data that requires them? What about *defensible disposal*? How will you audit access to a Hadoop cluster, and how will you show an auditor that when it comes to your governance policy, you do what you say and say what you do? These security concerns should be a priority for every organization, from its chief executive, technology, and security officers to the frontline workers that save data to their USB sticks to work on at home late at night.

We're concerned. Very concerned. We are still regularly surprised by the conflicting responses that we hear around security when discussing Hadoop and Big Data. For example, one of us had a conversation with an application development manager for a large securities and exchange company. A division of their company had been involved in a public security breach and subsequent fine for that breach. When asked whether they were concerned about security and protecting sensitive data in their Hadoop environment, the manager said, "It's not a big deal; we will just lock down access to the server and put security on the files we load into Hadoop. We trust our end users." How quickly we forget. It is a little shocking to say the least! This happens all the time, and it isn't that these people are ignorant or lazy; they just aren't thinking security first—they are running with scissors. Although locking down servers and securing files is a good starting point, when you give individuals full access to the data, you are putting the data at risk. In other words, lockdown just scratches the surface when it comes to securing and protecting sensitive data.

One of the authors had a similar conversation with the chief technology officer (CTO) of a large, well-respected insurance company whose response was, "Hadoop is not even on the radar for us until we have a plan in place and can figure out how we are going to first secure that environment." This brought tears to the author's eyes—he is closer than the rest of us to security and takes it personally, or perhaps his policies are underwritten by them.

What is obvious to us is that not every organization has the same level of maturity when it comes to securing their Hadoop or Big Data environments. It's time that we all approach security with the same priority and that we all "buckle our seatbelts before driving the car."

The evidence is clear that security is an issue whose scale is much broader than a couple of massive breaches here and there. On any given day, you can use an Internet search to dig up a new breach. The fact is that data breaches are occurring all too often, cost both companies and individuals billions of dollars, damage reputations and livelihoods, shatter consumer confidence, and result in many corporations facing lawsuits, negative publicity, and regulatory fines that can put them at risk of bankruptcy. Even scarier is thinking about all the data breaches you never hear about that are not highly publicized or even made public. Frequent breach events underscore the importance of protecting and securing sensitive information in both production and nonproduction environments.

In this chapter, we discuss data security and focus on governance in Hadoop because there is so much attention being paid to this part of a Big Data platform. We cover what you need to know to protect, secure, and govern your data in Hadoop environments as it moves through the data lifecycle. And, finally, we describe a comprehensive set of security capabilities and services that are provided by the IBM Information Management portfolio through on-premise software such as those found in the InfoSphere Optim (Optim) or InfoSphere Guardium (Guardium) suite of products, or the IBM DataWorks public cloud service catalog.

But make no mistake about it, and it bears repeating: Whether data resides in HDFS, an RDBMS, NTFS, DFS, or YCWDFS (your computer whiz daughter's file system), or whatever file system alphabet soup you can think of—governance matters. There are security methods that can already be implemented to protect data no matter where it lands, and this includes Hadoop. These security methods are being used today on other distributed and mainframe RDBMSs, by many of the same clients who are considering Hadoop as a viable platform to house data.

This chapter also defines and weighs the pros and cons of various security approaches and introduces you to the IBM portfolio of services that can be used to establish, enforce, and implement data governance policies and rules; mask sensitive data; monitor and control access to data; and protect data at rest. These control and refinery services can be leveraged on premise through traditional products or consumed as a service in the cloud. They are (or will be) integrated into a hybrid cloud strategy where work can burst from the ground to the cloud and land back on the ground with an integrated and consistent set of data protection services. For example, the managed analytics service that we talked about in Chapters 3 and 8, dashDB, includes some basic refinery services from the IBM DataWorks catalog. It could be the case that as a data set is bursted into the dashDB service, it has to undergo some masking processing, and that work is stitched into the data flow process and consumed as a service.

Securing Big Data in Hadoop

Data can be secured and protected in many ways. In this section, we cover the most commonly used data governance methods for securing and protecting sensitive data in Hadoop environments. Sensitive data includes personally identifiable information (PII), financial data, customer or employee information, intellectual property, and more. When you're done reading this section, you'll say, "These methods have been available for a long time in the SQL database world!" That's correct, and if they are available there and those platforms store data, then they should be available for Hadoop (and other NoSQL ecosystem databases) too.

Culture, Definition, Charter, Foundation, and Data Governance

An effective data governance strategy should start with a culture change (if needed) or its reaffirmation: "This organization is going to put data governance at the forefront of everything we do." It has to come from the top. Culture isn't an easy thing to shift. The problem with governance is that most organizations do it as something to check off on a list. However, what most people don't realize is that you can create regulatory dividends from your governance investments and leverage the efforts for other uses too. Such messages are integral to your culture shift.

We think it's important to define data governance so that everyone has the same understanding of what it means to the business. Here is the Wikipedia definition (http://en.wikipedia.org/wiki/Data_governance):

> *Data governance is an emerging discipline with an evolving definition. The discipline embodies a convergence of data quality, data management, data policies, business process management, and risk management surrounding the handling of data in an organization. Through data governance, organizations are looking to exercise positive control over the processes and methods used by their data stewards and data custodians to handle data.*

The most important parts of this definition are the phrases "embodies data policies" and "business process management." Establishing data governance policies (the what, the how, and the rules) should occur before implementing any data governance activities (this is the policy stuff we talked about in Chapter 11). Ironically, this step is typically an afterthought and gets overlooked by most organizations. It is not a difficult task, but it can be time consuming and resource intensive to accomplish.

Simply put, you cannot govern what you do not understand. If you are not prepared to invest in the required due diligence, take the time to define and establish what the data governance policies and rules are needed for and publish them across the organization so that everyone not only has access to the policies, but understands them too; how else do you expect those responsible for managing the data to protect it properly, or even to care about it? We believe that a charter can embody these concepts, and we recommend you document the journey to a charter for all to see and embrace.

Ensuring the clear definition and corporate understanding of your organization's data privacy policies provides a substantial return on investment; however, these benefits cannot be experienced unless the business commits to making it happen. If this kind of investment is made up front, then policies and rules on how data is governed and protected can be clearly established, made accessible from anywhere at any time, be well understood throughout the organization, and be enforced and implemented by the data stewards and custodians who are responsible for the data.

Services in the IBM InfoSphere Information Governance Catalog (IGC) provide all of these capabilities. The IGC aligns business goals and IT for better information governance and trusted information. It is an information governance encyclopedia with a comprehensive and intuitive set of services to manage and store data governance, including business, technical, and operational metadata. It has the capability to establish and define business policies and rules, assign ownership to those who are responsible for enforcing and implementing them, and catalog and store them in a central repository for easy access by everyone who needs access to this manifest from anywhere at any time. In short, it empowers the next generation information architecture that we introduced you to in Chapter 4.

What Is Sensitive Data?

After reading Chapter 4, you will likely agree that in the (very near) future, a substantial amount of information being placed into Hadoop will be classified as sensitive and that only authorized and privileged users will be allowed to access and view it. Before we review the methods that are available to protect sensitive data, you should understand what sensitive data is.

Sensitive data is defined as any information that can be used on its own or with other information to identify an individual. You will often hear it referred to as *personally identifiable information*. As you can imagine, there are many kinds of information that could be classified as PII: your name, address, location, email address, cell phone (the IMEI is a unique identifier), and so on.

The definition of what constitutes sensitive data varies by country and even by state or province within those countries. In the European Union (EU), for example, the definition of sensitive data is much broader and extends to identifiers such as trade union membership and even political beliefs. There are cultural issues that vary geographically too. For example, "Right to be Forgotten" policies are making their way through certain European countries. Countries such as Germany and Luxembourg tend to have broader definitions of private data than other countries such as Canada and so on. You should assume that any data about an identified or identifiable individual is considered to be personal data.

For example, another kind of PII is personal health information (PHI), which is any information that is related to an individual's health, condition, diagnosis, or treatment. In the Unites States, this information is governed by the Health Insurance Portability and Accountability Act (HIPAA), which contains national standards for electronic healthcare transactions and national identifiers for providers, insurance plans, and employers. One of the first steps in protecting data is to understand your organization's privacy policies and to identify what is considered sensitive within your organization, because of either legislation or good corporate citizenship. This has to be done upfront before the fact and not after it.

The Masquerade Gala: Masking Sensitive Data

Data masking, also referred to as *data obfuscation,* is the process of transforming real data values into fictional values while maintaining the original format of the data so that it is contextually correct. For example, if you mask a credit card number, your analytics environment might need to preserve the first four numbers because they identify a certain credit card provider such as American Express or Visa. In this case, you might want to fictionalize only the remaining numbers in the credit card. Data masking is used extensively to protect PII and, specifically, the identity attributes of an individual.

Don't confuse *data redaction* with data masking. Data redaction either completely removes or hides (all or a portion of) the data by replacing it with characters that have no meaning, such as a string of asterisks or an image that completely obscures the data. Think about the classic blacked-out government document in a scandal investigation—such a document is said to be *redacted.* Redaction is widely used to protect sensitive information contained in documents, forms, and images. It is also used in production environments because it does not physically change the real data values, only what the end user sees. The set of services that you can find in the IBM DataWorks service catalog includes (or will include) these services for off-premise redaction as well as other data protection services such as masking.

Data masking is primarily used in nonproduction environments for testing purposes so that sensitive data is not exposed to application developers, testers, or anyone who is not authorized to see the real data. The data in these environments needs to look real and remain valid and usable to maintain its testability throughout the process.

You will sometimes find data masking in production environments, although it is not as common as redaction. In this case, displayed result sets on user interfaces, not the underlying data, are masked. This is commonly referred to as *dynamic masking* or *masking on the fly*. Nonauthorized users see a masked version of the data, not a redacted version. If you plan to mask production data, you must ensure that the real production data values are not physically changed. For example, it might be the case that before you burst data into the cloud for use with a public analytics service such as IBM dashDB, you call one of the IBM refinery services to mask that data and then operate on the data and return results to the end user. If your industry regulations stipulate that data cannot leave the premises without some kind of obfuscation, you invoke this service, but when the data lands on the ground, it is restored to expected values.

Data Masking Methods

There are many different ways to mask data. Whatever method you choose, it's imperative that it be done by using consistent and reliable methods that not only produce masked data values and preserve the format and content of the original data values, but are also documented and curated across the enterprise too. Data masking is not just the process of simplistically scrambling characters to make the original data value look unrecognizable. Otherwise, your test buckets would likely fail, because the application code is expecting data values that have the same format as the original data. For example, masking a phone contact that is used in a test bucket to auto-dial a phone number if fraudulent activity is suspected on a credit card isn't going to work if you replace `314-804-3211` (this is a random generated number, so don't call it) with `abc-def-ghik`.

The following services and capabilities are essential to any effective masking strategy for sensitive data:

- Substitute real values with fictional values such as names and addresses by using replacement data that is provided from trusted sources such as national postal services from different countries.

- Use hashing algorithms to ensure that you select the same consistent replacement data based on a key value or a set of key values. This is important to ensure referential integrity across multiple data environments. For example, if you want to ensure that `Rick Buglio` is masked to a different name such as `John Smith`, but always the same masked name, you can use a hashing algorithm and assign a hash value that consistently identifies `Rick Buglio`, like an employee identification number or some other unique identifier. Of course, the hash table must be secured, but this is a great way to ensure that your application test cases won't break down for certain kinds of context-dependent data.

- Use intelligent algorithms that are designed for specific types of PII such as national identifiers (U.S. Social Security numbers, Canadian social insurance numbers, and so on), personal identification numbers (PINs), email addresses, phone numbers, driver's license numbers, credit cards and their associated verification numbers, dates, ages, and so on. These algorithms are context-aware with respect to the data that is being masked and produce a repeatable or random masked value that is fictional but contextually correct. Repeatable means that every time the original value is encountered and the same algorithm is applied, the same masked value is produced. As its name implies, a randomized masking service generates a contextually correct masked value, based on the type of data, but the algorithm generates a random value that is not based on the source value.

- Provide the ability to construct custom data masking methods through the use of scripts or custom code to do additional processing on data values before, during, or after data masking. The additional processing uses programming techniques such as conditional logic, arithmetic functions, operating system functions, data manipulation and transformation functions, decryption and encryption, and so on.

All of these masking methods can be valid and effective; choosing one over the others depends on what your data masking requirements are and what type of data you are masking.

The Optim Data Privacy solution, with its granular services that are composable on or off premise through IBM DataWorks, provides all these capabilities and more to mask structured data that is stored in relational database management systems and a majority of nonrelational data stores, including Hadoop. Think about how important this is to your polyglot environments (Chapters 2 and 4). It makes sense to have a consistent business policy that centrally controls the masking of data. If the PII data happens to land in Hadoop and work its way into an in-memory analytics database service such as dashDB that is surfaced to the line of business (LOB), why should time and effort be spent on redefining masking rules or perhaps missing them altogether in one persistent data store? The set of masking services that are offered both on and off premise by IBM enables you to have a consistent and persistent masking strategy across almost any data asset in your environment.

Optim Data Privacy includes a wide variety of methods to mask data in Hadoop. For example, it can be used to mask data in CSV and XML files that already exist in HDFS, even if that data comes from RDBMS tables and is converted into these (or other) data transfer formats. Optim masking services can be used to mask data from an RDBMS and then load that masked data into Hadoop, or can be used to extract and mask Hadoop data and then load it into an RDBMS or the NoSQL stores we talked about in Chapter 2.

Policy-Driven Data Privacy

So far in this chapter, we have given you some working definitions and considerations when it comes to implementing a data governance culture and working with sensitive data. We discussed the importance and usage of data governance policies and rules, as well as the various data masking methods and technologies that are available to establish, enforce, and implement them. Combining well-defined policies with automated software solutions provides organizations with a policy-driven on-premise or off-premise data privacy approach to proactively protect sensitive data and remain agile in the face of an ever-changing world of data privacy.

The data masking capabilities that are available through the on-premise or off-premise IBM Information Management portfolio are tightly integrated with the business metadata, policy, and rule capabilities of the IBM Information Governance Catalog. This synergy delivers an unprecedented policy-driven data privacy approach to protect sensitive data that can be directly applied to Hadoop distributions such as IBM InfoSphere BigInsights for Hadoop (BigInsights), the Cloudera Distribution for Hadoop (CDH), Hortonworks Data Platform (HDP), other Hadoop distributions, and non-Hadoop NoSQL or SQL environments. These services empower data stewards and custodians who are responsible for protecting sensitive data to use the Information Governance Catalog data privacy policies, data classification terms, and rules that were specifically designed to classify and mask sensitive data—*no matter where they reside*. They enable the automatic classification of data elements as sensitive, apply a best-practice data masking function to that data, and enable the rich set of IBM masking services to implement and enforce the data masking policy. Figure 12-1 gives you an example of just how powerful this integration work is.

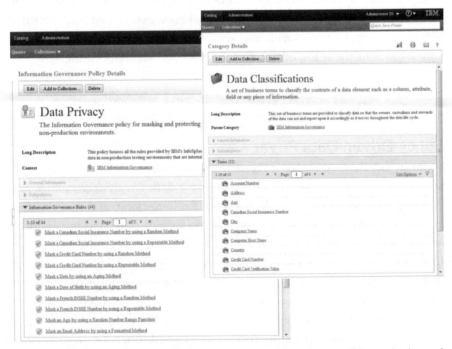

Figure 12-1   *IBM Information Governance Catalog: data privacy policies and rules and data classification information in one place for your enterprise*

In Figure 12-1, you can see multiple capabilities that are offered by the IBM Information Governance Catalog. On the left side of this figure is a large number (greater than 40) of predefined data privacy rules that you can use to mask sensitive data. For example, there is a random method to mask a Canadian social insurance number (SIN), credit card number masking that uses repeatable or random methods, and more. Using this capability through the IBM DataWorks cloud service, you could mask a Canadian SIN and wherever that data lands (perhaps, in a cloud storage service), it is obfuscated.

On the right side of Figure 12-1, you can see that the Information Governance Catalog has a Data Classification category that contains a number of rich services with defined data classification terms that can be used to mask sensitive data such as account number, address, credit card verification number, and more.

Figure 12-2 shows the tool set's designer interface, which has an integrated view into the Information Governance Catalog that empowers you to review, understand, and use the data classifications to mask sensitive data.

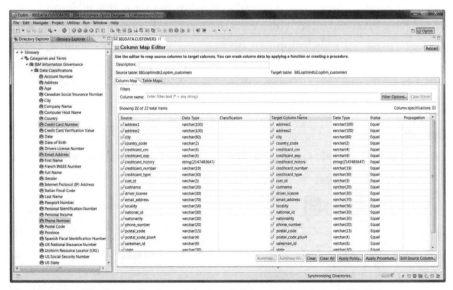

Figure 12-2 *The Optim Designer interface is integrated with the Information Governance Catalog.*

It might not be obvious at first, but the capabilities that are shown in Figure 12-2 should astound you. The figure shows a data steward leveraging a web-based management interface to apply enterprise-defined data privacy classification terms and masking policies to columns in Hive (part of the Hadoop ecosystem) through simple drag-and-drop operations. These services automatically classify the column, identify it as sensitive, and then apply and enforce the IBM best-practice data masking privacy service to mask the data based on its classification. You can also add your own custom data masking services that implement masking rules to protect sensitive data and host them here too. Think about that. Using an enterprisewide corpus of masking policies that can be applied across the polyglot data environment through simple drag-and-drop gestures. If that phone number exists in Hive, DB2, or Oracle, a simple gesture applies the same policy across those repositories. Folks, this is ground breaking.

Figure 12-3 showcases an example of a Data Privacy Compliance report that can be generated from the service's operational dashboard.

This report makes it easy to track the status of data privacy policy compliance across the enterprise. It reports on what columns (by table and data store) have been classified with a data masking policy applied, classified with no data masking policy applied, unclassified with a data masking policy applied, or unclassified with no data masking policy applied. Understand what is happening here: The report is discovering compliance metadata for

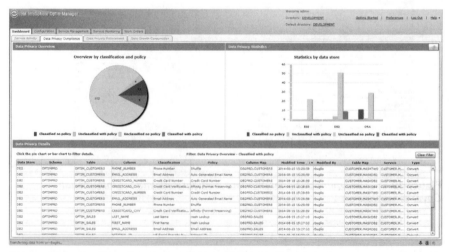

Figure 12-3   *An example of a Data Privacy Compliance report*

you to help you curate and govern your data assets. The report also provides an overall status for those columns that are fully compliant and protected, as well as alerts for those that are not. Finally, the report identifies whether a data masking service has been assigned to implement the data masking policies.

This integration delivers a cross-enterprise, end-to-end, policy-driven approach to data privacy that enables organizations to easily define and establish data privacy policies, publish them for everyone to understand, and then enforce and implement them to protect sensitive data.

Don't Break the DAM: Monitoring and Controlling Access to Data

Data activity monitoring (DAM) is a technology that monitors access to data and activity within a data store—it looks for anything unusual and can generate alerts based on a set of policies. It also captures and records database events in real time and then correlates the captured data to provide a comprehensive set of audit reports and graphical depictions of the information. If a user attempts to access data for which they are not authorized, a DAM solution can automatically terminate the request, log the user off the system, and send out an alert notification. Monitoring can be accomplished in numerous ways, such as by reading database audit logs, by sniffing the network for database traffic and transactions, or by directly reading a database engine's memory structures. These methods provide an invaluable service to detect and prohibit attacks and intruders by producing the forensic data that is needed to investigate data breaches.

Data activity monitoring is popular in the SQL RDBMS world. At this point, we're convinced that you'll also believe it needs to be just as popular in the NoSQL world too, including data repositories such as Hadoop. With the "opening" up of data access environments such as HBase, Hive, and Hadoop through SQL, there are more and more users accessing the data that resides in these NoSQL (and other) data stores—which makes DAM even more important!

Hadoop is delivering insights for many organizations. However, security risks remain high despite the hype. Although some Hadoop distributions do support various security and authentication solutions, there was not a truly comprehensive DAM solution for Hadoop until IBM introduced it with the

IBM InfoSphere Guardium Data Activity Monitor (Guardium DAM) services. Considering that even robust and mature enterprise RDBMSs are often the target of attacks, the relative lack of controls around Hadoop makes it a target, especially as more sensitive and valuable data from a wide variety of sources moves into the Hadoop cluster. Organizations that tackle this issue head on, and sooner rather than later, position themselves to expand their use of Hadoop for enhanced business value. They can proceed with the confidence that they can address regulatory requirements and detect breaches quickly, thus reducing overall business risk for the Hadoop project—they can run with scissors, but this time the scissors are sheathed and safe.

Ideally, organizations should be able to integrate Big Data applications and analytics into an existing data security infrastructure, rather than relying on homegrown scripts and monitors, which can be labor intensive, error prone, and subject to misuse. Guardium's data security services take care of most of this heavy lifting for you. You define security policies that specify which data needs to be retained and how to react to policy violations. Data events are written directly to a hardened manifest, leaving no opportunity for even privileged users to access that data and to hide their tracks.

Out-of-the-box reports and policies get you up and running quickly, and those reports and policies are easily customized to align with your audit requirements. Guardium services can dramatically simplify your path to audit readiness by providing targeted, actionable information. A scalable architecture and support for a wide variety of data platforms make it possible to integrate Hadoop activity monitoring with other database activity, giving security administrators an enterprisewide monitoring and alerting system for detecting and preventing threats.

Guardium DAM services can monitor, alert, and control access to data in Hadoop (it can access all kinds of NoSQL and SQL data stores, but the focus of this chapter is on the Hadoop ecosystem). These security services can monitor and audit data activity for Hive, MapReduce, HBase, Hue, Beeswax, and HDFS to help organizations meet regulatory compliance requirements. The services ensure that data access is protected by continuously monitoring and auditing events in real time, using pattern-based policies to detect unauthorized, suspicious, or malicious activity and then alerting key personnel. Monitored events include session and user activity; issued HDFS commands, such as `cat`, `tail`, `chmod`, `chown`, `expunge`, and so on; MapReduce job operations and permissions; exceptions such as authorization failures; Hive and HBase access and queries such as `alter`, `count`, `create`, `drop`, `get`, `put`, and `list`; and more. In fact, there is a whole Hadoop category for reports that includes the aforementioned operations and Hadoop ecosystem components, as well as canned reporting that tells you about exceptions and unauthorized MapReduce jobs, among other things.

Guardium DAM services also include a number of predefined policies to filter out the "noise" from Hadoop's well-known "chatty" protocols. For example, lots of Hadoop activity breaks down to MapReduce and HDFS: At this level, you can't tell what a user higher up in the stack was trying to do or who they are. Guardium DAM makes it more likely that you will understand the ongoing activities that are critical to securing your environment.

What's really nice about the Guardium DAM service is that it simplifies the path to audit readiness with targeted and actionable information. If you think that simply zipping up archived log data is going to satisfy most audit requirements, you are sadly mistaken.

Protecting Data at Rest

Encryption is the process of encoding data in such a way that only those who are authorized to view the data can read it. It converts data into what is known as *ciphertext*, a nerdy way of saying encrypted text. Data is encrypted by using an encryption algorithm, which generates encrypted or encoded data that can be read only if it is decrypted. The encoded data is an encrypted version of the original data that is unreadable by a human or computer without the proper key to decrypt it. A recipient of encrypted information can decrypt the information only by using a key that is provided by the originator of the encoded information. Encryption is a common and widely used method to protect information and is considered an industry best practice for protecting both data at rest and data in motion. If information is encrypted, there is a low probability that anyone other than the person who has the decryption key would be able to decrypt the information and convert it into a readable format. Encryption guards against unauthorized or malicious attempts to access data outside of established application interfaces, but it can also protect data that is being replicated, transferred, or transmitted to SQL or NoSQL data stores, lost or stolen, and this includes data in NoSQL ecosystems such as Hadoop.

IBM InfoSphere Guardium Data Encryption (Guardium DE) provides encryption capabilities to help you safeguard structured and unstructured data and to help you develop strategies to comply with industry and regulatory requirements. These services perform on- or off-premise encryption and decryption operations with only a minimal impact on performance. They also require no database, application, or network changes. Specifically, these services offer the following benefits:

- **Transparent, rapid implementation**   No application, underlying database, or hardware infrastructure changes are required to protect your data at rest.

- **Centralized key and policy management**   The service delivers a unified management system to help simplify data security management.

- **Compliance-ready capabilities**   It provides granular auditing and reporting to help you meet data governance requirements such as the HIPAA and PCI Data Security Standard (PCI DSS).

As you can see, Guardium DE services can assist in ensuring compliance and preventing data breaches for data at rest in Hadoop (among other data repositories). Data in Hadoop comes from multiple applications and is distributed across multiple nodes in the cluster; these services can allow access to only authorized processes or users and include file-level data access logging and alerting. Guardium DE transparently encrypts structured and unstructured files without the need to re-architect applications or the data. Integrated key and policy management is provided to minimize the administrative overhead and manage the protection of both structured and unstructured data, and more.

Wrapping It Up

We hope that after reading this chapter you are reminded about, or perhaps now fully appreciate, the vital importance of securing data, especially in Hadoop environments. In a Big Data world, it's even more challenging and imperative to safeguard PII and sensitive information to minimize the risk of data breaches and other unauthorized, suspicious, and malicious activities.

Hadoop data is different in many respects; the volumes are described with words such as massive, and the content and format of the data coming from new and different sources such as social media, machines, sensors, and call centers can be unpredictable. It's also true that a fair amount of data that will be (or is being) stored in Hadoop systems is the same production data that is used by organizations to run their critical business applications. Think back to the landing zones concept that we cover in Chapter 4. Governance is about the data being stored, not where it is stored; and if that stored data needs to be protected, it must be treated with equal importance and with the utmost urgency and sensitivity to secure and protect it properly, no matter where it lands.

The good news is that there are now proven methods for securing and protecting data in Hadoop. These methods have been available and used for decades in the SQL world across distributed and mainframe systems. They are reliable and can be applied to NoSQL and Hadoop systems to establish critical data governance policies and rules; mask, redact, or encrypt sensitive data; and monitor, audit, and control data access.

Today there are mature, industry-leading, on- and off-premise data security solutions from IBM that have extended their capabilities to support Hadoop environments.

13

Big Data Lifecycle Management

In the months leading up to the writing of this book, we've been struck by the number of times we've heard customers share stories about how their data volumes are rapidly increasing. One financial services customer marveled, "We bought a 25TB warehouse appliance two years ago, and at the time I never imagined we'd fill it. And now here we are, asking for more capacity." Over and over we hear about how a terabyte no longer seems like a huge amount of data.

Data governance and, in particular, lifecycle management were important before, but they become an even more significant concern with so much additional data to manage. This impacts every facet of the lifecycle. As data is generated, is sufficient metadata collected to enable analysts to find their needle in an increasingly larger stack of needles? Can the data integration strategy (transfer and transformation) keep up with the data volumes? Can the data quality tools handle the increased variations in the data sets being stored, as well as the high data velocity? As growing numbers of analytics applications are being developed, for Hadoop as well as relational sources, how can test data be managed consistently? And finally, can archiving facilities handle more defensible, flexible, and cost-effective solutions, enabling data to be taken off of warehouse systems in a governable manner, while having the archives stored in Hadoop where they can still be queried? In presenting key portions of IBM's data integration and governance platform, this chapter will answer all these questions for you, among others we are sure you have, and also show how IBM is enabling governance capabilities to be consumed as services in cloud environments.

A Foundation for Data Governance: The Information Governance Catalog

We've seen it more times than we care to remember: A company's line of business gets excited about Hadoop, works with IT to set up a cluster, and starts moving in data. The early returns are sometimes positive, provided they have the right expertise and tools, but it doesn't take long before problems start cropping up. As more data sets get moved into Hadoop, things start getting messy—efforts to keep directory structures orderly aren't cutting it. And if some of the key data administrators leave the business, much of the knowledge about which data sets were the real archives and which ones were the experimental sandboxes often leaves with them. After all, Hadoop does not have its own native metadata management platform. And what about more advanced issues, like knowing where the data came from and what state it's in (we call this lineage)? Forget about it. Hadoop has amazing potential for saving money with its cost-effective architecture and for making money with its ability to deliver new analytics patterns, but without proper metadata management, you're sunk before you get started. In fact, most of the data scientists we talk to spend more time on the integration of their data than the science of their data.

The IBM Information Governance Catalog (IGC) is a core component in the data zones model we described in Chapter 4, and can provide metadata management to Hadoop and other data stores. Whether you're improving data quality, mastering data, securing it, or managing it, you should *always* begin with efforts to understand your organization's data and defined governance policies. The IGC contains several components that help organizations understand and profile data sources; it contains unique services to blueprint information governance projects, discover data in its source systems (indeed, in a Big Data world, you need help sometimes finding data you didn't know existed and that needs to be governed), manage enterprise metadata, represent that metadata in business-friendly terms via a glossary, provide the ability to broadcast new data assets, and define governance policies, among other capabilities.

Shared metadata is the basis for effective data integration. By sharing a common definition of terms and data transformations at the enterprise level, an organization can quickly translate data from one system to another. In a fashion not dissimilar to how you would browse and buy shirt online, the IGC features tooling that enables analysts to browse through metadata collections and simply "shop" for the data sets they want to. You can see this interface in Figure 13-1. Once you've found a data set you're interested in, you can transfer it to your sandbox (on InfoSphere BigInsights for Hadoop, another database, or a cloud-based analytics service such as dashDB) for further analysis.

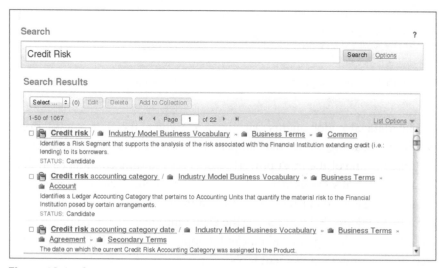

Figure 13-1   *Shopping for data in the Information Governance Catalog*

Once you've found a data collection you're interested in, you can explore the rich set of metadata, email users, provision replicas of the data for sandboxing purposes, and more. Figure 13-2 shows this exploration interface.

Effective sharing of metadata relies upon a common vocabulary, one that business and IT can agree upon. The IGC manages the business definition of the metadata—putting IT terms into a vocabulary that business users can understand. Because data comes from many new sources, it also comes with many new terms and in many new formats. In this era of Big Data, the need for a common vocabulary has never been greater.

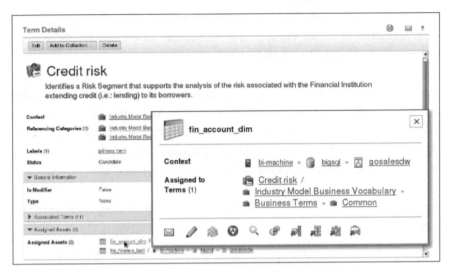

Figure 13-2 *Browsing metadata in the Information Governance Catalog*

Metadata also documents data lineage (where the data comes from), where it's heading, and what happened to it along the way. Data lineage metadata is one of the most powerful tools for building confidence in data, because when it's exposed to a business user, there is clear evidence that what's being looked at isn't just another unmanaged replica of some random data set. In Figure 13-3 you can see the Data Lineage view for a data set in the IGC. This data lineage metadata can be populated in the IGC as it's generated by ETL or data movement tools.

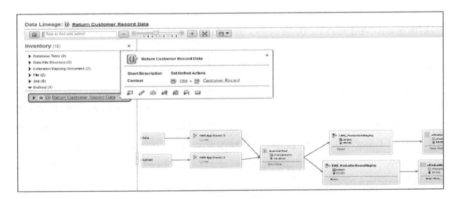

Figure 13-3 *Data lineage in the Information Governance Catalog*

One of the greatest challenges in information governance is developing policies. After all, you have to develop them in every system that manages and governs data. The IGC makes this easy for you, enabling you to define governance policies in plain language at the same time as you define metadata. This puts the definition of policies at the forefront when you should be thinking about them. Governance policies should not be an afterthought. The IGC provides business-driven governance by allowing business analysts and users to define governance policies.

The IGC provides metadata management for all facets of the data zones model we described in Chapter 4: both relational databases (from IBM and all other major vendors) and IBM BigInsights for Hadoop. To enable the modern architecture presented in the data zones model, a metadata management framework is critical. The IGC enables your organization to develop and maintain metadata, and equally important, enables the data consumers to browse and provision their own data sets.

Data on Demand: Data Click

One of the major trends we've seen in IT over the last few years is the growing importance of data scientists. This is the motivation for IBM to promote Hadoop as the shared landing zone in the data zones model from Chapter 4: Hadoop lends itself well to the kind of explorative analysis that data scientists regularly engage in. However, for Hadoop to be effective as a data exploration zone, data scientists will need to be able to easily explore existing data sets and provision their own data sandboxes. This is where Data Click lets data scientists do what their name suggests they ought to do.

A major benefit of the IGC's system of organizing and presenting the shared metadata is that analysts and data administrators can use it to quickly find the data sets they need. Once the data sets are identified, the data scientist (or line-of-business user for that matter) can open the Data Click service from within the IGC. There are a number of flexible data movement options in Data Click, enabling the data scientist to move data to another relational database system, to a Hadoop cluster, to a cloud storage service, and more (see Figure 13-4).

Once you've moved a data set using Data Click, it automatically creates metadata for this new instantiation of data, including its lineage and when the copy was made. Nice!

Figure 13-4 *Easy data movement with Data Click*

Data Integration

Information integration is a key requirement of a Big Data platform because it enables you to leverage economies of scale from existing investments, yet discovers new economies of scale as you expand the analytics paradigm. For example, consider the case where you have a heavy SQL investment in a next best offer (NBO) app. If this app were based on an SQL warehouse, it could be enhanced with the ability to call a Hadoop job that would look at the trending sentiment associated with a feature item stock-out condition. This could help to determine the acceptability of such an offer before it's made. Having the ability to leverage familiar SQL to call a function that spawns a MapReduce job in a Hadoop cluster to perform this sentiment analysis is not only a powerful concept; it's crucial from the perspective of maximizing the value of your IT investment.

Perhaps it's the case that you have a machine data analysis job running on a Hadoop cluster and want to draw customer information from a system that manages rebates, hoping to find a strong correlation between certain log events and eventual credits.

Information is often structured or semistructured, and achieving high-volume throughput requires a powerful processing engine. Your Big Data integration platform should provide balanced optimization for different integration and transformation needs, ranging from extract, transform, and load (ETL) to extract, load, and transform (ELT), which leverages the target system to process the transformations while providing the transformation logic, to transform, extract, load, and transform (TELT).

Some developers believe that new technologies, such as Hadoop, can be used for a multitude of tasks. From a batch and integration perspective, the Big Data world is characterized by various approaches and disciplines with Big Data technologies. This leads to a "build mentality," which assumes that everything can be built around the new technology. If you think back to when the data warehouse industry was in its infancy, many IT professionals attempted to build in-house integration capabilities using nothing but Perl scripts. Few would do that today because mature information integration technologies exist. The same pattern is playing out in Hadoop, with some believing that it should be the sole component for integration or transformation workloads.

For example, some folks propose that they should use Hadoop only to prepare data for a data warehouse; this is generally referred to as ETL. But there's a huge gap between a general-purpose tool and a purpose-built one, and integration involves many aspects other than the transformation of data, such as extraction, discovery, profiling, metadata, data quality, and delivery. Organizations shouldn't utilize Hadoop solely for integration; rather, they should leverage mature data integration technologies to help speed their deployments of Big Data. New technologies such as Hadoop will be *adopted into* data integration, and organizations indeed should utilize Hadoop for transformation processing where it makes sense—and it doesn't always make sense to use Hadoop for this work. So, while we think you'll find the need to use Hadoop engines as part of an ETL/ELT strategy, we are convinced you will also greatly benefit from the flexibility of a fit-for-purpose transformation tool set, massively parallel integration engine to support multiple transformation and load requirements, integration into common run-time environments, and a common design palette that's provided by a product such as InfoSphere Information Server for Data Integration (IIS for DI). In fact, this product's parallel processing engine and end-to-end integration and quality capabilities yield a significant total cost of ownership advantage over alternative approaches.

For example, if the transformation is full of SQL operations, IIS for DI can push down those operations into an IBM PureData System for Analytics appliance (formerly known as Netezza). Your integration platform should be able to not just automatically generate jobs to run on an Hadoop infrastructure or ETL parallel engine as required, but manage them with a common job sequencer too. IIS for DI includes connectors into Hadoop and a Big Data file stage (BDFS) container for data persistence and retrieval. A single data integration platform, such as the one provided by IIS for DI, gives you both capability and flexibility. IIS includes a multitude of prebuilt transformation objects and hundreds of functions, all atop a parallel execution environment that gives you the flexibility to use a myriad of technologies (including Hadoop) that are best suited for the task at hand. IIS for DI integrates with HDFS as both a source and a target system for data delivery. IIS for DI can also model certain integration tasks within an integration stage and specify the process to be performed on Hadoop, which would take advantage of Hadoop's MapReduce processing and low-cost infrastructure. This may be often used in ELT-style integration, where instead of the *T* being performed by data warehouse stored procedures, transformations are performed by a Hadoop system. IIS for DI also integrates with InfoSphere Streams (Streams), and it may accumulate insights or data filtered by Streams into a staged data file, which is then loaded to a target system (say a data warehouse for further analysis).

High-speed integration into data warehouses is going to be key, and IIS for DI delivers this capability as well. Figure 13-5 shows an example of an IIS for DI Big Data transformation flow. You can see that this job analyzes high-fidelity

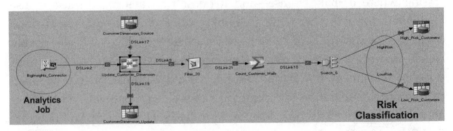

Figure 13-5   *A data-flow job that utilizes a combination of Big Data assets, including source data in Hadoop joined with DB2 relational data, and various transformations to classify risk*

emails (stored in Hadoop) for customer sentiment, and the results of that analysis are used to update a profile in the warehouse (for example, the Customer dimension); this is an example of risk classification based on email analytics.

Other integration technologies that are commonplace in today's IT environments (and remain important in a Big Data world) include real-time replication and federation. Real-time replication, utilizing a product such as IBM InfoSphere Data Replication (Data Replication), involves monitoring a source system and triggering a replication or change to the target system. This is often used for low-latency integration requirements. Data Replication has sophisticated functionality for high-speed data movement, conflict detection, system monitoring, and a graphical development environment for designing integration tasks. Furthermore, it's integrated with the set of IBM PureData Systems for high-speed data loading/synchronization and also with Information Server to accumulate changes and move data in bulk to a target system.

We believe that organizations shouldn't try to deliver enterprise integration solely with Hadoop; rather, they should leverage mature data integration technologies to help speed their deployments of Big Data whenever that makes sense. There's a huge gap between a general-purpose tool and a purpose-built one, not to mention that integration involves many aspects other than the delivery of data, such as discovery, profiling, metadata, and data quality. We recommend that you consider using IBM Information Server with your Big Data projects to optimize the loading (via bulk load or replication) of high-volume structured data into a data warehouse, the loading of structured or semistructured data into Hadoop, and the collecting of information that's filtered and analyzed by stream analytics. You can then load the data into a relational system (such as a data warehouse) and replicate data sources to a Hadoop cluster or other data warehouse.

Data Quality

Data quality components can be used to ensure the cleanliness and accuracy of information. IBM InfoSphere Information Server for Data Quality (IIS for DQ) is a market-leading data quality product containing innovative features, such as information profiling and quality analysis, address standardization and validation, and so on. It's fully integrated into the ICG, which allows you to develop quality rules and share metadata too. You can also use the IIS for DQ services while you're executing quality jobs on Information Server's parallel processing platform. Data quality discussions typically involve the following services:

- **Parsing**   Separating data and parsing it into a structured format.

- **Standardization**   Determining what data to place in which field and ensuring that it's stored in a standard format (for example, a nine-digit ZIP code).

- **Validation**   Ensuring that data is consistent; for example, a phone number contains an area code and the correct number of digits for its locale. It might also include cross-field validation, such as checking the telephone area code against a city to ensure that it's valid (for example, area code 416 is valid for Toronto; 415 is not).

- **Verification**   Checking data against a source of verified information to ensure that the data is valid; for example, checking that an address value is indeed a real and valid address.

- **Matching**   Identifying duplicate records and merging those records correctly.

Organizations should determine whether their Big Data sources require quality checking before analysis and then apply the appropriate data quality components. A Big Data project is likely going to require you to focus on data quality when loading a data warehouse to ensure accuracy and completeness, when loading and analyzing new sources of Big Data that will be integrated with a data warehouse, and when Big Data analysis depends on a more accurate view (for example, reflecting customer insight), even if the data is managed within Hadoop.

Veracity as a Service: IBM DataWorks

So far in this chapter we've mostly talked about governance and lifecycle management from an on-premise perspective. But as we described in Chapter 3, the Bluemix platform represents a service-oriented approach for working with data. The focus of Bluemix is to enable developers to quickly and easily build web-based solutions by piecing together Bluemix services. The beauty of this approach is that it's all about the developer: All the hardware, underlying software, and data are managed on IBM's SoftLayer cloud so the developer doesn't have to worry about it. IBM Watson Analytics is a similar sort of ecosystem, only its focus is on analysts, as opposed to developers. Watson Analytics brings together a complete set of self-service analytics capabilities on the cloud. You bring your problem, and Watson Analytics helps you acquire the data, cleanse it, discover insights, predict outcomes, visualize results, create reports or dashboards, and collaborate with others.

Since they're platforms that consume and produce data, both Bluemix and Watson Analytics need governance and integration tools. And the traditional software offerings we've talked about do not fit in this model. IBM's engineering teams are taking its rich data governance portfolio capabilities and exposing them as a collection of composite and data refinery services, known as IBM DataWorks. Figure 13-6 shows an example of some of the DataWorks services available for Bluemix and Watson Analytics. (Also note that some of the DataWorks services are part of dashDB.)

- **Simple Load Service** The Simple Load Service extracts data and metadata from source data and creates the same schema in the target database if it doesn't exist. Once the schema is created, this service loads the data into the target, offering high-speed data movement both at a bulk level and at a granular level. For data in files, as opposed to

Figure 13-6 *The Simple Load Service in Bluemix*

relational tables, this service will read a sample of the data to detect the schema and then create a corresponding schema in the target database. What gives this service additional credibility from a governance perspective is its ability to automatically capture the data design and collect operational lineage data. Cloud applications and analytics need governance too!

- **Masking Service**   The Masking Service masks sensitive data based on the Optim masking capabilities we detailed in Chapter 12. Masking support includes credit card numbers, Social Security numbers, dates, and more.

- **Selective Load Service**   The Selective Load Service does exactly what its name implies: It loads only a subset of source data into a target repository. The selection criteria can include constraints on the metadata (for example, only a certain schema, tables, and columns) and data values (for example, rows that meet a specified condition).

- **Standardize Service**   The Standardize Service reads a string, identifies "tokens" that have meaning, and then structures all identified tokens into a correctly formatted result. These tokens can be entities such as addresses, dates, or phone numbers.

- **Match Data Service**   The Match Data Service provides probabilistic matching to inspect multiple records, score the likelihood of a match, and return a single master record, based on user options. This is essentially a service-based offering of the Big Match product described in Chapter 14.

- **Profile Data Service**   The Profile Data Service analyzes the attributes of individual data records to provide information on cardinality, completeness, conformance, validity, and other characteristics. This enables analysts to understand the characteristics of data so they can better determine the confidence score in particular data values.

- **Combine Data Service**   The Combine Data Service extracts data from multiple sources, joins it (based on criteria defined by the user), and then loads the combined set into the target database.

Managing Your Test Data: Optim Test Data Management

Test data management should be a definite consideration when implementing a Big Data project in order to control test data costs and improve overall implementation time. Optim Test Data Management (TDM) automatically generates and refreshes test data for Big Data systems and has optimizations and tight integration with BigInsights and the IBM PureData System for Analytics (though it's used across all kinds of different vendors' repositoiries).

Optim generates right-sized test data sets; for example, a 100TB production system may require only 1TB for user acceptance testing. Optim TDM also ensures that sensitive data is masked for testing environments. It will generate realistic data for testing purposes (for example, changing Jerome Smith at 123 Oak Street to Kevin Brown at 231 Pine Avenue) but will protect the real data from potential loss or misuse. The possibility of data loss becomes even more real in the new era of Big Data. More systems and more data lead to more test environments and more potential for data loss. Optim TDM also has a tremendous cost advantage for self-service data generation capabilities. In summary, Optim TDM streamlines the test data process in a cost-effective manner.

A Retirement Home for Your Data: Optim Data Archive

One of the cardinal rules of data management is that for any data that's created, you need a plan to eventually destroy it as well—this is known as *defensible disposal*. Not planning for the full path of an information lifecycle is irresponsible because data cannot stay on active queryable systems forever—the costs to administer and provision it are simply not worth it if the data is no longer valuable. The natural lifecycle of data tends to be that it's in great demand early on, and as time goes on, people are less and less interested in it. There's a joke here about life being like that as well, but for the sake of both your happiness as a reader and ours as writers, we'll leave it alone. As data ages and it's no longer needed for regular reports, it makes sense to offload it from the relational database system it's on and move it to a less expensive destination. This less expensive destination could be tape, or it could be Hadoop as well.

Archiving relational data warehouses to ensure that only current information is stored achieves a number of goals. As we already mentioned, you can control costs as data volumes grow and also application performance, because less data means less content to parse through. Archiving, and eventually disposing of data, is essential to ensure legal compliance with data retention and protection regulations and to be able to audit compliance with data retention policies.

In the Big Data world, low-cost engines such as Hadoop offer the opportunity of a low-cost alternative for storing online archives to host colder data. While it's become easier to transfer data between Hadoop and other platforms, proper tools to manage the business process of lifecycle management and archiving are not widely available or mature outside IBM. That's where Optim comes in. It manages the lifecycle and the archiving process—discovering and profiling Big Data and tracking lifecycle milestones (when to archive) and automatically archiving Big Data from data warehouses and transactional databases. As part of its archiving solution, Optim provides visibility and the ability to retrieve and restore data if required and ensures the immutability of archived data to prevent data errors, which also complies with legal requirements for data retention and auditability. Optim can store archived data in a highly compressed relational database, in an archive file on a file system, or in BigInsights. And that latter integration point between Optim and Hadoop is a key one. Placing an archive file onto a Hadoop system provides low-cost storage, while also allowing data to be analyzed for different purposes, thus deriving insight from the archived files. It's no wonder why some of us refer to Hadoop as the new tape!

Wrapping It Up

For all the phases in the life of your data, IBM provides a range of mature tools to help you apply the principles of data governance based on your business requirements. The major benefit of IBM's suite of tools is the central storage of metadata in the Information Governance Catalog, which enables a far more seamless experience as data is transformed, moved, and selected for analytics. In addition, with IBM's emphasis on cloud-friendly deployments, many of these capabilities are now available as services as well.

14

Matching at Scale: Big Match

Every Hadoop vendor's marketing charts have the same bold proclamations about storing all kinds of data in Hadoop and then being able to analyze it. "Imagine the joy of your analysts!" the marketers cheer. "With the wonders of SQL on Hadoop, they'll be able to query across all your data sets, making new discoveries every day!" The IBM charts are no different, and our marketing folks say it too; in fact, this book says it too. But each time a veteran analyst hears those claims, the response is fear, not excitement. We've seen it ourselves in our customer work, and the question is always the same: "How (insert expletives here) can we easily query all our data in Hadoop *and* make correlations when both the data formats and the data are inconsistent?"

This is not a new problem, as anyone who's tried to run queries against relational databases from different organizations knows. That said, Big Data makes it a bigger problem because the amount, variety, and speed at which data arrives at your doorstep. IBM has solutions to overcome this problem, which is a key technical enabler for the landing zone architecture we described back in Chapter 4. As a result, there's a huge difference between IBM's claim about being able to easily query across these different data sets and competitors making the same claim. The key differentiator here is a data matching service called *Big Match*.

What Is Matching Anyway?

It's important to remember that SQL itself is not a magic bullet solution to data access problems. In relational systems, any analyst with at least a few years of SQL development experience will have felt the extreme frustration that comes when you correlate data from different data sets. This is because structural inconsistencies have been around for as long as organizations have been designing databases, and it's often not the result of poor DBA planning; for example, inconsistencies always happen with corporate merger activity because when you acquire a company, you get their data (with a different data model from yours). We've worked with large banks that, decades after a merger, still have inconsistent data models. When you've invested years into end-user applications and have reams of data, changing the data model is highly impractical and more often than not risky.

It's not just inconsistent data models that are a problem; it's the data itself. For example, Daenerys Targaryen is registered in the mortgage side of her financial institution's data center as "D. Targaryen" and in the personal banking side as "Dany Targaryen." When she signed up for an investment account, the clerk entered her birth date with the wrong year (likely out of fear—if you don't get the reference, watch *Game of Thrones*). Daenerys had first signed up for auto insurance with the same company when she was in her rebellious teen phase and was registered as "Daenerys Stormborn." Daenerys moved two years ago, and although she had her address updated in various institutional records so that she could continue getting mailings, the investment banking division did not get an updated phone number because she was too busy tending her dragons to call them.

As you can see, data that's formatted and stored in inconsistent ways would make it difficult for analysts to get anything done. SQL is a fantastic tool, but your joins only work when you can make apples-to-apples matches with your data. In the relational database world, we deal with this problem by using *master data management* (MDM) solutions. Organizations use MDM software and techniques to generate *master data,* which is the single version of the truth that analysts need to resolve the inevitable inconsistencies that crop up among their data sources over time.

The centerpiece of any good MDM offering is a *matching* engine. New data that is generated in operational systems is passed to the matching engine to find matches between the new entries and existing ones. When done properly, matching data entries is a resource-intensive and complex process. Consider the scenario with Daenerys Targaryen and her financial institution; if her records are to be properly matched out of the millions of other customer records, many sophisticated comparisons need to be made. The end result is the generation of master data, which would include a single record for Daenerys Targaryen, including all the data attributes about her. Let's say that Daenerys applied for a loan, and she added her email address to the loan's application form. After the loan application data is added to a database, this record will eventually pass through the matching engine. Daenerys' email address is seen as a new data point, and a corresponding update is made to Daenerys Targaryen's master data record. Linkage information is also written to the master data, which records the connections between the new data entries and the corresponding master records (these are also known as *golden records*).

A Teaser: Where Are You Going to Use Big Match?

There are great benefits to maintaining a single source of truth for your data center. As data is ingested into your databases, your ingestion systems can proactively cleanse their data by first searching for existing golden records. In addition to storing common fields (for example, customer names and addresses), different databases in an organization often collect fields that are unique. When a set of master data is built by matching data from many sources, the golden records are not just a single version of the truth, but they pull in the unique fields from all your sources, which gives you a full view of your customers (or whatever entities you're mastering). This is the Holy Grail for data analysts known as the *360-degree view* of the customer: Clients are going to be able to use Big Match to match customer data within any of their customer analytics initiatives using Hadoop!

We think that identifying patterns of fraud is going to serve as another major Big Match use case. After all, finding patterns of fraud in existing data includes looking for data that should not overlap (a individual with multiple passport numbers, the same frequent flyer number for two passengers on the same flight). This work is typically done with long-running, cumbersome SQL queries in a data warehouse. Big Match's probabilistic matching engine not only makes way for high-order matching (for example, a householding algorithm), but also is more scalable—we are talking tens of millions of matches per second here. A Big Match approach also provides the ability to do more what-if analysis, as well as incorporate unstructured data into the matching and attribute enrichment process.

Justice, child protection services, and homeland defense will be especially interested in IBM's Big Match capabilities too. For example, one challenge these departments have is finding overlaps between files received from multiple law enforcement agencies and comparing them against a central persons of interest database. Once again, in these uses cases you'll find the traditional relational technologies struggling; as transactions reach over two billion a week, it's not only challenging but expensive to keep up with the backlog of potential matches.

Connecting social data to party profiles is a huge opportunity to create fuller attribute profiles of any entity of interest—be it for retail, justice, campaign management, wealth management, and many other areas. Specifically, Big Match helps you identify advanced signals on customer needs (for example, a life event such as a birth or death); this isn't an easy thing to do across noisy social media and enterprise data at scale. The matches and insights generated here will help with the discovery of new predictive variables and new micro-segments.

There are plenty more examples we could share, and we share some more at the end of this chapter. In the sections that follow, we are going to tell you how Big Match works and why it works so well. In the meantime, remember that IBM Big Match enables clients to connect every customer touch point across a variety of massive volumes of information, empowering business analysts to act with confidence on a solid Big Data foundation for business information. It's a strategic shift from information management with an IT focus to a true business analyst focus—and that's definitely beyond the hype.

In this book we talk a lot about on-premise and off-premise services and the new buyers of IT; with that in mind, it should be easy to envision the kinds of matching services that will eventually be consumable over the cloud and as part of the Bluemix app development ecosystem (see Chapter 3 for details).

Matching on Hadoop

Now that we've walked through the generation of master data, you're probably thinking, "Hey, Hadoop would make a lot of sense as a place to do matching!" First, recall the landing zone pattern in the data zones model from Chapter 4: Having all your data land in one place is a really good starting point for any large-scale matching activity. This avoids a great deal of additional data movement and complexity. Second, matching is computationally expensive, and as the number of records grows, it can become impractical to keep the matching workloads on operational systems. Hadoop is a great fit here because it's good at large-scale operations such as matching, and can do so inexpensively. And if more capacity is needed, it's easy to add servers. Third, in thinking back to the 360-degree view of the customer, imagine the potential for incorporating data from nonrelational sources, such as social data or call center records. Hadoop can easily store these other data sets and make them available to matching technologies.

As with many good ideas, there's a catch. Remember that matching, at least when it's done right, is extremely complex. And the trouble with running complex operations at scale on Hadoop is that they need to be able to run in parallel. Although there are many matching engines for traditional relational data, you'll notice that outside IBM there are no mature, fully functioning matching engines available for Hadoop. So, what do we mean by "mature" and "fully functioning"? To give you an appreciation of the technology behind Big Match, the next section shows you the common approaches for matching, their benefits, and their limitations.

Matching Approaches

When you think back to the pain that analysts endure as they struggle to analyze data from different databases, the phrase "Necessity is the mother of invention" comes to mind. Given all that pain, the state of the art in data matching has advanced considerably. The following list summarizes the most common approaches to matching, ranging from the simplest to the most sophisticated approach:

- **Rules-based matching** Logical rules define when records match. This is an inflexible approach and does not yield good results for large data sets or when there are more than two or three data sources.

- **Rules-based fuzzy matching** More advanced than simple rules-based matching, this approach includes code to factor in typos and misspellings. This is still not sufficient to handle the complex, but common, scenarios that we illustrated with Daenerys Targaryen's example.

- **Scoring-based matching** Records are compared attribute by attribute, and a score is assigned for each attribute match. If the score reaches a certain threshold, a match is made. This approach is more advanced than a rules-based approach, but it still falls short because it does not account for things such as partial matches or nicknames.

- **Probabilistic matching** Probabilistic matching computes the statistical likelihood that two records are the same. Each record field is assessed by using statistical methods. This approach is able to find nonobvious data correlations.

What makes Big Match special is its probabilistic matching engine, which we describe in more detail in the next section.

Big Match Architecture

Big Match provides time-tested algorithms that run natively on Hadoop and can accurately link all customer data, across structured and unstructured sources, to provide matched information that consuming apps can act upon with confidence.

You are going to find Big Match is accurate because it uses statistical learning algorithms based on your data. It's also implemented in a manner that gives you a simple and quick path to value, as it comes with a set of customizable algorithms that turns months of codes into expert templates for you to calibrate the matching. One of the biggest advantages of enabling Big Match to run as a first-class citizen on Hadoop is performance: Companies can measure the time it takes to match initial data sets in minutes and hours as opposed to days, weeks, and some of them months, all thanks to Hadoop's distributed processing framework. Finally, Big Match is proven: It leverages the experience of over a decade of the core engine deployment and feature enhancement through organic development and acquisition of other domain matching engines. The following sections describe the components of Big Match, which are shown in Figure 14-1.

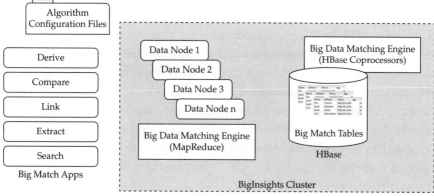

Figure 14-1 *Big Match components*

Big Match Algorithm Configuration Files

When planning how the matching should work, you can use the MDM Workbench tooling (see Figure 14-2) to tune tolerances and other aspects of the matching activities. You need to save your customizations as a configuration file to be consumed by the Big Match probabilistic matching engine.

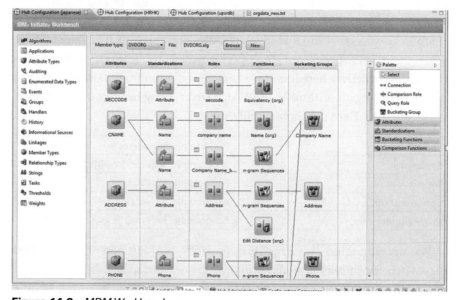

Figure 14-2 *MDM Workbench*

Big Match Applications

When you install Big Match on InfoSphere BigInsights for Hadoop (see Chapter 6), a handful of applications that can be run from the BigInsights app store are automatically laid down in the cluster. These applications handle preparation, matching and linking tasks, and can export a set of mastered data for consumption such as system-of-record data for a data warehouse. To know what to do, these applications consume the algorithm configuration file you generated from the MDM Workbench. Big Match also features an end-user interface that you can use to search for individual entities, such as customers.

HBase Tables

Before running the Big Match applications in BigInsights, you need to store the record data in HBase tables. There is an additional Big Match table in HBase where all the linkages from the processed records are connected with the originating record.

Probabilistic Matching Engine

The heart of Big Match is IBM's probabilistic matching engine. This engine runs on BigInsights as a collection of HBase coprocessors and MapReduce applications, which is how IBM's matching algorithms are implemented for Hadoop. (*Coprocessors* are low-level modules that run directly against HBase data—these are specialized high-performance applications that process HBase data exactly where it is stored, resulting in minimal data movement.)

The matching algorithms in Big Match cover a staggering range of matching techniques. Here are some highlights:

Phonetics	For example, Mohammed vs. Mahmoud
Synonyms	For example, Munenori vs. Muni
Translation	For example, Kawasaki vs. カワサキ
Concatenation	For example, de Roos vs. deRoos
Misalignment	For example, Kim Jung-il vs. Kim il Jung

The algorithms have been highly optimized—we have personally watched Big Match make *tens of millions of comparisons per second*. The workflow around the coprocessors has been finely tuned so that while records are being matched, the next records are loaded into memory.

How It Works

Big Match matches and links the data automatically as it is ingested. Before you run matching operations, you need to configure the attributes that you want to match (for example, a person's name, their phone number, and address) and the tolerances for matching. Big Match has a graphical configuration tool that you can use to generate the configuration files that the Big Match applications will consume. Following are the steps involved in the matching process:

1. **Load**   Ingest new records into the Big Match data table in HBase.

2. **Derive**   A Big Match coprocessor standardizes and compacts each record, optimizing it for statistical comparisons. A Big Match HBase coprocessor then performs rough calculations to find the set of potential matches (this is called a *bucket*).

3. **Compare**   A Big Match HBase coprocessor scores the comparisons from the bucket by using a number of statistical methods.

4. **Link**   Based on the results of the scoring, the Big Match linking application builds a set of discrete *entities*, where an entity represents an individual (or organization). The Big Match HBase tables are populated with master records and entity data that captures the linkages between the original records.

You can also run this process in batch mode by running the Big Match apps from the BigInsights console.

So imagine you've got records about your customers from multiple data sets, where you know there are inconsistencies for whatever reason (it could be different date formats, data entry mistakes, or any of the reasons we looked at with the Daenerys Targaryen example earlier). In addition, even within each of the data sets, you know there are instances where there are duplicate records for individual people. In short, this is a mess, and this is the normal state for most businesses storing customer data. What the linking application does is build a single set of entities representing individual people, and links each entity with all the matching records for each individual person.

Extract

After you have generated a set of master data, you can use Big Match to generate an up-to-date set of system-of-record data. You can do this by running the Big Match Extract app, which generates a set of delimited files that represents the system-of-record data. There are many uses for a trusted data set like this—for example, you can then load the system-of-record data into a warehouse to populate dimension tables.

Search

Having your customer data sets scored and linked with a master set of entities opens up many possibilities. There are many use cases, as you'll see later on in this chapter, where taking a set of different records and searching for the matching entity can be very useful. Big Match provides a REST interface for external applications to invoke probabilistic searches against the matched data. This REST interface is great for checking batches of records, but there are also situations where it would be useful for someone to manually search for matches one individual at a time. Big Match also includes an interactive matching dashboard (see Figure 14-3), where you can enter data points for people and see the corresponding records. As you can see in Figure 14-3, with an entity-based search, you can overcome data quality issues (like mistakenly swapping first name and last name) to get meaningful results. Other similar records will also be shown, but with lower scores.

Big Data Matching Dashboard							⊙ · IBM.
Input table	memgen ▾	**Entity Id**	**Score**	**First Name**	**Last Name**	**SSN**	**Birth Date**
		396041129524559890	75	JULIE	JACKSON	866-83-7218	1973-07-24
Algorithm	mdmper ▾	396041129524559890	75	JULIE	JACKSON	866-83-7218	1973-07-24
		396041129524559890	75	JULIE	JACKSON	866-83-7218	1973-07-24
Search Type	⦿ Entity	396041129524559890	75	JULIE	JACKSON	866-83-7218	1973-07-24
	○ Member	396041129524559890	74	JACKSON	JULIE	866-83-7218	1973-07-24
		396041440293146634	32	JULI	ARMSTRONG	216-48-4232	1973-07-24
Minimum Score:		396041166157639701	24	JOE	BLAKE	598-13-9893	1973-07-24
Search							
First Name	julie						
Last Name	j						
SSN							
Birth Date	1973-07-24						

Figure 14-3   *Interactive matching dashboard*

Applications for Big Match

Big Match originally grew out of a need for a matching engine that could be freed from the cost and scale constraints of relational databases. As is often the case when you move storage and processing to Hadoop with the goal of saving money, other possibilities come up that can help you *make* money. Earlier in this chapter we shared with you a couple of use cases where Big Match technology is well suited. Now that you understand this technology and how it works, we thought we'd share a couple of others and trust your newfound knowledge will find even more. Here's a run-down of some other usage patterns we've seen for Big Match.

Enabling the Landing Zone

As we've discussed earlier in the "Matching on Hadoop" section, storing the matching data and performing the matching processing work in Hadoop makes a great deal of sense. This is a perfect example of moving work to the platform with the best fit, which we covered at length with the data zones model in Chapter 4. With Big Match as an established part of the landing zone, your relational database systems are freed from having to wedge the massive burden of processing record matches into increasingly limited windows. In addition, by generating regular system-of-record extractions for use in warehouse dimension tables, Big Match furthers the pattern of the landing zone being used to refine data for use in data warehouses.

For the data scientist type of analyst, having the data sets in the landing zone linked to a nice, clean, system-of-record data set is an absolute dream. Without linked data between different data sets, discovery work would be tedious and time consuming.

Enhanced 360-Degree View of Your Customers

A major selling point for MDM solutions is the concept of building master records for your customers by factoring in all the attributes you've stored about them from many different tables and databases; this was cited by zealots as having a 360-degree view of your customers, but in looking back, it was 90 degrees at best. The problem here is that traditional MDM solutions did not factor in the wealth of information that's not stored in databases. This could be information from call center logs, forms, emails, and social media. While for the most part relational databases are heavily biased to tightly organized structured data, Hadoop doesn't discriminate on the kinds of data it stores.

Many companies talk a big game when it comes to analyzing text data (some people call it unstructured data), but once you look past their marketing slides and hard-coded demos, there's not much behind the curtain that you could get value from (think about the closing chapter in *The Wizard of Oz* as a good analogy). IBM Research has built an entity analytics engine that's capable of making sense of text data in a repeatable way, without requiring special programming. For example, from call center logs you could derive sentiment on how your customers feel about your offerings. Or consider social data: Twitter has become a public place for people to express their immediate reactions to the world around them. But how do you link Twitter accounts to actual customer records? With the combination of Big Match and IBM's entity analytics engine, it's now possible to automatically discover (assuming they were not provided to you) your customers' Twitter accounts. IBM Research worked with two nameplate clients to refine and iterate this technology: a large U.S. bank and large U.S. retailer—both with millions of customers. In both cases, Big Match was able to identify customers' Twitter accounts with 90 percent precision! (This means that for the millions of Twitter accounts that were each associated with a customer, there was 90 percent accuracy.) Of course, many customers don't have Twitter accounts, but for those that do, they represent a sizable sample of the full set of customers. This gives you a wealth of additional information about how different segments of customers feel about your products and services, but also attribute information such as hobbies, age, sex, and so on.

More Reliable Data Exploration

In Chapter 6, we talked a bit about Watson Explorer, which is a large-scale indexing and search platform designed to help people find information from multiple different sources of data. You can also build search-enabled applications for Watson Explorer, for example, an investment account manager dashboard, which would display customer information from many internal sources and then also show information about that customer's investments. In essence, an important component in these applications is the relationships between customers, their account manager, and their investments. IBM was able to further enhance these applications using Big Match by providing much more accurate relationship information for Watson Explorer to consume.

Large-Scale Searches for Matching Records

There are a number of industry-specific use cases involving batch search operations against scored and linked master data sets. While the use cases are often quite distinct, the pattern of actions is the same. An organization has a set of records and needs to know if there are similar or matching records in their existing databases. This is a tantalizing problem; it's painfully simple on the surface, but performing quality comparisons and running them against all of the organization's records is complex and involves heavy processing. The REST-enabled search API in Big Match removes any complexity, and Hadoop performs the processing with ease.

Imagine you're working in a government security agency, and you need to find persons of interest using only bits and pieces of information. In IBM, we may or may not have deployed Big Match solutions to enable millions of these kinds of searches to be run against repositories with billions of records. We'd tell you, but we'd have to silence you, and we want you to buy our next books.

In the health services industry, connecting prescribers for extended analytics is another Big Match use case. This is all about solving the challenge of connecting provider profiles to claim requests received from multiple vendors in the healthcare industry. Many clients today are unable to support new vendors because the extra demand requires significant changes to current architectures. What's more, each new large on-boarding brings with it extensive tuning and expense. IBM Big Match will simplify the on-boarding of new source systems, and the power of Hadoop gives assurances that there's enough room to expand when needed.

One of the largest health network information providers in the U.S. uses Big Match to enable insurance payers and pharmacists to make reliable decisions on issuing drug prescriptions. This is an area especially prone to fraud, with people trying clever ways to circumvent traditional checks and balances to get drug prescriptions they are not entitled to. One common tactic is for patients to go to multiple doctors to get prescriptions. Without a large-scale matching framework, this would be nearly impossible to detect. With Big Match, this company is able to take data from care providers, pharmacies, and insurance payers and maintain a large set of reference data. As prescription requests come into the system, the company can quickly score them and return recommendations to the insurance payers and pharmacies.

Wrapping It Up

Increasingly, businesses are storing operational data that captures their systems of engagement in Hadoop. This is often customer data, and where there is customer data, invariably there is complexity. Hadoop is an ideal platform to land system-of-engagement data, but if analytics users are to get any value out of it, a matching solution is essential. IBM has made its industry-leading probabilistic matching engine available in Big Match, which offers a matching solution that can run at Hadoop scale, and handle complex data.

In this chapter we shared with you a number of Big Match use cases. You also learned about how Big Match has a number of patterns that you can deploy to solve some of the more pressing business challenges today. We think you are going to find that while the details of the use case change from enterprise to enterprise or industry to industry, there's a repeating pattern that can unlock value in the data like never before. Take the knowledge you've learned in this chapter and start to think about how Big Match can help solve your pressing needs, and now you're taking Big Data beyond the hype.

Additional Skills Resources

InfoSphere BigInsights for Hadoop Community

Rely on the wide range of IBM experts, programs, and services that are available to help you take your Big Data skills to the next level. Participate with us online in the InfoSphere BigInsights for Hadoop Community. Find whitepapers; videos; demos; BigInsights downloads; links to Twitter, blogs, and Facebook pages; and more.

Visit **https://developer.ibm.com/hadoop/**

Big Data University

Big Data University.com makes Big Data education available to everyone, and starts a journey of discovery to change the world! Big Data technologies, such as Hadoop and Streams, paired with cloud computing, can enable even students to explore data that can lead to important discoveries in the health, environmental, and other industries.

Visit **http://bigdatauniversity.com**

IBM Certification and Mastery Exams

Find industry-leading professional certification and mastery exams. New mastery exams are now available for InfoSphere BigInsights and InfoSphere Streams.

Visit **www-03.ibm.com/certify/mastery_tests**

Twitter

For the latest news and information as it happens, follow us on Twitter:
@IBMBigData, **@Hadoop_Dev**, and **@IBMAnalytics**

developerWorks

On developerWorks, you'll find deep technical articles and tutorials that can help you build your skills to the mastery level. Also find downloads to free and trial versions of software to try today.

Visit **www.ibm.com/developerworks/analytics/**

Blogs

A team of experts regularly write blogs related to the full spectrum of Big Data topics. Bookmark the "Stream Computing" page and check often to stay on top of industry trends.

Visit **www.ibmbigdatahub.com/technology/stream-computing** or **www .ibmbigdatahub.com/technology/all**

This is part of The Big Data & Analytics Hub (ibmbigdatahub.com) that is populated with the content from thought leaders, subject matter experts, and Big Data practitioners (both IBM and third-party thinkers). The Big Data & Analytics Hub is your source for information, content, and conversation regarding Big Data analytics for the enterprise.

IBM Data Magazine

IBM Data magazine delivers substantive, high-quality content on the latest data management developments and IBM advances, as well as creates a strong community of the world's top information management profession-als. It vividly demonstrates how the smart use of data and information advances broad business success, providing the context that enables data management professionals at all levels to make more informed choices and create innovative, synchronized, agile solutions. The magazine's clear, in-depth technical advice and hands-on examples show readers how to imme-diately improve productivity and performance. At the same time, expert commentary clearly articulates how advanced technical capabilities benefit the people and processes throughout an organization.

Visit **http://ibmdatamag.com**

IBM Redbooks

IBM Redbooks publications are developed and published by the IBM Inter-national Technical Support Organization (ITSO). The ITSO develops and delivers skills, technical know-how, and materials to IBM technical profes-sionals, business partners, clients, and the marketplace in general.

Visit **http://ibm.com/redbooks**